About the Author

A specialist in western and northern Canadian history, Bill Waiser was Yukon historian for the Canadian Parks Service in the early 1980s. He joined the Department of History at the University of Saskatchewan in 1984 and served as department head from 1995 to 1998. Bill is the author, co-author, or co-editor of seven books, including the popular *Park Prisoners: The Untold Story of Western Canada's National Parks* and (with Blair Stonechild) *Loyal till Death: Indians and the North-West Rebellion*, which was a short-list finalist for the 1997 Governor General's literary award for non-fiction. He has served on the council of the Canadian Historical Association (1997–2000), with particular responsibility for archival issues (access, privacy, and census), and is presently a member of the board of directors of Canada's National History Society. Between 1999 and 2002, he hosted a weekly history series, *Looking Back*, on CBC Saskatchewan TV's supper hour news broadcast. He also co-authored (with CBC producer Paul Dederick) the book based on the television series: *Looking Back: True Tales from Saskatchewan's Past.*

All Hell Can't Stop Us

The On-to-Ottawa Trek and Regina Riot

Bill Waiser

Cover and interior design by John Luckhurst / GDL
Edited by Roberta Coulter
Copyedited by Alex Rettie
Proofread by Joan Tetrault

The publisher gratefully acknowledges the support of The Canada Council for the Arts and the Department of Canadian Heritage. We acknowledge the financial support of the Government of Canada through the Book Publishing Industry Development Program (BPIDP) for our publishing activities.

Printed in Canada by Friesens

03 04 05 06 07/ 5 4 3 2 1

First published in the United States in 2003

National Library of Canada Cataloguing in Publication Data

Waiser, W. A
All hell can't stop us : the On-to-Ottawa Trek and Regina Riot / Bill Waiser.

Includes bibliographical references and index.
ISBN 1-894004-88-4

1. Riots—Saskatchewan—Regina.
2. Depressions—1929—Canada.
3. Unemployed—Canada—History. 4. Canada—Economic conditions—1918-1945. 5. Regina (Sask.)—History.
6. Canada—History—1918-1939. I. Title.
FC578.R44W34 2003 331.13'7971'09043 C2003-910412-5
F1034.W34 2003

Fifth House Ltd.
A Fitzhenry & Whiteside Company
1511-1800 4 St. SW
Calgary, Alberta, Canada
T2S 2S5

Fitzhenry & Whiteside
121 Harvard Avenue, Suite 2
Allston, MA 02134

1-800-387-9776
www.fitzhenry.ca

For my sister and brother,
Gail and Tom,
who, like me, are children of parents
who came of age at the start of the Depression

Wherever they go they feel they are not wanted.
There is no work, no hope, no place for them.
They are *Canada's Untouchables.*

—Rev. Andrew Roddan, 1932

One of the happier moments of the trekkers during their stay in Regina.
Saskatchewan Archives Board R-A 21749-2

CONTENTS

PREFACE

All Hell Can't Stop Us

Exhibit 284 is a bullet. It falls harmlessly out of the end of an envelope onto a desk in the reading room at the Saskatchewan Archives Board. Charles Lord, who ran a photography supply business in downtown Regina, found the mushroomed slug outside the Cornwall Building on 2 July 1935, the morning after the riot. Exhibit 122 is another bullet—its shape intact—wrapped in cotton batting inside a small round pillbox. It was removed from the neck of porter John Rothecker during emergency surgery at the Regina General Hospital; the bullet had just missed the Regina citizen's spinal cord, but he would still require weeks of treatment. The rest of the over three hundred exhibits from the Regina Riot Inquiry Commission are no less intriguing. There's a faded meal ticket for the Clayton Cafe, one of many restaurants that fed hungry On-to-Ottawa trekkers during their forced three-week stay in Regina. There's also the slightly tattered membership card issued to Constable D. F. Taylor, who joined the trek after another mounted policeman working undercover had been exposed.

Most of the exhibits are letters and telegrams—many between Assistant Commissioner S. T. Wood, the senior Mountie in Regina, and the Royal Canadian Mounted Police commissioner in Ottawa, or between Conservative Prime Minister R. B. Bennett and his Liberal foe in Saskatchewan, Premier Jimmy Gardiner. The correspondence offers some insight into why the march to Ottawa ended in bloodshed: while the politicians wrangled over the trek, the police made preparations to bring it to an end by force.

There are also several lists: the demands that the trekkers were taking to Ottawa; the names of those injured during the fighting at Market Square and in downtown Regina; even the number of broken plate glass windows. Absent, though, from the Saskatchewan Archives holdings, are some of the larger items entered as evidence during the inquiry hearings: a chunk of brick, a block of wood, a section of metal pipe, a collection of makes hift clubs, police batons, a used tear gas grenade, a dented riot helmet, and more bullets.

The collection of Riot Commission exhibits, all but forgotten, are from a period that many older Canadians recall nostalgically. It was the Great Depression, a time when the world seemed to have been turned upside down. There were record-low wheat prices and record-high unemployment, dust storms and grasshopper plagues, relief camps, boondoggling, and the dole. The 1930s pushed a reluctant federal government toward a larger public role, while spawning new political parties and wry epithets, such as "Bennett buggies" and "Bennett burgs," in honour of the prime minister. No one who lived through those "ten lost years" was untouched, not even those who had a job. Many learned to make do with the little they had and saved everything—from string to rags to old nails—because it might prove useful some day. Surviving the so-called Dirty Thirties was like earning a badge for perseverance, and many wear it proudly today.

But there was also a darker, uglier side to the 1930s. The Bennett government, together with the RCMP, looked upon dissent, no matter how peaceful or justified, as a possible threat to the country and its traditions and values. In particular, they regarded the single, homeless unemployed with unease, fearful that they might be seduced by the lure of communism. They responded with force. Indeed, the violence of the period stands in stark contrast to the popular image of a peaceful Canada. In 1997, many Canadians were shocked when Sergeant Hugh Stewart of the RCMP, armed with a large canister of pepper spray, waded into a group of picketing students at Vancouver's APEC conference. In the 1930s, though, the mounted police routed protesters with batons, riding crops—and guns. Three times the Mounties were called upon by Ottawa to deal with unrest in Saskatchewan during the Depression, and three times they provoked a riot with deadly results. Jimmy Gardiner, then a federal cabinet minister, was quick to recall during the 1937 Ontario provincial election campaign what had happened when the Bennett government sent the RCMP into Estevan in 1931, Saskatoon in 1933, and Regina in 1935: "Property was destroyed, heads cracked, and gaols and hospitals filled."[1]

The On-to-Ottawa Trek was one of these instances of police violence. When one thousand relief camp strikers clambered aboard freight trains in Vancouver in early June 1935 to take their grievances directly to Ottawa, they had no idea that the trek would acquire a momentum and symbolism that went well beyond what is sometimes described as a simple regional protest movement. In fact, the men were initially more concerned with keeping the trek intact as they headed east through the mountains. Their goal was more than half a continent away, and during their first few chilly hours atop the freight cars, the future and what it held for them probably seemed as dark as the night before them. But once the men reached southern Alberta and rolled toward Saskatchewan, picking up new recruits at every stop along the way, the trek epitomized all that was wrong with the federal government's handling of the single homeless unemployed during the Depression. Here were hundreds of young men, many still in their teens, headed to Ottawa to try to secure a living wage and decent working conditions, defiantly singing:

Scorn to take the crumbs they drop us;
All is ours by right!
Onward, men, all hell can't stop us;
Crush the parasites![2]

But the trekkers *were* stopped—and the hell they faced was the RCMP, acting under orders of the Bennett government not to allow the men to proceed beyond Regina. For two tense weeks in the Saskatchewan capital, the mounted police and the trekkers played a game of brinkmanship, daring each other to make the first move. By the end of June, however, the men grudgingly conceded that there was no way out of Regina and that it would be foolhardy to engage the Mounties. Ending the impasse, though, proved equally difficult. The Bennett government insisted that the trek be disbanded on its terms—through a special holding facility on the outskirts of the city. But when the men balked at the proposal, seeing it as a trap, the RCMP, with the assistance of the Regina City Police, decided to pluck the leaders from a peaceful public rally at Market Square on Dominion Day. The raid quickly degenerated into a pitched battle between the police and trekkers and citizens, which spilled over into the streets of downtown Regina. Order was not restored until the early hours of the next day, but only after the city police emptied their guns directly into a crowd of rioters.

The toll from the Regina riot was two dead—not one, as usually reported—hundreds injured, and thousands of dollars of damage to the city. These statistics, however, are only part of the story—one that has never been completely told. Although the Saskatchewan government held a public inquiry, and almost two dozen trekkers went to trial, the full truth about the events surrounding the trek and riot was sacrificed in favour of a simple, comfortable conclusion: The On-to-Ottawa Trek constituted a threat to the cherished Canadian principles of law and order and, as such, had to be stopped by any means at any cost. This conclusion was not surprising, given the apparent radical nature of the event. But it missed the broader significance of the trek. Far from being a sinister Communist plot, the march eastward captured the profound sense of crisis that gripped the country during the 1930s. The individual stories of the trekkers—the feelings of personal failure and utter despair—could have been the stories of many other ordinary Canadians. It was if their own Depression experiences were being played out before them as the men headed to Ottawa to confront the prime minister over his relief policies. The Bennett government and the RCMP, however, refused to look beyond the Communist rhetoric of the trek leaders to see the real motivation for the movement. They failed to understand why people from different backgrounds and political sympathies readily identified with "the boys" and what they were doing. Instead, the government and the police chose brute force over a reasonable solution to the Regina impasse and provoked one of the worst riots in twentieth century Canadian history. This tragic outcome certainly made the trek appear to be a revolutionary movement. But the revolution it sought was a better deal for the thousands of single homeless unemployed who faced an empty, hopeless future in federal relief camps during the Depression. That was the real crime—and it would have gone largely unnoticed if not for the On-to-Ottawa Trek.

ACKNOWLEDGEMENTS

All Hell Can't Stop Us greatly benefited from the assistance of several individuals and organizations. The staff of the Saskatchewan Archives Board, in particular Nadine Charabin, Janet Harvey, Tim Novak, Linda Putz, and Lenora Toth, responded to my many queries and always gave expert advice and direction. Jacki Andre proved to be a skilled researcher who made my job much easier because of her resourcefulness and thoroughness; her attention to detail—getting things right—helped the project in many ways. Steve Hewitt shared his vast knowledge of the Royal Canadian Mounted Police during the 1930s and offered critical feedback on the manuscript in its early stages. Mike Hayden kindly turned over his research materials on the topic. Murray Langgard handed me a black valise containing the "missing" 1935 Regina city police records during a meeting at Saskatoon's Bessborough Hotel in the fall of 1999. Justice C. F. Tallis of the Saskatchewan Court of Appeal took time from his busy schedule to recall members of the Saskatchewan legal community who were involved in the riot commission and trials. Lori Krei of Iowa provided background material about her great uncle, trekker Nick Schaack.

A number of people read the manuscript at various stages and responded with warm encouragement and valuable suggestions: Bill Brennan, Ken Coates, Howard McConnell, James English, Gerry Friesen, Jim Miller, and David Smith. I have been extremely fortunate to have had such help. A special thank-you is owed to Bill Brennan, who never tired of my many questions about Regina. Naturally, any possible errors of interpretation or fact are my own.

Financial assistance for the research and preparation of *All Hell Can't Stop Us* was secured from the University of Saskatchewan President's SSHRCC Fund and the University of Saskatchewan Publication Fund. Brian Smith of Articulate Eye drew the maps. Mike Waiser prepared the trekker list, while Jessica Waiser helped with the photograph cutlines. Matt Novack did the index. Kate's cats, Bits and Baby, probably had more fun playing under the huge map of 1935 downtown Regina than I did trying to sort out the movement of people the night of the riot. Marley provided regular doses of encouragement and the occasional glass of malt.

Fifth House Publishers waited a long time for this book. Charlene Dobmeier always interspersed her queries about the writing with support and interest. Her faith in me is greatly appreciated—and valued. Lesley Reynolds skilfully guided the manuscript through the editing and production stages.

Finally, my parents came of age came of age during the Depression. My mother, Jean Ritchie, was nineteen at the time of the Regina Riot and had quit school years earlier to help her family in Toronto. My father, Ted, wandered western Canada in search of work in the early 1930s before spending the winter of 1933–34 in a federal relief camp in Hope, British Columbia. He returned home, at age twenty-one, to Lyleton, Manitoba before the big camp walkout in the spring of 1935. Doing this story has helped me better understand and appreciate why my mother always double-checked—item by item—the cash register slip from the grocery store and why my father always bathed in an inch of water. It's too bad they are not still alive so that I can tell them.

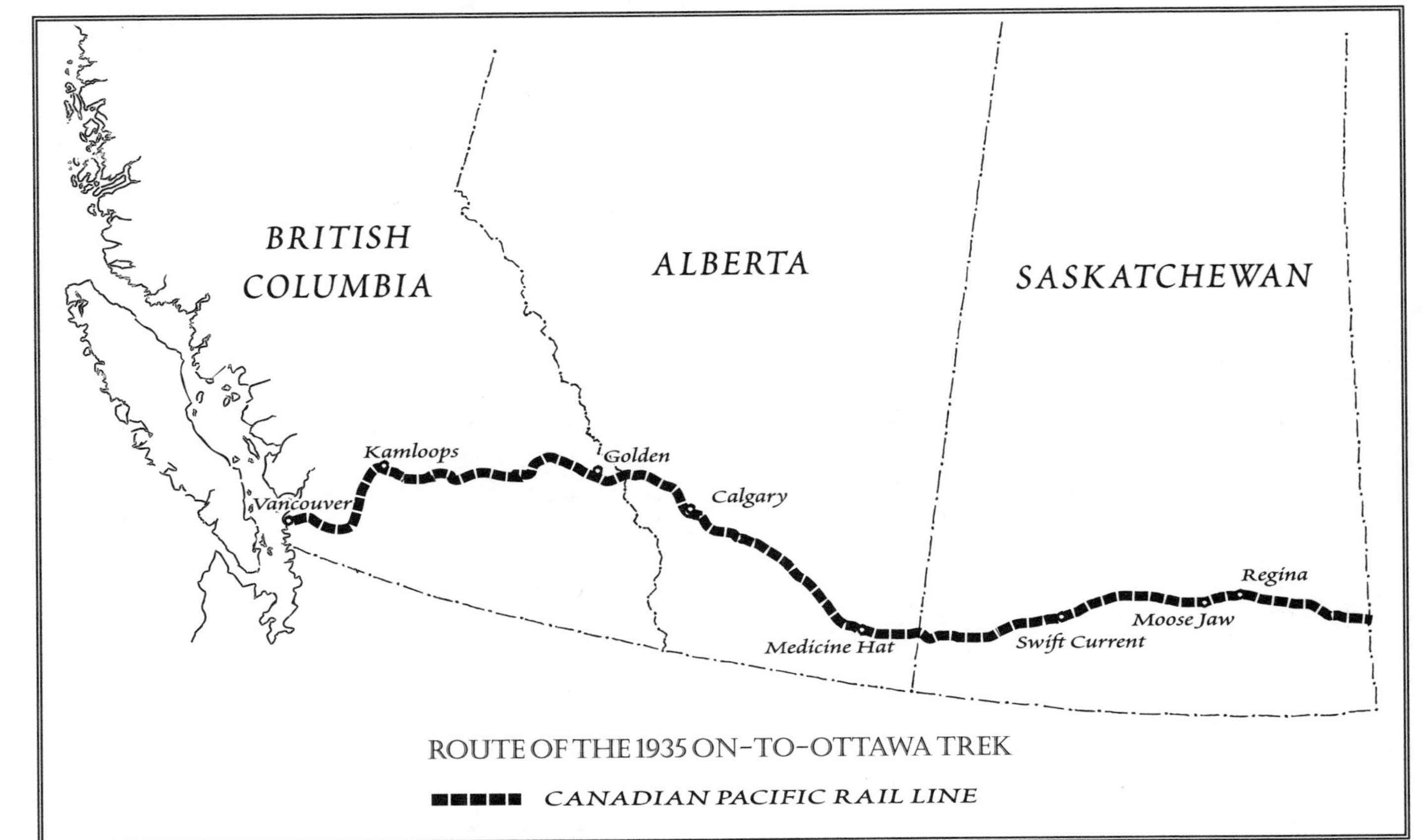
BRITISH
COLUMBIA
ALBERTA
SASKATCHEWAN
Kamloops
Golden
Calgary
Vancouver
Regina
Moose Jaw
Swift Current
Medicine Hat
ROUTE OF THE 1935 ON-TO-OTTAWA TREK
CANADIAN PACIFIC RAIL LINE

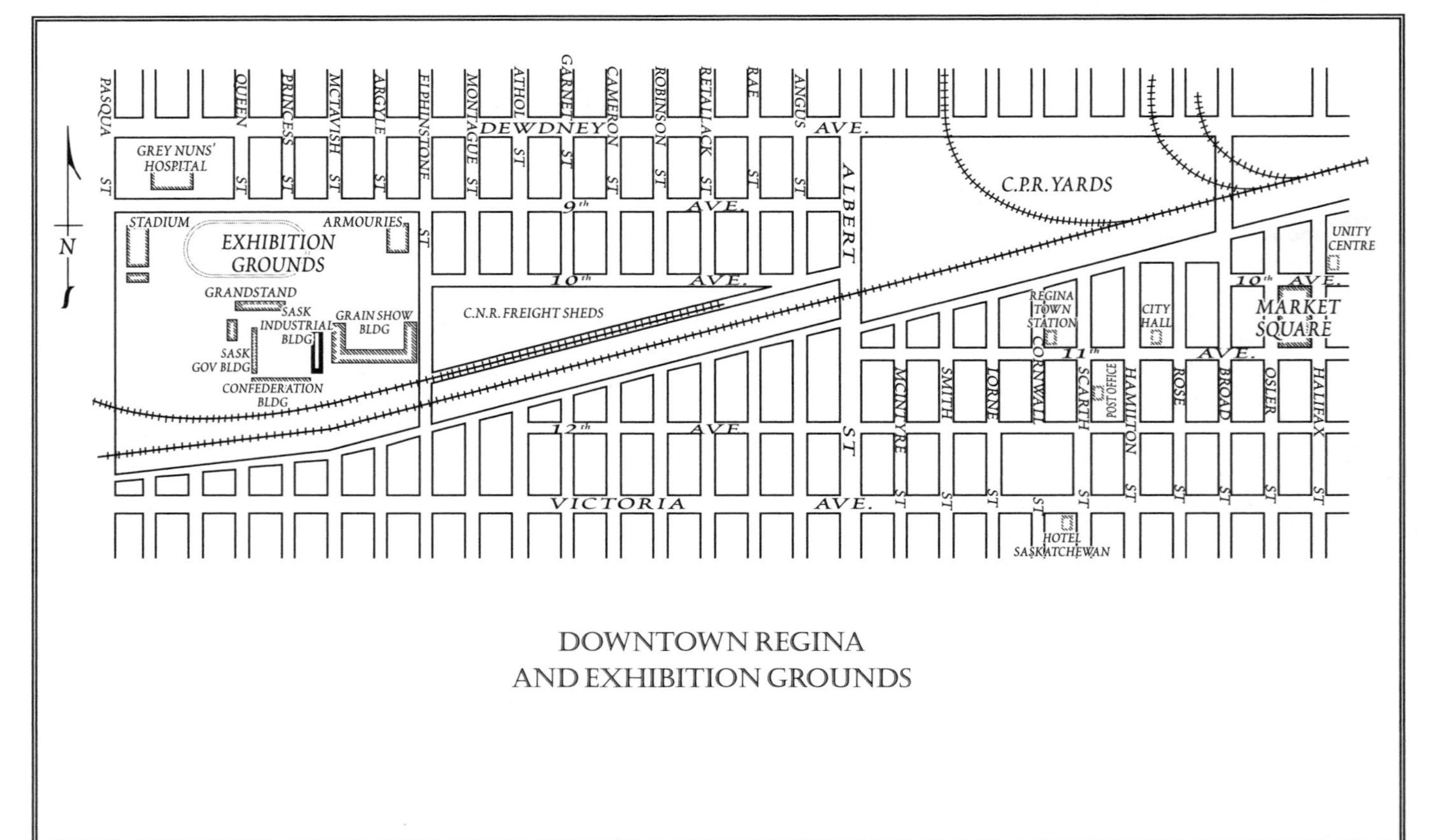

DOWNTOWN REGINA
AND EXHIBITION GROUNDS

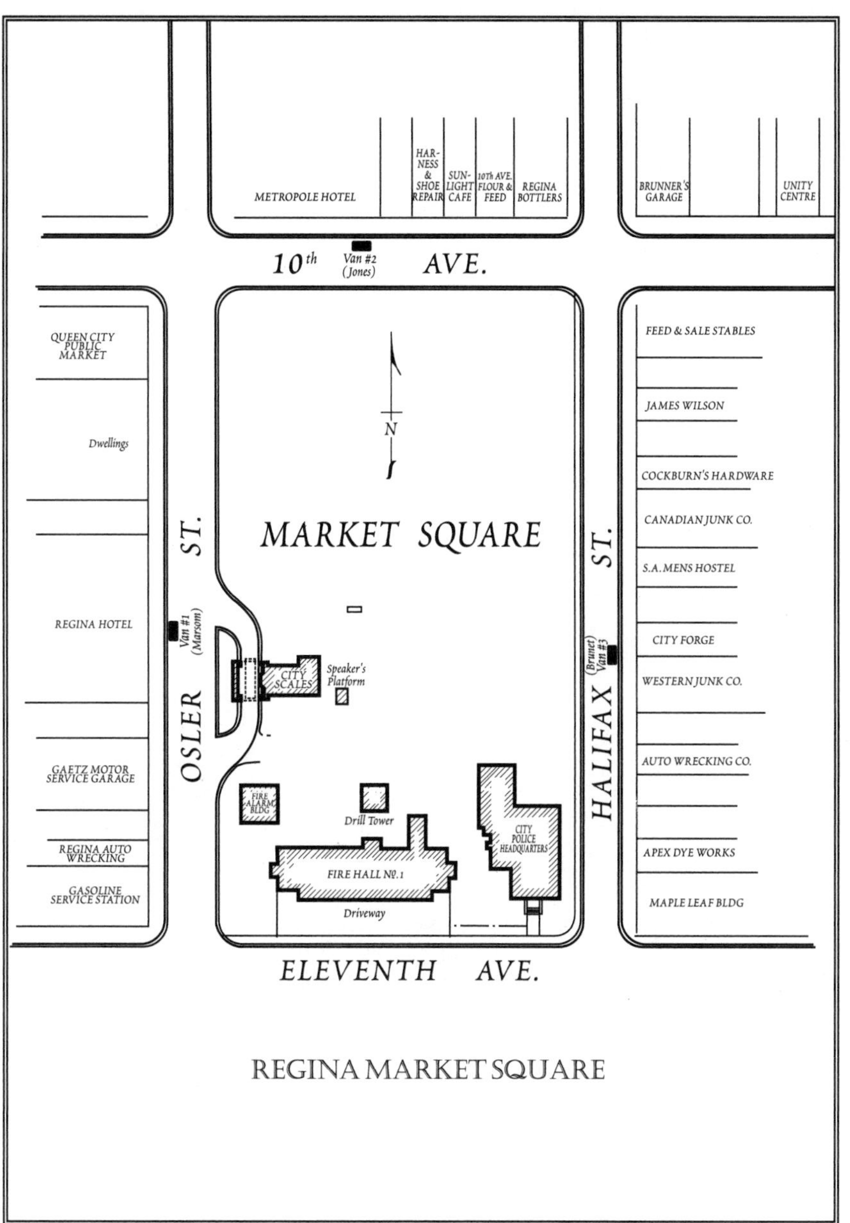

REGINA MARKET SQUARE

INTRODUCTION

We're Going to Ottawa

The smoke of the engine first announced their approach that morning. Then came the piercing squeal of the fifty-car freight as it slowed to a stop near the Elphinstone Street crossing in Regina. An overnight storm had just lifted, and in the first light of day the world seemed to stand still. Then, with a nod from trek marshal Jack Cosgrove, who was perched on the engine tender facing backwards, tens, and soon hundreds, of cold, rain-soaked men clambered down from the boxcars and shook off their stiffness. As the men, numbering around fifteen hundred, gathered up their few belongings and formed themselves into their divisions, a small clutch of sleepy well-wishers broke into a special welcome song that they had been practising for days. The two groups then exchanged some friendly banter before the division captains called for order in the ranks. Upon another signal, the men quietly began to march in unison, four abreast, north on Elphinstone Street and then west along Dewdney Avenue towards the exhibition grounds. At the head of the procession walked Cosgrove, his clothes and face blackened with soot from the train ride. At his side, in an old brown suit, strode trek leader Arthur "Slim" Evans, who had gone ahead by bus the night before to finalize arrangements for the men and was waiting, like an expectant father, when the eastbound freight pulled into Regina.[1]

❖ ❖ ❖

That the On-to-Ottawa Trek even reached Regina was testimony to the Canadian government's failure to deal with the country's single homeless unemployed during the Great Depression. In early April 1935, hundreds of dissatisfied, disillusioned men walked out of federally run relief camps throughout British Columbia and descended on Vancouver in a bold attempt to reverse their dead-end lives and bring about some kind of "work for wages" programme. But no one wanted to assume responsibility for the men, least of all the federal government, which believed that the Communists had orchestrated the protest and consequently refused to negotiate, let alone provide any support. At first, the "strikers," as they were dubbed, eked out a hand-to-mouth existence, thanks to the sympathy and kindness of Vancouver's citizens. But as the stalemate dragged on week after endless week and more and more men slipped away from an increasingly hopeless situation, the strikers decided to go to Ottawa and lay their grievances directly before the government.

An estimated one thousand On-to-Ottawa trekkers left Vancouver by freight train over a two-night period in early June. No attempt was made to stop them. Police and government authorities confidently assumed that the proposed trek was nothing more than a desperate bid to prevent the collapse of the Vancouver strike and that the resolve of the men would melt away like the snow in the interior mountains. Even Prime Minister R. B. Bennett, convinced that the Communists had misplayed their hand, announced that his Conservative administration would simply watch from the sidelines. There was no apparent need to do anything; the near breakdown of the trek at Kamloops seemed to suggest that it was nothing more than a crazy scheme. But the same kind of organizing zeal that had kept the strike going in Vancouver soon took over, and various committees now worked to ensure that the trek ran as smoothly as possible whatever the circumstances. The men also came to realize that they would never reach their goal, never get to Ottawa, unless they came together as a disciplined unit. They were no longer an aimless group of individuals, hitching a ride on a train, headed for nowhere, but men with a plan—and a mission.

Just as the freight the men were riding gained momentum as it rumbled down the Alberta foothills onto the prairies, so too did the trek as it headed towards Calgary, the prime minister's home riding. The sheer audacity of the men stirred the imagination of those who had suffered through five terrible years of drought and depressed wheat prices. Here were hundreds of young men—who could have been their own sons—headed to Ottawa to tell the country's political leaders that they were not doing enough to help ease the hardship and deprivation.

The Bennett administration, however, saw things differently, especially after the trekkers held local relief officers hostage until the provincial government agreed to provide meals for a few days. While many ordinary people understood the trekkers' sense of frustration and growing impatience, the federal government saw only an army of single homeless unemployed who had nothing to lose and could be expected to do anything. Though people were struck by their youth and referred to them as "our boys," the government regarded them as easy targets of Communist propaganda. And whereas ordinary citizens appreciated their good behaviour and no-nonsense organization, the government feared that the trek's outward appearance as a peaceful, orderly protest was only a mask for their real, more sinister, motives.

As the trek continued east from Calgary, the Bennett administration hurriedly began to make plans to bring it to an end. Indeed, a sense of urgency now informed Ottawa's response. Not only had the ranks of the trekkers swollen to fifteen hundred because of the addition of a number of new recruits from Alberta, but hundreds more were expected to join in Winnipeg. The federal government consequently turned to the Canadian Pacific and Canadian National railways, which up to then had been willingly transporting the men, and secured their co-operation. On 12 June 1935, the day the trek entered Saskatchewan, Ottawa's plan was in place: the railways would complain that the men were trespassing on their trains and in response to their plea for federal help, the Royal Canadian Mounted Police would be instructed to stop the unlawful movement at Regina. The next day, in a prepared statement read before the House of Commons to bolster police action, the minister of Justice branded the trek a Communist plot whose very purpose was "to disturb the peace, order, and good Government of Canada by unlawful means." Ottawa had no alternative but to intervene and derail the trek before it was too late.[2]

The trekkers first learned about the government's decision when they reached Swift Current on 12 June. Determined not to be intimidated, the men pushed on to Moose Jaw, where they were warmly greeted by hundreds of curious citizens gathered at the train station and along the streets. That reception deeply troubled Ottawa.

The Conservative government had another problem on its hands: Jimmy Gardiner, Liberal premier of Saskatchewan. Gardiner branded Bennett's decision "the most diabolical conspiracy ever perpetrated on the people of any province or any city." He was infuriated by the federal order to dump the men on the doorsteps of the provincial capital, like unwanted waifs, and insisted that the railways were obligated to take the men out of Saskatchewan since they had brought them in. He also deeply resented federal interference in provincial affairs—he was not even consulted—and predicted that the massing of the mounted police could lead to only one outcome—a riot. But Gardiner's ranting and hand wringing were dismissed as partisan theatrics, and all the Saskatchewan government could do was prepare for the arrival of the trek.[3]

The trekkers started for Regina in the early morning hours of Friday, 14 June. They had spent the previous day hunkered down at the Moose Jaw exhibition grounds, trying to keep dry during a steady rain, while the trek leadership considered their next move. At a public rally at 7:00 P.M., it was finally announced that the trek would continue eastward around 2:45 A.M. on the next available freight, a CPR cattle train. The decision, coming after the uncertainty of the past few days, seemed to galvanize the men's determination to complete their journey—even if the trip to Regina brought them only forty miles closer to Ottawa. They were also ready to do battle with the police if the trek was interfered with in any way, and could count on the additional muscle of several hundred recruits who had joined since Calgary. The most immediate challenge, though, was the first major thunderstorm of the summer, complete with lightning, which thoroughly soaked and chilled the men as they huddled atop the swaying boxcars on the trip to Regina.[4]

When the CPR freight stopped at the Elphinstone Street crossing at 6 A.M. on Friday, 14 June, most of Regina was just waking after a fitful night because of the storm. It would have been a perfect time for the RCMP to round up the tired trekkers, who were in no condition to offer much resistance. But surprisingly, the only policeman in evidence that morning was Inspector Fred Toop, a twenty-seven-year veteran of the Regina city police. Because of the national publicity the trek had garnered over the past few days, Assistant Commissioner S. T. Wood of the RCMP had decided to keep his troops at the Regina depot—at the ready if needed. Their absence that morning did not mean, though, that the mounted police were not getting ready for the expected showdown. The arrival of the trekkers was monitored not only by two plain-clothes Mounties, but also by Constable Henry Cooper, who was working undercover and had joined the trek at Moose Jaw. The CPR had also placed a secret agent among the men, in addition to several railway police who accompanied the freight train to Regina.[5]

Under Toop's watchful eye, and with several newspaper reporters tagging along, the trekkers headed for their temporary home, the exhibition grounds just west of downtown Regina. The sound of the men singing "Hold the Fort, For We Are Coming" as they headed north along Elphinstone Street soon brought people scurrying to windows or onto verandahs to watch the seemingly endless procession. Their number was overwhelming; in a way, they were like an army of occupation, meeting no resistance as they marched through the city. But, it was a ragtag army at best. Many still wore the telltale relief camp sweaters and khaki pants that they had been living in for weeks on end. The men also sported all kinds of footwear, mostly worn out, and a wide variety of hats, including a pith helmet. A lucky few had goggles, now worn atop their heads, to protect their eyes from the smoke and cinders on the trains. They also carried an odd assortment of luggage, from knapsacks to boxes to bundles wrapped in blankets and tied with rope. There were even a few cats and dogs, tucked under arms or clutched inside coats.[6]

What struck the reporters covering the story that morning was the trekkers' youthfulness and apparent nationality. Most of the men were in their early twenties, while several more were no more than teenagers, including at least one fifteen-year-old. Those over thirty were an exception. The majority also seemed to be from good Anglo-Saxon homes—certainly not the kind of people that were normally associated with being "red." The next largest group—but still a minority—were from eastern or central European backgrounds, in many cases the children of pre-World War I immigrants. There was at least one Indian, two blacks, and an Asian. The other noteworthy thing about the men was their gritty determination—as evidenced by the writing, On to Ottawa, many of them had on the backs of coats and sweaters or on hats.

Most of the marchers, when quizzed, refused to say much. But one young trekker gladly volunteered that they expected to stay in Regina for no more than three days and that they were prepared to meet force with force. "We're going to Ottawa. You can bet on it," he told a *Regina Leader-Post* reporter with an air of certainty. "We are going to Ottawa." This conversation elicited stern words and reproachful looks from some of the other men, and the speaker fell silent, except to repeat one last time, "We are going to Ottawa."[7]

Jack Cosgrove was equally tight-lipped. When asked whether he was in charge, he calmly replied that all decisions were made by committee. When pressed for further details because of his clipped answers, he politely but firmly told one dogged reporter to step aside and not to walk with him. When the man persisted, he calmly repeated the request, his slate blue eyes betraying his irritation. Little did reporters realize at the time that the man with the tired eyes walking at Cosgrove's side, mistaken for an aide, was actually trek leader Slim Evans.[8]

At the exhibition grounds, the trekkers headed for the stadium, where Toop stood waiting at the entrance. As the men streamed into their new home, they were immediately hit by the smell of the freshly spread straw on the floor. Several started mooing like cows, and a ripple of laughter went through the column. Under Cosgrove's supervision, the men formed up along the east side of the stadium. Those who broke rank were sent back into line with a growl; he also shouted at repeated intervals that there was to be no smoking inside the building. Once the last man was in place, Cosgrove mounted a central platform, decorated in red, white, and blue, and announced to a thunderous cheer that a meal would be served around 9:00 A.M. He also repeated his ban on smoking and suggested that the men try to get some sleep.[9]

The trekkers, exhausted from their overnight trip, dropped their gear and broke into small groups. While some chatted quietly, others headed for the promised soap and hot water in an outside corridor. Many tried to find a comfortable spot on the straw for a nap or simply a rest. A number were nursing colds and sore throats because of the rain of the past few days. But there would be no sleeping until a group of Regina unemployed, standing on the seats at the north end of the stadium, had finished serenading the men with "The Internationale." One of Cosgrove's last duties was to assign pickets to the stadium entrances for security purposes. He then doffed his sooty coat and hat and, grabbing a towel, headed for the washstands to clean up. Not even jokes from the men about living in a barn distracted him. He might have just led the trek into a maelstrom, but the trouble would have to wait.[10]

CHAPTER ONE

The Iron Heel of Ruthlessness

"On July 3rd 1870, the oceans seethed. At Hopewell, N.B. the earth groaned. Above, the heavens parted in fire. A babe was born into the comfortable household of Mr. and Mrs. Bennett. All who saw the little creature marvelled, not so much at its beet-red face and bellowing voice, but because of a strange phenomenon: For in one pudgy fist the child grasped a bag of gold, and on one pink foot grew a cast iron heel." That is how the Canadian Labour Defence League, a front for the Communist Party of Canada, satirized the birth of Conservative prime minister Richard Bedford Bennett in a 1934 pamphlet. For the past four years, Bennett had been fighting a war on two fronts and losing both campaigns badly. One of his enemies was the Great Depression, which had laid siege to the Canadian economy and was battering down prices to record lows while laying waste to traditional markets. The other enemy was the Communists, whose small guerilla army not only seemed to be everywhere, but whose tactics of confrontation grew bolder the more they came under attack. Bennett initially concentrated his considerable energies on defeating the Depression—he had promised in the 1930 general election to end unemployment or perish in the attempt. But as the Depression showed few signs of weakening, he increasingly came to blame foreign agitators and subversives for the growing unrest in the country. Suppressing dissent consequently became as important to Bennett as restoring the economic health of the nation—to the point where he came to regard the unemployed as a threat to the Canadian way of life.[1]

❖ ❖ ❖

If anyone could solve the economic malaise that descended on Canada in late 1929, it appeared to be Richard Bedford Bennett. Selected to head a demoralized Conservative Party at a Winnipeg convention only two years earlier, the New Brunswick–born Bennett seemed to have all the credentials for restoring the prosperity that many Canadians had come to know and enjoy during the heady 1920s. The schoolteacher-turned-corporate-lawyer was one of the most successful businessmen of his generation—a millionaire who held shares and directorships in several of the country's leading companies and financial institutions, such as Imperial Oil, Canada Packers, Imperial Tobacco, and the Royal Bank. He could also boast a diverse political apprenticeship which spanned a quarter-century, from his days in the old North-West Territories assembly to a spell in the Alberta legislature, to the House of Commons backbenches, to two brief stints in the cabinets of the short-lived Arthur Meighen governments of 1920–21 and 1926. But what distinguished Bennett, what made him so appealing as a leader in the first dark days of the Depression, was his overpowering personality. He was a gifted orator, according to one of his biographers, who spoke "with a torrent of words." He also had a quick, incisive mind; a natural ability to digest myriad facts and information and then coolly cut to the heart of an issue. It was his commanding presence, though, that impressed most observers. Whereas his arch-rival, Liberal leader William Lyon Mackenzie King, came across as a genial though somewhat dull career politician who always remembered to say his prayers, the tall, portly Bennett exuded a seemingly limitless confidence and optimism that suggested all would be well again—sooner rather than later. And why not? Here was a man whose relentless drive, industry, and thrift had served him well in the business world—why not apply the same talents to a country mired in a deepening recession?[2]

Bennett was not without his warts. He had a fierce sense of duty, so much so that he virtually ran a one-man government—introducing bills, dominating debates, and speaking for his ministers in the House of Commons. Colleagues were reportedly afraid to confront him, unnerved by his trademark glare. When a newspaper editor accused Bennett of treating his cabinet ministers like "office boys," he shot back, "That's all they were!" It was jokingly suggested that Bennett, found talking to himself during a walk on Parliament Hill, was holding a cabinet meeting. He was also prone to executive decisions—the kind more in keeping with the corporate boardroom and balance sheets—and never really did understand that Canadian politics required the art of compromise. Bennett liked to attack problems, meet issues head-on, all in the interest of doing some good. This dictatorial manner, what one reporter called "his belief in his own star," served to mask his generous nature. It also made him appear cold and distant, when in reality he found the trust of the public to be a heavy burden. According to his political philosophy, government was to provide stability, whether it be in the streets or on the financial markets. Despite his public persona, Bennett was awkward around women and, like King, never married. He also chafed at criticism and was easily angered, and yet his larger-than-life character made him an easy target for ridicule. While he was serving as solicitor for the Canadian Pacific Railway in 1905, for example, the *Calgary Eye Opener* published two derailment pictures and then a photograph of Bennett overlined "Another CPR Wreck." This mocking continued into the House of Commons in the 1920s when a Liberal opponent suggested that he "had the manners of a Chicago policeman and the temperament of a Hollywood film star." Bennett also led a solitary, if not blinkered, existence—a carry-over from his Calgary years when he travelled between his rented one-room apartment, his office, the law courts, and the hotel where he took his meals. He perfected a similar lifestyle in Ottawa: "The Chateau Laurier, where he slept, the Rideau Club, which he frequented, and the East Block on Parliament that contained his office, all lay within a quarter mile of each other." His only break from the job was an occasional morning swim in the indoor pool at the Chateau Laurier.[3]

Bennett, the so-called "knight of the foothills country," lost little time preparing to battle the "bogey of unemployment."[4] No sooner had he smote the ruling Liberals in the 28 July 1930 general election than he convened a special September session of Parliament to introduce two emergency measures to deal with Canada's worsening trade and unemployment problems. In an effort to protect the Canadian manufacturing sector from foreign competition and therefore save jobs in the industrial heartland, he hiked the protective tariff to its highest level since its introduction in 1879. He also provided twenty million dollars in emergency relief assistance to the provinces on the understanding that the aid was a temporary, one-time measure that did not represent any new obligations on the part of the federal government. The prime minister adamantly refused to entertain the idea of direct relief—"the dole" as it was called at the time—on the grounds that it would corrupt the recipients.

Bennett's actions mirrored conventional wisdom at the time. Other countries were scrambling to protect their domestic economies through restrictive trade practices, and Canada had to defend itself in the same way. Besides, unemployment had been a persistent feature of Canadian life since the late nineteenth century, and it was widely expected that the worst of the Depression would be over by the following spring when the new unemployment relief act was scheduled to expire. There was no apparent need, then, to abandon traditional practice in favour of bold new initiatives. It made more sense to continue to balance the budget in order to maintain international confidence in Canada's currency and creditworthiness. The alternative—spending money to get the economy moving again—was unthinkable.[5]

But the Depression was not going to go away so easily or quietly. In the 1920s, while Great Britain and the rest of Europe were recovering from the destruction and dislocations of the Great War, North America roared to unprecedented heights of growth and prosperity. The international demand for the products of the United States and Canada, however, collapsed in the late 1920s under the weight of the rebounding European economies. Worldwide overproduction led to lower prices. The famous stock market crash of October 1929 was a symptom, not the cause, of this instability in the world economy. And the situation went from bad to worse when countries tried to shore up their own economies by erecting high tariff walls at the expense of other, equally vulnerable economies.

Canada was one of the first casualties. Much of its prosperity in the 1920s had been fueled by the sale of primary products and semi-processed goods. Now, on the eve of the new decade, the economy was hit with a double whammy: international demand for these exports not only declined, but prices dropped as well. Wheat is a good example. At a time when wheat accounted for one-quarter of the dominion's total export trade, the price for Number 1 Northern, Canada's highest grade of spring wheat, plummeted from $1.03 in 1928 to a mere 29 cents in 1932. The fall in prices had a "multiplier effect," like ripples sent out by a stone tossed into a quiet pond. But in the Canadian case, stalled export sales and low commodity prices sent shockwaves through the entire economy, pounding retail, service, construction, and transportation industries, while displacing thousands of workers. In the face of this deluge, Bennett's much vaunted tariff wall offered limited shelter. Without doubt, it protected the manufacturing sector and saved jobs there. But it did little for those businesses and industries whose very livelihood depended on a strong export market. In the end, a high tariff served only to intensify the regional impact of the Depression.[6]

The other complicating factor, one that was not fully appreciated at the time, was Canada's growing economic integration with the United States. Most of the development and expansion in the 1920s had been financed with American dollars, and when the United States began experiencing its own economic woes, this investment evaporated—with painful consequences. What might have been no more than a short, severe recession turned into a prolonged, deepening depression, and the Canadian economy remained in poor health until the ailing United States was on the mend.[7]

Bennett's other major policy—emergency relief assistance—would also be found wanting as the ranks of the unemployed continued to swell through the winter of 1930–31. But even if the government had had some inkling about the depths to which the country would fall, it is doubtful if anything different would have been done to ease the growing crisis. Part of the explanation was the popular Canadian attitude to unemployment and the unemployed. Prior to the 1930s, unskilled workers rarely enjoyed a regular pay packet. They provided the raw muscle in agriculture, forestry, construction, and shipping, and whenever international demand for staple products went flat, they were dismissed in large numbers. Because of the country's immigration policies before the Great War and in the late 1920s, unskilled workers also had to compete with thousands of new arrivals each year, while employers had the luxury of a large pool of labour at their disposal, which kept wages low. Work was also seasonal; jobs in several sectors of the economy came to an end with the onset of winter. Yet despite Canada's long experience with unemployment, it was widely believed before the Depression that a healthy person without a job was lazy. Work could always be found by accepting a job at a lower wage or by turning to the land; in fact, one of the constant refrains during this period was that there was always work to be had on the farm.[8]

There was no unemployment insurance in Canada at the time. Employers in the 1920s, especially farmers worried about rural depopulation, argued that if an individual was provided with any kind of income support, then the individual would not only stop looking for a job, but others would be actively discouraged from seeking work as well.

This is not to suggest, however, that the destitute went without any kind of help. Canada administered a relief system in the early twentieth century that was grounded in the English poor laws of the 1830s, in particular the principle of "less eligibility." Relief assistance was deliberately designed to be less attractive than the worst job that society had to offer. Under such a system, a person was effectively forced to keep working and turned to relief only as a last resort. Even then, the person carried the stigma of personal failure and disgrace. The needy had to solemnly vouch that they had no other resources to fall back on—such as a bank account, personal belongings, or a relative—and that they were completely destitute. "I've seen tears in men's eyes," a former Calgary relief officer remembered, "as though they were signing away their manhood." Government authorities and welfare experts justified this policy on the grounds that it was shoring up the moral underpinnings of Canadian society by preserving the work ethic. It seemed that the unemployed needed discipline more than they needed to be fed, clothed, and sheltered.[9]

Under the terms of the legislation creating Canada, the 1867 British North America Act, the provinces were solely responsible for the financing and distribution of relief. That's why Prime Minister Bennett, in announcing relief assistance during the special September 1930 parliamentary session, insisted that the federal government was not taking on any new duties, but simply providing temporary aid until March 1931, when the worst of the economic storm was expected to be over. The way in which the emergency funds were to be distributed also reinforced the idea that relief was a purely local matter. The twenty million dollars in federal money was specifically earmarked for new public works, on the strict condition that three-quarters of the total cost of any project had to be financed by the provinces and municipalities—25 and 50 percent respectively. This requirement might have been acceptable during prosperous times, when there was a tax base to support municipal improvements. But the continued adherence to the notion of local responsibility during the early 1930s, as if it was some sacred principle, made a mockery of the situation. Cities, already struggling with ballooning relief rolls, somehow had to find the extra cash to pay their share of a new building, road, or bridge. More often than not, in order to qualify for the federal programme, they turned to boondoggle projects—make-work exercises that required no machinery and no material, and that had no meaning. In Winnipeg, for example, unemployed men spent their days picking dandelions from city boulevards.

Prime Minister Bennett reconvened Parliament in mid-March 1931. His prediction of a speedy recovery seemed like a poor joke, and no one was laughing. While the international prices for Canadian commodities were in free fall, the weekly tallies of the unemployed reached unprecedented amounts. Even with the fiscal and psychological deterrents of the relief system, the number of jobless had quickly overwhelmed the limited resources of municipal agencies. An estimated 15 percent of the labour force was out of work; the number would grow by another 2 percent in the next two months. Despite the bleak outlook, the Conservatives naively asserted that, although the recession was particularly persistent, traditional solutions would ultimately prevail. In the interim, in keeping with the government's ad hoc approach to the Depression, another dose of emergency assistance was prescribed—the Unemployment and Farm Relief Act. Like its predecessor, the act not only affirmed that unemployment was fundamentally a local matter, but placed a time limit on the availability of aid. The tap of federal assistance was to be shut off the following spring. What was different about the legislation, however, was that the amount of money available for unemployment relief was left to the discretion of the government. It could spend whatever was deemed necessary to fight the Depression without first securing parliamentary approval. The act also continued the sharing of the cost of public works, but this time the federal government would provide 50 percent in matching grants. If near-bankrupt provinces and municipalities were unable to finance a relief project, a magnanimous Ottawa would lend them the money so they could fulfill their obligations under the act. But the most controversial feature of the legislation was the assertion—in the formal title of the act and repeated in several clauses—that the ruling Tories were vested with "the powers necessary to ensure ... the maintenance of the peace, order and good government of the country." It even imposed a one thousand dollar fine and/or a maximum three-year prison term for those found in violation of the act.[10]

Bennett personally introduced the new relief legislation on 29 July 1931, just five days before the session was scheduled to come to an end. He made no apologies for targeting groups who were using the current crisis to infect the nation with "their pernicious political doctrines" and vowed to "free this country from those who have proved themselves unworthy of Canadian citizenship." Liberal Opposition leader Mackenzie King appreciated the need to contain the spread of subversion, but warned that unemployment relief was being confused with the maintenance of law and order—the matters should be handled separately. He was also uneasy about the scope of the legislation and, waving a copy of the 1914 War Measures Act for dramatic effect, observed that "my right hon. friend is asking for precisely the same powers" in a peacetime measure. Bennett, however, saw no confusion. Nor did he consider the act an abuse of executive power. "This is a land of freedom," he lectured the House, "where men may think what they will and say what they will, as long as they do not attack the foundations upon which our civilization has been built ... the institutions and customs under which we live."[11]

In many respects, the 1931 relief legislation was in keeping with the standard approach to dissent and unrest since the end of the First World War. In the wake of the 1917 Russian Revolution, the Canadian government dreaded the export of communism to the shores of North America, fearing that it would imperil a society made weak and vulnerable by the sacrifices of the war years. It seemed cruelly ironic that the nation was just coming of age, having proved itself on the bloody battlefields of Europe, only to face the insidious Bolshevik menace. Sir George Foster, a minister in the wartime government of Robert Borden, perhaps best captured the mood of those anxious days when he confided to his diary: "What a seething time it is in the world ... certainly the foundations of things are being uprooted in a thousand ways." The "Red Scare" even found its way into advertising. The National Drug and Chemical Company marketed "gophercide" with a cartoon of an endless line of expressionless gophers, parading on their hind legs, carrying placards such as, "Give us wheat or give us death." The quarter-page ad warned, "The Annual Bolshewheatie Parade is scheduled to march on your new wheat sprouts. The tender green shoots of growing grain will be at the mercy of this horde of hungry raiders—unless you break up the march with gophercide."[12]

That some kind of revolt was imminent seemed a real possibility in May 1919 when a general strike paralyzed Winnipeg for six weeks. The disaffected workers were seeking some control over their industrial lives. It would be determined later that they had legitimate grievances and reasonable demands, but in using the weapon of a mass shutdown they gave substance to the idea of an international conspiracy led by radical aliens. And the federal government, as frightened of the Communist scourge as was the business community, used the Royal Northwest Mounted Police to brutally crush the strike.

It also took swift legislative action to stifle the spread of bolshevism. Amendments to the Immigration Act, approved by both chambers of Parliament and the Governor-General in less than an hour, allowed for the detention and deportation without trial of any immigrant who was still not a Canadian citizen and who advocated the overthrow of the government by force. Section 98 of the Criminal Code made it illegal to belong to any organization that sought to bring about change in Canada by the use or threat of force. It was an extraordinary piece of legislation, not simply because of its broad definition of seditious activities, but also because it assumed that the accused were guilty until they could prove their innocence. As one labour historian has aptly observed, "The Cold War began in 1919, not in 1946."[13]

This anti-red crusade continued through the 1920s. Secretly founded in a barn in Guelph, Ontario in May 1921 and taking its direction from Soviet Russia, the Communist Party of Canada pursued a strategy of "boring from within" the established trade union movement for the better part of the next decade. These efforts netted only a few thousand members—mostly Finnish,

Ukrainian, and Jewish immigrants—certainly not enough to topple the government and usher in a proletarian dictatorship. But numbers did not matter as much as its revolutionary message, and most Canadians saw communism as an alien growth, something sinister that threatened to eat away at traditional values and undermine the state, the church, and the family. It was not the kind of political doctrine that good, loyal citizens of the British Empire would knowingly embrace or advocate. The RCMP consequently closely monitored the work of party activists—and anyone suspected of Bolshevik sympathies—and prepared weekly security bulletin reports for Ottawa's consumption.

Their efforts were no match, however, for the ever-vigilant Toronto city police, who were determined in the late 1920s to beat the reds into submission—even at the expense of freedom of speech. Believing that immigrants from central and eastern Europe harboured the Bolshevik virus, the police banned public meetings in any language other than English. When this order was overturned by the court, the police made it illegal to use any hall for a Communist gathering. And when the Communists turned to the streets for their meetings, the police arrested them for vagrancy or obstruction, but only after they had been first roughed up. In the end, though, these bullying tactics served only to make martyrs of the party's foot soldiers at a time when the moribund party seemed headed for extinction.[14]

If possible, the fear of communism became more palpable during the Depression. Taking advantage of the massive layoffs and accompanying hardships, the Communist Party of Canada—with a vigour and relevance unparalleled in its short history—went on the offensive in what it saw as the critical battle for the hearts and minds of the Canadian working class. Through its umbrella organization, the Workers' Unity League, the party tried to sign up labourers in traditionally non-unionized sectors of the economy and force recognition strikes, whatever the chances of victory. Any cooperation with existing labour groups or political parties was now considered a betrayal of its revolutionary cause. In another bold move, it also was the first and only group to attempt to organize the country's unemployed, under the banner of the National Unemployed Workers Association, in a common fight against the bastions of power and wealth. These proselytizing efforts attracted followers, especially in Canadian cities, if only for the simple reason that the Communists held out the prospect of hope in place of growing despair. Joblessness was not the consequence of personal failing, but the collapse of the capitalist system. And the rugged individualism at the heart of the relief system would lead to a "ragged" individualism, unless collective militant action was pursued. "Organize unemployed councils," the Communists urged. "Fight, Don't Starve."[15]

These words inspired hundreds of unemployed workers across the country as they marched on relief offices, held street-corner demonstrations, or circulated petitions—all under the careful direction of Communist organizers. The response was immediate and predictable. Alarmed by the organization of the jobless, the political and legal establishment interpreted their demands as the first step on the road to revolution. Their protest had nothing to do with their predicament but was clearly the handiwork of foreign agitators who threatened the moral fabric of the country in provoking the unemployed. And they needed to be quashed. Sir William Mulock, chief justice of Ontario, who had first been elected to the House of Commons in 1872, spoke for many Canadians in an after-dinner speech in early February 1931, when he bitterly condemned Communists as "conspirators, atheists, destroyers of family, who would rob all citizens by any degree of force, up to that of murder." That same month, Mayor Ralph Webb of Winnipeg, who had spent four years overseas with the Canadian Expeditionary Force, publicly called for a ban on the Communist Party of Canada. An exasperated Simon Tolmie, premier of British Columbia, wanted to go even further; tired of Communist antics, he proposed the deportation of foreigners without even a hearing.[16]

Prime Minister Bennett was personally haunted by the spectre of communism, as is evidenced by the number of files on the subject in his voluminous correspondence. A staunch supporter of the British connection and a fervent Methodist, he regarded bolshevism as nothing less than a blight on the future of the nation and vowed shortly after his 1930 election victory to crush the Communist Party and its nefarious disciples with an "iron heel of ruthlessness." Nothing shook him from this pledge. As the British secretary for the dominions later commented on his dealings with the Canadian leader: "The Russia menace became an obsession with him."[17]

Yet in stamping out the reds, Bennett exaggerated the menace and its influence. He instinctively tended to see any form of public dissent or demonstration as part of a larger Communist-inspired plot. That's why he deliberately combined the issues of unemployment relief and law and order in the 1931 Unemployment and Farm Relief Act. The line between the jobless and the Communists had become blurred. It's also why—just six days after the start of the new parliamentary session in March 1931—the federal minister of Justice began cooperating with the Ontario government to bring about the arrest of the Communist leadership under section 98 of the Criminal Code. The most revealing episode, however, was Bennett's heated confrontation in mid-April 1931 with a thirty-five-person delegation that had come to Ottawa to present a Communist-sponsored national petition calling for non-contributory unemployment insurance. After personally demanding and writing down the names and addresses of all of the delegates, as if they were in trouble, the prime minister exploded: "Never will I, or any government of which I am part put a premium on idleness or put our people on the dole!"[18]

To put an end to this kind of subversion, and at the same time ensure the kind of domestic stability envisaged in the 1931 relief act, Bennett decided to strengthen the RCMP. He started at the top. Going outside the force for only the second time since 1873, he appointed fifty-two-year-old Major-General James Howden MacBrien as the new commissioner effective 1 August 1931. The tightly wound, at times impulsive MacBrien was perfect for Bennett's purposes. A decorated Great War veteran and former chief of the general staff of the Canadian army, he regarded a strong military as fundamental to Canada's future security and had even advocated compulsory military training for all Canadian males, starting from the age of six. In the words of a career Mountie, "He didn't believe in weakness." MacBrien also feared that post-war civil unrest, unless checked, could be the undoing of the country, and he was not immune to sending troops into labour disputes, as he did in the Cape Breton coal fields in the 1920s. But what made him attractive to Bennett, what made them kindred spirits in a sense, was his rabid anticommunism. Not only was he a renowned red-baiter—he once denounced them before an American audience as a "reptile menace"—but he was deeply suspicious of anyone with leftist views. It is little wonder, then, that the new commissioner enjoyed a close relationship with the prime minister and was given free rein to build the RCMP into a formidable bulwark against communism.[19]

Just ten days after MacBrien's appointment, the mounted police, along with their Ontario provincial counterparts, raided the homes and offices of several prominent Toronto-area Communists, including the Soviet-appointed leader, Tim Buck. The operation was designed to "strike a death blow at the Communist Party," and the notorious section 98 of the Criminal Code was the chosen weapon. It was akin to a legal sledgehammer. The Crown easily convicted all eight defendants of being officers and members of an unlawful association. The appeal court, headed, ironically, by Sir William Mulock, upheld the five-year sentences in Kingston Penitentiary, including the recommendation of deportation for the foreign-born. Newspapers heralded the demise of the party—to the quiet satisfaction of the Canadian public.[20]

But MacBrien and Bennett did not stop there. It was not enough to declare the Communist Party of Canada illegal and put the ringleaders behind bars. Something had to be done about the continuing protest of the unemployed. If the "ultimate good of the nation" was to be saved from the "subversion ... steadily creep[ing] over the land"—as one Mountie at the time claimed—then the force needed more muscle. Bennett concurred. On 16 December 1931, by order-in-council, the government quietly increased the force by three hundred men and provided another quarter of a million dollars for riot equipment, including tear gas. The Opposition did not get a chance to question this expenditure until the following February when the estimates for the new fiscal year were tabled in the House of Commons. J. S. Woodsworth, one of a handful of Labour members, was appalled by the implications of the cabinet order. "It looks very bad to me," he warned above the shouts of "nonsense" and "shame." "Surely the government is not taking the position that the way to settle this unemployment question is to shoot down those who are unemployed."[21]

Woodsworth's comments may have been exaggerated, but Bennett's behaviour on 3 March 1932 suggested that there was a element of truth to them. A national convention of unemployed, meeting in Ottawa, wanted to send a small delegation to deliver some resolutions to the prime minister. Bennett grudgingly agreed to receive the men on the outside steps of Parliament, but only after Commissioner MacBrien had placed twenty policemen with side arms around the buildings and another mounted troop of thirty behind the Centre Block. It seemed that revolution was afoot—or at least those in power believed so. "Who would do less," Bennett asked in the aftermath, "than to take adequate precautions for the purpose of preventing a mad rush upon this chamber?"[22]

Mitch Hepburn, a Liberal backbencher and future premier of Ontario, was not so understanding. Always provocative, Hepburn suggested that the government was bolstering the mounted police because of the growing public backlash over broken election promises and claimed that Bennett's real unemployment policy was "the mailed fist." Ernest Lapointe, a former minister of Justice in the King cabinet, was much more sarcastic. He wondered aloud whether the increased police expenditure was "the reason for the fine parades we are witnessing on different occasions around the parliament buildings."[23]

Prime Minister Bennett had reconvened Parliament a month early so that the life of the current unemployment act could be extended to the end of May. The Depression seemed to have tightened its grip on the country over the winter, and the outlook for the spring was bleaker than at any other time in the past two years. But Bennett still clung tenaciously to the idea that recovery was just over the horizon, and that perseverance and sacrifice were needed until then. He faced a growing problem, though, with government expenditures outstripping sources of revenue; despite a potent mixture of deep spending cuts and hefty tax increases, the government still risked running a large deficit. In order to maintain some semblance of a balanced budget, Bennett announced a new relief policy. As of May 1932, there would be no more public works projects except in western Canada's national parks, where the labour was used to build roads and tourist facilities. Instead, he adopted the cheaper course of direct relief or welfare—something he swore he would never do—with the federal government paying one-third of the costs and covering provincial obligations where necessary. The exact arrangements were to be spelled out in individual agreements signed with the provinces. It was the closest that Bennett had come to admitting defeat.[24]

The other controversial piece of legislation that spring, approved by the House before the final reading of the new relief bill, was an amendment of the RCMP Act. The government justified the revisions on the grounds that the Mounties had recently resumed policing work in Alberta and Saskatchewan after the provinces' brief experiment with provincial forces and it was consequently a good time to update the legislation. What some members found troubling, however, were two clauses: one empowering the commissioner to appoint special constables "to make arrests or . . . for purposes of discipline or any other purpose in the public interest"; the other providing for the temporary employment of civilian constables—without pay—whenever requested by a government department. These amendments sounded much like the provisions in the 1931 Unemployment and Farm Relief Act, whereby the Bennett cabinet was given broad, arbitrary powers in the interests of peace, order, and good government. Now these same discretionary powers were being vested in the RCMP commissioner.[25]

J.S. Woodsworth, a lifelong champion of civil liberties, was constantly on his feet during third reading of the bill. Gravely concerned about the centralization of police powers, he argued that peaceful protest had a place in democratic societies and that repression only played into the hands of the Communists. He also found it peculiar that the government was enlarging the powers of the mounted police at the very time it was embarking on a new relief policy. Justice Minister Hugh Guthrie, a one-time Liberal who had changed his political stripes in 1917 to sit with the Tories, neatly sidestepped the criticism by reminding the House that the Mounties were known for their fair and general application of the law and that the new powers were to be used only during an emergency. He also explained that Commissioner MacBrien had personally requested the changes because they could be "useful" to the state.[26]

The new relief and mounted police acts were signed into law the same day; in fact, they can be found in the Canadian statutes for 1932 in consecutive chapters. That unemployment relief and expanded police powers had been paired together—like opposite sides of the same coin—was not accidental.

By the spring of 1932, the Bennett government was in retreat, effectively routed by the stubborn persistence of the Depression. Not only had the prime minister been unable to end unemployment—as he had solemnly promised Canadians in the 1930 election campaign—but he had been forced to backtrack on his spirited pledge never to introduce the dole. Like a prizefighter who has known only success in the ring, he had been badly staggered in the opening rounds. But he stubbornly fought on to ensure that the growing ranks of the unemployed did not become addicted to relief—it had to be kept as demeaning as possible. He could also count on the support of the mounted police, who were more than willing to trade punches with the unemployed, especially if the Communists were involved in some way. It was bad enough that the Canadian way of life was under assault from the Depression. Marches and rallies, coming at a time of national crisis, smacked of sheer bolshevism. But taking action against the Communists and the jobless in the name of law and order was not a simple matter of seeing protest as illegitimate. As Canada suffered through the third year of the Depression, many in authority began to regard the Communists as *the* source of the problem. Commissioner MacBrien said as much in February 1932. "If we were rid of them," he told a veterans' gathering in Toronto, "there would be no unemployment or unrest in Canada."[27] This was the same man who would be called upon by the prime minister three years later to end Canada's greatest protest movement of the 1930s.

CHAPTER TWO

The Royal Twenty Centers

On Thursday, 6 October 1932, the Gentleman Usher of the Black Rod solemnly led members of the House of Commons into the Senate chamber, where they joined other invited guests to listen to the Governor-General read the speech from the throne. The stately ceremony contrasted starkly with the world beyond Parliament Hill. While the aristocratic Earl of Bessborough, resplendent in his vice-regal uniform, confidently outlined the Conservative government's plans for the new session, tens of thousands of single homeless Canadians roamed the country looking for work, food, and shelter. Almost another million owed their daily survival to government assistance, as the unemployment rate continued its steady ascent, which would not peak for another six months, when it reached a staggering 30 percent.

R. B. Bennett, entering his third year as prime minister, probably did not appreciate the contradiction that day in the Senate, for he stubbornly clung to the belief that individual sacrifice and perseverance were sure to break the back of the Depression. Yet the prime minister remained deeply troubled by the menace posed by the unemployed. With characteristic impatience, while Bessborough droned on, he whispered to General Andrew McNaughton, chief of the army general staff, that he was interested in his relief camp scheme and wanted the proposal on his desk the next morning. Two days later, the Governor-General signed an order-in-council establishing work camps for an initial two thousand men to be run by the Department of National Defence (DND). The Bennett administration, after years of evading responsibility for the country's transient unemployed, had finally taken action. But even though the experiment was universally applauded at the time, the relief camps would come to symbolize all that was wrong with Ottawa's handling of the unemployment crisis and ultimately put some of the inmates and the government on a collision course.[1]

❖ ❖ ❖

They were Canada's untouchables. And they seemed to be everywhere. They lined up for endless hours in soup lines or outside relief offices, waiting to be fed or perhaps offered a few hours' work. They were at back doors, cap in hand and pride in their pocket, asking if there was anything they could do to earn a meal or some unwanted clothing. Or they were in rail yards, coming or going, alone or in small groups, hoping that things would be better at the next town down the line. It was a harsh, often demeaning, existence, made worse by the numbing sense of waste and utter desolation. "Wherever they go they feel they are not wanted," explained a Vancouver minister in 1932. "There is no work, no hope, and no place for them."[2]

No one seemed to want to help Canada's single homeless unemployed, and the problem was getting worse. By the fall of 1932 and the failure of yet another prairie harvest, it was estimated that there were one hundred thousand homeless souls wandering the country, atop freight cars, on the backs of trucks, or on foot, trying to survive as best they could. Many of the people behind the numbers were single men, including Great War veterans, who until the Depression had eked out a living in Canada's resource sector, moving from job to job and from region to region, depending on the season and the demand for their services. There were also several thousand young people, fresh-faced teenagers who had quit school to help support their parents and then left home so that they would not be a burden. Some were no more than children. And there were a few women, without family or any other means of support, who naively hoped for a new start in some other place.[3]

Most transients, as they were called at the time, gravitated to larger cities in their quest for work and, more importantly, relief. They were initially granted minimal emergency assistance, but the demands of the needy soon became so overwhelming that many western Canadian cities faced the prospect of bankruptcy if they continued to help the transient homeless in addition to their own citizens. In May 1932, for example, the Royal Canadian Mounted Police worriedly advised the federal minister of Labour that the relief bill in Edmonton for the past winter had exceeded half a million dollars and was expected to rise dramatically now that public works programmes were to be discontinued. This kind of expenditure could not be sustained, even with special supplementary funding from Ottawa. On 1 July 1932, Edmonton, in concert with Calgary, stopped providing relief to any single men, local or transient. The situation was little better in neighbouring British Columbia, a kind of mecca for unemployed single men because of the West Coast's milder winters. The province was awash with so many transients by the fall of 1931 that the Vancouver chief of police wanted the Bennett government to pull men from all west-bound trains and place them in special holding camps along the Alberta–British Columbia boundary.[4]

For Canadian municipalities desperately struggling to remain solvent as the Depression deepened, the simplest and most obvious way to reduce their welfare rolls was to have Ottawa assume responsibility for transient relief. After all, the mobility of the homeless meant that they did not belong to any particular city or province, but rather fell under federal or national jurisdiction. But as long as Prime Minister Bennett hid behind the Canadian constitution and continued to disclaim any direct responsibility for the unemployed, urban centres were forced to cull their relief lists by enforcing strict residence requirements. Only those who had lived in the same municipality for six successive months were eligible for assistance. This strategy may have saved scarce relief dollars, but it effectively sentenced the single homeless unemployed to a life of constant movement and uncertainty. Since there was no work at home, they moved about the country in a determined but fruitless search for a job, but they couldn't get relief in towns along the way because of the residency requirement. They were a fluid mass of individuals trying to make sense of what was happening to their world, when not trying to figure out where to go or what to do next. There was little time to put down roots, even in the makeshift hobo jungles that sprang up on the outskirts of communities.

Private church-run charities would normally provide only a watery meal and then the men were expected to move on. The soup kitchen in Sudbury, Ontario, for example, was housed in a damp, dimly lit basement, offering little shelter from the winter weather. "The tables were covered with ice, and beans, and pieces of wet bread," recounted Great War veteran Ronald Liversedge. "The floor was ankle deep in sludge, and at the out-door into the alley at the back, there was always a ... guard to see that nobody threw the valuable food into the garbage can."[5] City and railway officials, meanwhile, constantly harassed the transients—often at cross purposes. Local police would shoo the men away rather than arrest them as vagrants, while special patrolmen, known as railroad bulls, chased them from freight yards back towards town. It was as if the men carried some deadly plague unknown to civilization.

Even though the various levels of government could not agree who was responsible for the single homeless unemployed, there was no shortage of ideas of what to do with them. It was suggested, for example, that all transients should be issued identification numbers as part of a national registration programme and be assigned to a particular municipality for the duration of the Depression. Another proposal called for the establishment of mass feeding stations throughout western Canada, housed in such places as the former Edmonton penitentiary. Using a line of reasoning more appropriate to draught animals than men, it was argued that the vast pool of unemployed workers would be needed when the economy recovered and that they deserved at least to be fed in the interim. The most popular solution, especially among civic and provincial authorities, was placing the men in camps—effectively removing them from already overburdened urban centres. As a Winnipeg delegation explained to a besieged Senator Gideon Robertson, the federal minister of Labour, during his tour of the four western provinces in June 1931, the city faced a no-win situation. If local officials agreed to feed transients while other communities sat on their hands, then men would naturally be drawn to Winnipeg and quickly overwhelm relief services. But if the city continued to deny assistance to hungry homeless men on the grounds that they were a federal responsibility, then the situation could turn nasty. The message was not lost on a sympathetic Robertson—

somehow, he advised the prime minister, transients had to be removed from the cities before trouble erupted, and the best way appeared to be relief camps. As he bluntly told his boss, "young men can hardly be expected to starve quietly."[6]

Bennett, for his part, was certainly well aware of the suffering wrought by the Depression. His official papers overflow with gut-wrenching letters that are a testament to human perseverance. One unemployed veteran, for example, forced to sell his Great War medals, wrote in frustration, "Making for USA to obtain a crust withheld here." But the prime minister was flatly opposed to any camp scheme that even hinted at any federal responsibility for the unemployed, let alone transients. All he would do was provide emergency funds under the provisions of the 1931 relief act, so that the western provinces could run their own work camps, sometimes in cooperation with the national parks service. Ottawa, in the meantime, pursued its own policies to try to reduce the number on relief. Reaching back in time to an earlier Canada, the federal Department of Immigration and Colonization encouraged the unemployed to take up land, in the romantic belief that working backs and hands would never be idle in a rural setting. The same department, at the urging of western Canada, also embarked on an ambitious deportation programme—what one author has characterized as "shovelling out the redundant." Under a 1919 amendment to the federal Immigration Act, any non-naturalized immigrant who was convicted of vagrancy, or who became a public charge simply by applying for relief, could be deported. Immigration officials now wielded this sweeping provision like a giant dragnet to get rid of foreign relief recipients in the thousands. Ironically, many of these same people had been brought to western Canada only a few years earlier by the country's two major railways as part of an agreement with the federal government. The threat of deportation was also deliberately used to scare away, if not discourage, relief applicants. In Saskatchewan, for example, destitute foreigners were required to sign a form agreeing to voluntary deportation at any future time before relief was granted. By such means, many immigrants were forced to get through those dark years without any governmental assistance if they wanted to remain in the country.[7]

These two federal policies did little more than underscore the bankruptcy of the Bennett government in devising ways to handle the growing unemployment problem. The back-to-the-land campaign secured few converts, while the deportation crusade barely dented the number of single homeless. Many destitute individuals probably kept on the move in order to evade a possible deportation order. By the fall of 1932, it was readily apparent that something else needed to be done. But what? In an apparent fit of frustration, the prime minister had instructed the RCMP to pull transients from trains, beginning in mid-July. But this order had only aggravated the situation since the provinces refused to prosecute the detrained men for vagrancy—there was not enough jail space for all of them, let alone funds to feed and maintain them. Western municipalities, in turn, smarting from the lack of consultation and the federal insensitivity to their plight, angrily responded to the police action by publicly demanding the immediate establishment of federal camps. Others joined the chorus, particularly renowned social worker Charlotte Whitton who had been commissioned by Ottawa to assess the nature of the unemployment crisis on the prairies. Finally, in the days leading up to the new parliamentary session in early October, Bennett grudgingly acknowledged that Ottawa had to move in the direction of relief camps. And the man who had convinced the prime minister that the time had come "to deal with homeless unemployed men so that discipline may be enforced" was the chief of the Canadian army general staff, Andrew McNaughton.[8]

Rugged-looking Andy McNaughton was a Canadian war hero. His unconventional use of artillery during the Great War had helped Canadians win the battle of Vimy Ridge and secured his promotion to brigadier-general at the age of only thirty-one in 1918. Thereafter, his star was in the ascendant. Appointed to several key postings, including a stint at National Defence headquarters in Ottawa, McNaughton was soon recognized for his cool decisiveness, natural intelligence, and organizational skills, and named chief of the general staff in January 1929. But the general seemed more at home in the company of scientists and engineers—as evidenced by his later appointment as president of the National Research Council—and he turned an inventive eye to the growing unemployment crisis during the Depression.[9]

Canada's unofficial corps of single homeless unemployed offended McNaughton's keen sense of efficiency and purpose, all the more so after he observed first-hand the startling magnitude of the problem while inspecting military centres across the country during the summer of 1932. He saw wasted lives at every turn and concluded that something had to be done—and soon—to avoid a future of certain unrest. It was only a matter of time before the jobless became tomorrow's "storm troopers of revolution." McNaughton's answer to getting the men off city streets and out of breadlines was seductively simple. Upon his return to Ottawa that September, he met with Wesley Gordon, Robertson's successor as minister of Labour, and proposed the creation of a national system of non-compulsory work camps to be administered by the DND. In exchange for their work on various military projects, men would be fed, clothed, and sheltered until the economy began to recover and they could resume a more normal life in Canadian society. There the matter rested until the prime minister mentioned the government's interest in the scheme to McNaughton at the opening of the new parliamentary session in early October.[10]

Bennett's change of heart was understandable. Not only was the prime minister keeping an eye on the still climbing unemployment numbers—the September rate was a lofty 28 percent of the Canadian workforce—but he respected and valued the general's sober assessment of the situation. What particularly resonated with the prime minister, however, was the connection between camps and the rule of law. "If we had not taken this preventative work," McNaughton would later claim, "it was only a matter of time until we had to resort to arms to maintain order."[11] This suggestion that relief camps would defuse a potentially explosive situation appealed to Bennett, especially since he regarded unemployment and subversion as two heads of the same monster. It was also an argument that would be repeatedly used in the future to fend off any criticism of the camps, no matter how valid.

The relief camp scheme that the Governor-General signed into law on 8 October 1932 was a modest undertaking. No more than two thousand homeless men were to be put to work under the direction of the DND, repairing the Halifax and Quebec City citadels, as well as clearing twenty-four landing fields in eastern Canada for Trans-Canada Airways. That the size of the programme was kept deliberately small reflected the fact that the camps were a limited experiment. Bennett, for example, insisted that the cost of maintaining the men, including their daily allowance, free tobacco, and medical care, should not exceed a dollar per man per day. This cautious beginning also probably accounted for the Conservative government's decision to activate the programme by order-in-council, instead of debating the matter in the House of Commons. It did not make sense to draw too much attention to the initiative, especially when the government was not only a reluctant sponsor, but a temporary one. The camps were authorized to run only until the expiration of the 1932 relief act. Still, the creation of the DND camps enjoyed popular support, if only because Ottawa was finally taking steps to assist some of the country's transient unemployed.[12]

The other noteworthy feature of the relief camp programme is that women were not part of the relief equation. This neglect of the female unemployed was a reflection of the place of women in the Canadian workforce. Women's employment outside the home steadily rose during the booming 1920s; by the end of the decade, almost one in every five workers was female. But this greater participation rate could not mask women's role as labour's second-class citizens. Seventy percent of female workers toiled at boring, repetitive, generally non-unionized jobs—such as the match and textile industries. They were paid lower wages and worked longer hours than men, and were regularly laid off without a thought about their welfare. The second-largest group of women were employed in the service sector, mostly as clerks and domestics, where they had little prospect of advancement or promotion. Even in the professions there was segregation; women tended to be nurses and teachers, but rarely doctors and lawyers.

These attitudes about women's work carried over into the Depression. Canada administered a "gendered" relief policy—any assistance was specifically designed for unemployed men, while women were regarded as dependents within the family unit. In fact, in the early 1930s, there was a cranky public backlash against women and girls in the workplace. In the public's mind, they were collectively blamed for causing the unemployment crisis, accused of being "bread snatchers and home wreckers." "Wouldn't national life be happier, saner, healthier," asked Mederic Martin, a member of the Quebec government, in a September 1933 *Chatelaine* article, "if a great many ... men could be given work now being done by women, even if it meant that these women would have to ... go home?" It is little wonder, then, that the sense of national emergency associated with the problem of the single homeless unemployed did not extend to women, even though they were part of the transient population. The care of the female jobless was a family duty, the responsibility of fathers, brothers, even uncles or male cousins, but certainly not the state.[13]

McNaughton's relief camps were in operation in central and eastern Canada within a month. That still left tens of thousands of transients stranded in western cities with winter fast approaching. To ease this festering problem, Prime Minister Bennett provided the National Parks Branch with an initial two hundred thousand dollars to operate work camps for the single homeless in mountain and prairie national parks—including Banff, in his Calgary West home riding. He also reluctantly decided in late October 1932 to provide funding—to a maximum of forty cents per man per day—for provincial camps for the transient unemployed.[14]

Bennett looked upon the cost of transient relief like a charitable donation; it was intended to get the jobless through another bleak winter until the following summer, when it was hoped the economy would rally and the problems of the past three years would go away. But then the bottom fell out of the economy. By March 1933, the unemployment rate hit a record 30 percent; in human terms, an estimated 1.5 million Canadians, more than half the 1931 population of Quebec, existed on some form of relief assistance.[15]

The stubborn persistence of the Depression ended the brief experimentation with federal relief camps. On 31 March 1933, the same day another new relief act came into effect, the Bennett government authorized the first instalment of what would eventually amount to nearly nine million dollars over the 1933–34 fiscal year for DND relief camp operations. With the federal public works programme discontinued and no other alternative except direct relief, subsistence camps were now embraced as official government policy. Over the next few months, with Ottawa's unreserved blessing, a zealous General McNaughton moved swiftly to consolidate responsibility for the single homeless unemployed under his absolute control. No detail escaped his attention. It was as if he was going to war again, only this time with a motley army of society's cast-offs who had been on the losing end of life over the past three years. His one demand was that they be physically fit and willing to work. In exchange, he promised that the days of enforced idleness, the curse of the transient, would come to an end.[16]

By March 1934, the general's salvage operation seemed to be turning things around. Over the winter, almost twenty thousand men had been recruited for federal work projects in every province except Prince Edward Island. Given McNaughton's belief that Canada's preparedness for war was sadly lacking, military projects, many at established bases across the country, dominated the work list: hangars and aerodromes, training camps and barracks, radio-beacon stations and rifle ranges. An ambitious road-building programme was also undertaken in British Columbia in cooperation with the provincial government. Fifty-four camps supported forty highway projects, a reflection of the large number of transients who had descended on the province.

The camps were organized and operated along military lines; not even supervisory officers in civilian clothes could disguise the fact that the army was in command. This emphasis on order and discipline was seen as necessary given the large number of men involved and the demands of the work. It paid dividends. Despite claims to the contrary, the camps proved reasonably productive, as evidenced by the project summaries in the final departmental report on the programme.[17]

McNaughton, ever the idealist, promoted the DND relief camps as a kind of tonic intended to restore the morale and vigour of the transient unemployed. Men broken in spirit would go into the camps and emerge healthy, hardened, and hopeful. The supposed healing powers of the camps, however, were effectively negated by what was expected of the men and what they received in return. In the interests of providing work for as many as possible as cheaply as possible, the men were required to do as much as they could by hand. Heavy machinery was used only sparingly. The government insistence on keeping costs down compounded the problem by limiting the use of construction materials. So too did the Canadian trade union movement, which demanded that the camp workers perform only unskilled labour. In several instances, then, the men tackled heavy, back-breaking projects that would never have been undertaken by shovel and wheelbarrow were it not for the government's misguided belief in the need to keep them busy. The most notorious project was Project 51, described as "Canada's gulag," in the Lac Seul district of northwestern Ontario, where some two thousand men spent several miserable months, knee-deep in muskeg or snow, clearing the marketable timber from along fourteen hundred miles of shoreline before the level of the lake was raised by a dam. Such menial labour was bad enough by itself. What made it especially demeaning, though, was the twenty-cent daily allowance. "It affronted human dignity as little else could have done," author James Gray remarked about the failure to pay a decent wage. "It was just the right size to be insulting." A former camp member was much more biting in his criticism. "We were slaves," he bitterly complained. "What else would you call a man who is given twenty cents a day and is expected to believe their bullshit that he is an important part of the country?"[18]

The camps were also little better than jails. The single homeless unemployed were supposed to be admitted on a voluntary basis. In reality, if they wanted relief they had no choice but to enter a camp or try to survive by their wits. Once there, they faced an empty future—endless days of heavy toil with little to show for it. They had no idea how long they would remain there. Nor did they have any connection with the world they once knew. From one monotonous day to the next, nothing changed for the men, and the unnatural, stagnant conditions of camp life steadily ate away at their self-identity. "All the fresh air and sunshine you could stand," recounted a former worker, "but no women, no music, no streets and people, no place to buy anything... and no sounds of streetcars and kids playing. Just the wind through the fir trees, it blew all the time.... After a while you forgot what you looked like." It did not really matter, then, how the projects progressed, let alone how the camps were administered. The men were overwhelmed by the sense that society seemed to have forgotten about them and did not care about them: "They just wanted us out of sight, as far out of sight as they could manage." The utter despair was perhaps best captured by parliamentarian C. G. McNeill when he described the camps as "human scrap heaps" during a House of Commons debate: "There you find young men with no outlet for their talents, no hope of regaining their rightful place in the life of the community."[19]

The feeling of hopelessness that had consumed the transient's every waking moment now took root in the relief camps. Worse than sadly ironic, it was tragic. The DND programme, in the words of McNaughton's biographer, was intended to "conserve the nation's manhood" through work that would "capture the imagination of the men." Instead, camp life only aggravated the gloom and resignation that had gripped the men for much of the Depression. Some decided that life had been better on the road, even with all the uncertainties, and secured their release or simply slipped away without permission. Others stopped working or refused to take orders and were promptly discharged.[20]

Those who remained for any length of time in the camps grew increasingly despondent and distraught—perfect targets for the Communist Party of Canada, which quickly moved to take advantage of the men's vulnerability, when other groups ignored their plight, by organizing the Relief Camp Workers' Union (RCWU) under the auspices of the Workers' Unity League. Here was the second irony. General McNaughton had argued from the beginning that transients were easy prey for the Communists as long as they remained in the cities and that they could best be protected under his relief camp scheme. But the camps, in bringing men together in isolation, actually proved a perfect setting for the activities of Communist organizers. Not only were the men essentially a captive—and in many cases, receptive—audience, but the military structure of the camps probably facilitated the spread of the party's radical message.[21]

Once the Communists gained an initial foothold in the camps, they did everything they could to encourage unrest and resentment. Granted, this work would not have been as successful if not for the general dissatisfaction of the men. But the Communists pushed the simmering discontent to another level by deliberately playing upon the government's failure to pay a living wage and the men's profound sense of disillusionment. They were determined to undermine the camps as part of their larger campaign to discredit the capitalist system. They consequently took up the cause of the relief workers, not to alleviate their troubled existence, but to promote their own political ends. Communist agitators moved about the work projects, often under assumed identities, talking about "slave camps" and mocking the men as "the royal twenty centers." Exactly how many men joined the RCWU is not clear. But the Communist message undoubtedly struck home, if only because it offered hope—an answer—when no one else seemed to care. They were certainly successful in stirring up trouble. During the 4-year life of the camps, there were 359 strikes, demonstrations, and disturbances, while 17,391 men or 10 percent of the total camp population were discharged for disciplinary reasons.[22]

McNaughton's answer to the growing dissension in the camps was hard-nosed. Thankful for the labour and unable to see beyond the merits of his original scheme, he pushed for the creation of special "camps of discipline" for so-called agitators who had been expelled from the regular relief camps and were now suspected of causing trouble in cities. Since the largest number of discharged men tended to be concentrated in British Columbia, it was first suggested that the provincial government build more prison space for this purpose. When the province balked, the general entered into secret negotiations in the fall of 1934 to turn the experimental forestry area on East Thurlow Island, off the British Columbia coast, into an internment centre. Nothing came of the idea.[23]

Prime Minister Bennett, in the meantime, began to doubt the continuing viability of the camps, especially when he began to be identified with their shortcomings. "R.B.," a participant in the programme recalled, "those initials to us meant Rotten Bastard." On 29 May 1934, in a telephone conversation with McNaughton, the prime minister suggested that the time had come to quit the scheme because of all the bad publicity, especially in comparison to the response to what President Franklin Roosevelt was doing in the United States with his Civilian Conservation Corps programme. The general bluntly replied that the camps were the alternative to bloodshed on the streets and that to release the men with the country still deeply mired in the Depression was a recipe for disaster. Bennett seemed satisfied, but not for long. On 18 July, only days after the cabinet approved another large injection of funds into the camps, the prime minister warned McNaughton in a private meeting that the camps had become a political liability. In response, the general once again raised the spectre of revolution—only this time arguing that there would be grave consequences for the government if troops had to put down any disturbance. Bennett was no fool, nor had he gone soft on subversion. If the most senior military officer in the country was worried about pending insurrection, then he had a responsibility to protect the public. For the remainder of the year, a record amount of money flowed into DND camp operations—almost ten million dollars for 1934–35—and the total project population passed twenty thousand men for the first time that winter.[24]

The Bennett government's decision to keep the relief camps operating was not made in isolation. At the same time that McNaughton had been defending the camps as a kind of safety valve, Commissioner MacBrien, his counterpart with the RCMP, had been warning that the threat of subversion seemed to have coiled itself more tightly around the country than ever before. Not even the arrest and conviction of the leaders of the Communist Party of Canada in 1931 had made any apparent difference. "Through the selling of strikes and creating discontent," Commissioner MacBrien cautioned, "the Communists are really doing more harm now than they did parading in the streets."[25]

These fears had prompted MacBrien, in consultation with McNaughton, to recruit and equip a secret three-hundred-man riot squad, skilled in bayonet use and crowd control with horses, at the Regina training depot. Some of the first graduates were assigned to other western divisions, while the remainder of the special squad was kept in Regina, ready for dispatch at a moment's notice.[26]

The mounted police also kept a close watch on the growing ranks of the unemployed for any signs of unrest, real or imagined. A Mountie, for example, worked undercover in the Edmonton relief office during the early 1930s, filing detailed reports, some of which ended up on the desk of the prime minister. Because of the assumed link between ethnicity and radicalism—thinking common to both police and government—a good deal of this surveillance activity was directed at immigrants from continental Europe. One senior Mountie even suggested that many of the country's problems could be resolved if Ottawa simply amended the Immigration Act—he saw no reason why naturalized immigrants, those who had become Canadian citizens after five years, should be exempt from deportation.[27]

This police activity complemented relief camp operations. While the

DND camps were designed to save transients from the clutches of Communist agitators, the RCMP worked to prevent, frustrate, and if necessary respond to the red menace. It also meant that the Bennett government could not pour funds into the relief camp scheme alone. As part of its two-fisted approach to containing dissent, it also had to give the RCMP the means to crush protest, or the country might never be the same again. In the budgetary estimates for the 1933–34 fiscal year, Ottawa consequently proposed to spend roughly $5.5 million on the mounted police. It was a sizeable amount, and almost $2 million more than the force had received the previous year. Hugh Guthrie, the minister of Justice, taking his cue from the RCMP commissioner, forcefully defended the extra expenditure by claiming that it was necessary to bolster the police if they were to deal effectively with the Communist challenge. "I do not wish to be an alarmist," he told the House in his best boy-scout fashion, "but it is always well to be prepared." Angus MacInnis and A. A. Heaps, two members of the new Co-operative Commonwealth Federation party, were not swayed by the argument and chided the minister for interpreting the frustration of the unemployed as sedition. "This is no way to handle the situation which is confronting us," MacInnis countered, "and if we continue it, the result will be disaster." Guthrie, however, dreaded the Communist scourge as much as the prime minister, and he was back in Parliament the following spring asking for the same amount of funding for the mounted police for another year. The request once again raised concerns, particularly from a Liberal backbencher who asked whether the government was afraid "that the country may be kidnapped." But the general sentiment in the House was that the Mounties could be trusted to act judiciously, to do the right thing.[28]

This belief would be tested in the spring of 1935, and the source of trouble would be the DND camps, ironically one of the country's safeguards against violence on the streets. Prime Minister Bennett's decision not to cross General McNaughton, but to keep the relief projects in operation meant that the camps became the focus for much of the deep-seated bitterness of the single homeless unemployed during the worst years of the Depression.

Humiliated by the poverty of their situation and feeling betrayed by a government more concerned with where they were than with how they lived, the men grew increasingly frustrated and angry. The Communists, through the organizational efforts of the RCWU, seized upon this restlessness and gave it shape and voice; the sense of profound hopelessness gave way to mass retaliatory action. The protest began innocently in the form of minor disturbances and demonstrations, but soon escalated to work stoppages and strikes. By early 1935, the growing militancy of the relief camp workers threatened to provoke a showdown with the mounted police and possibly with the militia—exactly what the Communists were pushing for. It was only a question of where and how soon.

CHAPTER THREE

Work and Wages

"Let us go forward in the coming struggle," roared the 19 March 1935 edition of the *Relief Camp Worker*, "with the only weapon that gets results ... organized militant action!" This was the second time in four months that the district leaders of the Relief Camp Workers' Union (RCWU) had called for a general strike in British Columbia. But this attempt would be different from the earlier mass walkout in late December 1934, which had collapsed because of poor planning. With the strike date set for 4 April 1935, union organizers fanned out across the province in a coordinated effort to facilitate the movement of men to Vancouver, while another group readied the city for their arrival. Nothing would be left to chance—a situation that was not lost on local politicians and officials, who watched the strike preparations with a sense of alarm, if not visions of disaster. Yet even though hundreds of relief camp workers descended on Vancouver in early April and stubbornly held their ground for almost two months, the much anticipated showdown with the Royal Canadian Mounted Police never materialized. Part of the reason was the behaviour of the men, coached by their leaders to avoid trouble at any cost. More important, though, was the reluctance of both the federal and provincial governments to assume responsibility for the strikers and do something about the occupation of the city. The Bennett administration steadfastly claimed that the men fell under provincial jurisdiction once they left the Department of National Defence (DND) camps and that Ottawa would become involved only if British Columbia requested assistance. The province, on the other hand, blamed the men's presence in Vancouver on federal policies and refused to do anything that would precipitate a clash with the strikers. Ironically, this jurisdictional wrangling served to confirm what the relief camp workers had been complaining about since the first days of camp operations: that no one cared about their welfare. It also meant that confrontation with the mounted police would have to wait until another day in another place.

❖ ❖ ❖

That British Columbia would become the epicentre of relief camp unrest was hardly surprising. Not only had the province had the most men in the largest number of camps from almost the beginning of the federal programme—more than the three other western provinces combined—but it was here that the RCWU first took root and flourished in mid-1933. In fact, despite efforts to create a national following, the Communist-affiliated organization was essentially a provincial body. This mixture proved a potent one, and became even more so as the numbers of transients continued to pour into British Columbia as the Depression worsened. During a three-week period in the late fall of 1933, for example, the Alberta Relief Commission counted more than fourteen hundred "rod riders" travelling by rail across the southern half of the province and found that two people were headed westward for every person going in the other direction. Relief policies in neighbouring provinces contributed to the migration. Once the DND camps in Alberta reached their capacity in the early fall of 1934, excess men were sent to British Columbia as part of a special arrangement with the federal government. The city of Winnipeg, meanwhile, distributed twenty thousand posters throughout Manitoba that September with the stern warning in bold letters, NO RELIEF FOR SINGLE MEN. The message was brutally ruthless: unless the single unemployed found a winter job in the country, they were to go elsewhere.[1]

The RCWU could not have asked for a better situation than they found in the isolated relief camps of British Columbia. Thousands of frustrated, alienated men were aching for some kind of salvation, and union organizers promised it in the form of defiance. Soon there were work stoppages over the camp meals, the DND clothing allowance, and the lack of recreation facilities. Sometimes the men struck in sympathy for those who were being evicted from the camps. All told, there were one hundred disturbances in the British Columbia camps in 1934—twenty-seven in the month of December alone![2]

Any success was tempered, however, by the fluctuating membership of the RCWU. It was one thing to sign up the single homeless unemployed, but another to keep them wedded to the cause, especially when many would sooner move on to follow up the prospect of real work. Union activity was also hampered by the ban on camp grievance committees—a deliberate attempt by General McNaughton and the DND to restrict, if not prevent, the work of agitators. Any individual who had a complaint had to come forward on his own to the camp foreman; the usual outcome was eviction and blacklisting as a troublemaker.[3]

The RCWU leadership consequently decided to escalate its battle against Canadian relief policy, and in early December 1934 called for a massive walkout from the British Columbia camps. Hundreds of relief workers spent the Christmas period in Vancouver, while a small delegation led by twenty-four-year-old Matt Shaw, RCWU district secretary, tangled with Liberal Premier Duff Pattullo in Victoria. Pattullo, a former Yukon official turned Prince Rupert politician, had come to power only a year earlier on the promise of extending the power of government to ease the province's economic and social problems—what he dubbed his Little New Deal—and was no fan of the Bennett administration. But he had neither the resolve nor the means to address the federal relief camp woes, least of all to satisfy the delegation's key demand for a work and wages programme. All the premier would do was call for a special federal investigation into the camps. The strike, in the meantime, collapsed, sending hundreds of disappointed men back to their camps early in the new year.[4]

Pattullo's recommendation for a camp inquiry or commission had been repeatedly voiced throughout the latter part of 1934. But each time the matter was raised, General McNaughton shot it down with the same precision that he had brought to gunnery during the Great War. The general was not about to question his own creation, especially when he believed that all would be well in the DND camps if not for the nefarious handiwork of a few Communists. Nor was he willing to compromise and agree to have the camps transferred to the authority of another government department. He wanted any recognition gained from the programme to fall to the Canadian military and was worried that another department would bend to the pressure to close the camps. Ottawa, for its part, was initially happy to let the stalwart McNaughton answer the camp critics and debunk the need for an inquiry.[5]

McNaughton's response to the December mass walkout and concerns about future demonstrations was typical. In a draft telegram prepared for Prime Minister Bennett's signature, the general advised a member of the Vancouver Board of Trade that single homeless men had been placed in relief camps at the request of the provinces and that life inside was "fair and reasonable having regard to all circumstances," but that the federal government's responsibility for the men ended if they chose to leave. He also attributed any trouble to "subversive organizations whose one object is to destroy a system established for the care of the men until such time as they could be reabsorbed into industry." In this way, McNaughton fought back the commission question. But it was a strategy which did nothing to defuse the constant complaints emanating from the camps. Over time, the stonewalling would become a liability for the Bennett administration—as would the general.[6]

The RCWU decided to test the federal government's resolve again in the early spring. This time, the strike would be better coordinated, beginning with a weekend conference in Kamloops in mid-March 1935. It would also get outside help in the person of Arthur "Slim" Evans, the district organizer for the Workers' Unity League (WUL). Although the Toronto-born Evans was forty-five when he convened the Kamloops meeting, he had already lived a lifetime of labour activism. As a fellow Communist would later remark, "Nothing outside of working class struggle held any interest for him." Apprenticed as a carpenter, Evans drifted in his early twenties to the midwestern United States, where he became involved in radical labour activity, often at a personal cost. In 1913, during the lengthy Ludlow, Colorado, miners' strike, he was wounded in the leg by a machine gun bullet and thereafter walked with a pronounced limp. In 1919, shortly after his return to Canada and his recovery from the Spanish flu, Evans was appointed the new British Columbia/Alberta representative for the One Big Union, a revolutionary industrial union spawned in the turbulent months after the Great War. This work was cut short in 1923 when he was charged with theft of union dues—he apparently used the money for local relief in Drumheller—and was sentenced to three years in the Saskatchewan penitentiary; a petition from the miners he supposedly robbed secured his early release.[7]

Evans moved to British Columbia in 1926, the same year he joined the Communist Party of Canada. Here, he proved a tireless worker—first for the National Unemployed Workers' Association and then for the WUL—trying to organize fishermen, miners, relief camp workers, and any other disaffected group that would listen. "His pet subjects," in the words of a secret RCMP internal memo, "were the Bennett Starvation Government and his stools, the RCMP." By 1932, Evans's movements and his speeches were constantly being monitored by police—to the point where he had become almost an obsession. "This man seems to be establishing himself as quite a danger," complained the commissioner of the British Columbia Provincial Police, "and if there were any way of removing him it would help considerably." The RCMP were more than willing to oblige in the fall of 1932. But it would be another year before he was arrested and sent to Oakalla prison for advocating the overthrow of the government by violent means. By coincidence, he was released in mid-December 1934, while the first province-wide relief camp strike was underway.[8]

Evans was opposed to the federal relief camps from their very creation. In October 1932, the same month that General McNaughton's plan was embraced by the federal cabinet, he not only began to attack them as slave camps, but proposed the creation of a separate relief camp workers' union under the WUL umbrella. At Kamloops on 10 March 1935, he convened a meeting of delegates from RCWU sub-districts in British Columbia, along with representatives from various WUL affiliates, and recommended that a second mass walkout be organized for 4 April. It was a risky venture, coming as it did on the heels of the other unsuccessful strike, but it was apparent to the meeting that mass action was the only way to move the unsympathetic

Bennett government and perhaps win some public support. Besides, Evans inspired confidence, if not loyalty, among the group; he had been fighting these battles for years—going to jail if necessary—and was respected for his commitment to the radical cause. If anyone was going to make this gambit work, it was he.[9]

Evans rightly recognized, though, that devotion to the cause would not be enough by itself. He saw that the strikers would need something to keep them together, to keep them going, if this second walkout was not to suffer the same fate as the first. The conference consequently adopted seven major demands: a work and wages programme, with a minimum wage of fifty cents per hour for unskilled workers; workers' compensation; an end to DND control of the camps and to the blacklisting of discharged workers; elected camp committees; non-contributory unemployment insurance; the right to vote for all camp workers; and the repeal of section 98 of the Criminal Code and other related pieces of federal legislation. These demands, along with the announcement of the 4 April strike date, were published in the 19 March issue of the *Relief Camp Worker* and would become a rallying cry for the next three months. They also had broad appeal and could not be easily dismissed as subversive.[10]

The news of another Vancouver strike greatly distressed British Columbian politicians and business leaders, all the more so since it was the federal government's relief policies that were at the heart of the unrest. But even though Premier Pattullo warned Ottawa about possible rioting and bloodshed in the streets and repeated his demand for a formal inquiry into the camps, General McNaughton remained unmoved. Not even a damning assessment of the situation by Major-General E. C. Ashton, commander of Military District 11, made any difference. There would be no federal investigation as long as McNaughton continued to have the ear of his political masters.

This influence was threatened, however, on 7 March when the prime minister, already laid low by a severe respiratory infection, suffered what was believed to be a mild heart attack. The overtired, overweight Bennett was confined to bed rest for the next four weeks and then, seeking to escape the stress of the past few years, left on an extended state visit to Great Britain to attend the silver jubilee celebration of King George V. He would be away until the middle of May. In his absence, seventy-eight-year-old Sir George Perley, a hold-over from the Robert Borden war cabinet and the senior statesman on the government side of the Commons, took over the reins of power. He was likely chosen because he would not challenge Bennett's leadership. One of his first tasks was to attend to the pending Vancouver relief camp strike, and he seemed prepared to defer to McNaughton, including having him draft stiffly worded replies to Pattullo on behalf of the government as the strike deadline loomed. At a cabinet meeting on 28 March, however, Perley blinked and decided to appoint a three-man inquiry into the federal relief camps in British Columbia. The commission, to be headed by W. A. Macdonald, a retired provincial supreme court judge, was activated by order-in-council on 1 April.[11]

If Perley believed that the appointment of the Macdonald commission would defuse the strike, he was sadly mistaken. Evans and his team of organizers were not so easily appeased. Throughout the last two weeks of March, they had worked feverishly to prepare for the arrival in Vancouver of over one thousand men from the camps; they were expected to be joined there by several hundred others who had either been blacklisted from the camps or declared physically unfit for admission. The demands of providing for such a large group were daunting, particularly given the circumstances, but billets and food were found—in many instances, thanks to the generosity of Vancouver citizens who supported the men's cause. All was ready, then, when the first camp strikers, encouraged by the early spring weather, reached Vancouver around 5 April. Soon hundreds followed, eventually forming four divisions of about four hundred men each. Several representatives from each division made up a central strike committee, while a smaller strategy committee decided policy. There was also a publicity committee and several other division subcommittees. As Steve Brodie, one of the leaders of division three, later remarked, "We had committees for everything. We couldn't slice a loaf of bread into five bologna sandwiches without appointing a committee to see it was done according to plan. Discipline was an absolute must."[12]

This strong sense of community—what one participant in his memoirs called "The Family"—pervaded the strike during its time in Vancouver and gave the hundreds of men a new-found meaning in their lives. Without doubt, it was a natural consequence of their shared experience in the relief camps, their common hardships on the road. But the strike leadership deliberately cultivated this common purpose to strengthen the bonds among the men: they organized the strikers into divisions in which individuals were answerable to their fellows for any indiscretion; they sought approval from the rank and file of any decisions made by senior strategists; and they posted pickets in the Vancouver rail yards to discourage men from deserting the strike. Evans and his lieutenants knew full well that a large, united body could not be easily intimidated, but could use its size and strength to secure concessions. It was equally important, though, that the strikers avoid even the hint of violence in order to maintain popular support and avoid repression. The strikers had to walk a fine line, but the combination of solidarity and discipline paid dividends, as evidenced by the proceeds from an illegal "tag day" on Saturday, 13 April, when an incredible $5,500 was collected on the streets of Vancouver and surrounding communities. Evans could not resist tweaking the authorities and asked the city police to guard the money over the weekend until it could be deposited in a bank. When two constables arrived at strike headquarters, Evans took great delight, exclaiming in their presence, "Moscow Gold, Moscow Gold."[13]

How Ottawa initially responded to the camp walkout was complicated by a pair of "warring generals." In mid-April, RCMP commissioner James MacBrien went to Vancouver on his own initiative to assess the strike situation. He had every right to be there, especially since the mounted police might become embroiled in any future trouble. But MacBrien muddied the waters by suggesting to the minister of National Defence—McNaughton's boss in the federal cabinet—that the relief camps be replaced by some kind of work for wages programme. McNaughton, who had been junior to MacBrien during the Great War and was different from him from in many ways, was stunned by the recommendation. It not only flatly contradicted accepted government policy, but went right to the heart of his credibility. He retaliated by attacking MacBrien's judgement. The police commissioner should have had the "good sense" to confer with those who had been grappling with the problem before he put forward his "half baked ideas." He also took the matter before cabinet in a special meeting held at the home of Acting Prime Minister Perley on 19 April. For McNaughton, the choice was painfully obvious: the government either held its ground and dealt with the Vancouver strike for what it was—the work of Communist agitators—or did an about-face and embarked on a work for wages programme which he estimated would cost a hefty fifty million dollars per year. There was really no choice. The cabinet agreed and reaffirmed its commitment to McNaughton's hard-line approach—a victory that he telephoned to MacBrien on the West Coast later that same day, along with the warning that he was "in for serious trouble" because of his interference. Two weeks later, Perley wisely decided to bring the sparring to an end and invited the two generals to his office to see if an understanding could be reached. By the time they left, McNaughton had been named the government's point man, while MacBrien would be watching from the rear, at least for the time being.[14]

The strikers, in the meantime, worked hard to win over the public while forcing government authorities to act on their demands. All kinds of tactics were employed. Matt Shaw, the head of the publicity committee, organized a large thank-you parade through downtown Vancouver the day after the successful tag day. He also secured a private interview with the retiring Governor-General at the train station and walked with Lord Bessborough for about ten minutes outside his private railway car, regaling him with stories about camp life and the utter desperation of the men. There were also huge public rallies at the local arena and in Stanley Park, where several hundred, sometimes thousands of local citizens joined with the strikers in pursuing their cause. Naturally, May Day was celebrated with louder voices and more revolutionary enthusiasm than usual. But the most remarkable event was a Mother's Day gathering in Stanley Park when about three hundred women encircled more than one thousand strikers in the shape of a heart. The stunt may have been sentimental, but there was no mistaking the symbolism—these were "our boys."[15]

Bolder action was taken on two other occasions. On 23 April, a large group of parading strikers decided, on a whim, to snake dance through the Hudson's Bay Company department store. When confronted by the local police, they sat down and blocked the entrances and the aisles, trapping customers and the police inside with them. Some knocked over display cases. They then moved on to Victory Square, where they rallied around the war cenotaph, surrounded by hundreds of curious citizens and more police. When the mayor panicked and read the Riot Act, the crowd peacefully dispersed, including the strikers who marched away in formation. The next act of defiance was more carefully coordinated. On Saturday, 18 May, while divisions one and two roamed downtown, threatening to occupy another business, division three swept into the Vancouver Library and Museum. There they remained, hunkered down among the books and the displays until an exasperated mayor promised several hundred dollars in relief funding for the strikers. As one of the division leaders would later recall, "The echoes were already being heard down in Ottawa."[16]

On the surface, these incidents pointed to only one possible outcome: a bloody clash between the strikers and the authorities. Many certainly believed that it was only a matter of time before violence erupted. Harry Stevens, the maverick Conservative MP for Vancouver Centre who had served as Bennett's minister of trade and commerce up until October 1934, took a swipe at Acting Prime Minister Perley for the federal government's continuing insistence that the care of the striking men was purely a local matter. "I submit that such position is no longer tenable," he rebuked his former cabinet colleague, "and is, in fact, provocative."[17]

J. S. Woodsworth, the leader of the new Co-operative Commonwealth Federation party and a staunch civil rights advocate, said much the same thing in a Toronto speech, but added that Ottawa was deliberately spoiling for trouble: "I believe some of the authorities would almost welcome a few riots, because it would give them a chance to bring on their force."[18]

Perhaps the most agitated about what might happen was the newly elected mayor of Vancouver, the embattled Gerry McGeer. At the beginning of the April walkout, McGeer had complained that there were already too many people going to bed hungry in the city without it having to feed several hundred extra mouths: "Our national government is apparently anxious ... to wage war on people but unfortunately unwilling ... to wage war on poverty." But when federal authorities refused to show any sympathy for his situation, let alone extend a helping hand, he did an about-face and injected the vocabulary of revolution into the dialogue. In a radio address a few days after the fracas in the Hudson's Bay store, the mayor damned the strikers as part of a larger plot to install a soviet-style government. He made similar accusations after the men had extorted money from the city by occupying the library and museum—and pushed him around in the process. In a heated telegram to Prime Minister Bennett, fresh home from his trip to England, McGeer charged: "Communist organizers and agitators ... have been able to organize substantial numbers who are openly flouting constituted authority ... force will have to be resorted to maintain order ... we cannot hold the situation any further."[19]

Mayor McGeer's doom-and-gloom comments were little more than political posturing. Granted, an estimated fifteen hundred relief camp strikers were parading up and down the streets of the city. There was also serious labour trouble brewing on the Vancouver waterfront, where hundreds of longshoremen threatened to walk off the job any day and become the first recruits in a rumoured general strike. But the city—and the province, for that matter—did not want to move against the strikers if they could avoid it. This reluctance to act did not necessarily mean that British Columbia officials sympathized with the plight of the men. Rather, they were not about to do Ottawa's dirty work, especially when the strike revolved around conditions in federal relief camps. If the city or provincial police were to arrest and jail the camp workers, then they would essentially be accepting the blame for the failure of the camps, something they were not willing to do under any circumstance. McGeer's waving of the red flag was designed to provoke the federal government into dealing with the strikers and did not represent a true reading of the situation in Vancouver that spring. Yes, there were Communists busily at work among the disaffected, trying to evoke a class consciousness, but to suggest that a proletarian revolution was on the horizon was another matter entirely.[20]

Prime Minister Bennett did not rise to the bait. By the time he returned to Canada and took up his seat at the cabinet table on 20 May, there was every indication that the relief camp walkout was on the rocks. Just the day before, Major-General Ashton, the officer commanding Military District 11, had predicted that the strike would probably collapse in the next thirty-six hours, as evidenced by the growing number of men applying for readmission to the camps. There was no need, then, for Ottawa to bloody its hands. McNaughton's strategy of refusing to take any responsibility for the strikers and waiting them out appeared to have won the day. In fact, the only dissenting voice remained RCMP commissioner MacBrien, who had reversed himself in May and was now calling for the men to be rounded up and sent to internment facilities.

Victory seemed less assured, however, when Ashton reported a few days later that local Communists had convinced the relief camp strikers to hold out for a possible general strike led by Vancouver's longshoremen. The Bennett government had been quietly preparing for this eventuality for several weeks, especially after the dock workers had earlier debated a sympathy strike in support of the relief camp workers, and had over one hundred Mounties at the ready to supplement the city and provincial police forces. All Ottawa could do now was watch and wait. The prime minister, however, decided to dump McNaughton at the first opportunity for getting his government into such a fine mess.[21]

Ironically, it was the strikers who defused the charged atmosphere in Vancouver. After almost two months in the city, the relief camp workers were no closer to getting any of their demands acted upon by any level of government. They were also rapidly running out of funds, and there was only so much support that the beleaguered citizens of Vancouver could be expected to provide. The strikers were like uninvited houseguests. Worst of all, their numbers—and therein, the source of their negotiating strength—were rapidly falling away, as dozens decided to return to the camps or move on. Not even the prospect of support from the longshoremen could hold them.

The strike committee consequently had to do something to salvage the walkout or the relief camp workers would have nothing to show for their time in Vancouver. After some internal wrangling, it was decided to put the question directly to the men whether the strike should be continued. The result was announced at a pivotal afternoon meeting at the Avenue Theatre on 30 May: more than two-thirds of the 909 ballots cast favoured continuing the fight. But the bigger question was what to do next. The charm of the strikers' snake dancing was wearing off, and Mayor McGeer was dead set against providing any more relief. Besides, almost half the original strikers had already abandoned the walkout, as evidenced by the number of votes.

It was at this critical juncture that a motion was put forward which would galvanize the strikers' flagging spirits. Arthur Evans claimed that he was the originator of the idea that the men take their grievances to Ottawa and confront the Bennett government. Trekker Ron Liversedge, on the other hand, attributed the proposal to a nameless striker who stood up at the special meeting and calmly suggested, "Let us go to them." Whatever its source, the men embraced the trek as the answer to their dilemma and quickly approved it with a rousing unanimity that had been missing over the past few weeks. "The strikers were very enthusiastic," Evans later recounted. "If applause would do it they would have taken off the roof of the building."[22]

Police and military officials dismissed the trek idea as nothing more than a shameless attempt to forestall the inevitable collapse of the strike for a few more days, somewhere in the mountains beyond Vancouver. "Properly handled, this trek will melt away," the Vancouver police chief confided to General Ashton, "as men I have talked to say it is planned to save the face of their leaders, who let them down so badly." But they were not going to prevent the men from leaving the city, especially if it meant they would be removing themselves as potential allies in the anticipated longshoremen's strike. Ottawa could not have asked for a better outcome.[23]

Ironically, the Communist Party of Canada agreed. A front-page editorial in *The Worker*, carrying the headline "Trek to Ottawa Not Advisable," warned that the battleground was in Vancouver and that to leave the city would lead to "the liquidation of the strike." If anything, party leader Tim Buck argued, the relief camp men and the Vancouver working class should form a united front to further the militant struggle.[24]

The strikers, however, had been fed a steady diet of this rhetoric for weeks and had nothing to show for it. At least, in going to Ottawa, they could force the Bennett government to deal with their grievances. But the trek was a bigger gamble than the walkout. Ottawa was more than three thousand miles away by rail, and the strikers had less than one thousand dollars in their pockets to help get them there. Nor could they expect much help along the way, if Mayor McGeer's attitude was any indication. Not only did he refuse permission for a tag day to raise funds for the trek, but he also turned down a request to help send three strike delegates ahead to Ottawa.[25]

These were considerable challenges, and they would not be easily overcome. But what took hold of the strikers, what seemed to have stirred their imagination, was the sheer audacity of the scheme. For almost two months, Ottawa had turned a deaf ear to their demands—as if the men did not exist. Prime Minister Bennett was now going to learn that both the men and their grievances were real and could no longer be ignored. This sense of mission became even more acute once the Macdonald Commission issued its report on the B.C. relief camps on 31 May, the day after the decision to go to Ottawa had been approved. Even though the commission readily admitted that a deep dissatisfaction had coloured its hearings, it concluded that the camps "have reasonably fulfilled the object of their establishment." In fact, it took issue with the men's complaint that they were "a forgotten group." "We did not find evidence to substantiate this opinion," the report argued using a perverse kind of logic, "but are convinced that such a feeling exists in the minds of the men." The commission also refused to consider the striking men's seven demands, on the grounds that these issues were beyond its authority and were more a matter for the government. This last point was held up by the strike leadership as the reason that the men were going to Ottawa. As Evans later explained, the "hot cakes and foremen" commission "did not deal one iota with the demands of the strikers.... It is the hopelessness of life that these people are kicking about, not the camp conditions. They want to live like human beings with decent wages." These sentiments were echoed by thirty-six-year-old George Black, who had emigrated to Saskatchewan ten years before and like many others had drifted to British Columbia in search of work. "The whole idea of the trek ... was no pleasure trip," the Scottish immigrant recounted in his no-nonsense fashion. It was "rather ... to prove to the whole people of Canada that ... the camps were absolutely unfit for human habitation."[26]

The first batch of strikers, numbering 831, climbed aboard the nightly Canadian Pacific seaboard freight on 3 June. They probably had a spring in their step, for this trip, unlike countless others before it, was heavy with meaning. Two smaller waves followed over the next day: 195 men on a

Canadian National eastbound freight just after midnight and another 350 on the late evening CPR freight.[27] The entire group, now reduced to three divisions because of defections over the past few weeks, was to rendezvous less than a day's travel away at Kamloops at the junction of the North and South Thompson rivers. Just a handful of policemen watched the departure of the men. No attempt was made to stop them; on the contrary, officials were pleased to see them leave and ride off into oblivion. This sense of victory, however, was based on the assumption that the men were already beaten, and had been for years. It now fell to the trekkers to prove them wrong.

CHAPTER FOUR

Makin' History

The gentle swaying of the boxcars and the clickety-clack of the wheels proved hypnotic, and many quickly nodded off. But it was a fitful sleep that first night of the trek. Although relieved to leave Vancouver and the seemingly hopeless situation behind them, the men now faced an even bigger challenge: travelling en masse by rail more than half-way across the country to confront the prime minister about his draconian relief policies. Many probably quietly shuddered at the long days ahead, all the more so as the train knifed through the cold night air of the mountains. Even if they made it through the Rockies, there was still the wilderness of northern Ontario waiting for them. But despite a disappointing beginning, the On-to-Ottawa Trek soon took on the aura of a crusade. What began as a strike against federal relief camps would be transformed by the trek into a popular movement against the Conservative government's handling of the Depression. The trek was like an accusatory finger being wagged in Bennett's face, telling him that unemployment was a national crisis and that the days of evading responsibility were about to end. This symbolism was not lost on the communities that welcomed the men like modern-day folk heroes as they headed east on their mission. Nor was the prime minister unmoved. As the trek gathered momentum while crossing the southern prairies, Bennett decided that it had to be halted in Regina.[1]

❖ ❖ ❖

Few people gave the On-to-Ottawa Trek much of a chance of making it through the mountains. Despite rumours of a punitive force being hurriedly dispatched to the interior to pull the men from the trains, neither the Royal Canadian Mounted Police nor the British Columbia Provincial Police did anything to interfere with the trek as it headed for Kamloops. It was simply assumed that the men, after several frustrating weeks in Vancouver, lacked the resolve to continue their protest for much longer and that many would abandon the trek at the first opportunity, perhaps on the very first morning. Federal officials were equally convinced that the trek was destined to fail and publicly acted as if they did not care or even know anything about it. When the matter was first raised on the floor of the House of Commons on 5 June, W. A. Gordon, the minister of Labour, smugly responded on behalf of the government, "we have no knowledge of it.... The only information ... is what appears in the press." He also assured the House, somewhat half-heartedly, that the mounted police "would watch such a performance as these men are apparently staging" as part of their regular duties. What Gordon apparently did not realize, though, is that RCMP commissioner James MacBrien, as a precaution, had already telephoned Canadian Pacific Railway headquarters in Montreal the day before "to ask if the [railway] could take any action to halt the march to the east." Robert Manion, the minister of Railways, repeated the request by telegram, noting "it is the desire of the government that everything that is possible be done to prevent [the trekkers] being carried by the railways."[2]

The Communist Party of Canada was not much more optimistic about the chances of the trek succeeding. Putting up a brave front, the party claimed in the 4 June 1935 edition of *The Worker* that the men had to leave Vancouver because food resources had been exhausted there, and that the trek would be similarly imperiled unless mass feeding stations were set up along the route. "A trek to Ottawa," the paper argued in an apparent reversal of its initial position, "will bring the two-month-old struggle to a new front and rally greater national support." The Communists, however, were not prepared to back up these words with action and forbade Arthur Evans to accompany the trek. According to an internal mounted police report on the situation in Manitoba, the party was still upset by the decision to abandon the Vancouver strike and viewed the decision to go to Ottawa as a terrible blunder. "Starting out for Ottawa without the consent of the National Office showed lack of discipline and displayed weakness on the part of the leaders in not being able to control the unemployed and confine it as a provincial matter," local Communists reportedly complained. "There is no one in Winnipeg who seems optimistic about the outcome of this trek.... No one seems to be keen about joining up with them." But like the mounted police, the Communists could not dismiss the trek completely and at Evans's own urging sent him ahead to see what he could do to facilitate the movement of the men eastward. It was a short leash, though. Evans was to travel only as far as Golden and then return to Vancouver.[3]

The trek, meanwhile, seemed likely to fulfill the gloomy predictions. Although the train engineers tried to be as accommodating as possible—by making frequent, unscheduled stops, for instance, to allow the men to pee from atop the boxcars or have a smoke—the same could not be said of the reception awaiting the men at Kamloops. When Evans reached the ranching and fruit-growing centre on 2 June, he found to his disappointment that the local party organizer was away and that nothing had been done to prepare for the arrival of the men. To make matters worse, the mayor not only refused a tag day to raise funds, but suggested that if the men were intent on staying for any length of time, they could sleep beside the railway tracks. A frustrated Evans pleaded his case and then headed for Golden shadowed by the local mounted police.[4]

The first group of trekkers followed two days later, "stiff, sore, tired, and very hungry." Surprised by the lack of any welcome, they ignored the mayor's edict and did a quick canvass of the town for food and cash donations before settling down for the night in the local park. It was here, while the men were sitting around campfires talking among themselves or getting ready to bed down, that the trek found its unofficial battle song. "Comrade" F. Marsh, who had kept the books during the Vancouver strike, began to play "Hold the Fort," on the concertina that was his constant companion. As the music drifted through the park, the men stopped what they were doing and began to sing the words—a few at first and then more and more until the refrain was reached and all joined in:

Hold the fort for we are coming,
Union men be strong,
Side by side we battle onward,
Victory will come.

From that night forward, Marsh played the tune at every opportunity, and the men readily broke into song as if the lyrics were written especially for the trek.

We meet today in freedom's cause,
And raise our voices high

The song provided a sense of purpose for the men and their struggle, a sense of solidarity against a common enemy. It would be sorely needed in the days ahead.[5]

The main body of trekkers was supposed to wait at Kamloops until the two smaller groups that had left Vancouver a day later caught up with them. But the men were so demoralized by their reception that Jack Cosgrove, a Great War veteran who had been given the nod as trek marshal, decided to push on down the line before their grumbling and bitching became an open revolt. "It was here that the breaking point was just about reached," trekker Ron Liversedge later remembered about the stopover in Kamloops, "and the first time since our strike started that ... our self-discipline [was] thrown to the winds." The situation at Revelstoke, a mining and forestry community on the Columbia River, was little better. While the freight stood idling for them, the men hurriedly wolfed down sandwiches and coffee at local restaurants before heading off again an hour later. One might easily have mistaken them for a swarm of invading locusts.[6]

The main trek party reached Golden, on the east arm of the Columbia River, in the early morning hours of Thursday, 6 June. After the near breakdown in Kamloops, the trek leaders had talked about how things would improve down the line, that they would get the kind of help they were going to need if they expected to get all the way to Ottawa. No one realized the importance of this more than Slim Evans. Determined to erase the memory of the Kamloops fiasco, he set to work in Golden, calling on his contacts in the area as well as canvassing the local farm community for donations. By the time the men detrained, a smiling Evans greeted them in a nearby park, proudly standing before a clutch of elderly women stirring washtubs of simmering stew. "I'll never forget that," Red Walsh confessed years later. "We got off the freight at four o'clock in the morning. I was so cold when I come [sic] off the roof of that boxcar I thought I was goin' to fall down." This miracle in the Selkirks—and that's how many regarded the meal—was exactly what the trek needed to shake off its doldrums. As the hundreds of men lined up to be served, with the rising sun as a backdrop, the tension and doubt of the past few days gave way to friendly chatter and lopsided grins. No matter what lay ahead, there was a profound sense that the worst was now behind them. It was if they had been reborn and anything seemed within reach.[7]

At a mass meeting following the meal, Evans announced he was needed back in Vancouver and he would be replaced by George Black, a representative of the Workers' Ex-Serviceman's League (the Communist equivalent of the Canadian Legion), who had been denied entry to the Department of National Defence (DND) camps for medical reasons. When some of the men wondered aloud about his qualifications, the tall, wiry former Black Watch soldier from Glasgow quietly stood and stared down any skeptics. Black's no-nonsense demeanour would be needed in the coming days. Although the trek had defied the odds-makers and made it as far as Golden, the success had come at a cost: more than a hundred men had slipped away since Vancouver. If the trek was to going to build some momentum and become a force, it would have to draw on the same kind of organization and discipline that had been a hallmark of the Vancouver strike or the defections would continue and the trek ultimately fail.[8]

Evans, Black, and Cosgrove used the day in Golden to count heads and make adjustments to the three divisions, as well as to ensure that division captains and platoon corporals knew exactly what was expected of the men under their supervision. They also sent a small advance party ahead to make arrangements for the feeding and housing of the trek at a series of predetermined stops along the way. Nothing was left to chance.[9]

The next stop was Calgary, some 150 miles down the line—and 150 miles closer to Ottawa. It would also be the trek's last day in the mountains. But the upbeat mood of the men on leaving Golden was short-lived because of what lay ahead on the route: the famous spiral tunnels of the Kicking Horse Pass. This was not the first time that the trek had passed through a major railway tunnel. Just beyond Revelstoke, the men had spent several long, uncomfortable minutes sucking in the poisonous smoke from the engines in the Connaught Tunnel, a five-mile tunnel that had been excavated below Roger's Pass in 1916 because of avalanche problems in the area. The spiral tunnels were different, though. Built between 1907 and 1909 because of the steep grade of the "Big Hill" on the west side of the Kicking Horse Pass, the twin tunnels, each more than half a mile in length, spiraled around and underneath themselves like a giant corkscrew. Together, they posed a real danger to anyone hitching a ride on a boxcar, let alone several hundred men perched atop an entire freight. For the first time, there were genuine fears for the safety of the trek, so much so the train was deliberately stopped outside Field while two local mounted policemen and a railway man cautioned Cosgrove and Black about the danger ahead. The men prepared themselves as best they could. Some placed wet handkerchiefs over their faces to guard against the smoke and heat, while the lucky few with goggles made sure that those fit snugly over their eyes. All clung tightly to the catwalk, as the freight groaned around the curves. "It was hot in the tunnels," Irven Schwartz recalled. "First there was a blast of cold and then a real blast of heat and finally the smoke came back. You think you're not going to live."[10]

As the men endured their taste of hell, the trek began to attract national attention, if only because it was going to make it out of the mountains. The *Ottawa Citizen*, for example, had initially likened the men to "refugees." But once it appeared that they might actually get to Ottawa, the newspaper claimed it was "superficial" to dismiss them as "good-for-nothing nuisances" and try to keep them at bay. "They are an active and significant manifestation of the economic palsy that has this nation in its grip," an editorial reminded government officials. "Moreover, they are fellow Canadians and human beings." *The Worker*, on the other hand, conveniently forgot its earlier lukewarm support for the trek and called on labour groups across the country to rally behind the "relief camp boys" and their demands. "Arrange to meet them at the railroad terminals," it implored. "Organize mass meetings and demonstrations to greet them. Establish feeding stations, collect foodstuffs and money to help them on the next lap of their journey." The Communists looked upon the trek as an ideal vehicle to unite the labour movement under their influence and at the same time portray those who refused to lend a hand as enemies of the working class.[11]

Even the prime minister, who had been silent about the trek since it had left Vancouver, finally outlined the government position when Ian Mackenzie, the leading Liberal from British Columbia, raised the matter during the daily question period in the House of Commons. "No complaints have been made by the railway companies against these trespassers," Bennett reported on 7 June, "and until such time as such complaints are made, the provincial authorities are not ... disposed to take any proceedings against these men." He also indicated that the federal government was "ready and willing" to render assistance, but only if asked to do so by the provinces. When Mackenzie asked whether Ottawa had received any such requests, Bennett dutifully responded that Alberta officials had complained by telegram about the impending arrival of the men, but that they had not asked for help. "Obviously it is hardly necessary to say that we are not in a position to render any assistance until such complaint is made," he concluded, "and that matter ... is one that rests ... with the provincial authorities." These comments were identical to those Bennett had made a few weeks earlier when the Vancouver relief camp strike appeared to be getting out of hand. "There can be no trifling with anarchy, there can be no playing with chaos," he solemnly told Parliament on 21 May, but quickly added that the federal government would not—could not—get involved "except at the request of the provincial authorities." The On-to-Ottawa Trek consequently served to intensify the squabble between federal and provincial governments over which was responsible for dealing with the unemployed. While Bennett steadfastly held to the doctrine that the disciplining of the men was a provincial matter, the provinces were prepared neither to stop and arrest men who were going to Ottawa to protest federal policy nor to admit that they could not handle the situation. As one historian has observed, the Communists could not have asked for better propaganda than the spectacle of different levels of government publicly bickering over the trek.[12]

At about the same time the prime minister was making his pledge in the Commons not to interfere with the trek, Jack Cosgrove led the men into Calgary. At 4:00 on the afternoon of Friday, 7 June, a fifty-car CPR freight, with its human cargo, slowed to a stop at Tenth Street West, near the Mewata Armouries. On a signal from Cosgrove, approximately 750 men climbed down from atop the boxcars, neatly formed themselves into their three divisions, and then marched off, four-abreast, along the south side of the tracks to Victoria Park, the site of the Calgary Stampede, where they were to be billeted under the exhibition grandstand.

Cosgrove's return to his home town was a triumphant one. Although born in Scotland in 1899, he had been raised and educated in Calgary before volunteering—at fourteen—for overseas service at the start of the Great War. He spent the next five years in a Canadian uniform, mostly in the trenches of France, where he was wounded at the Somme, and then served another seven years in the American cavalry. The experience made him a crack shot—he was a candidate for the Canadian Bisley rifle team—but it did nothing for his job prospects, and he eventually ended up in a British Columbia relief camp in 1933. Now, as trek marshal, he was proudly leading his own army of unemployed through downtown Calgary with a police motorcycle escort. The attention rivaled that of his former school teacher, William Aberhart, who was about to lead the new Social Credit party to a landslide victory in the Alberta provincial election.[13]

The trekkers, or "tourists" as they were jokingly called in the local newspapers, were scheduled to spend three days in Calgary. But all the advance party was able to secure at a special city council meeting that same afternoon was the use of the grandstand for housing the men; Mayor Andrew Davison offered no bedding, no soap and towels, and no food. This last need was critical, especially since the two smaller groups of trekkers, numbering around two hundred, were expected to arrive in the city on another CPR freight about two hours after the main party. The mayor, however, refused to feed the men—or even grant a permit for a tag day—on the grounds that the care of all single unemployed in Alberta rested with the provincial government, not the city. The trek leadership took the decision in stride. Once the men had washed off the soot and grime in the nearby Elbow River, they were called together in their platoons and given fifteen cents each to purchase a meal of meat and potatoes that had been hurriedly negotiated at a number of neighbourhood cafes. The men had earned the treat. But something had to be done to secure relief for the next few days or the stay in Calgary would be a short one.[14]

George Black and the strike committee tackled the food question head-on Saturday morning. As the city started to stir, dozens of men with tin cans took up positions on downtown street corners and started soliciting donations from people going to work or on their way shopping. This illegal tagging was apparently part of a larger strategy to see how far they could push things without being pushed back. The night before, Matt Shaw, a member of the trek advance party, had made a plea for food and clothing on a local radio station. Now, with the tag day, the trekkers were taking their cause directly to the public, and at the same time testing whether the city was prepared to enforce its decision of the day before. When the Calgary police did nothing to stop the men collecting money, Black became even bolder. Knowing that any chance of securing temporary relief rested with the provincial government, he decided to lay siege to the downtown office of the Alberta Relief Commission and hold hostages if necessary. Shortly before noon, five hundred men formed up on Seventh Avenue, loudly chanting, "We want food!", while a smaller group of trekkers, numbering about eighty, snake danced around the building and blocked all exits. As a crowd gathered to watch the spectacle, Black and a handful of local supporters sparred inside with commission chairman A. A. Mackenzie. From the outset, the provincial official kept on insisting that relief funds were intended for Albertans only and that he had no authority to provide any assistance. The trekker delegation calmly countered that no one would be allowed to leave the building as long as the men outside went hungry. After two tense hours, Mackenzie finally relented and with the approval of the provincial government, agreed to cover the cost of two meals per day for the next three days. When news of the victory was announced outside, the men cheered and then marched back to the exhibition grounds without incident.[15]

Saturday's fund-raising efforts replenished the trek's near-empty coffers. Not only had the province been forced to provide $600 in meals, but the tag day had collected $1,302. Yet the real beneficiaries that day were the men. Initially wary of the trekkers and their motives, Calgary citizens were struck by the innocent youthfulness of those tagging on the streets. Many were little more than teenagers and could have been their sons, grandsons, or brothers. They were also amazed by the organization and discipline of the marchers, especially during the relief office episode, when not a single demonstrator broke rank or even responded to the catcalls from the appreciative crowd. "We had reports that these strikers were a rough bunch," one bystander told a reporter, "but when we saw how orderly and well behaved they were everyone warmed up to them." This sympathy for the men and their cause sharply contrasted with Calgary's treatment of its own unemployed during the 1930s. Whereas local protest was generally dismissed as Communist propaganda, the trekkers' demands—and their decision to confront the prime minister about them—came to be seen as both reasonable and legitimate. The *Calgary Albertan*, for example, seemed to speak for many citizens when it calmly downplayed the apparent connection between the trek and the Communist Party of Canada. "To be quite frank," an editorial confessed, "we don't care very much."[16] W. J. Stevens of the CPR believed that all the talk about the trek being a revolution on wheels was nonsense. "Do not believe intention of group leaders one of armed resistance and violence," he wired Montreal headquarters. "Do not think they are in possession of arms or weapons of any kind."[17]

The men also learned an important lesson from their experience on the streets of downtown Calgary that Saturday. Ever since leaving Vancouver, the trek leaders had been counselling the men to exercise self-discipline and bite back on their anger and frustration. It was not until reaching Calgary, however, that their conduct was really tested for the first time. And they passed brilliantly. They not only won some much-needed relief, they also won the support of the public—the two things the trek required if it was going to make it all the way to Ottawa.

Saturday's activities were capped with an evening meeting at the exhibition grounds, at which an estimated one thousand Calgary citizens listened to Matt Shaw explain the reasons behind the strike and the decision to go to Ottawa. The twenty-four-year-old Shaw, with sandy hair and grey eyes, was something of a "poster boy" for the trek. Born as John Surdia in Regina in December 1910 and trained as a mechanic, he had left home at eighteen and bumped from job to job, first in Ontario and then Manitoba, before taking to the road at the start of the Depression. He even changed his identity in the hope that he would have a better chance at work if his name sounded less foreign. But Matt Shaw fared just as poorly as John Surdia, and his experience in several relief camps hardened him beyond his years, to the point where he became actively involved in the struggle to secure a better deal for the single homeless unemployed. It seemed a natural calling. As chair of the publicity committee during the Vancouver strike, he exploited every opportunity to talk about the situation in the federal relief camps and the need for meaningful solutions. Now, as a member of the advance team, Shaw was well on his way to becoming the most famous trekker in the country, as he carried the story of the men's plight to a wider audience. It was a message he delivered with conviction and passion, if the cheers and applause that punctuated his remarks at the Calgary rally were any indication.[18]

Sunday was another busy, but more relaxed, day for the trekkers. In the morning, many washed their clothes in the Elbow River, hanging them to dry in nearby trees, while others lined up to be shorn by Bob Campbell, a former Toronto barber who still carried his electric clippers in his bag. Later that afternoon, led by a police motorcycle escort, the men marched to St. George's Island on the Bow River, where a number of local labour organizations hosted a picnic in honour of the trek. There was a concert band, hampers brimming with food, and a general feeling of fellowship as the men intermingled with citizens and shared their personal stories. A few of the younger boys were even invited home for supper.

The day ended with a closed meeting at the exhibition grounds, held in part to welcome about 150 new recruits from Edmonton. One of the more light-hearted moments came during the reading of congratulatory messages, when Red Walsh, who was chairing the programme, was passed a note from a woman outside the stadium entrance. Shaking his head in disbelief, a smiling Walsh announced that a group of women wanted to ease the loneliness of the men by joining the trek. The note suggested that an effort would be made to find a woman for every man on the trek. The offer provoked a roar of laughter and guffaws, but was decisively turned down by a show of hands when put to a vote. The men apparently believed that they would be asking for trouble if women were allowed to accompany them.[19]

Even without the female recruits, the number of trekkers continued to grow over the weekend as word of the march eastward spread. Dozens of single homeless unemployed deserted nearby federal relief camps and headed to Calgary, while about one hundred local citizens decided to sign up for the ride to Ottawa. The new men, including those from Edmonton, were assigned to a new fourth division headed by Sven Uden. They quickly learned what it meant to be members of the trek. While marching in formation through downtown Calgary to the rail yards early Monday evening to catch a ten o'clock freight, some of the new recruits at the end of the column broke rank and starting horsing around with people lining the sidewalks, especially the girls. Stewart "Paddy" O'Neill, one of the organizers of the Vancouver strike, was immediately dispatched to put an end to the ruckus and barked at the men to get back in line or get off the trek. "What the hell's going on here? Have you bastards gone mad?" the Newfoundland Great War veteran roared, "Do you think we've spent years building our organization to have you come and wreck it?" That was the end of any discipline problems.[20]

As the trek prepared to leave the city, military authorities pegged the strength of the movement at thirteen hundred—slightly less than the number of men who had originally set off from Vancouver at the beginning of the month. Despite the defections, the trek leadership had every reason to be pleased. Not only had the stop in Calgary been a remarkable success, but the very idea of going to Ottawa had assumed a credibility and popularity beyond the men themselves. Why else would an estimated one thousand to two thousand well wishers come to see the trekkers off that Monday night? They were not leaving empty-handed. Enough people had answered Matt Shaw's radio appeal for food, clothing, and blankets to fill a boxcar. Twenty-four hundred sandwiches, prepared from donated supplies, were distributed to the men as they sat in their divisions in the grass, watching their freight being made up. Even after George Black had given the signal to board, a few people ran up to the train and handed small parcels to the men as they took their place atop one of the fifty cars. As the engineer opened the throttle and the drag began to move, Jack Cosgrove, standing amid a shower of swirling cinders on the tender, waved goodbye to his grey-haired mother. Ron Liversedge was more reflective; with the crowd cheering the trek on its way, he privately wondered how Calgary could ever live down the "stigma" of electing R. B. Bennett.[21]

The trek's departure for Medicine Hat made a showdown with the federal government all the more likely. Indeed, some kind of trouble was already being anticipated. On the morning of 7 June, the same day the trekkers were scheduled to arrive in Calgary, members of Lord Strathcona's Horse suspended a training exercise at their Sarcee base to take up quarters at the Mewata Armouries. It was no coincidence that the trekkers were deliberately detrained there later that afternoon, instead of at the Calgary rail yards. The federal troops remained at the ready over the weekend, but were never sent out, even during the siege of the Alberta Relief Commission office, because the province never formally requested their assistance. Such a request was not forthcoming, according to Colonel S. T. Wood, assistant commissioner of the RCMP, because the police did not have "sufficient strength to deal with the situation"—there were only sixty city police and thirty Mounties in Calgary that weekend. The police were consequently reduced to reluctant bystanders, an uncomfortable, humiliating role that left a bad taste in their mouths. It was something that they would not let happen again. They would be ready next time.[22]

Police, military, and government authorities, in the meantime, decided that the trek had to be stopped. It was one thing for the trekkers to rail against federal relief policies, but quite another matter when their protest was attracting growing public interest, if not support. Before the trek even left Calgary, then, it was being portrayed as a threat to the peace and order of the country. Superintendent E. W. Bavin of the Calgary RCMP detachment, for example, told Assistant Commissioner Wood on 10 June that "there would be serious consequences unless action were [sic] taken to stop the trek" and that it was "clearly a revolutionary movement." The commander of Military District 13 made a similar report to Department of National Defence headquarters: "Militant action will be taken by men any time demands are not acceded to." The most troubling assessment was offered by A. A. Mackenzie, the provincial relief official who had been held hostage by the trekkers. "They expressed themselves as hopeful of being sufficient force when reaching Ottawa to take over the Government, if necessary," he wrote the federal minister of Labour about what he had learned during his time as a "prisoner." He also warned that other groups across the country could be counted upon to adopt similar tactics if the trek was successful. "This would create an impossible situation," he argued, "and I see no prospects [sic] of bringing such tactics under control." To this end, he deeply regretted that there had not been enough police in Calgary to force a showdown with the trekkers and prevent "their first victory ... before public sympathy was aroused."[23]

How the federal government proposed to respond to this disturbing information, Bennett was not saying. In a letter to Premier R. G. Reid of Alberta, the prime minister simply repeated his earlier statements that Ottawa's hands were effectively tied unless help was specifically requested. But surviving railway correspondence suggests that the Conservative government was preparing to order the RCMP to pull the trekkers from the trains. On 6 June—the day before the enunciation of Bennett's hands-off policy—D. C. Coleman of the CPR had advised the minister of Railways that he and Commissioner MacBrien had discussed the trek and that the corporation "would cooperate to the full extent of its power in any measures which the police might take in dealing with situation."[24]

That something was being contemplated was confirmed four days later by a headline in the *Calgary Herald*, which reported that "sources" in Ottawa "Indicate Gov't Has Decided on Action." It is also apparent that the prime minister looked to MacBrien—and not General McNaughton, the creator of the relief camp scheme—to come up with a plan to deal with the trek before it became unstoppable. One month earlier, Bennett had recommended MacBrien for a knighthood, calling him "perhaps the greatest soldier Canada produced in the Great War." Sir James looked upon the honour as "a recognition of the valuable services rendered by the Royal Canadian Mounted Police during the past few years" and promised "to help as much as possible in these difficult times." Dealing with the trek would be his first real test.[25]

The trekkers, for their part, had more immediate concerns. No sooner had the freight left Calgary than a stiff wind blew up and rain began to fall in torrents. The men atop the boxcars huddled together to try to stay warm, but their blankets and clothes were soon drenched. Whenever the train stopped during the night, a group quickly gathered around the huge pistons of the locomotive in an attempt to warm their chilled bodies. Others crowded in the small waiting rooms, if only to get out of the driving rain for a few minutes. At one station, a young trekker, without hat or blanket, pleaded with the agent to give him his paper lunch bag so that he could cover his head. They were a sorry lot by the time the freight finally pulled into Medicine Hat shortly after dawn, but the advance team had done its work, and hot coffee and sandwiches were waiting for them at a nearby park. They stopped their shivering for a loud cheer and then pounced on the food as if they had never eaten before.[26]

The mayor of Medicine Hat tried to discourage the trek from stopping in his city by offering two hundred dollars if it just kept on going. But the leadership turned down the bribe. Ever since the men had emerged from the mountains, there was a real sense that they were going to make it to Ottawa, that their movement had acquired an unstoppable momentum. "I thought we were makin' history," bragged Red Walsh. "No doubt about that." This belief that they were part of something special forged a common bond among the men, a steely enthusiasm that not even a night of cold, driving rain could dampen. And they were not about to pass up a chance to march through the streets of Medicine Hat and generate more support and secure more recruits. In fact, a series of scheduled stops, more in keeping with a promotional tour, was planned across the prairies. This concern with publicity also probably accounts for the fact that *Toronto Star* reporter James Kingsbury, who had accompanied the trek since Vancouver, was invited in Calgary to ride on the tender with Black and Cosgrove. They wanted the rest of the country to know first-hand about the men and what they were enduring in the name of making things better for Canada's unemployed.[27]

There was also a practical reason for spending a day in Medicine Hat, besides the need to recover from the cold, rainy ride. The men still believed that Slim Evans was the best person to lead the trek and had wired the Workers' Unity League in Vancouver at the first opportunity to plead for his return. The Communists, who had been making the trek front-page news in

The Worker, readily agreed and sent Evans speeding eastward on the first train. It was hoped that he might be able to rejoin the men before they left Calgary, but then it was decided to wait for him at Medicine Hat. He finally arrived, clad in his trademark carpenter's overalls, while the men were temporarily camped at the local athletic park. The handsome Evans, with a square jaw and dark hair stylishly parted in the middle, could have been a movie star in another life, but he would have been typecast as an obsessed labour organizer. "Because of the fire burning in him all the time," explained trekker Steve Brodie, "he never had an ounce of fat on him." It was this consuming passion for the working class and the Communist Party that made Evans such a dominant force, and Black gladly stepped aside so that he could take his rightful place at the head of the trek.[28]

It was while the men were resting in Medicine Hat—still in Alberta—that the Bennett government moved to put an end to the trek. Around 2:00 P.M. on 11 June, Commissioner MacBrien of the RCMP telephoned Assistant Commissioner Wood with the news that the trekkers would not be allowed to proceed beyond Regina, that the two railways were cooperating fully, and that reinforcements would be sent to the Saskatchewan capital as soon as possible. He repeated this information in a telegram later that afternoon, with the stipulation that "all possible preliminary arrangements to be made but scheme not to be put into action until further instructions received from here [Ottawa]." MacBrien's decision to stop the trek in Saskatchewan's capital was partly a reflection of his faith in Wood's command. The son of a career Mountie and a descendant of both Zachary Taylor, the twelfth president of the United States, and Jefferson Davis, the president of the Confederacy, the forty-six-year-old Wood had the traditions of the force bred in him. He grew up in the barracks in Dawson City in the early twentieth century, when the Mounties' word was the law, followed in his father's footsteps to Royal Military College, and then joined the police as an inspector upon graduation in 1912. Wood served in the Arctic after the Great War—supervising the first Inuit execution at Herschel Island—before being placed in charge of the British Columbia division in 1931 and posted to Saskatchewan two years later as assistant commissioner. Something of a loner who eschewed the spotlight, he had a reputation as a "strict disciplinarian" whose "only hobby

[was] his work." He also disliked anyone different. He was a virulent anti-Communist and once referred to Jehovah's Witnesses as "poison toadstools." MacBrien could not have asked for a better soul mate.[29]

It was not the first time during the Depression that the RCMP had been used in Saskatchewan to deal with a difficult situation. In September 1931, a handful of inexperienced Mounties shot three men dead on the streets of Estevan, when they intercepted a peaceful march by striking coal miners and their families and provoked a riot. Although the police would later claim that they did not draw their weapons until attacked, a newspaper photograph clearly shows the constables, with guns in hand, lined across the parade route. The gravestone for the three dead miners in nearby Bienfait reads "Murdered by the RCMP." A year and a half later, in May 1933, the police started another riot when they tried to forcibly remove some fifty "trouble-makers" from the Saskatoon relief camp. The only fatality was a police inspector who fell from his saddle and struck his head while being dragged helplessly by his horse. These two instances of police brutality would have an important bearing on how the Mounties chose to deal with the trekkers in Regina. In both cases, the RCMP deliberately dismissed any sense of grievance or complaint, no matter how legitimate, in favour of attributing the unrest to a few reds. Inspector W. J. Moorhead, who commanded the mounted police at Estevan, reported that the trouble in the coal fields, including the riot, was the work of foreigners. Assistant Commissioner Wood, in a similar vein, blamed the Saskatoon riot on agitators who had infiltrated the camp. The police also refused to take any responsibility for inciting the violence. Instead, they insisted the use of force was not only unavoidable but would become increasingly necessary as long as the Communist scourge was at the door. They had to be up to the challenge. In the immediate aftermath of the Estevan riot, for example, Commissioner MacBrien wanted to ensure the force was adequately equipped to deal with any future large-scale protest and asked the army to send three hundred bayonets and thirty thousand rounds of ammunition to the RCMP training depot in Regina. Recruits also began to receive instruction in handling riots, in particular how to use horses for crowd control.[30]

MacBrien's directive to get ready to stop the trek in Regina sent Wood into overdrive. As late as 6 June, the day before the men reached Calgary, the Mounties' number two man in the country knew so little about the trek that he had to ask whether the strikers were travelling as legitimate passengers or riding the freights. But once he learned how the men were headed en masse to Ottawa, he contacted MacBrien about what was to be done, only to be disappointed that no action was to be taken unless a province specifically asked for help. In fact, on 10 June, he regretfully told the commander of the RCMP D Division in Manitoba that the trek, despite its Communist hue, would be allowed to pass through Saskatchewan. MacBrien's call the next day was consequently something of a surprise, but a welcome one, and Wood ordered outlying detachments to search all trains and arrest any transients headed to Regina. He also appealed for police reinforcements and riot equipment from Alberta and Manitoba. The need for additional men was particularly acute, since both the training depot and F Division were well below strength because of the number of Mounties of all ranks who had been sent to Vancouver to deal with the unfolding drama there. And Wood knew full well that he would need a large, heavily armed force if he was going to take on an unemployed army which might number as many as two thousand by the time it reached Regina.[31]

There was also a personal matter at play here. Wood had been commander of British Columbia's E Division in September 1932, when the police were trying to find a reason to lock up Arthur Evans for his organizational work on behalf of the Communists. He would not let this second chance slip away, especially after the force had been publicly embarrassed in Calgary. Ironically, one of the Mounties who would be waiting for the trekkers' arrival in Regina was the brother of Slim Evans's wife, Ethel.[32]

The trek took to the rails again the morning of Wednesday, 12 June, and after an uneventful ride from Medicine Hat, reached Swift Current shortly after noon. Most of the town turned out to witness the train's arrival. So too did Charles Woodsworth, a newspaper reporter disguised as a transient. The *Winnipeg Tribune* had sent Woodsworth to Swift Current to join the trek, and the military-like organization of the men made quite a first impression on him. "I expected them to swarm across the tracks and invade Swift Current like a mob," he confessed. "Instead, they formed fours immediately on descending from the cars, waited until all sections of the hobo army were ready, and then marched townwards in real army style." Like others before him, Woodsworth was struck by their youthfulness: "They are, almost without exception, young men. Most I guess to be in their twenties; many are youngsters of 16 to 17." He also offered a rare glimpse into their survival techniques, noting that men carried blackened cans and glass pickling jars as part of their gear. "The cans are used for cooking ... along the line," he reported, "and the jars for carrying water."[33]

The men, swinging their arms in unison, strode down the main street of Swift Current to the athletic grounds, where the local unemployed association welcomed them and offered their support. It was here that the leaders first learned of the government's decision to stop the trek in Regina, prompting Evans to go ahead on his own to the Saskatchewan capital to find out more. It is not clear how the men were informed, but it was undoubtedly on their lips—and their minds—as they took turns eating in shifts at the local restaurants. They then marched back in formation to the station to board a waiting freight that had been deliberately held for them. This time, though, they had company. The box cars were loaded with horses and cattle, and as the hundreds of men took their positions above them, the frightened animals neighed, bellowed, and stomped.[34]

Commissioner MacBrien, in the meantime, had wired Colonel Wood that same morning, formally authorizing him to prevent the movement of the trekkers east of Regina. The order coincided with the arrival of W. A. Mather, general manager of the CPR's western lines, who personally handed the assistant commissioner a letter, dated 11 June, in which he complained that the large number of trekkers riding freights constituted a "direct menace" to the company's operations and asked for mounted police assistance in removing the men from trains. Wood lost little time responding. He immediately dispatched Inspector G. C. P. Montizambert, along with two carloads of undercover police constables, to Moose Jaw to monitor the trekkers and find out how many men were involved. He then met with Canadian Pacific and Canadian National police officials to decide how the eighty-five railway police who had been hurriedly summoned to Regina could best be deployed in and around the city to ensure that no trekker would be able to leave by rail.

Their actions were to be backed up by 240 non-commissioned officers and constables, divided into four troops, that the mounted police were massing in the city. To facilitate their handling of the trekkers, Wood issued a general memo to inspectors and sergeants to review crowd-control measures, especially the coordination of mounted and dismounted men. He also reminded them that the Communists practised the politics of provocation and that any police violence would only increase public sympathy for the trekkers. To this end, he instructed that "No member is to carry *loaded sidearms or ammunition*."[35]

While police preparations were underway, the trekkers, now numbering about 1,350, rode into Moose Jaw just before sundown to the boisterous cheering of large crowds at railway crossings and overpasses. The men shouted and waved back, their teeth gleaming from faces darkened by coal dust and smoke. Once the freight came to a stop, the men patiently held their places until given the order to dismount. They then smartly formed into their divisions and marched, four abreast, to Ross Wells Park, where they cleaned up before enjoying a late supper in the city's restaurants.

On one level, the trek had become a travelling road show or theatre, bringing out the curious, the jaded, and the bored. It is quite likely that many in the crowds in Moose Jaw that evening had come to catch a glimpse of the men before the looming showdown in Regina, now that Ottawa had decided to stop the trek. But on another level, the trek resonated with Depression-weary western Canadians. They identified with the hundreds of mostly young men and their stubborn determination to get answers by riding en masse by freight to Ottawa. They also marvelled at their orderly behaviour—something that had become legendary as the men headed across the prairies—and wondered what federal authorities were so worried about. Even RCMP inspector Montizambert, who had been sent to Moose Jaw to spy on the trek, privately admitted that the men gave no cause for police intervention. So too did Inspector Chesser of the CPR police: "They are a fine type of men and well disciplined ... [I am] puzzled at the hold the leaders seem to have on them." The most generous assessment was offered by Woodsworth of the *Winnipeg Tribune*. "They are a loveable bunch of boys," he wrote after spending a day with them. "There is nothing menacing about them."[36]

But the Bennett government viewed the situation much differently. On 13 June, the day after the trek reached Moose Jaw, J. S. Woodsworth rose in the House of Commons at the start of the day's business to call for an emergency debate on the federal decision to stop the trek at Regina. The Communist Party had been publicly calling for this kind of support for the past week, taking every opportunity to savage the Co-operative Commonwealth Federation (CCF) leader in the editorial pages of *The Worker* for his refusal to join a united front. But Woodsworth's intervention had more to do with the violation of the men's civil rights than with silencing his Communist detractors. If the government forcibly detained the trekkers, he predicted in the House that afternoon, "there is bound to be a clash resulting in bloodshed."[37]

Hugh Guthrie, the minister of Justice, was determined to limit criticism of the government's handling of the trek and challenged the urgency of the motion, sarcastically noting, "If we were to discuss this question at each of the points where these marchers may determine to halt I think we would interfere seriously with the business of this house." But the Opposition persisted. "If it is not urgent, why should the government give an order to stop the march?" pointedly asked Angus MacInnis, the CCF member of Parliament for South Vancouver. "If it is not of public importance, why should the government give an order to stop the march?" The speaker quickly ended further debate by ruling the motion out of order. When a frustrated Woodsworth appealed for a formal vote, the decision of the chair was easily upheld.[38]

That was not the end of the government's manipulation of the issue. Only minutes later, a question was lobbed in the direction of Guthrie so that he could read a prepared statement into the record. After incorrectly reporting that the men had already reached Regina, the Justice minister declared that the trek "has been organized and is under the direction of certain Communist elements throughout Canada." He then went on to explain that the trekkers had been trespassing on trains since leaving Vancouver, that the railways lacked the means to deal with such large numbers of men, and that the RCMP had been asked to help resolve the problem. Guthrie's remarks were clearly intended for public consumption. He characterized the unemployed army as a "distinct menace" and made repeated references to the need to uphold "law and order." But when questioned about recent events in

Calgary, he seemed to be caught flat-footed, claiming to have "no information whatever ... to anything that transpired [there]." Was this the same cabinet minister who had overseen a major expansion of the mounted police to deal with subversion and civil unrest?[39]

Back in Moose Jaw, the men were coping as best they could with a rainy prairie spring day—and the thought of what lay ahead. They had spent Wednesday night sleeping on the bleachers at the exhibition grounds or bedded down in the local curling rink. They awoke to a steady rain, and by the time they walked downtown in gangs to have breakfast, they were thoroughly soaked. The wet weather chased many back to Ross Wells Park, where they huddled in small groups in the stands or underneath them, talking and smoking while waiting for a decision from the strike committee about their next move. Others sought shelter under store awnings and passed the time window-shopping. A few were handed tin cans and sent out in the rain to tag on street corners. Their cry, "Help the camp strikers ... on to Ottawa," heard throughout the day, would net almost four hundred dollars.[40]

That afternoon, three thousand trekkers and citizens filled the grandstand for a public rally held, ostensibly, to thank the city for its support. But the real target was the Bennett government and its henchmen, the mounted police. In fact, just as Hugh Guthrie wanted to make the government's position known before any trouble erupted in Regina, so too did the trek leadership—even if it was in the rain and mud of a Moose Jaw park. Fiery Paddy O'Neill opened the meeting by recounting the circumstances behind the Vancouver strike and the decision to go to Ottawa. "I'm here to tell the police that they better keep their hands off the relief camp strikers," he thundered to the enthusiastic roar of the trekkers. "We are going through with the march and we don't care if we have to go in our stockinged feet." The affable Matt Shaw followed with a stinging indictment of the relief camps and all that was wrong with them. "We have been called agitators," he shouted, "but can you blame us for being agitators after being condemned to a living hell for four years?" He also warned that the young men who dominated the ranks of the trekkers were dead set on taking their demands for work and wages and an end to the slave camps to Ottawa: "If they attack us, we are not going to lay down and take it." Slim Evans, just back from Regina, pursued this same

Prime Minister Bennett *(left)* and Liberal Opposition leader William Lyon Mackenzie King were bitter political adversaries.
NATIONAL ARCHIVES OF CANADA PA148532

Prime Minister Bennett surrounded by his cabinet ministers in his Ottawa office.
NATIONAL ARCHIVES OF CANADA C9076

is scheduled to march as soon as your new wheat sprouts. The tender green shoots of growing grain will be at the mercy of this horde of hungry raiders—unless you break up the march with GOPHERCIDE.

NOW is the time to rid your fields of Gophers; before the new wheat comes up; before any damage can be done.

Gophercide

Gets the Gophers Every Time

GOPHERCIDE is Strychnine, without strychnine's bitter taste. It is strychnine that dissolves in warm water without the use of acids or vinegar. In other words, GOPHERCIDE has all the deadliness of strychnine, without any of the disadvantages of ordinary strychnine.

A package of GOPHERCIDE, dissolved in half a gallon of warm water, will poison a gallon of wheat; this wheat will kill about 400 gophers, because gophers like the taste of it and will eat it eagerly.

Go after the Gophers NOW. Get GOPHERCIDE—soak the wheat in it and sprinkle the poisoned grain in and around the holes. Never mind the weather: rain doesn't affect GOPHERCIDE.

Chemical Analysis of Manufactured Poisons reported by Andrews and Cruickshank, analytical and consulting chemists to the Deputy Minister of Agriculture, Regina, shows: Gophercide contains ten times the quantity of Strychnine of all other preparations examined.

National Drug and Chemical Company of Canada, Limited

MONTREAL, WINNIPEG, REGINA, SASKATOON, CALGARY, EDMONTON, NELSON, VANCOUVER, VICTORIA and EASTERN BRANCHES.

"The Annual Bolshewheatie Parade,"
Saskatoon Daily Phoenix, 7 February 1920

Saskatchewan-born General Andrew McNaughton, who proposed the idea of federal relief camps for Canada's single homeless unemployed, photographed by Karsh in 1942. NATIONAL ARCHIVES OF CANADA PA164285

Hobo jungles sprang up outside towns and cities across Canada in the early 1930s.
NATIONAL ARCHIVES OF CANADA PA202354

Workers, equipped with shovels and wheelbarrows, at the Dundurn relief camp in Saskatchewan in June 1933.
NATIONAL ARCHIVES OF CANADA C35656

Reverend Andrew Roddan, author of *Canada's Untouchables*, helps distribute food to transients in Vancouver.
NATIONAL ARCHIVES OF CANADA C27902

The Communists equated General McNaughton's scheme with the creation of slave camps. *THE WORKER*, 11 NOVEMBER 1932

Turn the Royal Commission Into a Tribune! **--By Avrom**

The findings of the federal relief camp commission served to strengthen the resolve of the striking men to take their grievances to Ottawa. *THE WORKER*, 6 APRIL 1935

Toronto-born Arthur "Slim" Evans, an avowed Communist, led the Vancouver relief camp strike and later the On-to-Ottawa-Trek. GLENBOW ALBERTA ARCHIVES NA-36334-7

George Black, a former Black Watch soldier from Glasgow, was one of the trek leaders. SASKATCHEWAN ARCHIVES BOARD R-B9020 DETAIL

Matt Shaw, whose real name was John Surdia, was a fiery speaker on behalf of the relief camp strike and later the trek. SASKATCHEWAN ARCHIVES BOARD R-B9020 DETAIL

The On-to-Ottawa trekkers quickly acquired a momentum and symbolism beyond that of a simple regional protest movement. The CPR cooperated as much as possible to facilitate the movement of the men eastward through the mountains.
CITY OF TORONTO ARCHIVES SC 244-2181

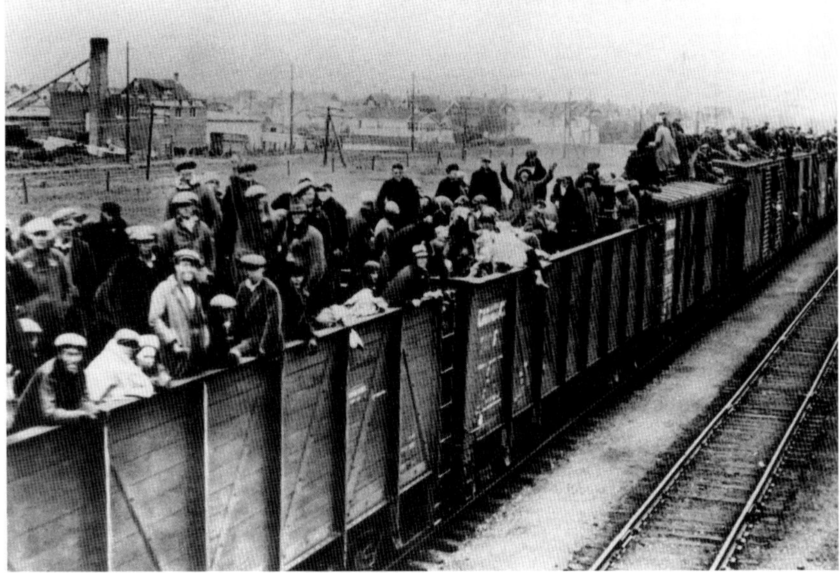

The trekkers—cold, wet, and exhausted—pulled into Regina at 6:00 A.M. on Friday, 15 June 1935. CITY OF TORONTO ARCHIVES, SC 244-1682

Colonel Wood's decision to make the arrests at the Market Square meeting ultimately led to the Regina Riot.
NATIONAL ARCHIVES OF CANADA PA203199

General James Howden MacBrien was handpicked by Prime Minister Bennett in 1931 to lead the RCMP fight against communism.
NATIONAL ARCHIVES OF CANADA PA203197

NOTICE

In the absence of the leader of the Marchers at the Stadium Friday morning, the following notice was handed by the Railway Companies' representatives to Bert Canaven, who stated that he was qualified to receive it and would undertake to see that it got to the leader of the Relief Camp Strikers:

REGINA, 14th JUNE, 1935.

To Whom It It May Concern:

We are instructed to inform you that no person or persons will be permitted to further ride on the trains of the Canadian National Railways or on the trains of the Canadian Pacific Railway without authority or without holding proper transportation entitling such person or persons to do so.

It is requested that you will accept this notice and refrain from unlawfully boarding or riding on the trains of either Railway Company, and that you will notify and instruct those that may be associated with you or under your directions not to unlawfully board or ride on any train of either Railway Company.

We are further instructed to inform you that if you or those associated with you further persist in unlawfully riding on the trains of either Railway Company, the proper authorities will give every assistance and use every means available to ensure that the law in this respect is observed.

You are requested to disperse and return to your respective homes. If you will do this the Railway Companies will take up with the Dominion authorities the question of providing some means by which you can so return.

THE CANADIAN NATIONAL RAILWAYS.
THE CANADIAN PACIFIC RAILWAY.

An unknown trekker and his dog. *REGINA LEADER-POST*, 13 JUNE 1935

Below: Cadets training at the RCMP Depot in Regina. NATIONAL ARCHIVES OF CANADA PA41411

Above: On 14 June 1935, the day the trek reached Regina, Canada's two national railways finally announced that they would no longer carry the men eastward. SASKATCHEWAN ARCHIVES BOARD R-A9413

The trekkers marched from the exhibition grounds to downtown Regina their first morning in the city. *Regina Leader-Post*, 15 June 1935

Exhibition stadium served as the trekkers' temporary home in Regina for three weeks. *Winnipeg Evening Tribune*, 15 June 1935

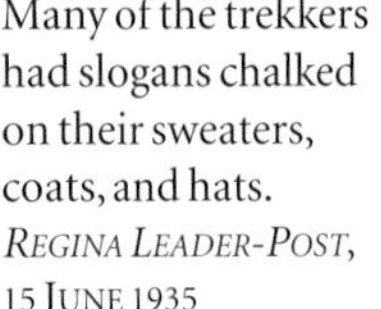

Many of the trekkers had slogans chalked on their sweaters, coats, and hats. *Regina Leader-Post*, 15 June 1935

A young trekker solicits a donation from a Regina citizen on one of the city's downtown streets. The trekkers' illegal tag day in Regina netted almost fifteen hundred dollars. *Regina Leader-Post*, 15 June 1935

Saskatchewan attorney-general Tommy Davis asked for a copy of the phantom federal order-in-council preventing Regina citizens from assisting the trekkers.
SASKATCHEWAN ARCHIVES BOARD R-B8266

Premier Gardiner returned from his farm on the holiday Monday, 1 July, to meet a trekker delegation at his office in the late afternoon. He regarded the federal government's decision to stop the trek in Regina almost as an attack on the province.
SASKATCHEWAN ARCHIVES BOARD R-A6030

Robert Manion (left), the minister of Railways, and Robert Weir (right), the minister of Agriculture, are greeted by W. A. Mather, western manager for the CPR, at the Regina station. Weir was Saskatchewan's only representative in the Bennett cabinet; Manion would succeed Bennett as federal Conservative leader. *Regina Leader-Post*, 17 June 1935

A pensive Evans (far left) listens as Jack Cosgrove addresses Manion (left) and Weir at the Hotel Saskatchewan meeting. *Regina Leader-Post*, 17 June 1935

Below: The trek delegation photographed en route to Ottawa. *The Worker*, 27 June 1935

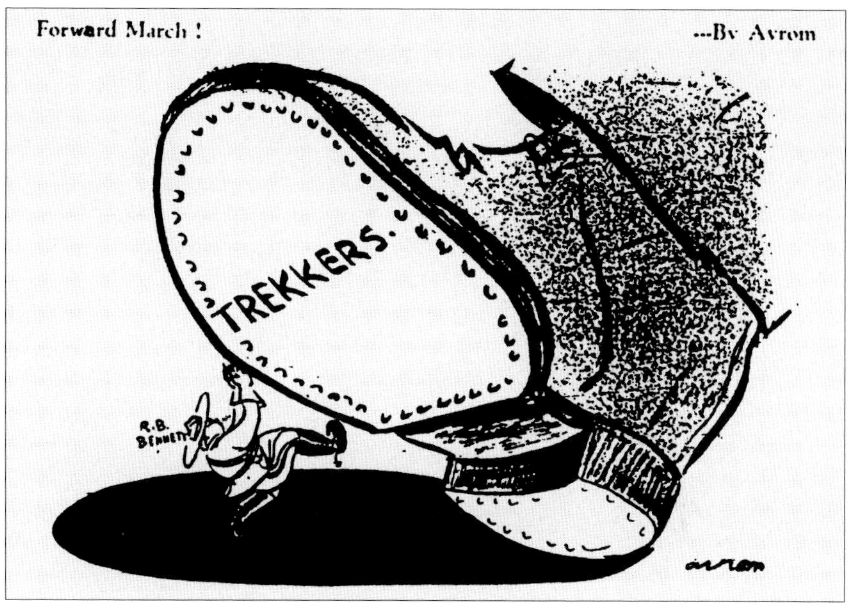

Above: The Communist Party of Canada called for a nation-wide Ottawa trek following the breakdown of negotiations with the Bennett government. *The Worker*, 27 June 1935

Below: "Get Back Into That Camp, You…!" *The Worker*, 2 July 1935

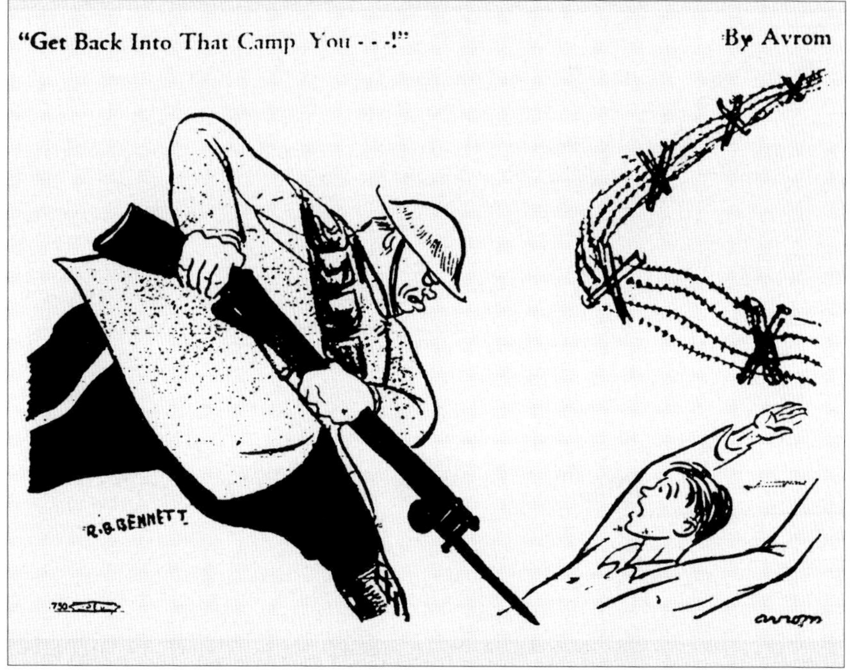

Above: The Citizens' Emergency Committee sponsored several Regina rallies in support of the trek. SASKATCHEWAN ARCHIVES BOARD R-A27560-1

Below: A late-June rally on Regina's Market Square in support of the trekkers. SASKATCHEWAN ARCHIVES BOARD R-A27560-2

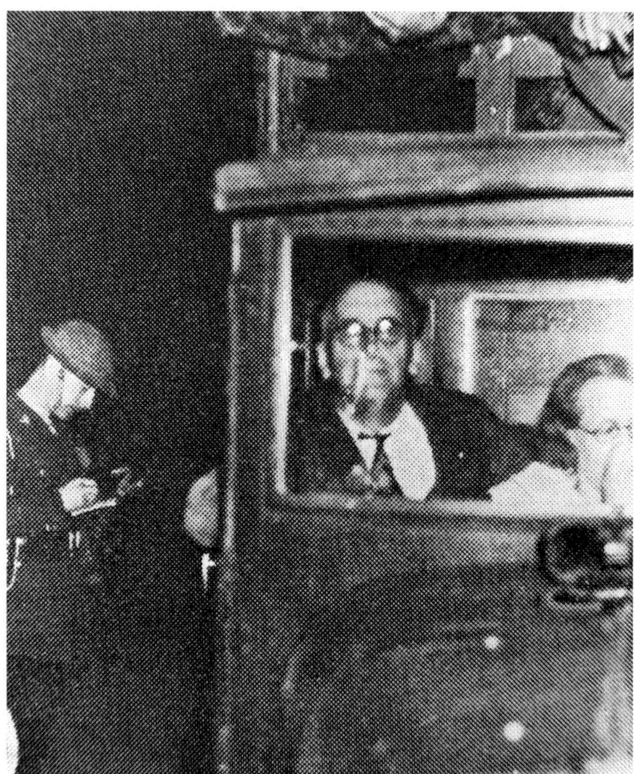

Reverend Samuel East was part of the convoy that failed to break through the RCMP blockade of the city on 27 June. SASKATCHEWAN ARCHIVES BOARD R-A9840-2

Below: A smiling Jack Cosgrove is arrested by the RCMP on 27 June during an attempt to leave Regina by truck. SASKATCHEWAN ARCHIVES BOARD R-A9840-1

Stewart "Paddy" O'Neill, one of the Ottawa delegates, would later die fighting for the Republican side during the Spanish Civil War.
SASKATCHEWAN ARCHIVES BOARD R-A7867

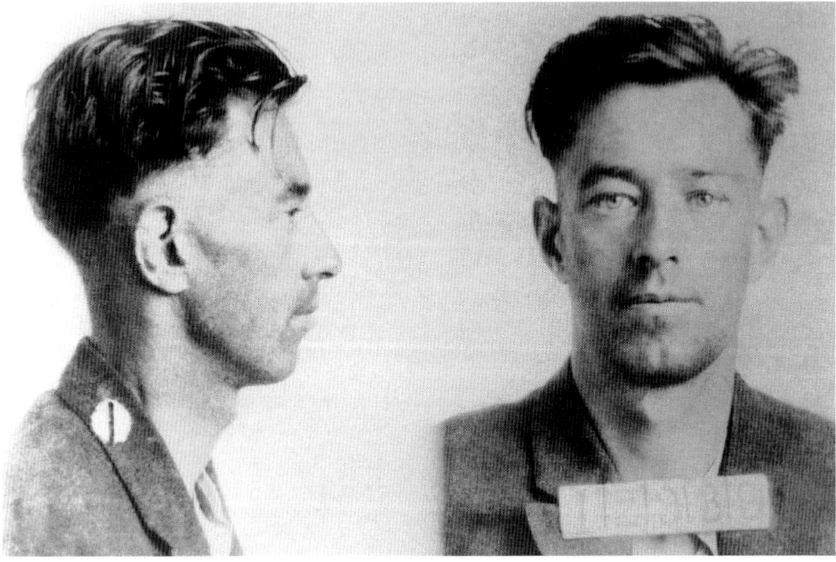

Trek marshall Jack Cosgrove was charged with being an officer and member of an illegal organization. The case never went to trial.
SASKATCHEWAN ARCHIVES BOARD R-A7868

theme, but with a decidedly Communist spin; he argued that the trek was symbolic of the larger class struggle and that worker solidarity was the only way to break the power of "pot-bellied political heelers" and "financial parasites." This war of words would get only worse over the next few days.[41]

The men spent the early evening getting ready for Regina. At a closed mass meeting at the park at 7:00 P.M., the trek leadership created a fifth division, under the iron hand of O'Neill, to deal with overcrowding in the other four. One of the new trekkers included RCMP constable Henry Cooper, alias Henry Ward, who had spent time undercover in the nearby Dundurn relief camp and had travelled to Moose Jaw with Montizambert the day before. The leaders also talked in detail for the first time about the blockade in Regina and what would be expected of the men. "There are reports that some of you are not observing discipline," Evans admonished the new recruits. "Unless we maintain order we are not going to retain the public's sympathy.... If there are any men here who do not want to obey orders then we want them to leave now." This rebuke was reinforced by Black and Cosgrove, who, true to their military training, sternly cautioned that any "monkey business" or hooliganism on the trains or in the streets would lead to expulsion.[42]

Evans then left by bus for Regina, for the second time in as many days, to help prepare for the arrival of the men, now estimated to number nearly fifteen hundred. At 12:30 A.M., after waiting for what seemed to be an eternity in the mud-filled park, the trekkers were called into formation and marched to the train station. There, they patiently waited two more hours in steady rain until their freight was finally ready, then struggled aboard for the forty-four-mile trip to Regina. The scene was eerily reminiscent of their departure from Vancouver ten days earlier: they were setting off in the night, with no one to see them off, and uncertain as to how far they would get. At least one thing had been settled. There would be no turning back.[43]

CHAPTER FIVE

They Had Better Keep Away

As the trekkers rode through the early morning hours of Friday, 14 June, the sky cracked, then boomed with thunder, followed by flashes of lightning and sheets of heavy rain. It was a fitting omen. For the past few days, Saskatchewan premier Jimmy Gardiner and Prime Minister R. B. Bennett had been engaged in a heated public spat over the federal decision to halt the On-to-Ottawa Trek in Regina.

The ever-vigilant Gardiner, believing that his province had seen more than its share of deprivation and suffering during the Depression, had been prepared to help the trekkers in any way he and his government could—as long as they kept moving out of Saskatchewan. After all, it was the Conservative government that had created the problem, and it was up to Bennett to fix it. But when the premier learned to his horror that the men were to be pulled from the trains in Regina, he blasted the move as political interference of the worst kind and confidently predicted that there would be a clash, with the provincial capital as the backdrop.

The prime minister, on the other hand, maintained that his government was simply acting in an area of federal jurisdiction, even suggesting that his Liberal rival was not prepared to see law and order upheld in the country. It was not a time, as far as Bennett was concerned, for worrying about provincial sensibilities. It was more important that the trek come to an end—even at the cost of violence.

❖ ❖ ❖

The task of saving Saskatchewan from the Depression initially fell to the new Co-operative government of Dr. J. T. M. Anderson. The provincial Conservatives, with the support of the Progressive Party and a handful of independents, had ended twenty-four years of uninterrupted Liberal rule in 1929, only to be saddled with the twin scourge of record-low wheat prices and prolonged drought. It was a formidable challenge for a government of any political stripe, something that was driven home in 1931. Total farm net income went through the floor, slipping to less than $36 million, while ninety-five (roughly one-third) of the province's rural municipalities faced their third consecutive year of crop failure. Premier Anderson, who had bravely tried to uphold provincial standards during the first two years of his mandate, was reduced to vowing in a Yorkton speech in July 1931 that "no one in Saskatchewan would be allowed to starve." One month later, he put his promise into action and established a nonpartisan agency to oversee the distribution of emergency assistance to the province's farm community.[1]

The Saskatchewan Relief Commission provided direct relief (food, fuel, clothing, and medical aid) and agricultural support (such as feed, seed, and fodder) to try to keep families on the land and producing a crop in the event that international wheat prices rebounded. It was an expensive rescue operation. During what was supposed to be the commission's only year of activity, total expenditures amounted to $18.7 million, almost evenly shared between the federal and provincial governments. It was sorely needed. Nearly 50 percent of the rural population, or roughly three hundred thousand people, were assisted in one way or another. In fact, the demand was so great and the outlook so bleak that the commission dispensed relief for another two years, on the understanding that strict economy would continue to be observed and that any advances would technically have to be repaid. This aid was supplemented by the Saskatchewan Voluntary Rural Relief Committee, an umbrella group of church and other charitable organizations which solicited donations of fruit, vegetables, and other foodstuffs from other provinces (including salt cod from the Maritimes) and then arranged for carloads to be shipped by the railways free of charge. In 1931 alone, 249 boxcars were distributed to distressed areas.[2]

Yet even with this extra help, the hardship of those years could not be eased. Thousands of dust bowl refugees grudgingly admitted defeat and abandoned their farms or small-town businesses for other parts of the country and the promise of better days; it was the beginning of an out-migration from the region that continues to this day. Others fled north, with the assistance of the province, to start over again in the parkland region along the southern edge of the forest belt. Those that remained behind eked out a miserable existence as best they could, but at a terrible cost.[3]

The Depression also walloped Saskatchewan's cities—something that has been largely overlooked, if not ignored, because of the tendency to view the province in simple agricultural terms. Yet almost one-third of Saskatchewan's 1931 population lived in urban areas. Because these cities and towns acted primarily as agricultural service centres, businesses floundered, unemployment soared, and tax arrears mounted. What made the crisis worse is that the province's major cities were already hobbled by the huge debt they were carrying from the reckless over-expansion before the Great War. Saskatoon, for example, had grown from a mere 113 people in 1901 to 12,000 ten years later; local boosters dubbed it the "wonder city." Prince Albert, on the other hand, set its sights on becoming the "white coal" capital of western Canada and poured millions of dollars into developing the hydroelectric potential of nearby La Colle Falls and related improvements in the city. But when the real estate and construction boom fizzled during the winter of 1912–13, prairie cities were left with a colossal financial headache that had not lessened by the onset of the Depression. The case of Prince Albert was particularly tragic. Not only did the city declare bankruptcy in 1919, but it did not finish paying for the half-completed power dam across the North Saskatchewan River until the 1960s.[4]

The exact number of urban unemployed during the early 1930s is difficult to determine because statistics from the period provide only the number of individuals assisted for any given year and fail to capture those who refused, or were denied, a helping hand. But the bottom line is that there were far too many needy people calling on the limited resources that municipalities had to offer. By 1932, almost one in every five persons in the province's cities depended on direct assistance, a situation that remained constant until the latter part of the decade.

The Anderson government tried to reduce the municipal burden by establishing relief camps, under the auspices of the Saskatchewan Relief Commission, for the single homeless unemployed in Regina and Saskatoon. It also cooperated with the federal government in establishing a farm-placement programme in the fall of 1931 to get several thousand displaced workers out of the cities and onto the land, even if they had limited or no agricultural experience. Anything that reduced urban relief rolls was understood to be better than maintaining men in idleness. But the problem for the cities remained the large numbers on the dole—1933 relief expenditures were forty times those of 1929! Fortunately, the lion's share of these costs was financed by Ottawa in the form of grants or by the province which covered the better part of the shortfall at the expense of a ballooning deficit. Still, the municipalities could not completely elude their responsibility and had to mortgage their future by heavily resorting to debentures.[5]

Regina, home to almost a third of Saskatchewan's urban population, was one of the casualties of the Depression. Indeed, the decade dashed any lingering hope that the city would become the pre-eminent city in western Canada. Founded on Pile of Bones or Wascana Creek in 1882 as the new capital for the North-West Territories, and named in honour of Queen Victoria, Regina enjoyed the advantage of being on the Canadian Pacific Railway main line across the southern prairies. But its most famous asset, apart from being the seat of the territorial government, was serving as the new national headquarters for the North-West Mounted Police following the closure of Fort Walsh in the spring of 1883. Thereafter, Regina was as much a garrison town as it was a government one. A steady stream of recruits passed through the training depot, while a large contingent of Mounties, including the commissioner, was stationed there permanently.[6]

Regina's regional dominance was confirmed in 1905 when it was named—despite an aggressive challenge from upstart Saskatoon—capital of the new province of Saskatchewan. Flush with the great hopes of the new century and fueled by the developing wheat economy, the predominantly British Protestant community began to take on the appearance of a modern Edwardian city, complete with the construction of a new domed legislative building and the planting of thousands of elm trees along prosperous residential avenues. The population, meanwhile, multiplied almost fifteen-fold between 1901 and 1911, from 2,250 to over 30,000, thanks to a flood of immigrants the likes of which would not be seen in Canada again until the 1950s. If Saskatchewan was destined to be the wheat province, then Regina would be the wheat capital.

The 1912–13 recession brought these heady days to an abrupt end. Regina, like its other western counterparts, had grown too much, too fast, and would spend the 1920s trying to consolidate the urban landscape. There were a few major building projects during the decade, but generally the downtown core saw little change. Vacant lots served as a reminder of what might have been. Even more symbolic was the transfer of police headquarters to Ottawa to coincide with the creation of the Royal Canadian Mounted Police in 1920. This loss was tempered, however, by the fact that Regina remained the training depot for the new force—no small concession when it is realized that the barracks were the city's number-one tourist attraction throughout the 1920s.

But any sense that the city's fortunes would rebound was snuffed out by the Depression. The collapse in agriculture inevitably spilled over into construction and retail trade, and as sales dried up like much of Saskatchewan's southern farmland, Regina businesses cut staff in a desperate bid to stem the hemorrhaging. By July 1931, almost one in four adult male workers had lost his job. These numbers translated into a rocketing relief bill for the city—from around fourteen thousand dollars in 1929 to nearly a half-million dollars in 1934. They also compounded a severe housing crisis. Unlike Saskatoon and Moose Jaw, which lost citizens during the first half of the 1930s, Regina's population continued to grow—to the detriment of the unemployed. With construction at a standstill, there were fewer affordable places for people to live. Some relief was provided through the renting of empty office space or basements in downtown stores, but by the end of the decade Regina was one of the most overcrowded cities in Canada. According to a 1938 survey, 7.4 percent of all families lived in one room; the national average was 2.5 percent.[7]

Such conditions might have been expected to cultivate unrest. But the Regina labour scene was "a bastion of ... moderation" during the inter-war years. Trade unionists were a minority among workers and consciously pursued a conservative agenda during the Depression. They were more interested in holding onto their own jobs than signing up new members, especially if it meant locking horns with the business community. And although the city gave its name to the manifesto of the new Co-operative Commonwealth Federation (CCF) party, local labour activists—best described as Christian socialists—shunned any radical tactics in favour of reforming Regina's relief system through the municipal franchise. Their initial success at the polls—three of the ten city council seats were occupied by labour aldermen by 1932—was quickly countered by the formation of the pro-business Civic Government Association, which successfully ran candidates committed to economy and retrenchment. This healthy tension between the moderate left and the city's business and professional elite became the hallmark of civic politics during the first half of the 1930s. Civic politics were taken seriously, but there were no deep divisions—only differences over how best to deal with the Depression. Even when labour briefly secured control of city hall, it pursued a cautious fiscal policy.[8]

The one major exception to this generally peaceful scene was on May Day 1931, when the Communist-affiliated National Unemployed Workers' Association held a Friday night rally on Regina's Market Square that attracted a reported ten thousand people. Trouble erupted when several onlookers, incensed by the unfurling of the red flag, attacked the paraders as they attempted to march along downtown streets. While both sides jeered and taunted one another, faces were bloodied and banners torn down. It took city police almost three hours and several arrests before the fighting was finally halted and some semblance of order restored. The incident served as a warning of how mob violence could overtake a large crowd under the right circumstances. It also raised the question as to why the city issued a parade permit when several groups had threatened violence—unless, of course, the police wanted the Communists to sustain a beating.[9]

The Anderson government tried to help Regina meet its relief obligations by contributing several hundred thousand dollars to make-work projects in the city, as well as paying one-third of the cost of direct assistance—more than a million dollars. But as with other provincial governments with the misfortune of being in power during the early 1930s, it really did not matter what the governing Conservatives did to ease the impact of the Depression. Since they held office when the economy began its steep descent, they were readily identified with the bad times.

James Garfield Gardiner, the Saskatchewan opposition leader, did not help matters. Popularly known as Jimmy, Gardiner had the distinction of being the only sitting Saskatchewan premier to be defeated in office. He did not like the honour. He was also worried that his 1929 defeat might cost him the mantle as federal Liberal leader Mackenzie King's prairie lieutenant, and he was determined, for the sake of his political future, to deliver Saskatchewan to the Liberal fold once again. Instead of extending a hand of cooperation to deal with the worsening crisis, then, Gardiner attacked the credibility of the Anderson government at every opportunity, even accusing the new premier of breaking his election promises before the new legislature was convened. Such partisan theatrics came easily to Gardiner, who believed that every good Liberal had a duty to save the province from Conservative tyranny. In fact, from Gardiner's perspective, just being a Tory was a knock against a person.[10]

The Liberal strategy during the early 1930s was to highlight Conservative "extravagance." Having led the province at a time of relative prosperity and balanced budgets, the Gardiner Liberals charged that Saskatchewan was on the road to bankruptcy thanks to the huge deficits that the new government was racking up. People clearly needed help, the Liberals argued, but the path chosen by the Conservatives was not the way to go; if anything, Anderson's policies made the hard times only worse. "If this orgy of extravagance is to be maintained," asked Liberal stalwart Dr. J. M. Uhrich in the legislature in May 1931, "what will eventually become of the province?"[11]

This message was carried over into the general election that Premier Anderson finally set for July 1934. The Liberal platform, with one eye on the new socialist Farmer-Labour Party (later the provincial CCF), advocated less spending—not more—claiming that the province had "already experienced five years of extravagance." But the deciding factor was not the emphasis on retrenchment but party organization. While the Conservatives had been preoccupied with solving the province's woes—and being dragged down in the process—Gardiner had been busy rebuilding his formidable election machine. The result was one of the most lopsided victories in Saskatchewan electoral history. The Liberals won in a romp, denying the Conservatives a single seat in the legislature.[12]

The fifty-one-year-old Gardiner was no stranger to Saskatchewan politics. First elected in 1914, the teacher turned politician had faithfully served in the cabinets of two premiers before ascending to the leadership of the Liberal dynasty in 1926. His diminutive size—he stood only five foot, three inches—and tedious manner of speech belied his many talents. He was not one to be underestimated. He had a sharp mind for detail, loved the adversarial game of politics, and carried himself with firmness and purpose. But more than anything else, according to his biographers, he was a "relentless Liberal," who remained true to traditional Liberal policies. How he would deal with the Depression, after repeatedly calling for economy during his days on the Opposition benches, would be one of his biggest tests.

Ironically, it was a challenge of his own choosing. Less than two weeks after his election victory, Gardiner headed to Ottawa to receive the blessing of Mackenzie King and claim his crown as prairie kingpin. King, sensing his own victory at the polls was only months away, encouraged the Saskatchewan premier to leave provincial politics to run in the next federal election. But Gardiner demurred, asking for time to get his new government up and running. It was as if he was still smarting from his 1929 defeat and wanted to prove to the electorate that he could do a better job than Anderson in wrestling the Depression into submission.[13]

Gardiner had his hands full. The 1934 wheat harvest was the smallest since 1920, while nearly one hundred and fifty thousand men, women, and children—almost three times more than in neighbouring Manitoba and Alberta—were on direct relief in dried-out areas. Conditions in the cities were just as bleak. An estimated 20 percent of Regina's population, for example, survived on relief, while the city's tax arrears topped one million dollars. One of the most telling comments on how badly the province was hurting was supplied by young Margaret Bichel of Cactus Lake, about 140 miles due west of Saskatoon. Margaret had learned that children living in southern Saskatchewan had received twenty-five cents for Christmas 1934, and with her best penmanship, asked for the same amount from the premier for herself and her brothers and sisters.[14]

Gardiner's answer to the province's woes was to bring the administration of relief more directly under government control. Little time was lost dismantling the Saskatchewan Relief Commission. By mid-August 1934, the Department of Agriculture would attend to agricultural aid, while a new Bureau of Labour and Public Welfare administered direct relief; a new cabinet relief committee was also formed to ensure that departments were spending wisely. This action reflected Liberal criticism over the past five years—and a desire to set a course different from that of the Anderson government—but it remained to be seen whether distress would be more effectively alleviated. One newspaper likened Gardiner's relief policy to Christopher Columbus: "He didn't know where he was going when he started. When he got there he didn't know where he was. When he got back he didn't know where he had been."[15]

In keeping with his desire to restore the financial health of the province, Gardiner assumed the treasurer's portfolio in addition to his job as premier. This double duty meant that he would have to negotiate a new relief agreement with the government of R. B. Bennett—a sensitive undertaking since Saskatchewan could meet its responsibilities only with federal aid. Gardiner, however, despised the Conservative prime minister—and not simply because of his political leanings. The Saskatchewan premier was convinced that Bennett had financed the activities of the Ku Klux Klan in the province in the late 1920s, arousing the latent ethnic and religious hatred that had brought his government down in 1929. That there was no documentation to support this claim did not matter; Gardiner clung to the belief until his dying days. Ironically, what he did not know at the time—and what might have actually contributed to his 1929 defeat—was that Bennett was the secret owner of the *Regina Daily Star*, a new Conservative paper launched in 1928 to target the long-entrenched Liberal government. These examples suggest there was bad blood between the two men well before Gardiner toppled the Anderson government in 1934. They also underscore the new premier's predicament. He had to get much-needed aid from an unfriendly government and at the same time work to defeat that government.[16]

At about the same time Gardiner resumed power, the Bennett government adopted a new way of funding relief assistance. Up until the spring of 1934, Ottawa covered one-third of provincial relief costs, regardless of the total amount. Bennett now wanted to place a cap on these expenditures by paying a fixed monthly grant. A separate agreement would be negotiated with each province on the basis of need. Gardiner privately preferred that the federal government assume complete responsibility for direct relief, but gladly accepted the notion of a monthly payment, especially since the province would decide where the money would be spent. The sticking point was the size of Saskatchewan's grant. In August 1934, the Bennett government informed Gardiner that he could expect to receive two hundred thousand dollars per month for direct relief. Naturally, the province could have done with more. But exactly how much more was not known until the government began tallying up the cost of yet another crop failure. According to the estimates, it would take between eight and ten million dollars to save an estimated forty-five thousand farms in drought-stricken areas—from supplying feed, fodder, and seed to relocating families and their belongings. Gardiner initially requested a five-million-dollar federal loan to meet the most urgent needs. But when the prime minister and the federal minister of finance, in an exchange of telegrams, questioned Saskatchewan's proposals for dealing with the agricultural crisis—going so far as to suggest that the province was making the issue a political one—Gardiner travelled to Ottawa in late October to confront Bennett. There, before the federal cabinet, he described the situation in Saskatchewan as "a national calamity" and repeated his request for emergency assistance. Otherwise, he suggested, it was up to the federal government to deal with the problem, given the importance of wheat to the national economy. Bennett balked at the idea of Ottawa administering agricultural aid. He also had to admit that without help Saskatchewan would likely default. But it took three days and several hours of sparring over how relief in the province was being managed before Gardiner was finally sent home with three-quarters of a million dollars.[17]

The Saskatchewan premier's struggle to secure farm aid aggravated the already poor relationship between Ottawa and Regina, especially since the federal contribution fell far short of the needs of the province. But things turned even nastier the following spring when federal finance minister E. N. Rhodes accused the Gardiner government of being careless in the distribution of federal relief funds. A blistering 30 April 1935 letter to the premier listed a number of apparent abuses—individual cases where relief should never have been advanced—and then repeated Ottawa's earlier concern over the disbandment of the Saskatchewan Relief Commission. "The system seems not only to have been faulty," Rhodes scolded his provincial counterpart, "but was rendered more inefficient by failure to exercise adequate inspection and control." Gardiner defended his government at length, arguing that the general success of the agricultural relief programme, under which thousands of farmers had been helped, more than outweighed a few irregularities. But the damage had been done, and Rhodes's threat to suspend future assistance only hardened Gardiner's dislike of the Bennett government. The Saskatchewan premier was extremely territorial when it came to the affairs of the province, and for Ottawa to question the integrity of his government was a slap in the face.[18]

This acrimony did not bode well for how the two governments would cooperate in dealing with the On-to-Ottawa Trek. A little more than a month after Rhodes had sent his bullying letter to Gardiner, the relief camp strikers began their odyssey to Ottawa. Initially, Regina was not prepared to help. On 4 June 1935, the day the trekkers reached Kamloops, Regina mayor Cornelius Rink warned, "They had better keep away if they figure the city is going to feed them and look after them while they are here." But once the men made it to Calgary and it became apparent that they would soon invade Saskatchewan, the Gardiner government stepped in to facilitate their passage across the province. At a 10 June meeting attended by Premier Gardiner, Mayor Rink, and other civic officials, Tom Molloy, the commissioner of the Bureau of Labour and Public Welfare, announced that the provincial government had decided to treat the men as transients. Cities could spend up to forty cents per day (the equivalent of two meals) in feeding the men on the understanding that they would be reimbursed by the province. This arrangement came two days before the trekkers' advance delegation reached Regina. In other words, even before the Gardiner government was asked for help it was ready and willing to do what it could to see the men on their way.[19]

Gardiner's sense that he had protected Saskatchewan did not last long. The very next day, 11 June, RCMP assistant commissioner Wood hurriedly met with the premier in the late afternoon to tell him that a decision had been made to stop the trek in Regina. A stunned Gardiner protested the lack of consultation, but he was powerless to do much more, especially given the speed at which events were moving. In a telegram to the premier later that same day, W. A. Mather of the CPR declared the men to be trespassers and asked for the "assistance and cooperation of your Province ... to put an end to this practice." Colonel Wood returned to the legislature the next morning to report that his orders were now official, and that the mounted police were to remove the trekkers from the trains and place them in a special holding camp. He also carried copies of reports on the disturbing events in Calgary. Gardiner, still angry about the turn of events, responded that any police action would surely lead to violence, and that the real tragedy would be that the trouble would be none of Saskatchewan's doing. He also mused out loud that if the railway companies refused to carry the men beyond Regina, the province might arrange to take them by car and truck to the Manitoba border. Whether the premier was bluffing is debatable, but Wood certainly took him at his word and warned the commander of Manitoba's D Division to be ready.[20]

Gardiner next moved to engage the prime minister. After consulting with his cabinet, he sent a tersely worded telegram to Ottawa challenging the federal government's authority to use the mounted police to stop the trekkers. "CPR delivered these men in Saskatchewan en route to Ottawa," he summed up the government's position, "and we expect them to carry them through." Gardiner then huddled with Mayor Rink, the Regina police chief, and J. W. Estey, the acting attorney-general, while waiting for Bennett's response. It was not long in coming. By mid-afternoon, the prime minister wired Regina, calmly noting that the request to stop the trekkers had come from the railways and asking for the province's cooperation in putting an end to their illegal riding of trains. This notion that the trek, after making it through the mountains without interference, was now breaking the law as it headed across the prairies strained the premier's credulity. In fact, he knew from Mike McCaulay and Bill Hammill, the trek advance men who arrived in

Regina earlier that morning, that the railways had been as accommodating as possible in moving the men eastward. Gardiner used this information to go on the offensive. He dispatched a second wire to Ottawa that went directly to the heart of Bennett's credibility. According to information that the Saskatchewan government had gathered, he stated, the men were not in any sense trespassers and stopping them really had nothing to do with unlawful travel. He sent a similar message to the CPR's Mather, who had come to Regina to meet with the premier and present the company's case for the removal of the trekkers. After recounting what he had learned from the advance team, Gardiner suggested that the railway company had a duty to "carry these men through this Province in view of the fact that they do not belong here." Finally, he issued a press release that reproduced the exchange of telegrams between Regina and Ottawa, and invoked Bennett's public pledge, made only days earlier, that Ottawa would get involved only at the specific request of a province. "He has never been asked by this province to interfere," Gardiner growled, "and we would ask him to keep his hands off the policing of this province."[21]

Prime Minister Bennett should not have been surprised by the intensity of the Saskatchewan premier's reaction—anything less would have been uncharacteristic. But Gardiner was not his major worry at the time. When Bennett returned to Ottawa in mid-May 1935, following his lengthy recuperative trip to England, he was ready to withdraw from political life. Any idea of retiring had to be quickly shelved, though, because of the stiff challenge to his leadership he faced from Harry Stevens. The former trade and commerce minister had been a thorn in Bennett's side—regularly chastising the government for not bringing about meaningful reform—ever since he had resigned from the cabinet in October 1934. Now, as the next general election drew nearer, the popular backbencher threatened to split the Conservative party, if not wrest control of it away from Bennett. The prime minister consequently decided to remain at the helm of the ship of state, even though there were good medical reasons for him to find a quiet harbour. Indeed, one biographer describes him as "a man who came alive in adversity." Galvanized by what he perceived as Stevens's treachery, Bennett reached deep down inside to find his old self—not the tired, beleaguered leader of the past few years—

and stood ready to defend his record against all enemies. He was gamely supported by his sister Mildred, who had come north from Washington with her no-surrender attitude, determined to see her brother lead the country into the election.[22]

It was against this backdrop that Prime Minister Bennett had to cope with the On-to-Ottawa Trek. When he returned to the House of Commons on 20 May 1935, the Vancouver relief camp strike was already in its second month. Although he told a correspondent that "the situation would be entirely different" if he were dealing with the men, he took comfort in the reports that the strike would soon disintegrate. And when the men decided to head to Ottawa, he, like many other observers, dismissed the trek as an ill-fated gamble. It is too easy, however, to attribute the prime minister's position solely to his belief that the single homeless unemployed were a provincial responsibility once they left the camps.[23] He had another urgent problem in the form of Harry Stevens. That was his real quarry in late May and early June, not some relief camp strike on the West Coast. There was no reason, then, to tangle with the strikers when the more important fight, his much anticipated showdown with Stevens, was on the horizon.[24]

The unexpected success of the trek introduced a new dynamic. If the men made it to Ottawa, then Bennett would have a second conflagration on his hands at the same time he was trying to put out the Stevens fire. In fact, from the government's perspective, a mob of hundreds of angry young men protesting on the steps of Parliament could pose a real danger, especially given the revolutionary tenor of the movement. This prospect was driven home when an extremely upset Dr. George Stanley, the Conservative MP for Calgary East, arrived in Ottawa on 10 June to speak to the prime minister. Stanley had witnessed the trekker occupation of the Calgary relief office and left immediately by train for the capital to warn his boss about the gravity of the situation.[25]

Bennett, however, had effectively tied his hands with his statement in the Commons on 7 June that he would not interfere with the trek unless a province asked for help. He had to find another reason, then, for federal involvement, and at a meeting on the morning of Tuesday, 11 June—the same day Commissioner MacBrien of the RCMP telephoned Colonel Wood in Regina—it was decided to find the trekkers in violation of the Railways Act, a federal statute. This plan would only work, though, if the two national railways declared the men to be trespassers—something they readily agreed to do, no matter how contradictory it appeared after they had carried the men through the mountains and across Alberta. The government also needed a place to stop the trek, and Regina, the home of the RCMP training depot and several hundred Mounties, seemed the most logical place. That the men would not get there for a few days also gave the mounted police some much-needed time to get ready. There is no evidence to suggest, however, that the federal government deliberately chose Regina because it was the home of a Liberal government. Granted, the chance to cause Gardiner a little distress was tempting, but Bennett was more interested in a quick resolution of the problem, not opening a war on a new front. The premier's behaviour, though, meant that he could not be trusted as an ally in dealing with the trekkers.[26]

Despite Gardiner's opposition, Ottawa continued to push the interpretation that the trekkers were trespassers and hence guilty of travelling illegally. Early on the morning of Thursday, 13 June, the day before the trek was expected to reach Regina, Bennett wired Gardiner that he had been "apparently . . . misinformed" about the men riding on the trains. Both national railways also took issue with the premier's reading of the situation and categorically denied that they had offered any assistance to the trek. An indignant Mather inaccurately claimed the CPR had not "stopped any train at any place or at any time to permit or facilitate these men reaching Regina in a body." But Gardiner's continuing insistence that he had evidence to the contrary revealed the weakness of the federal position: how did several hundred men, riding in public view atop boxcars, manage to get as far as they did?[27]

The other glaring difficulty for Bennett was that Saskatchewan—not Ottawa—exercised control over the RCMP in the province. Under the terms of a 1928 agreement, the Mounties not only took over provincial policing duties from the Saskatchewan Provincial Police, but enforced the federal Criminal Code at the instruction of provincial authorities. This jurisdictional question—whether Ottawa in fact had the authority to order the mounted police to stop the trek in Regina—had dogged the Bennett government from the beginning of its operation against the trek.

The prime minister had even sought the advice of the Justice Department. At a special meeting on 12 June, three senior officials of the department, including the deputy minister, met with General Andy McNaughton, chief of the army's general staff, to discuss a number of possible scenarios. It was the first and only time that McNaughton, the creator of the Department of National Defence (DND) camps, had been involved in discussions about the trek. Bennett seemed to hold him personally responsible for getting the government into such a mess, and his days as defence chief would come to an end in a matter of weeks. After McNaughton briefly outlined Ottawa's plan—as told to him by Commissioner MacBrien—the officials decided that it would be best if any action against the trekkers involved the provincial government. Otherwise, responsibility for any trouble would rest squarely with the federal government. They also discussed the problem of what to do with several hundred convicted men and after briefly toying with the idea of creating "camps of discipline," decided "it would be preferable to have any necessary action taken by the Province affected." Finally, they concluded that the Saskatchewan attorney-general would normally be the one to call Canadian troops into action, but that the federal government could do so if it first declared a national emergency and secured the approval of Parliament.[28]

It was the Bennett government's need to justify Ottawa's intervention that led to federal Justice minister Hugh Guthrie going before the House of Commons on the afternoon of 13 June and declaring the trek to be the handiwork of the Communists. The men were not ordinary trespassers. They were a red-infested movement—an unemployed army of Communist foot soldiers—defying "the laws of the country." Guthrie also tackled the question of who had control of the RCMP in Saskatchewan, noting that there was a special provision in the agreement with the province giving the mounted police the authority to enforce dominion statutes. The men had been trespassing upon railway property since leaving Vancouver and were therefore in clear violation of the federal Railways Act; Ottawa could therefore use the Mounties to pull the men from the trains before there was "serious damage to life and property." These arguments were designed to provide a kind of legal wedge for federal intervention. But ironically, there was really no great need to worry about the Saskatchewan government causing problems. That very morning, RCMP assistant commissioner Wood had written Ottawa headquarters, reporting that, despite the premier's bellyaching, he had "received no direct instructions from the Attorney-General of the Province to withhold any action in preventing relief camp workers from proceeding east."[29]

Gardiner spent most of Thursday portraying Saskatchewan as a victim. In response to Bennett's telegram claiming his information about the trek was wrong, the premier shot back that the men should be allowed to travel across the province, as they had been in British Columbia and Alberta, and not dumped in Regina. "If there is trouble while these outsiders are in Saskatchewan," he vowed, "we will hold you responsible." Gardiner also held a tell-all interview with James Kingsbury of the *Toronto Daily Star*, who had left the trek in Moose Jaw to see what was being planned for the men's arrival in Regina. He began by describing how Ottawa had been scrambling to find a way for Bennett to get around his non-interference pledge. He then listed several confirmed instances of railway cooperation and went on to explain that the provincial government was prepared to treat the men as transients, not trespassers. He also disclosed that Ottawa was massing a large mounted police force in the city without the consent or approval of Saskatchewan. For Gardiner, there could be only one outcome. "We will not be a party to creating all the conditions necessary for a first-class riot in the midst of this province," he said.[30]

The fault line separating Ottawa and Regina was reflected in the newspapers. The *Ottawa Journal* found it "extraordinary" that the trekkers had been able to travel as far as the prairies and did not look forward to them marching on Parliament Hill. "It would be better … to meet trouble more than half way," an 11 June editorial argued. "The men should be halted for discussions in the West, where they belong." Three days later, the paper called Ottawa's plan to stop the trek in Regina "a sensible decision." The *Saskatoon Star Phoenix* also initially questioned the wisdom of the trek: "It will not bring the results desired, for the Government there is not made that way. Instead it may create considerable trouble." But once the Bennett government ordered the Mounties to put an end to the march, the paper spoke of "dictatorial power, an inexcusable and unforgivable Hitlerian action." The *Moose Jaw*

Times-Herald, on the other hand, blamed the trouble on the failure of federal officials to act earlier in British Columbia: "If Ottawa could exercise its authority to stop them at Regina, it could, and should have, done so within the Province where the trouble started." The toughest talk came from Regina's *Leader-Post*. The paper's lead editorial on the morning of 14 June argued that Ottawa's handling of the trek was "typical of the bungling that has characterized ... the Government's handling of the unemployment situation from the start." It also reminded readers that exactly five years earlier in Regina Bennett had promised during the election campaign that he would not play with the lives of Canada's unemployed. "My heart was saddened," the paper mockingly recalled his words, "to hear that all they all ask is a chance to live to work. To live to work! That is what it means.... And they are denied it."[31]

How this simmering federal-provincial feud would affect the fate of the On-to-Ottawa Trek in the days ahead was anybody's guess. Certainly, the trek could count on support from Premier Gardiner. On 13 June, with the men hunkered down in Moose Jaw, trek leader Slim Evans had met with Saskatchewan officials in Regina and learned that the province was willing to provide food and shelter. But this help was given on the understanding that the men's stay in the capital would be a temporary one. As Gardiner would later confess, he did not care which way they went "as long as they got ... out of the province." It was also not clear how far the premier was prepared to go in seeing the men on their way. As he told the *Toronto Star* reporter, he could instruct the RCMP to ignore Bennett's edict, but when pressed for details, he was extremely coy about exactly what he would do. The other unknown was how the people of Regina, already hurting from five years of depression, would respond to the arrival the trekkers. It was one thing to have the men there for only a few days, but quite another matter if there was to be a bloody showdown with the mounted police. The one certainty was that Regina's little world would be a different one with the arrival of the trek, but exactly how different would depend on the trekkers, the Mounties, and—most importantly—the Bennett government.[32]

CHAPTER SIX

They Had Us Across a Barrel

The arrival of the On-to-Ottawa Trek in Regina had been anxiously anticipated for days. The trekkers had defiantly vowed that no one—least of all the Royal Canadian Mounted Police—was going to stop them, while the R. B. Bennett government was equally adamant that the men would proceed no farther than the Saskatchewan capital. Something had to give. But when the exhausted trekkers clambered down from their freight in the Regina rail yards early in the morning of Friday, 14 June, the Mounties were nowhere in sight. Ottawa had decided not to move against the men unless they attempted to board another train to continue their journey eastward. Until then, federal authorities would work hard to convince them to abandon their plan, all the while hurriedly massing a large punitive force in the event that more persuasive methods were needed. The trekkers, on the other hand, reluctantly took up temporary residence in Regina, trying to decide what to do next. They were trapped in the city, prisoners of the Canadian state, and knew that any attempt to break out would precipitate a showdown—something they were more than ready for. They also realized, though, that they had to work inside the box they found themselves in and portray the federal government and the mounted police as the aggressors, while courting the support of the Saskatchewan public. The stalemate that had characterized the Vancouver relief camp strike was consequently replayed in Regina in the middle of June. But the situation was entirely different from that in British Columbia. This time, the Bennett government was not prepared to be so patient with the men or their protest.

❖ ❖ ❖

For a city that did not want to serve as the battleground between the mounted police and the trekkers, Regina was remarkably well-prepared for the arrival of the On-to-Ottawa Trek. In fact, the city's welcome could be described as friendly, if not generous. Unlike other communities along the route, Regina had had several days' notice to get ready for the trek and what was supposed to be a brief stopover in the city. Jimmy Gardiner's Liberal government was also determined to do whatever it could to expedite the movement of the men through the province without incident. But what was even more important to the trekkers' reception was the emergence of the Citizens' Emergency Committee (CEC), a kind of who's who of the city's leading activists, including those of the radical left. On 13 June 1935, twenty-four organizations, along with several private citizens, held their first official meeting as the CEC, a broad coalition representing such diverse interests as the Young Communist League, the Regina Union of Unemployed (RUU), the Co-operative Commonwealth Federation (CCF), the United Church of Canada, and even the Milk Drivers' Union. Seven more groups had joined by the next meeting, bringing the total number of delegates to seventy-five. This turn of events probably brought a smile to the face of William Hammill, one of the trekker advance men who attended the committee's first meeting. For the past few days, Hammill almost had to resort to extortion to line up assistance along the route. Now in Regina, many were not only swept up in the drama of the trek but, in the words of Fred Boor of the Regina North-West Union of Unemployed, wanted "to make the stay of the boys as comfortable and pleasant as possible."[1]

By the time the trek rolled into Regina Friday morning, the Citizens' Emergency Committee had everything planned for the weekend. At Hammill's suggestion, a mass rally was organized for the men's first night in the city. The committee originally wanted to hold the event at the local armouries, but when military officials balked at the idea, it moved the meeting to the exhibition stadium where most of the men would be staying. An application was also made to the city clerk for a tag day on 15 June. This was the second request on behalf of the trekkers. Several days earlier, the RUU had asked for a permit, only to be turned down because Grey Nuns' Hospital was already scheduled to tag on that Saturday. But once a delegation from the committee apprised the sister superior of the situation, she called off the hospital appeal so that the trekkers could canvass for funds.

The committee also had ambitious plans for entertaining the men over the weekend. Free tickets to the movies were solicited, while boxing and wrestling matches were arranged for Saturday at the exhibition grounds. At the urging of the trek advance team, there was also to be a picnic on Sunday afternoon so that the public could meet the boys and hear their individual stories. The question was where. Having some fun at the expense of the military and mounted police, H. Cowan suggested at the committee's second meeting that the RCMP barracks was "the logical and appropriate place" for the picnic. R. R. Mackenzie of the Disabled Veterans' Association heartily agreed. "It's a ripping idea," he chortled. "The police could join in some little games." When the laughter subsided, it was decided to hold the picnic at Wascana Park, near the provincial legislature, or, in the event of rain, in the new Grain Show Building. The committee also selected M. J. Coldwell, a former Regina high school principal and leader of the provincial CCF, to speak on one of the local radio stations later that afternoon to publicize the weekend's events and solicit donations, especially food for Sunday's picnic. There seemed to be a common spirit among committee members that if they called on their many contacts in the city all would go well over the next few days and they would be able to "discourage police oppression."[2]

The RCMP were also ready for the arrival of the trekkers. Not only did Regina boast a sizeable contingent of Mounties, but Saskatchewan's F Division had one of the best security and intelligence-gathering sections in the country. Assistant Commissioner S. T. Wood also made sure that the Regina city police understood the gravity of the situation. On 12 June, he forwarded to Chief Constable Martin Bruton a secret report about the trekkers' bullying behaviour in Calgary, implying that they might resort to the same tactics in Regina. He also provided a copy of the Canadian Pacific Railway's request for help in preventing the men from trespassing. The Irish-born Bruton, who had served as chief since 1915, promised "the fullest co-operation," duly noting that it was "certainly within the duty and scope" of the city police to protect property and respond to any disturbance. But at the same time, the veteran police officer was not about to go looking for trouble and counselled his patrolmen to "exercise the greatest possible forbearance" in dealing with the trekkers. Colonel Wood also huddled with railway officials to figure out what should be done once the trek reached Regina. The simplest and most obvious answer was to cancel the two daily through freights—one at five in the morning, the other at eleven at night—from stopping inside the city, thereby denying the men a means of moving on. There was also the matter of officially informing the trekkers that their days of riding trains were over. W. A. Mather of the CPR wanted someone from the mounted police to serve the notice. But Wood was reluctant to do anything for the time being that might be construed as "provocative." This caution did not mean, though, that the RCMP was not prepared to tangle with the trekkers. It was no secret that reinforcements were arriving almost daily in Regina, nor that police were guarding the outskirts of the city as if it was under attack, preventing new recruits from joining the trek. As of 14 June, Commissioner MacBrien in Ottawa also expected twice-daily situational reports from Wood—probably the same kind that General MacBrien had demanded on the battlefield during the Great War. It was only a question of when and how the Mounties would move against what many in the force clearly regarded as a "revolutionary movement." Why else would the men be organized along military lines?[3]

The trekkers had plans of their own. Despite warnings about the police blockade, they looked upon Regina as just another way station on the road and expected to leave for Winnipeg by Monday at the latest. But by the time the trek reached the city shortly after dawn on Friday, 14 June, the men were in no condition to go anywhere, no condition to meet any resistance. Cold, wet, and exhausted from their early morning ride from Moose Jaw, they trudged, in fours, to the exhibition grounds. One reporter with a weakness for hyperbole likened their silence to "the menace of 2,000 sticks of explosives." In reality, though, all they wanted to do that morning was sleep for a few hours and eat a warm meal. The men lost little time settling into their new quarters at the stadium and, after washing up, many bedded down on the fresh straw for some welcome rest. Just before 10:00, they got their wake-up call—a driver from Parkdale Dairy Farm at nearby Pilot Butte pulled up with three large cans of donated milk. The men grabbed cups and tins and took turns dipping into the liquid and gulping it down. They were then called into their divisions and headed out to introduce themselves to Regina. As they marched east along Eleventh Avenue, in a line that stretched nearly half a mile, their chanting brought out hundreds of onlookers: "Where are we going? OTTAWA! Who's going to stop us? NOBODY!" Many of the men had the words On To Ottawa printed in chalk on the backs of their coats and jackets—even on their hats. A new slogan also appeared for the first time on the streets of Regina: "R.B. B. Ware." The column wound its way through the downtown before finally lining up with military precision outside the Unity Centre, home of the RUU, which would serve as trek headquarters. Slim Evans spoke briefly to the men from the roof of a nearby building, reminding them to attend the rally that night. His final words, "That is all for today," were followed by a mad scramble as hundreds of hungry trekkers, with meal tickets in hand, sought out one of the nineteen local restaurants that had agreed to feed them. The publicity committee, in the meantime, issued its first news release: a plea for clothing, especially shoes and socks. Pickets, wearing red armbands with a black letter P, also took up positions on street corners to ensure that the men did not get into any trouble. Regina might have been home to the mounted police, but the trekkers seemed ready to challenge that.[4]

The trek's arrival in Regina forced Premier Gardiner to become more deeply involved in the dispute between Ottawa and the men. He had spent the past few days ranting about federal interference while absolving the province of any responsibility if trouble erupted. But now that the trekkers were actually in the city and marching through the streets, his government actively tried to find a peaceful way out of the situation. At an early afternoon press conference at the legislature, he distributed a prepared statement which indicated that the Saskatchewan government had met with the trek leaders and asked them "to maintain order as long as they are in this province." And they were doing just that according to the premier. Not even the late morning parade was cause for concern. "There has been no necessity for police action so far," he confidently told a clutch of reporters in his office, "and we don't believe there will be any." Many of the scribes might have dismissed Gardiner's assessment as naive, if not blinkered. But what they did not know was that the acting attorney general had written Assistant Commissioner Wood that same day asserting Saskatchewan's control over the administration of justice in the province and ordering the RCMP to "take every precaution to preserve the peace"—even if provoked.[5]

The chances of the mounted police bowing to provincial authority at this stage were extremely low, but even more so after three Regina lawyers—F. B. Bagshaw, E. C. Leslie, and F. Somerville—sent the prime minister a frantic message after witnessing the downtown parade. Indeed, their telegram confirmed Ottawa's worst fears. The three Conservative party members had looked past the trekkers' youth, poverty, and empty lives to see a highly disciplined army that had been trained for "conflict with authority." They also accused Premier Gardiner of spreading "vicious propaganda" about the federal government and its motives, while doing absolutely nothing to rein in the men. Most disturbing, though, was the "public sympathy" for the trek and its demands; the people of Regina had been duped and did not realize that the "situation [was] really full of dynamite." And that was the real worry for the Bennett government and the RCMP. It was bad enough that the men had fallen under the spell of the Communists, but the movement had also taken, in Wood's words, "this city by storm."[6]

This popular support of the trekkers was nowhere more evident than at the Friday night rally. The CEC had arranged for special streetcar service to the exhibition grounds; by the time the programme got underway at 7:30, six thousand Regina citizens filled the bleachers along the east and west sides of the stadium and in the south-end gallery. Those unable to attend the meeting could listen to the speeches live over CKCK, Saskatchewan's first radio station. The men sat stretched out with their packs and bedding on the straw, under floodlights, in the central show ring—as if they were on display. Pete Mikkelson, president of the RUU and a future city alderman,[7] opened the meeting by naming all of the organizations that had come together to help the trekkers during their stay in the city. His announcement that the local Conservative and Liberal organizations had declined to send representatives elicited loud booing. George Black, one of the trek leaders, then took over, guided by a script that had been perfected since the men had left Vancouver. As he had done at every public meeting, Matt Shaw spoke first, vividly recounting the conditions in the camps and the reasons for heading to Ottawa. Gazing out across the packed stadium, he said it was plainly evident that "our problem has become a national problem" and called on the people of Regina to support the tag day and other trek activities. "We will not be trampled on any more," he declared.

A series of special greetings followed, each warmly applauded by the trekkers. Jack Guest, representing the youth of Regina, pledged "solidarity in the struggle for a decent living," while Mrs. Florence Theodor, speaking on behalf of women and mothers, defended the boys and their cause. M. J. Coldwell went even further, promising the "unqualified support" of the provincial CCF. "No power will be able to stop your onward march," he vowed to the cheers of the men ringing through the rafters. The only controversial note—which set the crowd abuzz—was when Reverend John Mutch of Knox United Church suggested there was no reason to go to Ottawa. The negotiations between the trekkers and federal representatives could easily take place in Regina. As was customary, Slim Evans spoke last. The trek leader reviewed the events of the past few months, dismissing the relief camp commission report as "contemptible." He also contrasted the orderly behaviour of the men with the heavy-handed tactics of the Bennett government and reported that there would be a house-to-house canvass to bring citizens out to see the trek on its way Monday night. "There are not enough Cossacks in the Dominion to stop us," he thundered, "if the workers ... unite in saying, 'Hands off the relief camp strikers.'" The three-hour meeting ended with a series of resolutions: one demanding that Bennett remove all obstacles in the way of the trekkers; one censuring the local Conservative MP for suggesting that the militia be called out; and one urging the federal opposition parties to use their influence to hold back the RCMP. As each was approved with a shout of "ayes," the tired trekkers leapt to their feet at Black's cue and roared their appreciation to the crowd. A Hollywood director could not have done better.[8]

Saturday 15 June was a day of maneuvering by all players. Premier Gardiner decided to go another round with Prime Minister Bennett and made his strongest statement yet about provincial control of the mounted police. "Would ask Ottawa to withdraw orders affecting the administration of justice in this province," he wired the federal leader, "and await a request for action from this Government should it be necessary to advance one." In asserting Saskatchewan's jurisdiction, Gardiner directed the prime minister to a letter sent by federal Justice minister Hugh Guthrie in the aftermath of the September 1931 Estevan riot. Two Saskatchewan residents, Louise King of Ratcliffe and Frank Hannah of Frobisher, had been seeking federal compensation after being accidentally wounded by RCMP gunfire during the melee. But Guthrie dismissed any responsibility for the claim, on the advice of department lawyers, because the Mounties were "an agency of the Province ... employed ... to maintain law and order." From the premier's perspective, Guthrie's 1931 letter effectively undercut the federal position, while bolstering his own argument that the handling of the trekkers—and the supervision of the mounted police—should be purely a provincial matter.[9]

The RCMP also reconsidered its plans in light of the Friday night rally. Worried that a sympathetic public might restrict the police's handling of the trekkers, Colonel Wood called on Reverend Mutch and grimly shared his fears about the situation. Not only had the city been invaded by a revolutionary movement, but Evans and several others had criminal records. Mutch swallowed the bait and delivered a scorching denunciation of the trek leadership from his pulpit on Sunday night. The other, potentially more serious, problem was Evans's announcement that he intended to use the public essentially as a human shield to "see the strikers out of Regina." MacBrien's response was to arrange for the Regina mayor or some other qualified official to be ready to read the Riot Act at the first whiff of trouble. If no one was willing to do it, Wood was to perform this duty "in your capacity as justice of the peace before commencing police action."[10]

The mounted police, however, would find a cooperative soul in Mayor Cornelius Rink. Something of a gadfly, the Dutch-born Rink had come to Regina early in the twentieth century to cash in on the real-estate boom and soon found his way into municipal politics. He failed in his first bid for mayor before the Great War, but won on a populist platform in 1933. Now in his early sixties, Rink seems to have come unhinged while the trek was in Regina—and for good reason. The trekker advance team had visited him at his office and apparently threatened that if they did not get what they wanted, there would be "three feet of blood on the streets of the City of Regina." Whether these exact words were used is debatable, but Rink was clearly spooked by the presence of the trekkers in Regina and was already carrying around a copy of the Riot Act in his pocket well before he was formally approached about being ready for trouble.[11]

The trek leadership decided to build on the overwhelming success of the public meeting and collect some much needed funds for the days ahead—despite the fact that the city had refused to grant a permit. It did not matter, though. Although Police Chief Bruton would later complain that the trek broke several civic by-laws by parading, tagging, distributing handbills, and placing posters—all without proper authority—the city police ignored the hundreds of taggers, with their donation cans and friendly banter, working the downtown streets and Regina neighbourhoods throughout the day on Saturday. The haul was incredible—almost $1,450 was collected. It was not only the largest amount ever raised in Regina in a single tag day, but the largest amount raised in any community, including Calgary, during the trek. Matt Shaw was ecstatic. "We find ourselves in a very fortunate position," he crowed to a fellow organizer back in Vancouver. "Public support is tremendous.... There has been no beating about the bush, they jumped right into the struggle."[12]

This sympathy for the trek drew dozens of citizens to the exhibition grounds that Saturday afternoon to meet the men and talk about their trip to Ottawa. People wanted to hear first-hand about their experiences and wish them luck in their quest. James Kingsbury of the *Toronto Star* was there as well, collecting stories about what was now being called "the army of despair" or "the unwanted generation." Most of the trekkers, he reported, "are under 25 ... Canadians ... and ask nothing more than a chance to work and make good." There was Bradley—first name unknown—who had trained as a doctor in Nova Scotia but was forced to enter a relief camp when his fledgling medical practice failed in Vancouver. Nineteen-year-old Leonard Brownstone was a former star football player from Winnipeg who wanted to study civil engineering one day. "I still retain my old-fashioned ideas," he told Kingsbury, "I want to settle down and raise a family." Harold Goodson of Edmonton had quit school at fifteen to work as a harvester and then crossed over the mountains to find work; he had spent the past few winters in a relief camp. Jim King and Bruce Hart had both left southern Ontario at the start of the Depression for the promise of a better future in the West; they were now headed back as trekkers. So too was Jimmie Fitzgerald, who had not been home to Toronto for years and wished that his folks knew he was on his way. There were others who preferred to keep their identity and past to themselves, as if they did not want their family or friends to know they were part of the trek. Japanese Fred Nogami would only admit that he had been born in Canada. Some refused to say anything at all. What struck Kingsbury more than anything else, though, was the mood among the men at the stadium. "There was no complaint," he noted. "There was despair among these young lads ... but there was hope and courage, too."[13]

The federal government, in the meantime, took steps to reassert control of the situation by finally moving to deal with the relief camp strikers and their demands. On Friday night, Prime Minister Bennett telephoned cabinet ministers Robert Manion and Robert Weir and told them that he was sending them immediately to Regina to meet with the trek leaders. The identical strategy had been employed sixteen years earlier to deal with another crisis in another western city. In May 1919, the Union government of Sir Robert Borden had dispatched two cabinet ministers westward to try to end the Winnipeg General Strike. Now, Manion and Weir were being parachuted into Regina on a similar mission: to defuse a Communist-led movement that imperiled the peace and order of the country.

Manion, a long-time parliamentarian and minister responsible for Canada's railways, was a logical choice for the task, given the reason for stopping the trek in Regina. The Fort William doctor and Great War veteran also took a hard line on relief. In his autobiography, *Life is an Adventure*, he spoke of a better Canada where people must be "courageously self reliant, eager to struggle for a living,... We must care for our people, but not turn them into perennial loungers." At the same time, Bennett did not completely trust Manion—he had entered federal politics as a Unionist Liberal—and his consensus style of politics. The prime minister also regarded him as another unworthy leadership contender, and the two had openly quarreled in the House in early June.[14]

Robert Weir's selection was more dubious. As minister of Agriculture, he represented Saskatchewan at the cabinet table. He had also been a popular Regina high school mathematics teacher before enlisting in 1916 and being wounded at Passchendaele. But he was largely a nonentity—a lightweight in Bennett's cabinet—and he returned to farming near Prince Albert after serving just one term in Parliament. He died tragically at his Weldon-area farm in 1939 when a truckload of barley tipped over and smothered him.[15]

Direct federal intervention, even at this late date, was widely applauded. The *Toronto Globe* considered it "wise to take ... a hand in the problem," while the *Montreal Gazette* was relieved Dominion authorities "have been stirred to a fuller appreciation of their public duty.... A great deal of harm would inevitably have resulted if this 'mission' had been allowed to follow its original course." Not surprisingly, Bennett's own paper, the *Regina Daily Star*, provided the strongest endorsement, noting that "nothing can possibly be gained by proceeding to Ottawa." It also warned to expect the worst if a settlement was not reached: "A peaceful crowd may quickly take on the nature of a mob.... Some of the leaders have stated they will brook no interference." The rival *Leader-Post*, on the other hand, offered some blunt advice to the government representatives: "So far as Saskatchewan is concerned ... [they] had better concern themselves with methods to get them out, and to get them out in the orderly fashion in which they came in."[16]

The news that two federal cabinet ministers were headed to Regina sent the strike committee into lengthy deliberation. For the better part of Saturday afternoon at the stadium, it hotly debated whether to meet with Bennett's emissaries or push on to Ottawa, regardless of the consequences. When Evans eventually emerged to speak to reporters, he calmly asserted, "We are quite willing to negotiate." But he also insisted that there had to be meaningful discussions. "If Manion is coming down here to talk about boxcars," he sarcastically remarked, "we are not interested." There also had to be a satisfactory outcome. If negotiations failed, then Evans declared the trek would resume its eastward march on Monday night with the support of Regina citizens.[17]

This tough talk was not idle bluster. As a seasoned organizer, Evans would not allow the trek to be boxed in by promises alone. It had to be made clear that if the cabinet ministers did not have the authority to reach a written agreement, then the trek's negotiators would walk away from the table. Nor were the trekkers prepared to fade away, "back to the hills," in Matt Shaw's words, if a deal could not be brokered. The trek had come too far, endured too much, to turn back empty-handed—even if faced with a police blockade. "If ... Bennett is prepared to supply transportation back west in order to hide the blot of Slvery [sic]," Shaw privately told his Vancouver friend, "we have said, 'Let him provide transportation right to Ottawa.'" At the same time, a meeting with Manion and Weir could not be avoided. Ever since the relief camp strike had been called in early April, the organizers had been seeking a meeting to put forward their six demands—that's why they were going to Ottawa. The strike committee could not, then, turn down the opportunity to talk to two of Bennett's ministers without hurting the trek's credibility and raising questions about its real purpose. In preparation for the meeting, though, the publicity committee hurriedly printed posters detailing the trekkers' demands and plastered them throughout the city; in large black letters, they called for "work with wages" and urged workers to "unite to do away with forced labour." Evans also announced that an eight-man negotiating team had been struck. The number was both symbolic and deliberate. In 1931, eight Communist organizers, including Tim Buck, had been jailed. Eight would now speak for the trekkers.[18]

The meeting with Manion and Weir was not expected to take place until sometime on Monday. That gave the men another opportunity to showcase public support for the trek at the Sunday afternoon picnic. The planning for the picnic was consequently just as important as that for the rally. The CEC lined up free air time on three local radio stations and approached the ministerial association about advertising the event during Sunday services. The biggest challenge, though, was securing enough food, something that the women on the committee gladly tackled. Mrs. Elizabeth Cruikshank of the Regina Council of Women, for example, convinced the city's bakeries to donate hundreds of loaves of bread, as well as cakes, doughnuts, and cookies. The canvass of other local merchants was equally successful—

enough to make more than three thousand sandwiches and gallons of lemonade, coffee, and tea. In the words of one of the organizers, "The response was magnificent."[19]

The picnic was originally to be held at Wascana Park, but the heavy rains of the past few days had made the grounds soggy, and the event had to be moved indoors to the Grain Show Building at the exhibition grounds. Despite the continuing rain, at least five thousand Reginans turned out with more than enough food for everyone there. The crowd actually may have been larger, but the estimates vary depending on those doing the counting. One thing is certain though—it was a huge success. There were so many people that it was hard to move about, while the din of the voices was so loud the Salvation Army Boys' Band could hardly be heard. But that did not matter, especially for some of the younger boys who flirted with the local girls and tried to get names and addresses.

At the end of the picnic, the citizens endorsed a telegram urging the Bennett government to withdraw the mounted police so that the trekkers could continue to Ottawa. Leaflets were also distributed calling on the public to assemble near the CPR freight yards around 10:00 on Monday night to see the men on their way. This last action was certainly incendiary, especially with negotiations pending. But as Evans told a *Toronto Star* reporter at the picnic, he was worried that the cabinet ministers' real mission in coming to Regina was to get the trek to disband. He had to find some way of finessing Bennett's representatives into responding to the trekkers' demands, and the threat to continue the trek seemed the best card to play.[20]

The RCMP took Evans at his word. Colonel Wood immediately contacted Police Chief Bruton and formally requested the assistance of the city police in protecting railway property. Bruton readily agreed, on the understanding that "there will certainly I trust be the fullest cooperation between us." The assistant commissioner also called together some of his more experienced officers at the training depot on Sunday morning to consider how best to prevent the trekkers from boarding a freight without provoking a clash.

It would not be an easy task. The Mounties recognized it would be nearly impossible to keep the men away from railway property, especially when the line west of the CPR station was unfenced. All they had to do was pour onto the track and force a train to stop with their numbers. The mounted police also did not want to be put into a position of having to use force—what they regarded as a standard Communist tactic—and end up being blamed for initiating the violence, while generating more public sympathy for the trek. What was most troubling, however, was the likely involvement of anywhere from one to ten thousand Regina citizens in breaking the blockade. In fact, Wood fully expected the organizers to use another Communist ploy, the deliberate recruitment of women and children to mingle with the trekkers in order to hamper police action. In retrospect, it would have been better to have rounded up the trekkers upon their arrival in the city.[21]

Wood eventually settled on a solution, but only after conferring with several local railway officials on Sunday night. The men would be allowed to board a train, specially despatched from Moose Jaw, that would take them east only as far as Pilot Butte, the next community along the line. Here, they would be removed by force and marched back along the railway right-of-way under guard to a new holding facility near Regina. The scheme had one glaring, potentially comical, weakness: the prospect of the men seizing control of the engine before the police could respond and heading across southern Saskatchewan at the controls of their own train. It also required the cooperation of the DND, which was expected to build the new camp. But with the support and advice of Inspector Chesser of the CPR police, Wood worked to perfect the plan. He did so in the knowledge that his original orders of 12 June, to stop the trek in Regina, were still valid. Although the acting provincial attorney-general had attempted to assert control over the police, Commissioner MacBrien deftly swatted aside the challenge, privately reminding Wood that the trekkers, as trespassers, were in violation of the federal Railways Act and hence the force was "within its rights … assisting in its enforcement."[22]

The Gardiner government, for its part, was placed in an extremely awkward position by Evans's plan to leave Monday night. Naturally, the premier wanted the men to move on, but not at the cost of a confrontation at the rail yards. Such an outcome seemed more than likely, though, especially when the Bennett government continued to argue that it enjoyed complete control over the mounted police given the circumstances. In a telegram to Gardiner on Sunday morning, Justice Minister Guthrie steadfastly maintained that the "general powers and authority of Mounted Police throughout Canada were not in any matter abbreviated or limited" when they took on "additional duty" in Saskatchewan in 1928. Simply put, it was their role to enforce dominion statutes. He also insisted there was "no analogy" between the Estevan strike and On-to-Ottawa Trek—they were "entirely different" matters—and called on the Gardiner government to do its part "to maintain law and order." Guthrie's rebuff left the premier with few options. He could—and did—continue to spar with the Bennett government, but to no avail. No amount of constitution-waving or dire predictions would budge Ottawa. Gardiner also sent yet another letter to Mather of the CPR, requesting that "these men be conveyed by your company beyond the boundaries of this Province." But the apologetic tone betrayed the premier's belief that he was probably wasting his time. The only glimmer of hope, then, rested with the two cabinet ministers reaching a deal with the trekkers—a topic the Saskatchewan cabinet likely discussed at a special meeting at the legislature on Sunday night. T. C. Davis, the attorney-general, had just returned to the capital from Winnipeg and Gardiner wanted to ensure that his minister was fully briefed about recent developments—and for good reason. Davis would be the government's point man in the days ahead. He was perfectly suited for the task. The son of a Saskatchewan senator and the former mayor of Prince Albert, Davis was not only one of the most senior members of the Gardiner government, but one of the most level-headed. [23]

Manion and Weir reached Regina at 7:00 A.M. on Monday, 17 June. They were expected to meet with the trek negotiators later that same day, most likely in the afternoon. But any hubbub about their arrival was eclipsed by the escalating tension over the trekkers' decision to leave that night. Tommy Davis called on Colonel Wood at the RCMP barracks in the morning to see what might be worked out, only to be told that Commissioner MacBrien, and not the province, was directing the police. A few hours later, Wood asked Davis by letter to arrange for the reading of the Riot Act "should the situation warrant same either tonight or thereafter." The attorney-general complied by sending Mayor Rink a copy of Wood's request, along with an excerpt from the appropriate section of the Criminal Code. The assistant commissioner also made plans for the deployment of his men. For the past day, there had been some debate whether the Mounties should put on a show of strength—as the trek had done its first day in Regina—to intimidate the trekkers and their supporters. But Wood realized that the group he was dealing with was not so easily cowed. Nor did he want to tip his hand at this point and reveal the actual size of the RCMP contingent. Instead, a thirty-man mounted detachment was to be posted behind the RCMP Town Station that evening, while four troops of men were to be concealed inside. All other mounted policemen were to stand by at the barracks with trucks ready to transport them if they were needed. The Regina police, meanwhile, were to wait at the city station. Only the Canadian Pacific and Canadian National railway police, about eighty strong, were to be positioned at the railway yards, where they were expected to respond to any trespassing in the first instance. But once the crowd had been engaged, the mounted and city police forces were to join the fray and attempt to drive the trekkers from east to west back towards the exhibition grounds.[24]

The assistant commissioner's preparations raised the real possibility of a clash in the city, something few wanted once the trek had reached Regina. In fact, Wood himself seemed attuned to this sentiment and had been trying to avoid a disturbance if at all possible. But if the trekkers were going to try to leave, he had orders to stop them. And he would gladly give them a fight, if he had to.

But did he really have to? This question ate away at Chief Bruton, who began to have second thoughts about stopping the men from leaving by train. "If a struggle should ensue," he candidly wrote Wood on Monday, "there would be grave danger.... Innocent citizens would suffer." The obvious answer for Bruton was not to route any train through the Regina yards that night, "thereby lessening the danger of injury or bloodshed." Wood agreed, and by the early afternoon had wired Ottawa about the change in plan: "Owing to large number of women and children at station tonight train will be canceled at last minute." This decision was not in any sense a retreat. Wood steadfastly believed that the trek was a Communist movement and was spoiling for a fight if and when he got the chance. He had also not given up on the idea of dealing with the trekkers just outside Regina and was ready to spring the trap. But the timing was not right, especially with the cabinet ministers in town, and he would have to wait.[25]

Ironically, the other group contributing to the sense of uneasiness was the CEC. At its daily meeting on Sunday, Mike McCauley, one of the trek representatives, reported that the men would be leaving the next night and called on the committee for help. The answer was quick in coming. "Let's get the people out to see the boys get on the freight," argued Pete Mikkelson. "No one has the right to turn this city into a battleground," added Alderman A. C. Ellison. "They don't dare." A motion was then passed, committing the CEC "to do all in its power to amass public support, lead the parade, and assist the boys in boarding the train east."[26]

When the matter was discussed again at the meeting the next morning, other suggestions were put forward: that the parade to the rail yards be advertised over the radio and that speakers be lined up to address the crowd until the men were on their way. But what was to be done, delegate William Cocks asked, if the CPR decided not to cooperate and provide a train that night? Within minutes, a three-person committee, including Ellison and Mikkelson, was empowered to approach provincial and civic authorities "to see to it that a train is supplied."[27]

The news was not encouraging when the committee reconvened later that afternoon. Although sympathetic to the delegation's wishes, Gardiner could not do much, especially since Saskatchewan had no means of enforcing any decision and the CPR had repeatedly refused the government's request to transport the men out of the province. The premier was also reluctant to foist the trekkers on Manitoba when their dispute was with the Bennett government. Undeterred, the committee voted to proceed with its original motion—a parade from the exhibition grounds to the rail yards followed by a public rally—regardless of the outcome of the meeting with Manion and Weir. "It is the desire of all fair-minded citizens that the body of strikers shall be allowed to depart as peacefully as they arrived," read the committee statement handed to the press. "We call upon the citizens of Regina to give the marchers a fitting send-off."[28]

Manion and Weir were well aware of this behind-the-scenes activity. A newspaper photograph showed them being greeted at the Regina station by

Mather of the CPR, who likely briefed them on the latest developments, including the Pilot Butte plan. Colonel Wood also secretly met with the pair mid-morning and suggested that the federal government could best control the situation if it assumed responsibility for the feeding and housing of the men. Whether the cabinet ministers actually believed, though, that the trekkers would carry through on their threat to leave that night is not known. But the possibility was there, and the trek leadership decided to turn the pressure up a notch by dispatching a five-man advance party to Broadview, the next railway divisional point east of Regina, to make preparations for the arrival of the men. Organizers in Winnipeg also lent their support, threatening Bennett's emissaries: "If BC marchers demands not complied with and force used to block trek Winnipeg will organize to continue march to Ottawa."[29]

Dr. Manion, the more experienced of the two politicians, probably expected this kind of posturing. But what stunned him was the attitude of the Saskatchewan government. As a courtesy to the province, the Railways minister invited the premier to meet with them late Monday morning in their suite at the stately Hotel Saskatchewan. Gardiner arrived at eleven, accompanied by Davis and Estey, and for the first part of the hour-long meeting was "quite friendly." But when Manion began to speak of the trek as "the beginning of a revolution ... one which would gradually lead to bloodshed" and appealed for "at least passive assistance," Gardiner became visibly upset. He angrily resented the takeover of the mounted police and the failure to be kept informed about federal actions. He also reminded Manion that over one thousand western farmers had descended on Ottawa in 1910 to protest national agricultural policy "and they didn't create a revolution." Why, wondered the premier, was this new march any different? What was most disturbing, though, was Gardiner's emphatic vow towards the end of the discussion to treat both trekkers and railway police as rioters if trouble erupted at the rail yards that night. "Attitude very ugly," Manion wired Bennett about the province's position later that afternoon, "and anything but helpful."[30]

The premier's performance served as the warm-up act for the headline event, the meeting with the trek delegation. Shortly after 2:00, Evans led his team into the hotel lobby, where they were directed by Manion to the Canadian Room in the basement. The minister also reported that about forty people from various organizations—including Mayor Rink and Attorney-General Davis—had been invited to attend the meeting, and asked if there was any objection. Evans welcomed an open forum, but agreed to participate only after being assured by Manion that he and his colleague had been empowered to deal with the trekkers' demands. Robert Weir took no part in these preliminary discussions. Nor did he say anything once negotiations got underway. He seemed uncomfortable with the circumstances that had brought him back to Regina and simply sat there and scribbled notes for the next two hours—more like an overpaid stenographer than a minister of the Crown. The two sides need not have bothered to bring their own recorders.[31]

Manion opened the meeting, introducing himself and Weir, and then called on the eight delegates to state their names for the record. Tony Martin went first, wondering if he should give his home address as the exhibition grounds, before reporting that he represented Division One. The others followed in quick succession, like a machine-gun round: "Mike McCauley, representing the Camp Workers' Union; J. Walsh, representing Division Two; R. Savage, representing Division Three; Peter Neilson, representing Division Four; S. O'Neill, representing Division Five; Arthur Evans, representing the Workers' Unity League, an organization to which the Relief Camp Workers was affiliated; J. Cosgrove, marshal of all the divisions."

Evans began his comments on a sour note, complaining that Ottawa had not bothered to inform the trekkers that it was sending two negotiators to Regina. He then outlined why the men had left the relief camps and how no one wanted to deal with their grievances. "We were made a political football," he declared. "That was the reason for this trip. At all times we have tried to open negotiations with the responsible authorities. That was denied us." He spent the remainder of his remarks explaining the trekkers' six demands, concluding with the hope that the delegation would finally get the chance to discuss them. When Manion asked if any of the other men wanted to speak, Tony Martin echoed Evans's frustration. "We are willing at any time—we have been in the past, and we are willing now—to negotiate these demands of ours," he added. "That was the basis of the trek to Ottawa—nothing else but that."[32]

Manion, speaking from a single page of brief points, responded that the government wanted "to be as reasonable as possible and ... at the same time ... avoid trouble." But he then proceeded to betray his lack of sincerity by claiming that the Bennett government could not have negotiated earlier because it did not know who was leading the men and what their demands were. He also maintained that the railways could no longer transport such a large group because they were worried about accidents. The delegation politely endured this claptrap, but when Manion began to talk about the world economic crisis, Evans was on his feet, blurting out that "political propaganda" was not appreciated. "The question," the trek leader pointedly warned the minister, "is whether you can discuss these proposals with us or whether we will carry on with our trek to Ottawa tonight at ten o'clock." Manion was annoyed by the interruption and countered that he had every right to make his statement and expected the men to keep quiet and listen. He then went on to describe how Canada was not alone in trying to find an answer to the unemployment problem and how the government wanted to give every young man, like each of them, the opportunity to earn a decent living through work. He made no real attempt to discuss their demands. Instead, he put forward two suggestions. First, he called on the leaders to look out for the interests of the younger boys on the trek and abandon any plans of leaving that night. "It would be a grave responsibility," Manion admonished, "to take a group like that and insist on putting them on trains, even to the extent of fighting with the police, possibly leading to bloodshed, which none of us want." As an alternative, he proposed that the trekkers send a committee—the same eight if they wanted—to Ottawa "to appear before the Government, the whole Government, and submit your case and receive the consideration of the whole Government."[33]

This offer dominated the rest of the discussion, with Manion pushing it as hard as he could without appearing overanxious. He said that the trekkers had a choice: they could either entrust their case to the two cabinet ministers, or better yet, send their own delegation to Ottawa at government expense. The rest of the men would remain behind in Regina to be fed and clothed by Ottawa on the understanding that they would not try to continue the trek or cause any trouble in the city. In an effort to win over the trekkers, Manion also pretended that it was a spontaneous idea—and a good one at that. "I am making ... a proposal which—quite frankly—has not been submitted to the Government at Ottawa," he pledged, "but I am so sincere about it that I feel the Government will uphold it." This statement was yet another fabrication on the minister's part, since Colonel Wood knew beforehand what was going to be proposed at the meeting.

But the problem for the trekkers was not Manion's lies, but the fact that they had been snookered. Evans had stated during his opening remarks that the men simply wanted their grievances discussed, and now Manion was offering them the chance to speak directly to the Bennett cabinet without the necessity of the trek. It was a brilliant move on the government's part, and Evans was left scrambling. He argued that the trekkers' demands were no secret. He insisted that the railways had always cooperated with the trek. And he maintained that all decisions had to be approved by the trek body. His biggest beef, though, was the kind of response a delegation might receive in Ottawa. "We believe that the mass of citizens of Canada aroused is the only weapon we can use to force authorities to act," he said, almost in desperation, "and if fifty went ... it would not 'fizz' on the authorities to the same extent." Manion downplayed this concern, suggesting that there was nothing to lose in going to Ottawa: "At the end of the week, if you were not satisfied with what you received from the Government, you would be back ... in just the same position; you would have your men ready to go to Ottawa." At this point Evans seemed to concede defeat and tried to get what he could from the minister. In particular, he wanted three meals per day for the men who stayed behind instead of the two twenty-cent meals the province was now providing. But Manion refused to enter into negotiations until he had an answer to his proposal. He would only agree to meet with Evans again later that night after the trekkers had discussed the matter.[34]

Manion immediately sent an assessment of the situation to his boss. Although "very well satisfied" with the meeting, he was still cautious about the outcome. "The position is quite delicate," he reported to Prime Minister Bennett, "not at all sure they will accept our proposition." He found the leaders to be "radicals of the most extreme type" and the public sympathetic to their cause. The trekkers, however, had no alternative but to accept the compromise that was being offered them. Red Walsh, one of the delegates, said it best: "They had us across a barrel. We couldn't turn it down.... If we refused them the newspapers would come out with banner headlines just slammin' hell out of us for refusing this when we had suggested it all along." So even though the question of going to Ottawa was debated, according to Ron Liversedge, at "the longest, most turbulent meeting ... we ever held," the decision was never in doubt. After a verbatim transcript of the afternoon's meeting was read aloud, the men agreed—albeit reluctantly—that the same eight who had met with Manion and Weir would make the trip to Ottawa. Some were worried, though, that the minister's proposal was simply a ruse to lure the leaders away to be arrested. Others also saw it as an attempt to force the break-up of the trek—something that Manion had alluded to in his remarks, when he hinted that transportation would be provided to any men who wanted to return home in the leaders' absence. The negotiating team shared these concerns and proposed several measures to preserve the integrity of the trek, as well as make the life of the men a little more comfortable. Little, if anything, could be done, however, to guarantee the delegation's safe return. They simply had to take Manion at his word.[35]

While the meeting was underway at the stadium, about two hundred Regina citizens gathered outside in preparation for the parade to the rail yards. It was still not known at this point whether the men would accept Manion's offer or go ahead with their plan to leave that night with a public escort. Nor did the trek leadership want to do anything to lessen the tension and uneasiness that had been building over the past day. Keeping Ottawa and the police guessing about their next move was one of the few instances where they still enjoyed some power.

Shortly after eight, trek marshal Jack Cosgrove informed Pete Mikkelson, who was supposed to head the parade, that their mass departure had been postponed, but that they still wanted to march through the downtown streets, despite the rain that was coming down. The citizens formed into a column, unfurled a large banner that read On To Ottawa, and began to walk east along Dewdney Avenue to Albert Street and then south to Victoria Avenue. The trekkers smartly followed in their divisions, loudly chanting "WE WANT WORK FOR WAGES," and singing songs. One of them was

"John Brown's Body," but in this version Bennett's body was "mouldering in his grave." As the parade worked its way downtown, several hundred people, including children, tagged along, while the streets were lined with anywhere from five to ten thousand onlookers.

Turning east on Victoria, the column passed the Hotel Saskatchewan, where Evans and the other seven representatives pushed their way through the crowd and slipped into the lobby to let Manion and Weir know whether they had a deal. At this point, the parade split in two. The marching citizens continued east, while Cosgrove pulled away and led the trekkers around the hotel in a circle several blocks wide. By the time Mikkelson and the others realized what had happened and rejoined the column, they found themselves at the rear. The Regina city police, meanwhile, had their hands full trying to deal with the traffic chaos.[36]

Inside the hotel, the trekker delegation waited a few minutes before being ushered into a conference room where they were warmly greeted by Manion, along with his sidekick Weir. The cabinet ministers wanted to know what the boys were singing. "Oh, just a half dozen songs," smiled Evans. He then said that he wanted to keep the discussion as brief as possible because he did not want to keep the men waiting. Evans reported that they were willing to go to Ottawa to present their case, but on certain conditions. He wanted three meals a day for those who stayed behind in Regina, as well as some new sleeping quarters to relieve the congestion at the stadium, especially since several hundred new recruits were expected from the Dundurn relief camp in the next day or so. He also insisted there be no attempt to interfere with or disrupt the trek. The younger men had no interest in going back home. Manion readily agreed to the terms, even joking at the end of the meeting that the delegates probably had enough money in their kitty to pay for their own meals on the trip.[37]

Evans and the others emerged from the hotel shortly after 10:00, just as the column was passing the entrance for a third time, this time snake dancing in a wave motion from one curb side to the other. As previously arranged, Cosgrove neatly marched the men into formation, filling an entire city block at Scarth Street just across from Victoria Park. Evans then mounted the bumper of a parked truck to disclose the results of the meeting with Manion.

"This is a tremendous victory for us," he shouted. "It is proof of the power of organization. But our success is largely due to the great amount of public support we have gained." At the end of his remarks, someone near the truck moved a resolution calling on the federal government to remove any extra mounted police from the city. "All in favour," called Evans, and the crowd yelled, "Aye." He then asked if anyone was opposed. "Bennett," someone quipped to the roar of laughter.[38]

Giddiness aside, the On-to-Ottawa Trek had enjoyed a remarkable few days in Regina. When they climbed down from their freight on Friday morning, the trekkers looked more like careworn refugees than a crusading army for Canada's single homeless unemployed. They also faced a formidable foe in the mounted police, who had been ordered to prevent the trek from proceeding beyond the Saskatchewan capital. But the enthusiastic support of Regina citizens, together with a number of well-conceived events, including the threat to leave, had turned the situation on its head over the weekend. Not only had they forced Ottawa to send two cabinet ministers to Regina, but a trek delegation would soon head east to negotiate directly with the Bennett cabinet. And it had all been achieved while being held prisoner by the Mounties. It remained to be seen, however, if their "tremendous victory" had a hollow ring. Despite the public sympathy for the trek and its mission, the men were no closer to Ottawa and Prime Minister Bennett still controlled the situation.

CHAPTER SEVEN

An Empty Gesture

By the third week of June, the On-to-Ottawa Trek seemed headed for a peaceful resolution. The "Regina truce,"[1] as one newspaper dubbed it, had effectively prevented a clash between the trekkers and the mounted police, while at the same time making it possible for a delegation to travel to Ottawa at federal expense to appear before the Bennett cabinet. There was even the suggestion the trek had fulfilled its mission by finally getting a hearing for its demands. But the Ottawa meeting quickly dissolved into a verbal slugfest that only aggravated the stalemate in Regina. The trekkers, incensed at their treatment at the hands of Prime Minister Bennett, were more determined than ever to resume their march, only this time with support from across the country. But getting out of the Saskatchewan capital was impossible as long as the city remained sealed off by the Royal Canadian Mounted Police. The federal government, at the same time, tried to bring the trekkers to their knees. Not only did Ottawa cut off relief to the men, it tried to force them into a new temporary camp outside Regina. One way or another, the trek was going to end in Regina—on federal terms.

❖ ❖ ❖

The trekkers' decision to accept the federal offer to send a delegation to Ottawa generated a huge national sigh of relief. A clash at the Regina rail yards on Monday night had seemed imminent—with citizens as innocent victims. The deal that had been brokered allowed both the trekkers and the mounted police to step back from the brink. It also raised for the first time hopes for a negotiated settlement. "The news from Regina is the best that has come out of the West," declared the *Montreal Star*, "A providential spirit of compromise and common sense has made its appearance." The *Ottawa Journal* was equally effusive about the agreement and what it meant to Canadian democracy: "There is nothing of lawlessness nor force ... [but] every evidence of a disposition by the Government to treat the strikers fairly, almost generously." Closer to the conflict, the *Regina Leader-Post* spoke of "a situation eased" and how Dr. Robert Manion, the minister of Railways, "warrants a word of commendation for his attitude in the negotiations." Even the Communist *Worker*, a declared enemy of Prime Minister Bennett and the Conservative government, embraced the agreement. "Victory is within our grasp," a front-page editorial thundered. "A signal victory has been won."[2]

Ironically, the pending departure of the trek delegation produced the first fault lines in the Citizens' Emergency Committee (CEC). At the regular morning meeting on Tuesday, 20 June, it was announced that the trekkers wanted a few speakers for the mass demonstration they were hosting at the stadium that night. Some committee members, though, believed they had fulfilled their purpose. "For the life of me," wondered Ralph Hesseltine of the Regina Trades and Labour Council, "I can't see why a send-off is needed for the eight men. It's just another form of propaganda." Pete Mikkelson, one of the driving forces behind the committee, countered that the rally was necessary to ensure that the public fully appreciated the trek and its mission. "The send-off is their business," he observed, "and they have invited citizens to participate." Another committee member then complained about the last-minute change in the proposed parade to the rail yards the night before and the failure to keep everyone informed of developments. This criticism prompted Hesseltine to note that there was no trek representative at the meeting. "Surely," someone chimed in, "they could send one man down here when they have 2,000." These divisions nearly undermined the coalition that had been so effective over the past few days, but in the end it was resolved to keep the committee "intact until the return of the eight delegates from Ottawa."[3]

The trek delegation had tickets for the nightly Canadian Pacific Railway eastbound passenger train, the Number Two, at 8:20. That left little time for the early evening rally at the stadium. Slim Evans, wearing new coveralls donated to him for the trip to Ottawa, spoke first. "The campers, after two months, have forced Bennett to act," he cried to the delight of the crowd. He then explained that any deal reached in Ottawa would have to be brought back to the men in Regina for approval and that the trek would continue if they were not satisfied—only this time with five to ten thousand men. "The government fears this army," he gloated. "It fears the march of the working class." Jack King, national secretary of the Co-operative Commonwealth Youth Movement and chair of publicity for the citizens' committee, followed with a simple thank-you. "You have aroused the citizens of Regina," he observed. "That is a remarkable achievement." Alderman Clarence Fines, a future provincial finance minister, shared these sentiments, confidently telling the men, "The government will accede to your demands."[4]

The most sentimental speech, more like a testimonial, came from the lips of sixty-six-year-old Reverend Samuel B. East of Regina's Rosemont and Wascana United churches. The British-born East had been present in Winnipeg in 1919 during the general strike and regarded the trek as yet another stage in the continuing struggle of the oppressed. But his fervour often got away on him. He reportedly wrote Soviet dictator Joseph Stalin that the cross superimposed over the hammer and sickle would bring about "a quicker solution of his problems, than any other method." And when he was elected to city council as a labour candidate in 1936, he announced from the balcony of Regina's city hall, "The reign of money is over and the reign of manhood has started." East told the trekkers that he had never been prouder than to be on the platform that night. "You're fighting my battle," he confessed, "my family's battle, the battle of the proletariat!" He then apologized for the negative comments that his colleague Reverend Mutch had been making about the trek and its leaders. As part of this smear campaign, East related how he had been told over the telephone that Evans had a criminal past. "How terrible," one trekker remarked to the laughter of the crowd.[5]

At the end of the speeches, trekker Gerry Winters innocently asked—as if he did not know the answer—"Do you want a parade?" Others began to chant, "Parade, parade," and soon the men were on the march to the railway station, singing "Hold the Fort." At the depot, the column neatly lined up in divisions, while hundreds of citizens, including many from the rally, gathered in the station or milled around outside. Regina native Matt Shaw, standing atop a truck cab, addressed the gathering. "Our delegation is off to meet the starvation government," he roared. "Today is a signal victory, the biggest since the blustering R. B. went into power." As the trekkers gave three cheers, the eight delegates, wearing white armbands with the words On to Ottawa in blue, strode through an opening in the crowd, into the station, and out onto the platform. They paused briefly for a photograph before boarding the waiting train and heading immediately for the comfort of the smoking compartment. It had probably been some time since many of them had last "rode the cushions," and they intended to enjoy themselves. Their safety was assured—there were no fewer than twenty CPR policemen along for the ride.[6]

The trek delegation was expected to be away six days. The men, in the meantime, were to be fed three times a day at city restaurants at federal expense. Cyril Burgess, a senior official with the Department of Finance based in Regina, was given the task of distributing the meal tickets. He was no friend of the trekkers. The day the men arrived in Regina, he had wired Ottawa that the trek was a Communist movement led by known criminals. He also complained that the attitude of the Gardiner government had prevented the police from dealing forcefully with the situation. Burgess handled his new job as if he was paying for the meals out of his own pocket and grudgingly issued the first batch of tickets for 1,700 men on Tuesday. This figure jumped the next day with the arrival of 204 men from the Dundurn relief camp, just south of Saskatoon. Some of the trekkers, used to eating only two meals a day, traded their third ticket for tobacco.[7]

Manion had also promised to deal with the crowded sleeping conditions. Almost half of the men were consequently relocated to a space under the grandstand, while the new Dundurn recruits were assigned to the Saskatchewan Government Building, also on the exhibition grounds. A request for seven hundred beds, however, was flatly turned down by Burgess. He would provide only new bales of straw to be spread over the old straw. Civic officials were in a more generous mood and supplied two thousand bars of soap, five wash tubs, and five wringers on Thursday. It was the first big wash day for the men since 9 June in Calgary. Dr. Hugh MacLean, a Co-operative Commonwealth Federation (CCF) candidate in the upcoming federal election, also held a clinic for the men and reportedly diagnosed sixty cases of venereal disease—5 percent of the trek population.[8]

Under the terms of the agreement, Evans had promised that the men who stayed behind in Regina would not cause any trouble in the delegation's absence. But keeping in line two thousand men who had little to do but wait proved difficult at best. "With the coming into our ranks of new elements we have been taxed to the extreme," Shaw wrote a fellow organizer in Vancouver. "Many of our leading Comrades are going almost day and night ironing out the newcomers and bringing them into line with the originals." The strike committee tried to keep a firm hand on the situation by establishing a 1:00 A.M. curfew and threatening to take away the membership card of anyone who missed picket duty or seriously misbehaved. It also worked with the citizens' committee to hold a series of special events, including a sports day and picnic at the exhibition grounds on the weekend.[9]

Local businesses and groups pitched in as well. The Capitol Theatre provided a batch of complimentary tickets to the movies (*Star of Midnight* starring William Powell and Ginger Rogers, and *The Bride of Frankenstein*), while baseball organizers treated the men to exhibition games between touring Japanese and American teams. The trekkers also did their best to keep busy while the delegation was away. One tried his hand at free-style poetry. "Soup for breakfast, Soup for dinner; Soup for supper," he scrawled on one of the fence boards at the stadium. "I swear when I swallow a chunk of bread I'll hear it splash." Another played a game for one of the local soccer teams and scored the tying goal in the dying seconds. Others spent hours poring over the newspaper and reading what was happening beyond Regina: two of the Dionne quints had stood for the first time; the Golden Gate Bridge in San Francisco was nearing completion; and Italy and the League of Nations were squabbling over Ethiopia.[10]

No amount of entertainment or other activity, though, could prevent some of the men going from door-to-door, begging for clothing and food in residential areas. There was also a rash of home burglaries the same week the delegation was away. It would be easy to blame the trekkers—as the mounted police did at the time—but internal Regina city police documents indicate that at least one petty criminal had joined the trek in Calgary in order to commit break-ins along the route. City police records also reveal that the Mounties handed Chief Bruton confidential information about Evans's criminal past and encouraged him to share it with the *Regina Daily Star* as part of a larger campaign to smear the trek and its leaders. But the police chief had his hands full fielding calls from anxious parents who reported that their sons were missing and suspected them of being with the trekkers.[11]

RCMP assistant commissioner Wood was one of the few people who seemed disappointed with the compromise Manion had reached with the trekkers. He had dearly wanted to put into action his plan of luring the men east to Pilot Butte and overpowering them, and continued to promote the scheme as the best way of preventing a clash in Regina. Until then, he used his extra troops along roads and rail lines to prevent other men from joining the trek. Ironically, one of these blockades snared a group of men in Moose Jaw that had deserted the trek and was heading westward. Another trekker who wanted out was not so lucky. Alex La Rocque from Estevan was struck and killed by a locomotive while crossing the tracks in the Regina rail yards. The engineer reported that he seemed to walk deliberately into the path of the train. The mounted police also continued to gather information inside trek ranks, but with a new agent. Constable Henry Cooper, who had successfully infiltrated the trek at Moose Jaw, had been identified by several citizens during the Monday night downtown parade. His exposure was not surprising, since he normally worked out of the Regina town station. In fact, he was lucky to have remained under cover for as long as he did. Cooper's replacement was twenty-four-year-old Constable Don Taylor of Winnipeg, who quietly joined Division Five under the pseudonym "A. Wing" the same day the Dundurn boys reached Regina. His usefulness was questionable. Although Taylor spent the next ten days among the trekkers, he was unable to recall the name of a single trekker several months later.[12]

The mounted police attitude towards the trek hardened—if that was possible—on 19 June, only one day after the trek delegation had left for Ottawa. Just the day before, the two-week-old longshoremen's strike in Vancouver had come to a head when the RCMP brutally attacked a march by the strikers to shut down all work on the waterfront. The police action provoked one of the worst riots in the history of the city. But the next day, Mayor Gerry McGeer sent a congratulatory telegram to Commissioner MacBrien, applauding the "splendid work" of the force and warning him "not to compromise with the present party in Regina." How the police responded to the Vancouver troubles signalled the way the Regina situation might also be handled, especially since the Mounties regarded both strikes as the handiwork of the Communists.[13]

The crushing of the strike also meant that those mounted policemen who had been rushed to the West Coast in early June were now available for duty in Regina. But it would be several days before these reinforcements could get to the Saskatchewan capital. The dispatch of the trekker delegation to Ottawa was therefore a blessing, in that it gave the police some much-needed time to get ready to deal with the trek once and for all. Commissioner MacBrien started this process, what he described as "firm action," on 19 June. Fully expecting the Ottawa negotiations to fail—"owing to the impossible demands"—he told Colonel Wood to prepare to move against the trek "to see that the laws of Canada are enforced."[14]

To facilitate this task, MacBrien promised at least seventy-five additional men from Vancouver and possibly another one hundred from eastern Canada. He also reported that the force was to be enlarged by one hundred new recruits, "most of whom will be sent into Regina and put into tents, if necessary." He expected them to be ready for duty after only two weeks' training. MacBrien was prepared to use whatever force was necessary to prevent the trekkers from reaching Winnipeg, where their numbers were expected to more than double. "You may rest assured," he solemnly concluded his instructions to Wood, "that all possible support, moral and physical, will be given to you to enable you to carry out this difficult task." These were not simply words of encouragement. The commissioner made his plans with the full knowledge and support of the minister of Justice.[15]

It is not known whether the trek delegation knew about the crushing of the Vancouver strike before they reached Ottawa. It probably would have made little difference. Stepping off their train at 4:40 A.M. on Friday, 21 June, the eight held an impromptu news conference on the station platform, while the lone Mountie who had been sent to meet them had to wait. "We are not going to be browbeaten by the government," Evans grimly told a handful of waiting reporters in the pre-dawn darkness. "If our demands are not met, that is Mr. Bennett's business—we will come anyway." The other delegates talked about conditions in the camps and the need for answers. "This is not just a matter of wheat cakes and grub," Evans added. "Thousands of young men are ... unable to lead a decent normal life. There is no chance for them to get married, to have their own homes or act like human beings."[16]

The RCMP officer then took the men to a small hotel, where, according to Red Walsh, they were the only guests. When asked for their addresses at the registration desk, they answered "British Columbia slave camps." Some of their first visitors were representatives of unemployed groups in Ontario and Quebec, who asked to be included as part of the delegation. But Evans turned down the request. He wanted to keep the meeting with the government focused on the trek and its six demands.[17]

The delegation expected to see Prime Minister Bennett that same day, but the meeting could not be scheduled until Saturday morning, 22 June, because of a busy legislative agenda. It was not a good week to call on the prime minister. On Wednesday, just two days earlier, Bennett had had his much-anticipated showdown with his leadership rival Harry Stevens in the House of Commons and skilfully skewered the former cabinet minister—"skinned the skunk" in his words—for his criticism of the government. Later that night, at a caucus banquet in his honour, he ended any speculation about his political future by announcing that he would be leading the Conservatives into the next election; only ill health would force him to step aside.[18]

This assertion of his control over the party would clearly have affected Bennett's mood. It was not a time for concession, let alone compromise. Instead, he was looking for an issue to hang the coming campaign on. The message he was getting from various sources that week seemed to be that law and order was just the issue he was looking for. On Thursday in the Commons, Justice Minister Hugh Guthrie read a telegram from Mayor McGeer into the record, hailing the mounted police for upholding "constitutional authority" in Vancouver.[19] There was also public questioning of the legitimacy of the trekkers' demands. The *Toronto Mail and Empire* reported the relief camp strikers' "so-called grievances have been thoroughly investigated and ... discovered to have little or no foundation." Frank Turnbull, the Conservative member of Parliament for Regina, was equally dismissive of the trek and privately urged Bennett, the day of his humbling of Stevens, to stand up to the delegation: "These men have no proper right and no proper occasion for the action they have taken." He also blamed the Gardiner government for not stopping the trek at the Alberta border. Then there was the matter of Evans's criminal past. No less than three separate statements about Arthur Evans's convictions were forwarded by the mounted police to the prime minister's office in the days before the delegation reached Ottawa.[20]

Robert Manion, who had negotiated the deal with the trekkers, was quite concerned about how Bennett would behave at the Saturday meeting. According to the Railways minister's autobiography, published in 1939, the Conservative leader was a "complex and contradictory character ... either coldly logical or highly emotional.... He seems determined too often to show himself at his worst." It was this "temperamental and explosive" side that Manion tried to reign in, and he sat down upon his return from Regina on Thursday and prepared a two-page letter to Bennett about how to handle the trek deputation. He argued it was crucial, especially for public consumption, for the prime minister to appear reasonable and suggested that most of the demands, with "some modifications," could be "accepted in a general way."

But if Manion expected Bennett to adopt a conciliatory approach in dealing with the delegation, he was sadly mistaken. It not only went against the prime minister's instincts—not to mention his political style—but even contradicted Manion's own reading of the situation in the West. In the same letter to Bennett, he described things as "exceedingly critical," not only in Regina but in Winnipeg as well, and predicted that if the trek was stopped, another would "immediately arise" in the Manitoba capital. He also claimed that the Communists were behind the trek, trying to use the unemployed to launch a revolution. "Strong measures will have to be taken to curb this movement," he cautioned. "Somehow the leaders should be got at." Nor did Manion expect the interview to go well. He indicated that the delegation did not want a "satisfactory agreement" and would likely try to scuttle the meeting. With comments like these, one wonders why Bennett simply did not find an excuse to arrest the eight men when they arrived in Ottawa.[21]

The late Saturday morning meeting between the federal cabinet and the trek representatives was convened in the prime minister's office in the East Block of the Parliament Buildings. Eleven of Bennett's ministers were at his side, including "a little shriveled-up guy" whose identity and presence puzzled the delegates. It was the elderly Sir George Perley, who had served as acting prime minister during the relief camp strike in Vancouver. Manion and Weir, just back from Regina, were also there. The one glaring absentee was the minister of Labour, Immigration and Colonization, and Mines, Wesley Gordon, who was opposed to the idea of the interview and refused to participate. Gordon, a lawyer from northern Ontario, had a reputation as a populist before entering politics. But at the cabinet table, the rookie MP argued for individual responsibility, while deportation numbers soared. Gordon believed that the trekkers should never have been allowed to leave Vancouver and even pooh-poohed the idea of sending cabinet ministers to Regina to meet with them. Force, in his opinion, was the only way of dealing with the relief camp strikers.[22]

Bennett, two weeks shy of his sixty-fifth birthday, sat in the middle on one side of the conference table. Wearing a swallowtail waistcoat and a winged collar, with a diamond stick pin in his tie, he exuded wealth and power—the two things that the men sitting on the opposite side of the table would likely never know. Indeed, the separation of the two groups was both real and symbolic. The only other person in the room, at one end of the table, was H. Oliver, a House of Commons recorder who prepared a verbatim transcript of the interview. There were no assistants, no police, no reporters—just the Canadian cabinet face-to-face with the official delegates of nearly two thousand homeless, unemployed men stranded in Regina. There was Jack Cosgrove, whom the men would have followed into hell and back again; Pete Neilson, a Danish immigrant who at thirty-eight was one of the oldest members of the trek; Robert "Doc" Savage, who proudly led the division populated by mostly blacklisted men; Stewart "Paddy" O'Neill, a fiery Newfoundlander who would be killed in battle two years later during the

Spanish Civil War; Mike McCauley, a natural organizer and one of the valued advance men for the trek; James "Red" Walsh, who provided one of the few first-hand accounts of the meeting; Tony Martin, who had escaped the poverty of London for the poverty of Canada; and Arthur "Slim" Evans, their revered leader. It was the first meeting between Evans and Bennett, and they glared across the table. They were like sporting legends playing against one another for the first time.

The prime minister controlled the meeting from the beginning. He started by asking the delegates to state their names, slowly moving from one man to the next as if he was back in his New Brunswick schoolroom taking attendance. He made no offer to introduce his cabinet colleagues, but simply inquired who would be speaking for the Regina delegation. At Bennett's invitation, Evans rose from his seat and explained at length—even though the meeting was supposed to last only half an hour—why the men had left the camps and what they were seeking. Bennett interrupted several times at first, mostly for clarification, but then remained uncharacteristically quiet as Evans outlined the six demands and the reasons for them. "We are empowered to accept any proposals you may wish to offer ... and we will take them back to the workers in Regina," he asserted. "If satisfactory, then some arrangements should be made for the safe return of these workers to the places where they came from. In the event that they are not satisfactory there will be a continuation of the trek to Ottawa." He concluded by referring to recent press reports that the RCMP were sending sixty additional men to Winnipeg and complaining that such action violated the Regina agreement. Manion spoke up at this point and claimed that the government had kept its word by remaining silent over the past week about the trek. He was the only one of the cabinet ministers to say something. The rest knew better. Bennett was in charge.[23]

When Evans finished his remarks, he suggested that other members of the delegation might have something to say. But before anyone else could speak, the prime minister began asking each of the men their age and place of birth. Only Evans was born in Canada, and even then, Bennett questioned that. All of the men, except Jack Cosgrove, claimed to be single, but that was inaccurate, since Evans was married with a daughter. Cosgrove, who had been busy keeping notes, then spoke for a few minutes about camp accidents before Tony Martin boldly announced, "We are ready to talk business on the six demands." Bennett began his remarks by taking a veiled swipe at Evans and the other men's attachment to the country. "With the exception of one of you, who has a record we will not discuss," he observed sanctimoniously, "you were born outside Canada." He then argued that the Conservative government had taken care of people during the Depression and that the men should be thankful for the shelter, clothing, and food provided by the Department of National Defence (DND) camps. Any unrest, according to Bennett, was the work of Communist agitators and their propaganda, and the men in the camps, including some in the room, were victims of that propaganda. At this point, the prime minister, who had managed to keep his famous temper in check, set aside any niceties and attacked the men's motives. "Now you ask for work.... You have not shown much anxiety to get work, not much anxiety to get work," he repeated. "It is the one thing you do not want. What you want is this adventure in the hope that the organization which you are promoting in Canada may be able to overawe the Government and break down the forces that represent law and order." He also angrily declared the trek would be stopped. "The police have moved west; they have moved east; they will move in increasing numbers wherever it is necessary to maintain law," he loudly asserted. "Take that down. Tell Mr. Cosgrove to take it down, Mr. Evans. Take that down."[24]

The prime minister's harangue drew Paddy O'Neill and Red Walsh into the fray. But it was Evans who ended up exchanging verbal blows. "You referred to us as not wanting work," the trek leader interrupted. "Give us work and we will see whether we will work.... Anybody who professes to be premier and uses such despicable tactics is not fit to be premier of a Hottentot village." Bennett calmly replied, "I come from Alberta. I remember when you embezzled the funds of your union and were sent to the penitentiary." "You are a liar," shot back Evans, "I was arrested for fraudulently converting those funds to feed the starving and ... if you say I embezzled ... I will have the pleasure of telling the workers throughout Canada I was forced to tell the premier of Canada he was a liar.... You are not intimidating me a damned bit." The two leaders continued to bicker over Evans's prison record, prompting

Cosgrove to intervene: "I take exception to any personal attack on this delegation and will not—" "Sit down, Mr. Cosgrove," Bennett ordered. "I will not," he declared. "Then you will be removed," Bennett warned. "Then the entire delegation will be removed," countered Evans. "Sit down, Mr. Cosgrove," Bennett demanded again. "I will when I have said this," the trek marshal held his ground: "I fought in the war as a boy fifteen years old. I have the interests of this country as much at heart as you have." "That is good enough," the prime minister lamely replied.[25]

The remainder of the meeting was devoted to the six demands. Bennett dismissed them all, insisting that the relief camps were fulfilling their purpose and would be kept in operation. "No young men have been better treated in better circumstances than these camps provide," he told the delegates. "Everyone knows that." This twaddle had Paddy O'Neill on his feet again, arguing with the prime minister, but Evans stopped him and suggested that there was no point interrupting anymore. O'Neill tried to hold his tongue, but finally lamented in frustration: "You could have told us all this by wire." Bennett sparred a little longer with the delegates before tiring of the game. "That is all that can be said," he moved to end the interview. "I want to warn you once more, if you persist in violating the laws of Canada you must accept full responsibility for your conduct." "And you also," Evans retorted. "I am prepared for that," Bennett acknowledged. "So are we," Evans came back.

The prime minister then asked the delegates to inform the trekkers that they would be able to return to their camps and that there would be work for them as the opportunity arose. But he cautioned them that any illegal riding of the trains would not be tolerated. Not to be outdone, Evans issued his own summary remarks. "We are confronted today with a greater responsibility than when we first came here," he observed. "Our responsibility is we must take this back to the workers and see that the hunger programme of Bennett is stopped." The prime minister then wished the eight men a good morning, ironically remarking, "We have been glad to listen to you."[26]

In retrospect, it is easy to suggest that Prime Minister Bennett should have made some kind of gesture, offered a few token concessions the delegates could have taken back to Regina to defuse the situation. After all, Robert Manion believed that five of the six demands could have been accepted with some negotiation, as indicated by his briefing notes, neatly penned on Privy Council letterhead in advance of the meeting. But before the Conservative government could reach some kind of agreement with the trek delegates, it first had to recognize them as the legitimate representatives of Canada's relief camp workers—something it could not do. Had not the minister of Justice stood in his seat in the House of Commons on 13 June, the day before the trek reached the Saskatchewan capital, and declared the march a Communist movement and a threat to law and order? And had not the prime minister vowed to crush this kind of subversive activity with his famous iron heel of ruthlessness? Recognition, let alone negotiation, was therefore impossible, especially with a general election only months away. It would have been a public admission that the government's heralded DND camps had been a miserable failure.

The other problem preventing meaningful dialogue that morning was that the two sides, as represented by Bennett and Evans, were worlds apart. Their differences made it impossible for them to talk to one another, to hear and understand one another. Ottawa was also nervous about the nature and extent of the challenge it faced. Was the trek headed to Ottawa to topple the government? Was it just the beginning of similar kinds of protests in other parts of Canada? Instead of trying to find a solution, then, the government deliberately chose to discredit the trek and its demands by attacking its leader. This strategy was age-old. In 1885, for example, the federal government had blamed the North-West Rebellion on Métis leader Louis Riel in order to ignore the grievances of his people. Now, fifty years later, Bennett was doing the same thing by highlighting Evans's criminal past and his slavish devotion to communism.[27]

The two sides came away with widely differing versions of the meeting. Evans claimed that an "arrogant, domineering, and cynical" Bennett had "barked" during their encounter. Red Walsh's published recollection was much the same. It reads like the delegates were going into a lion's den. "I knew we weren't goin' to get anything from the federal government," he confessed. Grote Stirling, the minister of National Defence, telephoned General Andy McNaughton that same evening to report on the meeting. McNaughton's cryptic, handwritten notes of the conversation offer one of the few assessments from the government side: "Evans & Delegation … name, age, res, orig … only 1 Cdn born … clash with Evans … Cosgrove put case well … McCauley bad actor … not violent except Evans … kept threatening take law into own hands." Perhaps the most accurate account was provided by a two-line memorandum that the CPR flashed to its offices across the country: "Prime Minister told Regina Committee nothing doing. Go back to your camps."[28]

The country's newspapers zeroed in on the fractious exchange between the two leaders, reproducing Evans's liar remark in bold headlines. But despite Bennett's unpopularity, there were limits to how far the trekkers could go, even in Regina. "If marchers should attempt to defy constituted authority," a *Leader-Post* editorial encouraged its readers, "Regina citizens must then take up their stand on the side of law, order, and the authorities who hold office." Many Canadians endorsed the prime minister's position, if the letters to his office in the aftermath of the meeting are any indication. "Better a strong hand now than when too late," wrote an Edmonton couple. The editor of the *Maple Creek News* agreed: "People capable of taking the long view know you are right.… The one thing those birds don't want is work.… Weaken before Evans and his crowd and we would soon have anarchy." Stockton General Merchants of Carlyle, Saskatchewan, offered congratulations and the "assurance that law and order will be maintained regardless of the attitude of the Sask. Govt." A letter from a Vancouver citizen commended Bennett's pluck: "I am glad to know that the rebels from the relief camps have now met someone who has the courage to tell them the plain truth." Even people who had never voted Conservative took comfort in how the prime minister had handled the delegation. "Never having supported you previously," one woman promised, "I will support your policy of firmness at the polls this time." Bennett must have been very pleased with himself.[29]

The trek delegation, on the other hand, was angry, if not bitter, about the meeting's outcome. Its worst fears had been realized, and it was determined to come calling again, only this time with twenty, maybe thirty, thousand men. At a Sunday night rally at the Rialto Theatre on Bank Street, just hours before the men left Ottawa, Evans declared to the delight of a crowd of about a thousand, "I am a member of the Communist Party and proud of it." He then announced with an air of defiance that the trek would resume as soon as the delegates returned to Regina. Cosgrove seconded the sentiment, noting that it might take several weeks to reach the capital, but they would be back—in force.[30]

This message dominated the delegates' return trip to Regina. At every major stop along the way, Evans would hold a meeting with local organizers on the station platform and then speak to the local press about the struggle in the days ahead. Nothing was held back. At one point, he described Bennett as "looking like a great big overfed toad," while in Sudbury, he evidently stated that the streets of Regina would run red with blood if the police clashed with the trekkers. Evans later denied the report, stating that what he actually meant was that Bennett was prepared to see the streets run red with blood. Whatever the truth, the RCMP actively considered arresting the trek leader before he returned to Regina.[31]

There was good reason to try to silence him. By the time the delegation reached Winnipeg on Tuesday, 25 June, Evans was predicting that fifty thousand men would march on Ottawa. The Communist Party of Canada actively promoted this crusade to unite behind the trekkers. An editorial in *The Worker* lambasted the prime minister's "monstrous" treatment of the delegation as an attack on the workers and youth of Canada. "Rally in the struggle to retain the last vestiges of democratic rights. Rally to the defense of the relief camp strikers," it urged. "The united action of the common people is imperative … to defeat this ugly menace." The same issue featured a cartoon of a fascist Bennett, complete with swastika and the words, "I HAVE SPOKEN."[32]

The mood in Regina, meanwhile, was anything but defiant. On Thursday, 20 June, the night before the delegates reached Ottawa, the trekkers, in cooperation with the CEC, had held a march from Market Square to the stadium, followed by a rally in support of the negotiations. All seemed hopeful. But early Saturday afternoon, when the first reports of the meeting reached the Saskatchewan capital, trek spokesmen refused to comment. By Sunday, Evans had confirmed the disappointing news, as well as indicated that preparations were already underway to turn the trek into a dominion-wide movement. This information was relayed to the men by means of a special strikers' bulletin. Again, though, the strike committee issued no official statement. The silence continued over into Monday, when a small delegation led by George Black, acting trek leader in Evans's absence, called on Premier Gardiner and Attorney-General Davis in the afternoon to determine if and how the Saskatchewan government could help the men out of their predicament. Black wanted to know who controlled the RCMP and what could be done by the province to spring them free. "We have to get to Ottawa," he pleaded. "I don't think we have any powers," Gardiner candidly confessed. Black responded that the men did not want to cause any trouble—that any talk of violence was coming from the other side. "We do not intend the battle to be anywhere," he pledged. The premier refused to say much more, except to ask the men to see him again "before you decide on anything definite."[33]

That night, the trekkers held a meeting to discuss the skirmish with Bennett. It was a relatively tame event, especially in comparison to past rallies. So too was the message: the men were to behave themselves and wait for the return of the Ottawa delegation. Matt Shaw of the publicity committee tried to put up a brave front. "Imagine the insulting attitude of that blatant Hitler," he wrote one of his buddies in Vancouver in the heat of the moment. "Rest assured that we will see to it that the vacillating and blustering forces of Bennett & Co. get away with nothing of the kind attempted by the Ottawa maneuver." But upon reflection, the cruel reality was that the promise of a hearing for their grievances was "an empty gesture." Nor was the trek any closer to Ottawa—and the chances of getting there grew more remote with each passing day. Shaw's sense of frustration came through a few months later when he publicly complained about the position the men had found themselves in: "It was ridiculous after all the trials we had gone through."[34]

The prime minister, still flushed from his spanking of the trek delegates, made an official statement about the Regina situation in the House of Commons on Monday, 24 June. He reported, with a solemn certainty, that the delegation's demands were unrealistic, that their leader was a crook *and* a Communist, and that the trek was really an "organized effort" to overthrow "constituted authority." He also announced that the Department of Labour would be establishing a temporary camp north of Regina to serve as a kind of demobilization centre for the trek. The men would be fed and sheltered there until they could be sent home or to their relief camp. It seemed as if the Conservative government was confident of winning the struggle with the trekkers and could now dictate terms with impunity.[35]

But deciding exactly how to proceed after the meeting had not been so easy. Upon learning on Saturday afternoon how Bennett had rebuffed the delegation, a somewhat panicky Colonel Wood had wired RCMP headquarters with a new plan for dealing with the trekkers: that they be immediately handed over to the DND in order "to secure control and liquidate the movement." The assistant commissioner was worried that the men might try to leave Regina—as early as that night—before the return of the delegates. Commissioner MacBrien called General McNaughton at home Saturday night about the proposal and met with stiff resistance. McNaughton, in no mood to help his rival, dismissed the scheme as "impracticable," if not "inadvisable." There were no troops stationed in Regina, only a small administrative staff, and any attempt to round up the men under the threat of force would prove "provocative." Instead, the chief of the general staff suggested it would be better to bring the trek to the troops, namely to the Shilo military base in western Manitoba along the CPR main line. But MacBrien did not want to see the men leave Regina and decided to seek the advice of the minister of Justice about his next move. McNaughton, sensing an opening, tried to take matters into his own hands later that night and instructed Brigadier H. E. Boak, the Regina-based commander of Military District 12, to let it be known that all men, except for known agitators, would be taken back into the camps. A similar offer attracted few takers during the first days of the Vancouver strike. But McNaughton now believed that the solidarity of the trek was beginning to crumble and that he could peacefully defuse the situation—and at the same time make MacBrien look bad—by extending a helping hand to the men.[36]

The question of what to do in Regina was sorted out by Monday morning, the day of the prime minister's statement in the House. General MacBrien had found a willing ally in the minister of Labour, who readily agreed to establish a temporary camp for the trekkers under the auspices of his department. The actual administration of the camp, however, would fall to the local military district, despite McNaughton's objections. Superintendent Hill of the local RCMP, together with a reconnaissance party from Military District 12, spent the day searching for a suitable site and eventually chose a pasture belonging to farmer Barclay Muir, about twenty miles north of Regina, between Craven on the Canadian Pacific line and Lumsden on the Canadian National. Men from the Dundurn relief camp were to start early the next day setting up army bell tents, erecting a barbed wire enclosure, and laying a water pipe to the nearby Qu'Appelle River. Federal officials, including the police, were convinced that many of the trekkers were basically good young men who had been misled by the leaders and did not fully appreciate the seductive dangers of communism. "A large percentage of boys ... joined this movement as they would have a circus," Wood had advised MacBrien a week earlier, "not realizing what it was all about or what was back of it." But even though it was now clear that the trek had no future, the men needed a helpful nudge to disband. The Bennett government consequently instructed Cyril Burgess late Monday afternoon to stop distributing meal tickets to the trekkers as of Wednesday morning, 26 June. If the men wanted to continue to eat at federal expense—in other words, if they wanted lunch that day—they first had to register for admission to the new temporary camp near Lumsden. Here, after a few days, they would either be sent home or back to their camp.[37]

The trek delegation was scheduled to arrive in Regina Wednesday morning, around the same time that federal meals at local restaurants would come to an end. It effectively meant that the men would have no time to consider the report of the delegates before they had to sign up for the new camp. These heavy-handed tactics did not sit well with the trekkers. They had already concluded that the trek had been stopped in Regina, and not someplace earlier, because it was the home of the RCMP barracks. They also questioned why the Bennett government had invited the delegation to Ottawa if it had no intention of considering their demands; it appeared that the police had gained an extra ten days to get ready to deal with them. The establishment of the temporary camp now raised a new fear. If the government genuinely wanted the trek to disband, then why did it matter where and how this process occurred? Why could it not be handled at the exhibition grounds—unless, of course, the Lumsden camp had another purpose? That seemed to be the case when

Burgess, in consultation with Colonel Wood, issued a public notice Tuesday afternoon, declaring the trekkers to be little more than Communist dupes and calling on them to provide "certain information" before being admitted to the special camp and "their final disposition." Reading between the lines, it seemed as if Ottawa planned to use the registration process to identify agitators and troublemakers—all the more so, since the mounted police were responsible for security at the new holding facility.[38]

On Tuesday afternoon, 25 June, Burgess set up the new office for the Lumsden camp inside the World's Grain Show Building on the exhibition grounds. Registration would officially commence at eight the following morning, while a handful of city policemen, backed by a troop of Mounties, patrolled the building and grounds. These precautions may have seemed excessive, but for the first time in the ten days since the trekkers had arrived in Regina, the RCMP were ready for—and expected—the worst. In the aftermath of Bennett's mauling of the delegation, there had been two days of emotional rallies in Winnipeg, where an estimated one thousand men were preparing to launch their own march to Ottawa. The meetings were disturbing in their own right, but even more so because of what was said at them. Tim Buck, the leader of the Communist Party of Canada, pledged his "wholehearted approval" of the idea of turning the trek into a national campaign, while a Labour member of the Manitoba legislature gloomily predicted, "We are sitting on the edge of a volcano." Such talk suggested that the long overdue showdown between the Canadian state and the Communists might finally be at hand. And the event that would likely precipitate the clash would be the trek trying to leave Regina, immediately after the return of the delegates, to unite with the Winnipeg forces.[39]

On Monday, then, in the same telegram detailing the creation of the temporary camp, an anxious MacBrien instructed Wood to stop the trekkers from continuing eastward by *any* means—car, truck, bus, even foot. He also cautioned him to watch for his old nemesis Buck, who was on a western speaking tour and might try to slip into Regina to take advantage of the trek. "If situation develops seriously," he wired, "permanent force will be called out to support police and state of emergency declared by the government." Wood, who had regained his composure from the weekend, assured

MacBrien that he had sufficient force to handle any situation, especially since the railway police could be sworn in as special constables. He also expressed profound disappointment with the attitude of the Saskatchewan government and readily acknowledged that Ottawa had to be poised to deal with the men and the threat they posed to law and order. Yet behind this brave talk, Wood too had reason to be nervous. The trekkers were reportedly toying with the idea of seizing a train, probably on Wednesday, when the Ottawa delegation returned. There were also rumours that two truckloads of Alberta organizers had arrived in Regina, while Buck was apparently on his way, if not already there.[40]

MacBrien felt vindicated by this news—the trek was showing its true face—and ordered the "largest mobilization" of F Division. Wood immediately called in all men on leave or off duty, and by including office staff from the depot was able to muster a force of about 340. On Tuesday afternoon he sent a squadron to the armouries nearby the exhibition grounds—where they remained hidden, in riot gear, to handle any trouble at the new registration office for the Lumsden camp. He also conferred with city and railway police to coordinate their efforts in dealing with any disturbance, especially at the rail yards. The three forces then held their breath and waited, but not much happened. The trekkers refused to pick up the last of the federal meal tickets for Wednesday morning's breakfast. Nor did any of them volunteer to go home. The only potentially provocative act was the surreptitious distribution of a handbill at the new camp, calling on the workers to "refuse to build the concentration camp.... Don't assist the government to defeat us." Everything seemed to be on hold, awaiting the return of the delegation.[41]

Slim Evans first learned about the government's latest moves by telegram only a few hours before reaching Regina. But by the time the train pulled into the station at 7:00 Wednesday morning, 26 June, he was ready with his own tough response. Cheered by the men, waiting in formation as he emerged onto the street, Evans mounted the front of a car and delivered a scathing account of the Ottawa negotiations and Bennett's bull-headed defence of the camps. "These tar paper shacks from which you came are better than the shelter of average citizens," he mocked the prime minister to the accompaniment of boos. "This from the man who lives in a five thousand dollar suite in the Chateau Laurier." Evans then accused the government of breaking the Manion agreement by cutting off meals before the delegation had reported. He congratulated the men for staying together despite the pressures to register for the new camp, and reminded them that their struggle for work and wages was just as important now as it had been when they decided to go to Ottawa. Only this time, they would not be alone. Camp walkouts were planned across the country, while a "Manitoba division" was ready to join the "Regina army." Support for the trek beyond Regina would be "every bit as great" as it had been since Vancouver, Evans bragged, and men "were ready to be on the firing line at Ottawa, when we arrive." The trekkers roared their approval and then marched their returning heroes back to the stadium. As they passed the front door of the Grain Show Building, they jeered and hooted. "I'm staying right here," yelled one, "until the police wear holes in the ground standing around."[42] Little did he and the others realize that the Mounties lay in wait in the nearby armouries, ready to pounce at the first sign of a disturbance.

Despite the defiant mood, the trekkers faced a difficult situation. They could draw on their own funds to buy meals at local restaurants—as they had done that morning—but the money would quickly be exhausted, especially when there were almost two thousand mouths to be fed. They also had to find a way out of Regina—and soon—or some might start registering for the Lumsden camp or just quietly slip away. Perhaps the biggest problem was that there were few avenues of help. The CEC could be counted on for organizing rallies and picnics and arranging entertainment, but feeding the trekkers at least twice a day was beyond its resources. Besides, all was not well on the committee. Members had wrangled at Monday morning's meeting over the wording of a proposed statement in support of the men. Henry Cowan of the CCF wanted the committee to affirm its commitment to work along constitutional lines to bring about a satisfactory end to the strike. Others objected to the word "constitutional" and thought "peaceful" would be more appropriate. Then someone successfully moved that the entire motion be withdrawn, prompting two members to threaten their resignation. It was finally agreed to refer the matter to a subcommittee to come up with suitable wording. "A lot of people are getting constitution jitters," Pete

Mikkelson sadly noted. "They're afraid now of what might happen since Bennett refused the demands." The committee did, however, decide to sponsor a public petition in support of the trek continuing to Ottawa. It also approved the sale of special lapel buttons, "Citizens' Emergency Committee—Save Our Youth," to raise funds for the men.[43]

At the committee's meeting the next day, the members had set aside their differences in favour of a pointed statement which suggested that Bennett, and Bennett alone, was preparing a violent end to the trek. "It is difficult to imagine a set of circumstances," the statement warned, "which could have been better calculated to incite a riot causing bloodshed and loss of life than the steps the prime minister has taken." This growing tension was confirmed by Reverend East, who produced an anonymous, expletive-filled letter, threatening to "fill him full of lead" because of his work on behalf of the trekkers. But other forces were apparently at work. To the amusement of the committee members, East read a second letter predicting the men would succeed. "Assurance of their victory came when Uranus recently moved into a certain position," a Winnipeg astrologer promised. "The planets will help them."[44]

Such prophecies aside, the trekkers' only real hope at this stage was that the province might come to their rescue. It was not an unrealistic expectation. The Gardiner government was still angry with the way it had been mistreated by its federal counterpart and looked upon the establishment of the Lumsden camp—without consultation—as another slight on a growing list. "We protest the formation of a camp in this province," Premier Gardiner complained to Bennett on Wednesday morning, "and would again ask federal government which permitted the march into this province and the railways who facilitated the movement to see that the marchers leave the province."[45]

The Ottawa delegation, along with a few other citizen and trek representatives, called on the premier shortly after its return to the city. The group had three basic requests: it wanted the province to feed and shelter the men, protect them from police interference, and fund their transportation to Winnipeg. Gardiner refused outright the third request—he was not going to foist the trekkers on Manitoba as Bennett had foisted them on Saskatchewan.

Nor could he do anything about the mounted police, since they were now taking their directions from Ottawa. Feeding the men also proved something of a problem. The premier reminded Evans that the trekkers had struck a deal with Manion—without involving the province—and if the federal government was now reneging on the arrangement, it was not up to him to provide meals. The only thing that could be done under the circumstances, he told them, was for the trekkers to apply to the city for relief as transients and for the city in turn to apply to the province for financial support. To facilitate this process, Gardiner immediately conferred with Mayor Rink, who readily agreed that the men could remain at the stadium, but admitted confusion about the continued feeding of the men. The premier also issued a press statement and sent another telegram to Bennett. Both stated that the trekkers were the responsibility of Ottawa and that the province would get involved only if requested to do so—ironically, the exact reverse of the prime minister's position when the trek first started.[46]

The Saskatchewan government's response to the trekkers' requests left them with only two options: call off the trek and disband or try to continue the march eastward. To register for the Lumsden camp—in effect, to surrender to the Bennett government—was out of the question. The preferred option was to complete the trek and continue the battle for work and wages. But how? Any attempt to leave by train would pit them against the mounted police, who could be expected to use the same brute force that had been unleashed against the striking longshoremen in Vancouver. Marching out of Regina on foot was also not the answer. It would take too long, expend too much energy, and require tremendous logistical support along the way. The only viable solution was to evacuate the men by car or truck, as far as Winnipeg if necessary. It was not a new idea. The Regina Board of Trade, along with several service clubs, had been prepared to chauffeur the men by motor cavalcade to the Manitoba border shortly after the trek had arrived in the city. But they backed away from the scheme when it was learned that Manion and Weir had been sent west to meet with the trekkers.[47] The trek leadership now revived the plan, only this time they would appeal to the public for trucks and other large vehicles to take them out of Saskatchewan.

The Ottawa delegation was scheduled to report on its meeting with Prime

Minister Bennett at a public rally at the stadium on Wednesday night. But the four thousand people in attendance, including several plainclothes policemen, were probably more interested in hearing about the trek's next move. Once again, there was a string of speakers, including Reverend East who likened the trekkers' hardships to those of Christ. Matt Shaw pleaded for money, a signal to send donation boxes through the crowd. Unfortunately, the $165.61 collected that night would not even cover the cost of the twenty-cent meals that had been negotiated for the men at city restaurants. Evans, the last speaker, talked for an hour. As had become customary, he methodically reviewed what the trek was all about and what the men were seeking. He then described how the prime minister's scandalous treatment of the trek delegation had made the men more determined than ever to continue their march.

To that end, he appealed to all Regina truck owners to report to the Unity Centre by ten the following morning; the trek was prepared to pay any driver to take a cargo of men to Winnipeg. As Evans told the audience, it was useless to attempt to leave the city by any other means. Nor did the men want to fight.[48] But in making the declaration that the trek would go on, Evans brought the anticipated battle with the mounted police one step closer to reality. Everyone there that night knew that the Mounties would respond—had to respond. The question was where, when, and especially, how.

CHAPTER EIGHT

The Time Is Opportune

From the moment the On-to-Ottawa Trek arrived in Regina, some kind of heavy-handed response was expected from the Royal Canadian Mounted Police. After all, the Bennett government had publicly declared the trek a revolutionary movement and had instructed the police to prevent the men from leaving the Saskatchewan capital, by force if necessary. The response finally arrived on 27 June, almost a full two weeks after the trek had been stopped in Regina. When the trekkers refused to register for the temporary Lumsden camp, choosing instead to try to continue their march eastward by truck, Ottawa had had enough. If they were not interested in the chance to disband at federal expense, not interested in the olive branch being offered, then they would have to contend with the sword. It consequently fell to the mounted police to break up the trek and disperse the men, something they had been spoiling to do ever since the Alberta relief office episode had embarrassed the force in Calgary. What this action meant, though, is that the Bennett government effectively took a back seat to the Mounties, who were blindly determined to crush the trek and, with it, the resolve of the men, at any cost. Both Commissioner James MacBrien and Assistant Commissioner Colonel Stuart Wood of the RCMP readily identified the trek with the larger Communist movement and were willing to do almost anything to strike a decisive blow against the organization and its agents. The days of restraint were over.

❖ ❖ ❖

The mounted police viewed the On-to-Ottawa Trek as little different from the two previous times they had been called upon in Saskatchewan in the early 1930s. In fact, the police seemed to have learned little from the fiascos in Estevan in September 1931 and Saskatoon in May 1933, except the need to be better prepared given the number of trekkers they faced. Assistant Commissioner Wood consequently placed several large orders for riot gear, including 150 police batons the day the trek delegation reached Ottawa.

He considered these preparations absolutely essential. The trekkers may have appeared peaceful and well-behaved, but they had to resort to violence to achieve their goal. That was the real threat, according to Wood, not some trumped-up complaint that they were illegally riding freights. This was more than a gut feeling. Nor was it simply a response to Slim Evans's reported statement in Sudbury that the streets would flow with blood if the trekkers were stopped. The mounted police had been trained to equate dissent with communism. According to the *RCMP Quarterly*, it was Canada's number one enemy, an insidious cancer capable of taking on many guises and exploiting every situation. It was not surprising, then, that well before the men reached Regina, Colonel Wood considered the trek a "Communists' catspaw," whose true purpose was not to improve the camps, but to overthrow the government by force. "It was carrying out the policy of the Communist party," he would repeatedly assert in the months ahead, "as a step in the revolutionary movement." He also regretted that the trek had been allowed to leave Vancouver and believed it was now up to his men in Regina to quash the march before it was too late. The alternative was anarchy.[1]

Stopping the men from continuing to Ottawa, though, was not so straightforward. On Tuesday, 25 June, the day before Evans put out the call for trucks to transport the men to Manitoba, Saskatchewan attorney-general Tommy Davis told Wood during a meeting at the legislature that the vagrancy section of the Criminal Code could not be applied to men travelling on foot or by motor vehicle, especially if the transportation had been authorized by the province. Wood was troubled by the advice and wired Commissioner MacBrien about the "legality" of his orders. MacBrien, in response, repeated his earlier directive, but this time added: "Dominion Government will declare national emergency to exist if necessary." This was

exactly the kind of assurance Wood had been seeking, and he immediate informed the attorney-general that Ottawa would be providing the leg authority to prevent the men from leaving the city by any means.[2] But wha Wood, or anyone else in Regina for that matter, did not know at the time wa that MacBrien was acting on his own initiative and had not bothered t inform the prime minister or any other government official. It seems th general thought he was at war again and did not want any complications getting in the way of his battle plans.

By the morning of Thursday, 27 June, the mounted police seemed to be everywhere in Regina. Two troops continued to stand at the ready inside the armouries, while another troop had taken over the camp registration office at the Grain Show Building and was now using it as a base to keep an eye on the movements of the trekkers at the nearby stadium. An unexpected bonus was the first volunteer for the Lumsden camp: fifteen-year-old Robert Wessel from Verwood, Saskatchewan, who had joined the march in Regina and was now afraid of what lay ahead. Carloads of Mounties also drove through the exhibition grounds throughout the day. This harassment, according to undercover policeman Don Taylor, proved unsettling and prompted many of the men to fashion crude weapons from whatever materials were at hand. Others wrote their names and addresses on pieces of paper they now carried in their pockets in case they were killed or seriously injured in any fight.[3]

Wood also dispatched a squadron of police to the provincial jail on the outskirts of the city to detain any trekker attempting to head east on the Winnipeg highway. One reporter mockingly suggested that police were even watching police that day. "Every vacant lot was a parking space for a police car," the *Leader-Post* noted. "There were uniforms and uniforms ... car after car of Mounties passed along the streets slowly bound for nowhere in particular."[4]

Premier Jimmy Gardiner, for his part, did not find anything amusing about the deployment of the police, especially when he knew from his attorney-general that the federal government was about to declare a national emergency. Nor did Prime Minister Bennett help his mood. The premier's morning began with a blunt telegram from Ottawa, in which Bennett insisted the Saskatchewan government need not worry about the

maintenance and care of the trekkers. A second, more incendiary telegram followed a few hours later—most likely in response to the news that the men intended to leave the province that day by truck. "I publicly appeal to you and your government to discharge your proper responsibilities in respect ... to law and order," Bennett urged Gardiner. "If you are unable to carry out your constitutional obligations and seek the assistance of the Dominion it will be furnished." This suggestion that Saskatchewan was somehow standing in the way of dealing with the trek enraged the premier, who, like the men, had effectively been handcuffed by the Bennett government for the past ten days. "Throughout the course of this matter," he shot back in bitter frustration, "your Government has acted without our knowledge, consent or concurrence.... You and you alone have prevented this government from fulfilling our constitutional responsibilities." The prime minister, however, never doubted the rightness of the decision to stop the trek and, in the continuing war of words, accused Gardiner of refusing "to cooperate to maintain the fabric of our society and the institutions of the country against the illegal threats and demands of Communists and their associates." The premier, a fierce competitor in his own right, deftly returned the volley. "Unfortunately this province had no problem until you imported one into Saskatchewan," he charged, "and took steps to see that it remained here." He also ridiculed Bennett for failing to stop the movement from leaving Vancouver, especially if it was so dangerous. But in the end, Gardiner knew that the federal government held the upper hand and reminded the prime minister that "while protesting your actions we [Saskatchewan] have assiduously refrained from interfering in any way with your orders."[5]

The trekkers, meanwhile, pushed ahead with their preparations to leave Regina. For the first time since the men had arrived in the city, trek leader Arthur Evans personally attended the regular morning meeting of the Citizens' Emergency Committee (CEC) and appealed for assistance in rounding up trucks. The committee readily agreed to arrange transportation, including sponsoring a radio broadcast at noon directed at local farmers. Evans then went for coffee at the Olympia Cafe, where he met with two local men, who refused to give their names but claimed to represent the business community. The men handed Evans ten fifty-dollar bills to help the trek

hire vehicles and said that there would be another equal instalment once half the men had left the city. There was even good news from the Saskatchewan legislature. Premier Gardiner told a trekker delegation that if the men were able to reach Broadview, about fifty-five miles east of Regina, the province would feed them.[6]

Evans had originally suggested that the truck caravan would leave Regina around 10:00 A.M. But the early departure proved unrealistic—there was not time to get together enough vehicles—and it was decided to postpone any attempt to break through the police blockade until later that afternoon. In the interim, the trek leaders did their best to keep the divisions intact and placed pickets at the stadium entrance to prevent any men who were having second thoughts about staying from leaving with their packs or other belongings. The pressure to desert had never been stronger, what with the police seemingly everywhere that day. General MacBrien also tried to make it easier for men to join the Lumsden camp by instructing Wood to announce it was no longer necessary to apply first at the registration office. Any trekker who showed up at the camp would be taken in and fed, no small inducement at a time when the men were now getting only two meals a day. The police also did their best to sow doubt in the minds of the men, especially the younger ones, by playing up the supposed link between the trek and the Communist party. MacBrien encouraged Wood to let it be known, even if it was only speculation, that convicted red Tim Buck was in the city directing operations.[7]

At 2:30 that afternoon, Division One, numbering about three hundred men, formed up outside the stadium, ready to board the trucks that were to take them to Winnipeg. Any sense of elation was cut short, however, by the news that the Manitoba government would not allow the trek to enter the province. There was also a problem securing vehicles for the trip eastward. Paddy O'Neill, for example, who had been sent to Moose Jaw, called to report that the RCMP were turning back any trucks he hired. The trekkers, no strangers to waiting, sat down in the grass and spent the rest of the afternoon sunning themselves or watching the seemingly endless stream of police cars pass through the exhibition grounds. One energetic individual hung an effigy of R. B. Bennett from a nearby telephone pole. Colonel Wood, on the other hand, used the delay to wire MacBrien that the time had arrived for

Ottawa to declare a national emergency. The commissioner immediately telephoned Wood to proceed with any seizures and arrests on the understanding that the government would be acting under the authority of the peace, order and good government section of the 1935 relief act—what critics termed the "blank cheque" provision because the government could take literally any action. With this verbal assurance from headquarters, Wood let it be known that Ottawa had empowered the police to prevent the men from leaving Regina by any means. He also called the legislature and had the attorney-general pulled from a cabinet meeting so that he could give him the news.[8] No one at the time contacted Ottawa for further details. It was simply assumed that the Bennett government had run out of patience.

The assistant commissioner's announcement, although not a complete surprise, seemed to stun the trek leaders. They were not sure what to do, except to avoid something foolish or rash. "We do not intend to fight," Matt Shaw solemnly told reporters, "The police have the weapons." At first, Evans approached the Canadian Pacific Railway about hiring boxcars or even an entire train to take the men out of Regina, but was turned down. It was then decided to try a small test run to see how the Mounties would respond. There seemed to be some question whether the mounted police could actually stop private vehicles carrying a few trekkers, especially if they held a provincial permit to take passengers to the Manitoba border. This view was apparently shared by someone in the provincial government, for not only were permits issued, but the motor vehicle office was kept open an additional two hours.[9]

At 9:30, with the trekkers singing "Hold the Fort," two cars and a truck pulled away from the stadium. Regina truck driver Jim Lennox and Co-operative Commonwealth Federation (CCF) activist Jack King drove the cars, one of which was donated by an unnamed woman. Frank Halaburd, a local poultry dealer, was behind the wheel of his truck—minus the chickens. At his side in the cab sat his wife and Reverend Samuel East, who acted as if he was on a divine mission. In fact, East had become something of a local folk hero to the men and, as he climbed into the truck at the stadium, one of the boys shouted, "We're moving east with East." The caravan headed first to the Unity Centre for last-minute instructions from Evans and then proceeded straight out Winnipeg Street to Highway 1, followed by dozens of curious citizens in cars, on bikes, or on foot. It is not certain how many trekkers were involved. One participant suggested that there may have been as many as twenty-five.[10]

At the highway, the three vehicles pulled into an Imperial Oil station to get gas. Here they were confronted by RCMP constable W. H. Foskett and his partner, F. D. Bolger, who had been watching the road in their patrol car for the past few hours. They were soon joined by Corporal J. Painter, who had been dispatched to the highway as soon as it was reported that several vehicles had left the stadium. The Mounties politely informed the drivers that they could proceed no further without being arrested and then called the Regina Town Station for back-up. While a large crowd began to gather, an indignant East challenged the authority of the police, brandishing the truck's permit. An apologetic Painter said he had been ordered to stop them. He flashed a smile when another rider quipped, "We are just out on a Sunday school picnic."[11]

At 10:15, Inspector J. T. Jones arrived at the gas station with two large vans. After first conferring with the police on the scene, he immediately asked who was in charge of the party. Trek marshal Jack Cosgrove, who had been riding in the lead car with Lennox, stepped forward and identified himself. Jones calmly announced that he was to detain all those travelling in the cars and truck. With that, about sixty Mounties in riot gear poured from the back of the vans. Most of the trekkers bolted in the growing darkness and were soon lost among the spectators, who began to boo and shout insults at the sight of the steel-helmeted police with their side arms and riding crops. In the end, only three trekkers were arrested: Cosgrove, Ivan Bell, and Ernest Edwards. Lennox and Halaburd were also detained, while Jack King, the third driver, managed to elude capture in the confusion. Reverend East was initially held, but then released that same night. The police did not want to make him a martyr. Those arrested were briefly interrogated at the RCMP barracks by Colonel Wood before being placed in cells for arraignment the following day. The most pathetic case was that of Frank Halaburd. Throughout his overnight detention, all he wanted to do was talk about his chicks and who was going to look after them. His wife refused to leave his side. Through tears, she told a constable, "I won't go, we mated together and we stay together."[12]

Evans learned of the police action by telephone while anxiously waiting at the Unity Centre to hear whether the blockade had been successfully breached. The call was like a body blow. The Bennett government had countered every move by the trekkers, kept them in check at every turn, regardless of the local support they enjoyed. There seemed to be no escape, only the prospect of being rounded up like cattle and herded into the Lumsden camp. In desperation, Evans sent a plaintive wire to his Manitoba contacts in the middle of the night. "Martial law practically in force here," he pleaded in an intercepted telegram. "We call upon Winnipeg and other camp strikers to commence trek to Ottawa at once to lessen pressure here." It was Evans's hope that if the hundreds of men waiting in the Manitoba capital to join the trek started their own march, then the police would have to divert men there. But the Winnipeg group, numbering about twelve hundred, would not be ready to move for at least two days, not soon enough to ease the situation in Regina. He would have to find some other way to keep the trek from the reach of the Mounties, if it was going to survive intact to fight another day.[13]

Premier Gardiner also had a fitful night. Just after dawn, he called Tommy Davis and told him to bring the assistant commissioner and a copy of his Ottawa instructions to his home as soon as possible. Wood arrived at his doorstep before 7:00 A.M. and handed the premier the telegram in which MacBrien declared that any action against the trekkers would be supported by government order. Gardiner apparently said little while he and his attorney-general examined the document, except that he would try to speak with the trekkers later that morning. Privately, the premier seemed ready to concede that the trek was finished, that the men would never take a step beyond Regina. He also knew that the incident at the filling station was tame in comparison to what might happen in the days ahead if the men refused to back down but openly challenged the Mounties. The best thing he could do, then, under the circumstances, was to try to reach some agreement with the Bennett government on the condition that the trekkers first went to the Lumsden camp. Gardiner put this idea to a small trek delegation that had hurriedly been summoned to his office around 9:00 A.M. He promised that the province would take the men's case to Ottawa, as well as ensure that they were properly treated at the new camp, but said that his government could effectively do little as long as they and the mounted police were at loggerheads. Evans balked at the offer, suggesting instead that the men might establish their own camp. Gardiner, though, was in no mood to bargain and asked permission to address the trekkers directly. Evans turned down the request, arguing that anything the premier wanted to say to the men should be said to the delegation.[14]

Half an hour later, the trekkers held their own meeting at the stadium to review what had happened the night before and decide on a course of action. The defiance of the last few days was now gone, but they were still not ready to roll over. The men consequently rejected the premier's proposal as nothing short of surrender. It was "absolutely insane," according to Evans, to count on the protection of the province as long as control of the mounted police rested with the Bennett government.[15] Besides, the trek leader had still not given up on the idea of negotiating with Ottawa and had to put the trekkers in a position whereby federal authorities had to deal with their demands. That would never happen, though, if the men continued to occupy the stadium. The police could easily surround the building at any time and turn it into a holding pen. It made more strategic sense, then, for the men to set up their own camp outside the city and try to continue to deal with the Bennett government from a position of organized strength. This had been a defining feature of the strike and trek ever since the men had walked out of the federal relief camps and descended on Vancouver in April. There was no reason to abandon it.

The men needed little convincing that morning to embrace Evans's recommendation that the trek set up its own camp. The experience of the night before had made them feel extremely vulnerable, and they were open to any suggestion that put some distance between themselves and the police, something that Gardiner's proposal could not guarantee. The preferred site for the camp was a five-acre parcel of land owned by Mrs. Francis Ryan, a Regina restaurateur, about a mile west of the city at Boggy Creek. Another possible location, about five miles to the east, had been considered but rejected because of the police restriction on travel in that direction. In order to feed the men at the new camp site, it was decided to appeal to the local farming community for donations. The trek also continued to rely heavily on the generous and enthusiastic support of the CEC. In fact, at the very time that the men were meeting at the stadium, Bill Hamill was before the committee, securing its pledge to sponsor a national fund-raising campaign, as well as a local food drive. This kind of assistance was not unusual, but it appears to have been motivated in part by a growing fear that the police would evict the trekkers from the stadium, a view shared by the local newspapers. Evans did nothing to squelch the rumour, if only because of the sympathy it might generate. But it had little to do with the real reason for setting up the new camp, namely, to use it as a base, in Evans's words, to "carry on a continuation of the struggle." Nor was the trek leader prepared to brook any interference. After the meeting had adjourned around ten, Gardiner and Davis arrived at the entrance to the stadium and asked to speak to the men before they headed downtown for breakfast. But Evans turned them away with the boast that the province's proposal had been unanimously rejected.[16]

The premier had good reason to try to get the trekkers to Lumsden, for he rightly sensed that the situation in Regina was about to enter a new phase. Around the same time that Gardiner and his attorney-general were wrangling with Evans, Commissioner MacBrien called Colonel Wood to advise him that the federal Department of Justice had retained local lawyers F. B. Bagshaw and A. G. MacKinnon to prosecute the five men arrested the night before. He also reported that the government wished to proceed against the leaders of the trek and would be relying on advice of the two solicitors, in consultation with the RCMP, to decide whether charges could be laid under section 98 of the Criminal Code. To facilitate this task, the commissioner was sending Staff Sergeant John Leopold, a former secret agent, to Regina with a briefcase of highly sensitive documents; he was not expected to arrive until the morning of Monday, 1 July. MacBrien repeated this information in a telegram ostensibly sent for confirmation purposes. But he added one crucial closing line: "You are authorized to take such action if and when you think time is opportune." The rounding up of the trek leaders and anyone else considered suspect would now be left to the discretion of Colonel Wood.[17]

The assistant commissioner was undoubtedly delighted with his new orders. From the beginning, he had regarded the trek as a revolutionary movement and its Bolshevik leader "a talking ass" who spouted propaganda. But he had been forced to wait—with the trek in his crosshairs—even though the men continued with the same antics in Regina that had made them such a menace as they crossed the prairies. This was about to change. Wood faced a new complication, though, if the men formed their own camp outside the city. He needed to keep the trekkers at the exhibition grounds in order to prevent the leaders from slipping away and eluding arrest. On his own initiative, Wood called a press conference late Friday morning and grimly announced that helping the trekkers in any way was now forbidden. "Farmers should be warned against assisting these men in setting up such a camp," he threatened. "Any person who supplies any form of accommodation ... transportation or food, will be prosecuted." When asked by the press about the legal basis for such a draconian measure, Wood explained that the Bennett government had passed an emergency order-in-council and that the police had been acting under this same order when they stopped the trekkers from leaving Regina by truck the night before.[18]

The threat of arrest, coming from the lips of the most senior Mountie in Regina, sent a chill through the city. Support for the trek was already beginning to slip, but Colonel Wood's warning drove a wedge between the trekkers and local citizens. The canvass of Regina homes for food donations was consequently a miserable flop. The men had to fall back on their rapidly diminishing resources. Local radio stations also refused to grant air time to George Williams, a CCF member of the provincial legislature, who had been scheduled to speak on behalf of the trekkers. The feisty Williams refused to be intimidated, though, and sent a statement to the national press: "If Mr. Bennett wishes to arrest those assisting the strikers, he will be able to find me in my office in Regina."[19]

The resolve of some of the other members of the CEC, on the other hand, began to crumble. At the committee's meeting the next morning, the Regina Trades and Labour Council refused to allow any further use of the Labour Temple out of fear that the building would be confiscated by the police. This was the same group which had publicly chastised the Bennett government less than a week earlier for its ham-handed handling of the trek: "These days, anyone who fights for better conditions is a Red."[20]

Such developments, in one sense, were not new to the men. They had learned from their Vancouver experience that public sympathy for their cause, let alone material assistance, could not last forever. But according to an observer, there was a fundamental difference between the two situations: "The trek had left Vancouver, it could not leave Regina."[21]

Tommy Davis was particularly intrigued by Wood's public remarks. The Saskatchewan attorney-general had seen a copy of MacBrien's telegram, and it said nothing about assistance to the trekkers being prohibited. He also likely knew from his contacts in Ottawa, if not from the morning papers, that Hugh Guthrie, the federal minister of Justice, had been silent about a government order in the House of Commons the night before when the situation in Regina was raised during a debate about increased military spending. All the minister did was issue a vague warning. "If the marchers persisted in their intention to violate the law," he calmly observed, "they would have to take the consequences." Davis decided to seek clarification and asked Guthrie for information about the phantom government decree "as I am unable to find any legal authority under which any such orders could be issued." Indeed, the 1935 legislation was quite explicit: the federal government could not act by order-in-council as long as Parliament was in session.[22]

Colonel Wood, meanwhile, was in complete command of the situation. He continued to send out patrols day and night to watch the highway and the rail yards for any attempt by the trekkers to leave the city. These efforts ironically netted a group of visiting horticulturists when their tour bus failed to stop at a roadblock Friday afternoon and was chased by several patrol cars. Wood's men also picked up three trekkers who wanted to enter the Lumsden camp. Twenty-six more were pulled from a westbound freight. Another deserter, twenty-one-year-old Robert Melville, was found wandering back alleys in search of food and arrested by the city police for vagrancy. Wood expected these desertions to climb, now that the trekkers' plan to establish their own camp had been sabotaged and the leaders were running out of options, not to mention food. Several of the defectors also reported that the trekkers were splitting into two factions, between those who wanted to carry on to Ottawa and those who wanted to get away from the trouble in Regina. The highlight of the day, though, was the late-afternoon arraignment of the five men arrested the night before—hopefully, for the police, the first of many such hearings at the RCMP Town Station in the days ahead. After some delay while E. C. Leslie replaced MacKinnon as one of the prosecutors, each man was charged with being a member of an unlawful association under section 98 of the Criminal Code and remanded for four days. Bail ranged from one thousand to three thousand dollars—certainly well beyond the means of the defendants or the trek. At the end of the day, a tired but smug Wood telegraphed MacBrien: "Situation very satisfactory."[23]

Saturday, 29 June, was a day of small victories for the trekkers. That morning, the federal Justice minister wired Tommy Davis: "No instructions have been issued to prevent persons rendering assistance to marchers." When a persistent Davis specifically asked about the government order that Colonel Wood had cited in support of police actions, Guthrie could not have been blunter: "No order-in-council of any kind has been passed in connection with the Regina situation." This revelation, far from comforting, alarmed the Saskatchewan attorney-general, for it suggested that RCMP commissioner MacBrien, and not Guthrie, was issuing instructions. "There must have been two people down there running affairs," Davis would later lament, "acting without knowledge of what one another was doing, or was going to do." The scapegoat for this mix-up was Wood, who was forced to clarify his public statement from the day before. But he remained unrepentant, even if his comments had embarrassed the government. "This action," he reasoned with MacBrien, "effectively stopped any active assistance being rendered the strikers.... I think the means justified the end." The commissioner evidently agreed, or at least realized he was equally implicated, for it was he who had misled Wood in the first place about what the Bennett government intended to do.[24]

An even bigger headache for the mounted police was working up charges against the trek leaders. Both government lawyers in Regina had determined that the Relief Camp Workers' Union was an unlawful organization and that the men's actions in Vancouver and Calgary appeared illegal. But Bagshaw and Leslie could not find enough hard evidence in the files at the RCMP depot to proceed against Evans and the other leaders. "The prospects at the moment do not appear bright" is how the situation was summed up for

MacBrien. Wood blamed the lack of material on the failure to place a member of the force among the trekkers before they reached Moose Jaw. Even then, the two undercover agents—first Constable Cooper and then Constable Taylor—had been recognized and recalled before they could gather much information. He also conceded that "the radical leaders had been very careful of their statements" during their stay in the city, and no matter how these statements were added up, they did not violate section 98. To remedy this shortcoming, Wood wired the Alberta and British Columbia divisions and asked them to forward any documents that could be used to support criminal charges. He remained confident that the arrests would be executed, but acknowledged that it would take a few more days than originally anticipated.[25]

This reprieve made no difference to the trek and its fate. The longer the stalemate in Regina remained unresolved, the worse it became for the men. Saturday marked the beginning of the fourth day the trekkers had been surviving on their own funds. Unless another source could be tapped, they would not be able to pay for any more meals beyond the holiday Monday. Entering the weekend, they apparently had less than twelve hundred dollars to keep them going. This sense that the end of the trek was at hand probably explains why eleven men came forward that morning to enter the Lumsden camp. Twelve followed the next day. Others continued to slip away in small groups and head west, while a few took the opportunity to store their packs outside the stadium. Henderson Bell of Bell Motors on Eleventh Avenue, for example, reported that a handful of the trekkers began to keep their gear at his garage in the event they had to leave the city. There was a growing fear among the men that they might be evicted from the stadium—and therein separated from their few belongings—in order to force them into the new federal camp. And by Saturday afternoon, this outcome seemed a real possibility. Evans, with cap in hand, had gone back to see Premier Gardiner and suggested that the province establish a camp for the men. But the premier rejected the proposal. Even though he deeply resented how Prime Minister Bennett had treated the province, he knew better than to take on the federal government, especially when it was freely using section 98. Nor did he intend "to adopt 1800 men mostly from outside the province as our special care."

Instead, Gardiner repeated his earlier offer to take the men's case to Ottawa if they first went to Lumsden.[26]

Federal officials, in the meantime, started to smell victory. Cyril Burgess, who was responsible for the Lumsden camp, told his Ottawa supervisor that something had to give: "Strike leaders discouraged at outlook while rank and file are becoming suspicious and restless." Colonel Wood was more cocksure about the future. "The whole attitude and demeanor has changed in the last 24 hours," he advised MacBrien in a lengthy, detailed assessment of the Regina situation. "I could force matters," he continued, "by seizing the Stadium and bringing about a clash with the strikers, but see no great advantage due to the fact that the next two days will see the movement definitely broken." The Regina *Leader-Post*, on the other hand, wanted to see things finally settled and called on the federal government to "solve the problem that it has presented for Regina and Saskatchewan." It was time to end the game of "hide and seek" that the trekkers and authorities were playing with each other: "To permit it to continue ... is bad for everyone concerned." Nor were the trekkers immune from the paper's chiding. In the same Saturday issue, a front-page editorial titled "THE END OF THE TRAIL" declared the likelihood of the trek getting to Ottawa or anywhere else to be nil and urged the men to disband. "The strikers, in the end, must obey the authority of the state as must every other citizen," it lectured. "There is no hope for them in trying to do anything else."[27]

The trekkers could at least count on the continuing support of the Communist Party of Canada. A 27 June editorial in *The Worker* accused Prime Minister Bennett of trying to win re-election "by spilling the blood of young Canadians ... thousands of young Canadian boys who can no longer live in the filthy, rotten slave camps." Two days later, the paper described the mounted police preparations as "warlike." These strong words, however, were not matched by material help, and Slim Evans's appeal for funds from the party's Vancouver office, according to internal police documents, went unanswered. Nor did national leader Tim Buck lend a hand, even though the police were convinced that he was in the city.[28]

The support of Regina citizens, except for a number of steadfast activists, had also begun to noticeably wane. At a rally at Market Square on Saturday night, sponsored by the Canadian Labour Defence League to raise funds for the defence of the five arrested men, no more than three to five hundred people attended. Provincial CCFer George Williams pledged his party's support for the work and wages programme of the trekkers before railing against the government's bald-faced attempt "to force the workers to capitulate through starvation." Reverend East, who had become a fixture on rally platforms during the past two weeks, went one step further and accused the prime minister of deliberately trying to provoke a clash so that he could unleash his "cossacks" in the name of law and order. He also assured his audience that no one was breaking the law by helping the trek.

Evans spoke last as usual, but made no attempt this time to mask the frustration that had been welling up inside of him for the past few days. In a rambling, at times bitter, tirade, he announced that it was he who was a member of the Communist party, not the five men who had been arrested under section 98 two nights earlier. He then lashed out at the police for tampering with his mail and derided Premier Gardiner for being "a spineless jellyfish, hanging on to the tail of Bennett's kite." The press was little better; he slammed local reporters as "mental prostitutes" and "slimy snakes." He concluded by appealing for funds so that the working class struggle could continue. But when the call came for donations—East pleaded with the crowd to donate one-dollar bills—only $58.36 was collected. It would buy some much-needed cooking supplies for the feeding stations that the trekkers had established at the stadium and Unity Centre.[29]

The outlook was even bleaker by Sunday. Several hundred men in Winnipeg were expected to start their own trek to Ottawa that day to help ease the pressure in Regina. But instead of heading to the rail yards, where they would have been challenged by the mounted police, they occupied a federal dining hall in order to extract relief from authorities.[30]

The other disappointment was an afternoon picnic at Regina's Wascana Park, near the Legislative Building. Although the CEC had actively promoted the event, there was barely enough donated food to feed the two hundred trekkers in attendance—a far cry from a similar gathering two weeks earlier. Colonel Wood briefly toured the grounds and sarcastically reported that he had trouble finding the picnickers. But he refused to relax his grip. His men still carried out round-the-clock patrols of the city and nearby highways. They even searched a circus train in the middle of the night before it was allowed to continue eastward. Two Mounties in plainclothes, Constables Bailey and Lovock, also began to follow Evans in preparation for his arrest. On Sunday morning, for example, they watched and made notes as he moved between Devon Lodge, a boarding house on Broad Street, the Olympia Cafe, where he took most of his meals, and the stadium. It is not known whether Evans was aware of the surveillance, but he was constantly changing residences every few days during his stay in Regina and never slept at the stadium.[31]

The holiday Monday was a day of decision for the mounted police and the trekkers. The day before, Commissioner MacBrien had called Wood and wanted to know if any arrests had been made; he urged him to take action "with as little delay as possible."[32] This extra pressure seemed unnecessary at the time, since it was plainly evident that the trek was on the verge of collapse. But MacBrien might have been worried that the men, like cornered animals, might resort to more desperate tactics. He was also probably anxious to serve the Conservative government. Not only had the Justice Department ordered the arrest of the leaders, but the prime minister had to call a general election in the coming weeks that could very well be fought on the issue of law and order. A personal matter might also have been at play here. Although his rival and the creator of the federal relief camp scheme, General MacNaughton, had served his last day as chief of the general staff on 30 June, MacBrien might not have been satisfied. He could have been motivated by the desire to see the dismissed general out the door with the knowledge that the mounted police, under his leadership, had won the battle with the strikers, something that had eluded MacNaughton earlier that spring. Whatever the reason for MacBrien's call to Regina, it placed additional weight on Wood's shoulders to do something about the trekkers.

The answer arrived that morning by train from Ottawa in the form of Staff-Sergeant John Leopold, who was quickly hustled off to the RCMP barracks before he was recognized. Leopold was no stranger to Regina or its more radical organizations. In 1913, the Bohemian-born Jew was one of countless thousands who emigrated to western Canada to begin a new life as a farmer. But when he failed as a homesteader in Alberta's Peace River country, he started a new career in 1918 as a mounted policeman. Leopold's recruitment might seem peculiar. His ethnic background, his religion, even his height—at five foot four inches, he seemed like a midget next to other members of the force—did not fit the mould of a Mountie of that era. But that's exactly why he was taken on. In the new Communist world, the mounted police wanted people who could work undercover and spy on continental European immigrants who supposedly carried the seeds of bolshevism. Leopold's linguistic skills and swarthy appearance—he was repeatedly challenged at RCMP headquarters for being "foreign looking"—made him an ideal candidate for this kind of work, and he was sent to Regina at the end of the Great War. There, Agent 30, as he was known to his police handlers, assumed the identity of house painter Jack Esselwein, and over the next decade wormed his way into the Communist party, even serving as secretary for the local branch. But the double life carried a great strain, and Leopold found solace inside a bottle. It was not until 1928, though, after he had been transferred to Toronto, that he was finally exposed and sent to the Yukon for his own safety. His expertise on communism, however, made him the star prosecution witness at the trial of eight Communists, including Tim Buck, in Toronto in August 1931. It was for this same reason that Leopold was now in Regina with a briefcase of incriminating documents about the party and its activities, and he immediately set to work with Bagshaw and Leslie to work up warrants against the trek leaders.[33]

The trekkers were also planning their next move that morning. At a special 8:00 A.M. meeting, the strike committee decided that it would be best, given the dead end they faced in Regina, to beat a retreat back to British Columbia. To leave the city, though, they would need to reach some kind of agreement, and it was decided to strike a five-man delegation—Evans, Martin, Morrison, Young, and Winters—to meet with the federal and provincial governments to see what arrangements could be worked out. These recommendations were endorsed an hour later at a general meeting where the men seemed resigned to their fate.

But getting federal authorities to cooperate was another matter. When Evans called Burgess to set up a possible meeting with both federal and provincial representatives, the civil servant readily agreed to see the trek delegation as long as neither Gardiner nor any of his cabinet ministers were there. Evans then called the premier, who had gone to his farm at Lemburg, about ninety miles from Regina. The trek leader explained that Burgess had turned down a joint session and then asked Gardiner if he would be willing to return to the city to consider a proposal aimed at resolving the deadlock. The premier promised to leave his farm after lunch and meet the trek delegation at the legislature late that afternoon.[34]

The face-off with Burgess got under way at 11:00 A.M. in the Grain Show Building. At his side, in plainclothes, sat Inspector Jones, the same RCMP officer who had overseen the arrest of the men who tried to break the police blockade. Another Mountie, Corporal Radcliffe, took notes. Evans spoke for the delegation and began by asking for relief if the negotiations were successful. But before Burgess would make any commitment, he wanted to know what the trekkers were proposing. Evans then explained that the men were prepared to leave the city under their existing organization and return to their point of origin—what he termed "a discretionary retreat"—if the federal government provided transportation, three meals per day, and medical attention. When Burgess responded that he had to consult with the Department of Labour, Evans repeated that the trek was ready to disband in forty-eight hours. It was then agreed to meet again at mid-afternoon and not to say anything to the press in the meantime.[35]

Evans's proposal seemed a sensible way out of the imbroglio, in that neither side would lose. It was also a surprising gesture for someone with the trek leader's Communist credentials. If Evans had followed the standard script—in other words, practised the politics of provocation—he would have led his men into a bloody showdown with the mounted police instead of trying to work out some kind of compromise with federal officials. It would appear, though, that he had become attached to the men and did not want to send them into a battle they could not win. He also seemed to recognize that any violence would wreck their cause, effectively undo everything they had achieved since leaving Vancouver.

But the Bennett government was not prepared to soften its stance towards the trek now that the men were finally within its grasp. It wanted nothing less than total capitulation, especially after it had spent the past few weeks tarring the movement with the brush of revolution and sedition. Nor were the mounted police willing to stand aside and watch the men return westward in their divisions to Calgary, Kamloops, and Vancouver, where they could possibly launch another, more ambitious, march on Ottawa in the near future. The Mounties had stopped the trek in Regina because it represented a threat to law and order, and it was their duty to subdue that threat, not turn their back on it.

Evans's solution to the impasse, then, was really no solution. The men had to accede to Ottawa's terms. When Burgess consequently forwarded the trekkers' offer to Ottawa, the deputy minister of Labour responded that the men were still required to demobilize through the new federal camp at Lumsden.[36]

Burgess met the trek delegation again at 2:30, but with reinforcements. Colonel Wood, dressed in street clothes, now sat at the table. Although Wood and Evans had known one another by reputation for several years, it was the first time the two foes had met face-to-face. Detective Inspector Walter Mortimer of the Criminal Investigation Branch of the RCMP was also there. The Regina-based Mountie had spent most of his career in Saskatchewan. He was a former member of the now defunct provincial police force and had participated in the 1931 Estevan riot.

Inspector Jones, who attended the morning meeting, had been given a new duty. He and a group of uniformed men were now watching from a nearby curling club in the event of a disturbance. As the trek delegation filed into the room, Evans asked Burgess about the identity of the two new men and was introduced to Wood and Mortimer. He then wanted to know if there was a response to his proposal. Burgess replied that Ottawa had not changed its position—the men still had to disband through the Lumsden camp. Evans reacted angrily and declared that the men would have to be dragged into the federal "concentration camp." Wood intervened at this point and accused Evans of wanting to take the trekkers back to Vancouver where they could cause more trouble. For the rest of the meeting, the pair squared off like an old bickering couple, while everyone else watched in rapt silence. The trek leader kept repeating that the men simply wanted to go back to the places where they had started, while the assistant commissioner kept insisting that the men wanted only to get back to the west coast. Evans then tried to secure a promise that any trekker who entered the camp would be immune from prosecution, but Wood scoffed at the suggestion. The climax came when a defiant Evans declared, "The trek will go on.... We will fight this to the bitter end." An equally resolute Wood countered with his own threat, warning that the men had to go to Lumsden or "take the consequences."[37]

Wood returned to the depot shortly after 4:00 P.M. and immediately telegraphed General MacBrien that the trekkers refused to be demobilized through the Lumsden camp. There was also something of a surprise waiting for him. After spending the day with Leopold reviewing the records of several men on the trek, Bagshaw and Leslie had determined that seven belonged to the Relief Camps Workers' Union and were thereby guilty of being members or officers of an unlawful association under section 98. The two lawyers were working up the warrants and supporting documentation when Wood returned from the meeting with Evans. After a brief conference, it was decided there was sufficient evidence in the affidavits to proceed. At 5:00 P.M., Police Magistrate W. B. Scott issued arrest warrants for Arthur Evans, Matt Shaw, George Black, Paddy O'Neill, Tony Martin, J. Clark, and P. Sullivan. He also approved search warrants for the Unity Centre and three private Regina residences. The time had come to act.[38]

The trek delegation, at the same time, had also made an important decision. After negotiations with the federal government had broken down, Evans went to a telephone booth on the exhibition grounds and called the premier's office. Gardiner had just returned from his farm and agreed to see the men at 5:00. The delegation arrived at the legislature early and had to wait outside, sitting on the front steps in the late afternoon sun, until the premier unlocked one of the huge oak doors with his own key to the building and led them to his office. Gardiner would later claim that the mounted police both knew that the trek representatives were there and that they were trying to reach an arrangement with the provincial government. Colonel Wood, however, flatly denied any knowledge of the meeting. It is quite possible that the police were caught up at that time in the preparation of the arrest warrants. They also wanted little to do with the Saskatchewan government, because they believed Gardiner could not be trusted to do the right thing. But it does seem peculiar that the Mounties could not keep track of the trek delegation and its movements, especially when Evans had been singled out for surveillance.[39]

The meeting with Gardiner and two of his cabinet ministers lasted over an hour. Evans described in detail what had happened that day and then outlined the same proposal he had put before federal authorities—but with one crucial change. He indicated that the trek was willing to be dispersed under provincial supervision. The premier, needing time to think things through, responded that he had to discuss the matter with the attorney-general, who would have to be called back from his cottage. He also wanted to consult with the cabinet and said it would take a few hours to call together the members who were still in the city. But he promised an answer no later than 9:00 the next morning.[40] The delegation left the premier's office around 6:15 and headed downtown to the Unity Centre. As they walked among the holiday crowd on the legislative grounds, they could take some comfort in the fact that Gardiner might be willing to help them out of their predicament—that if he made a deal, he would keep it. But little did they realize that everything now depended on how soon the mounted police executed the warrants.

Exactly twenty-three years earlier on the Dominion Day weekend, a powerful tornado swept through the same grounds, just missing the legislature but laying waste to much of downtown Regina. Another storm was now on the horizon, and it was gathering strength.

CHAPTER NINE

Just Like a Hailstorm

The shrill blast of a police whistle set off the deluge. The north garage door of the Regina city police station burst open and out poured thirty-one city policemen, yelling at the crowd to let them through and threatening to club anyone with the sawed-off baseball bats they menacingly brandished as they headed northwest across Market Square towards the speaker's platform. The large crowd, trekkers and citizens, panicked at the sight of the charging police and scrambled to get out of the way as best they could. But their escape was effectively blocked by the Royal Canadian Mounted Police who ringed the east, north, and west sides of the square and began to advance, in full riot gear, at the sound of the whistle. Some of the people broke through the Mountie gauntlet to surrounding streets and the relative safety of nearby stores and businesses, but the majority swept west to Osler Street, like a huge tidal wave, and then spilled north and south to Tenth and Eleventh Avenues. Plain-clothes detectives, meanwhile, pushed through the stampeding crowd and nabbed trek leaders Slim Evans and George Black as they jumped down from the back of the truck that was being used as a speaker's platform at the evening rally. Evans was quickly hustled off the square and shoved into the back of a waiting police van on Halifax Street. Black was escorted to city police headquarters and placed in one of the cells there. It had taken less than five minutes for the two police forces to clear the square and make the arrests—but at the cost of one life, hundreds injured, and thousands of dollars of damage.

❖ ❖ ❖

Although the On-to-Ottawa Trek had been stalled in Regina for more than two weeks, the decision to finally move against the leaders was a hurried one. Colonel Wood was personally "surprised" that government lawyers Bagshaw and Leslie had been able to work through Staff-Sergeant Leopold's material so quickly—he expected the process to take at least two days—and had even doubted whether they would find sufficient evidence to justify arrests. The issuing of the seven warrants, however, dissolved any remaining sense of restraint and caution by clearing the way for the Mounties to act—something Commissioner MacBrien had been demanding for days. Wood also believed the trekkers would never cave in to federal demands as long as Evans and his Communist cohorts held sway and that the movement had to be decapitated as soon as possible. "That was the idea of issuing warrants," he would later explain, "to remove the body of the trekkers from under the influence of those leaders." Wood was equally worried that the trekkers might try to occupy some building or even take hostages in order to force concessions from the federal or provincial governments. This prospect had first been raised by a Canadian Pacific Railway secret agent who had successfully infiltrated the trek in Moose Jaw and whose identity remains a well-kept secret to this day. Unlike the two undercover mounted policemen who had both been exposed after only a short time in trekker ranks, the railway secret agent not only successfully maintained his cover in Regina, but evidently served on the influential strike committee. On 26 June, the same day that the delegation returned from Ottawa, for example, he reported the trek leaders were considering the same kind of tactics that had been so successful in Vancouver and had told the men "if a showdown is necessary it might as well happen now." That showdown, Wood feared, would soon take place now that the trek had run out of food and funds, and the police had to strike first or face a more volatile situation.[1]

The question, though, was where to execute the warrants. Colonel Wood immediately huddled at the barracks with Detective Inspector Walter Mortimer and other members of the Criminal Investigation Branch (CIB), along with Superintendent C. H. Hill, commander of the Depot Division, and Superintendent R. R. Tait. The senior Mounties dismissed the idea of raiding the stadium and provoking a pitched battle, especially when it was rumoured the trekkers had armed themselves with makeshift weapons. Some of them undoubtedly remembered how a similar raid in 1933 had led to the Saskatoon relief camp riot. Grabbing the men during the night was also ruled out, and for good reason. According to Bagshaw, who sat in on the meeting with Leslie, "they did not know where these leaders were actually residing." They also rejected the possibility of plucking the seven men from the streets of Regina; not only did the leaders reportedly travel with bodyguards, but it was considered best to serve most, if not all, of the warrants at once and thereby prevent any of the targeted men from going into hiding or slipping away.[2] With this in mind, the officers hatched a two-part plan of action. They decided to look first for the seven men at the Unity Centre—what Wood derisively called the Communist Hall. If they were not there, then the arrests were to be made at the beginning of a public rally that the trekkers had called for Market Square at 8:00 that night.

The decision to apprehend the leaders at the Market Square meeting would prove to be the most controversial order of Wood's forty-year policing career. In fact, he would later publicly admit, "It was not a good place." But he could see no other option at the time. Wood was certain that the trekkers would stage a huge demonstration the next day, as they had done in Vancouver and Calgary. The only way to stop them was to deal the strategy committee a mortal blow. He also wanted to take the leaders by surprise in order to foil any resistance and reasoned, on the basis of the most recent public rally on 29 June, that the trekkers would not be at Market Square in any strength. The sheer size of the trek and orderly discipline of the men had been a constant concern for the mounted police for the past two weeks. Any confrontation, such as when the men threatened to march on the rail yards on 17 June, could easily have led to a riot. But with the trek now on the verge of collapse, the ranks weakened by desertions, Wood confidently assumed he could "quietly" arrest the leaders at Market Square without incident. What is not clear, though, is why he never considered serving the warrants at the *end* of the meeting, when the crowd began to disperse and there was even less likelihood of any trouble. It would appear that Wood wanted to put on his own show of force—one that rivaled that of the trek during its first day in the city—to drive home the message that Regina was the

Mounties' town and that the men had better capitulate to federal demands.[3]

Once the mounted police had decided how to proceed, Colonel Wood called Inspector Chesser of the CPR police about the pending arrest of the trek leaders and asked him to secure the rail yards. Chesser, in turn, relayed the latest information from his secret agent—that the strategy committee would be meeting soon to decide how to respond to the failed negotiations that day. The assistant commissioner interpreted this news to mean that some form of civil disobedience was inevitable and he became more than ever convinced of the need to act soon. Wood also tried to reach Martin Bruton, chief of the Regina city police, but found that he was spending the holiday at nearby Regina Beach after being told nothing was planned. Not wanting to lose any valuable time, Mortimer telephoned city police Staff Inspector Duncan McDougall at home and asked him to come to the RCMP barracks to discuss arrest plans for the trek leaders. While McDougall was changing into his uniform, he called Bruton's house and found that the chief had just returned to town. Bruton drove at once to the barracks and met Bagshaw and Leslie coming down the steps as he headed inside to Wood's office. But the assistant commissioner had already left for dinner. After some delay, Bruton finally found him at home around 7:10.[4]

These were the only officials that Wood chose to contact about his plan. He never sought Commissioner MacBrien's blessing, but simply followed his earlier directive to round up the trek leaders once the government lawyers had found sufficient evidence for arrest warrants. He also did not bother to advise any member of the federal cabinet, let alone the prime minister. Dr. Robert Manion, the minister of Railways and Canals, for example, was addressing a national radio audience at the very time that Wood was making his preparations. His words were eerily prophetic. "On a day like this and at a time when subversive activities are so apparent," he observed at the opening ceremonies for a new section of the Trans-Canada highway in the Lakehead area, "all true Canadians should be prepared to take their part in maintaining law and order." Wood also neglected to tell Premier Jimmy Gardiner, who was about to go into a hurriedly convened cabinet meeting to decide whether the Saskatchewan government would help the trek disband. This failure to inform provincial authorities was perhaps understandable, given Gardiner's apparent sympathy, if not support, for the plight of the trekkers. But the province would come to believe that it had been deliberately deceived. On Sunday, 30 June, Attorney-General Tommy Davis had advised Colonel Wood that he was going to his cottage at Fort Qu'Appelle for the remainder of the holiday weekend and wanted to know if the police were contemplating any action. Wood said no. The following day, around 11:00 A.M., Davis contacted Wood once again, this time through his assistant, and was assured there was no reason to return early from the lake. Davis consequently did not begin the three-hour drive back to the city until 5:00 P.M., the very time that the arrest warrants were being issued.[5]

After contacting the city and railway police, the RCMP put their plan into action. Around 6:00 P.M., Special Constable Mervyn Black of the CIB dispatched constables Percy Lovock and E. B. Bailey to watch for the leaders downtown. The pair had spent the past two weeks in Regina masquerading as trekkers and had come to know the key trek figures, especially Evans, by sight. But after searching the men's favourite haunts for an hour, Lovock spotted only Matt Shaw leaving the Unity Centre and heading east on Tenth Avenue. None of the six other wanted men were to be found—not even Evans, who left his meeting with Premier Gardiner at the Legislature Building shortly after 6:00 and travelled downtown by streetcar to the Unity Centre. There, he dictated a letter for Shaw and Reverend Samuel East, who had been selected to go to Toronto that night by train to represent the trek at an unemployment rally at Maple Leaf Gardens. Shaw then left the Unity Centre, under the watchful eye of Lovock, and headed to the place where he was staying to get ready to go to the train station. Evans followed shortly thereafter, around 7:00, walking west along Tenth and then north on Broad to the Olympia Cafe, a popular eating place for the trekkers. For some inexplicable reason, Lovock never saw Evans enter or leave the Unity Centre. Nor did Bailey, even though he went into the Olympia Cafe to buy some tobacco and asked some of the boys there about Evans's whereabouts. But RCMP detective corporal Norman McFarlane noticed the trek leader alone near the corner of Tenth and Broad and could easily have arrested him. Evans met George Black, one of the other wanted men, at the cafe for supper, and then the pair started to make their way to Market Square for the public rally. Black was apparently unhappy with the agenda for the meeting and complained to Evans as they walked along together. This sense of uneasiness had carried over from a five o'clock mass meeting at the stadium. Black, acting as chairman, had warned the men to be ready for possible trouble, that the pickets around the building were being doubled in the event the Mounties tried to forcibly evict the men. Little did he realize that there were bigger problems lying in wait.[6]

While Lovock and Bailey conducted their ineffectual search downtown, the mounted police busily organized the second part of the arrest plan. At his home, Wood explained to Chief Bruton that he had warrants for seven trek leaders and planned to execute them at the Market Square meeting at 8:15. When the city police chief questioned the wisdom of raiding a public rally, where there would likely be women and children, Wood produced a blueprint map of the area and indicated where his men were to be placed and how the arrests were to be effected. He then asked for the assistance of the city police in clearing a "safe passage" for the removal of the prisoners from the square. Although Bruton responded that there was not much time, he had been convinced by Wood that the plan could be executed "without trouble" and readily agreed to provide every available man. He immediately called Staff Inspector McDougall, now at the city police station, and instructed him to have all detectives and as many uniformed men as possible at headquarters by 7:45. Inspector Frederick Toop, who was on night duty that evening, began frantically calling all off-duty constables and ordered anyone he could locate to report to the station no later than 8:00. McDougall had already taken the precaution of holding back the ten uniformed men who were scheduled to begin their shift at 7:00. By the time Bruton arrived from the RCMP barracks, his men were changing from street clothes into their uniforms and being issued special hardwood batons. During a near riot on May Day, 1931, several constables had complained about the ineffectiveness of their regulation billies. In its search for a heavier, more persuasive weapon, the police department purchased fifteen-cent children's baseball bats at Woolworths and cut them down to serve as batons. It would be their first use.[7]

Inspector Mortimer, in the meantime, coordinated the arrangements for the arrest of the seven men. With the help of Acting Sergeant R. M. Wood, who coincidentally had been involved in the Saskatoon relief camp riot, Mortimer matched plain-clothes men with the leaders they knew. He also assigned men to carry out the search warrants at the Unity Centre and three private residences. In all, over thirty men from Depot Division would be involved. City police detectives were also to be on the square to help execute the arrest warrants, but not take part in the searches. To protect the plain-clothes men making the arrests and at the same time facilitate the removal of the prisoners, Superintendent Hill detailed three van-loads of uniformed men to take up positions along the east (Halifax Street), north (Tenth Avenue), and west (Osler Street) sides of the square by 8:15 P.M. Each twenty-seven-man unit was to remain inside its respective furniture van until the whistle sounded and then provide assistance if necessary.[8] For backup, thirty-four mounted men were to be posted at Osler Street and Twelfth Avenue, one block south of the square, while an additional twenty dismounted men were held in reserve at the Town Station at Cornwall Street and Eleventh Avenue. The balance of the Mounties would wait in readiness at the barracks, while fifty-five Canadian Pacific and Canadian National police would guard the rail yards and the Hotel Saskatchewan.

These were extraordinary preparations for an operation that was supposed to be carried out, at Wood's insistence, "without any disturbance." But many of the mounted policemen were experienced combatants. Inspector John T. Jones, a twenty-year veteran who commanded the three vans, with particular responsibility for van two on Tenth Avenue, had just returned from Vancouver, where he helped crush the longshoremen's strike; he was also the Mountie who arrested the trekkers and citizens who had tried to bust the police blockade the night of 27 June. Edmonton-based Inspector A. G. Marsom, in charge of van one on Osler Street, specialized in paramilitary training, while Sub-Inspector Joseph Brunet, the officer assigned to van three on Halifax Street, was a troop commander from Regina's F Division. All three inspectors had spent the past few days hunkered down with an armed force at the exhibition grounds, keeping the trekkers under observation. The mounted men were headed by Inspector A. S. Cooper, an English-born, twenty-six-year police veteran who had been involved in the 1919 Winnipeg General Strike and the 1925 Cape Breton coal fields riot. Like

Jones, he had been sent to Vancouver, but he was summoned back to Regina shortly after the arrival of the trekkers. His second-in-command was Sergeant-Major G. W. Griffin, another long-serving Mountie who had also been in Winnipeg in 1919, as well as participated in the 1933 Saskatoon relief camp riot. All uniformed men were dressed in khaki, with steel helmets, Sam Brown equipment with 45-calibre revolvers, and either leather batons or truncheons. A few, because of the shortage of batons, carried wagon spokes, while those in reserve at the barracks were given pick handles.[9]

At 7:30, Constables Lovock and Bailey called the barracks to report that none of the wanted men was at the Unity Centre or the Olympia Cafe. That left the Mounties no other choice but to proceed with their plan to arrest the leaders at Market Square. Before distributing the warrants, Mortimer briefed the plain-clothes men about the critical importance of making the arrests "as quietly as possible" and getting the prisoners off the square "as quickly as possible." He also instructed the three "van" inspectors to keep their men in the trucks until the whistle sounded and then use their discretion to decide whether to move onto the square. There was little doubt, though, that they were to advance at the first sign of trouble. At least one mounted policeman, Lance Corporal Jimmy Lemieux in van three, who would rise to the rank of deputy commissioner, understood that their job was to "disperse the crowd and push them off Market Square and keep them there as much as we could." None of the Mounties involved in making the arrests or providing back-up was issued ammunition for their sidearms—something senior officers checked before anyone left the barracks.[10] The same could not be said for the city police. They carried loaded 38-calibre guns as part of their standard equipment.

Inspector Mortimer, wearing a grey suit, headed downtown by car about 7:40 and after briefly stopping at the Town Station, drove to the city police headquarters at the corner of Halifax Street and Eleventh Avenue. The station was ideally located for the operation, since the north side of the building backed onto the square. But there was a certain irony. The station had been built by the city in 1931 as a relief project. Mortimer quickly reviewed the arrest plan with Chief Bruton and Staff Inspector McDougall. They were never shown the warrants, but were simply expected to cooperate. What they heard, though, was completely at odds with what senior Mounties would later claim. Both Bruton and McDougall believed the city police were to rush the speaker's platform and clear the square, regardless of whether their assistance was needed. In fact, when the chief, wanting to ensure that there was no misunderstanding, pointedly asked if all four police sections were to advance when the whistle blew, Mortimer apparently said yes. These, then, were the instructions the chief gave to twenty-eight men assembled in the station's garage at 8:00 P.M. As he spoke, three more constables hurriedly joined the group, pulling on their dark blue tunics and matching British-style bobbie helmets. Bruton told his men that they were to assist the RCMP in effecting the arrest of the trek leaders by clearing a path to the platform at the sound of the whistle. He also made it clear that even though they were to leave the garage with their batons drawn, in an upright position, they were not to strike anyone unless attacked.[11]

Colonel Wood, along with Superintendent Hill, left the barracks by car about five minutes after Mortimer. By the time he arrived downtown, the meeting was just getting under way, and he slowly drove once around the perimeter of the square, like a shark circling its prey. Wood had decided to make the chief constable's office his headquarters during the operation, and was just inside the doors of the police station, on the steps, when he met Inspector Mortimer, accompanied by Detective Sergeant Ewan McDonald and Detective Robert Bruce of the city police. It was 8:10. Mortimer informed the assistant commissioner that everything was ready. Wood gave his approval to proceed and then went down into the garage, where he joined Bruton watching the square from a north-facing window. Mortimer and his escort continued out the front door, passed between the fire hall and the police station, and then worked their way through the crowd on the square to a spot about forty feet southeast of the platform. The other plain-clothes men with their warrants found places nearby. Lovock and Bailey, as well as constables Cooper and Taylor, the two exposed RCMP undercover policemen, were also there to help identify the wanted men. None of these Mounties—except for Mortimer—were known to McDougall who would be leading the city police from the garage.[12]

The trekkers had put out the call for the Market Square meeting once it had been decided earlier that day to meet with federal representatives to see whether the deadlock could be resolved. The leaders were to report on the negotiations, as well as make a much needed appeal for funds. Posters reading "MASS MEETING TONIGHT, Market Square 8 P.M." were hastily printed and distributed throughout the city. Matt Shaw also prepared an "official statement" on behalf of the strike committee that was passed out on street corners and stuffed in mailboxes throughout the day. The two-page, mimeographed handout reviewed the purpose and history of the trek and then in hard-hitting language, accused the Bennett government of preparing to smash the movement with state forces rather than provide work and wages. It also defiantly declared the men would never enter the "Lumsden internment camp"—it was a trap—and called on the public to stand shoulder-to-shoulder with the trekkers to force the opening of meaningful negotiations and the provision of immediate relief. Shaw's words seemed intended to revive sagging trekker morale as much as put their case before the public. At one point he counselled, "Our position today is *not* a hopeless one."[13] But the statement also underscored the unwavering conviction of many of the men, some of them no more than teens, who had joined the trek to try to secure a better deal in life. They were not about to be starved into submission, not about to knuckle under to federal demands, despite the fact that a noose was being slowly tightened around their necks.

Market Square had served as Regina's public market place since 1892. The size of a full city block, it was little more than a large, dusty lot in 1935, with a scattering of debris and clumps of weeds here and there. There were two buildings at the south end facing Eleventh Avenue—the city police station and, just to the west, Fire Hall Number One. The city weigh scales were located on the west or Osler Street side of the square, almost in the middle of the block. The four sides of the square were surrounded by an assortment of businesses that reflected the city's role as a service centre: hotels, repair garages, junk dealers, and feed stores. There were also a number of vacant buildings and lots. The square had always been a popular meeting place throughout Regina's history. The trekkers had used it twice for public rallies before that evening. Exactly how many people were there that holiday Monday, though, is difficult to say with any certainty. The estimates range from several hundred to three thousand. The Mountie figures were curiously low, while many citizens tended to give numbers in the higher range. Chief Bruton and detectives McDonald and Bruce, three of the longest-serving members of the city police force at that time, pegged the crowd at twelve hundred to fifteen hundred, with less than half of them trekkers. This number is supported by the CPR secret agent, who reported that there were approximately four hundred strikers there at the beginning of the meeting. The most candid estimate was offered by Reverend J. F. Stewart of Carmichael United Church, who likened the crowd to "a very large congregation," "unfortunately" better than he got at his own church. Those trekkers not at the square were back at the exhibition grounds, watching the first game of a baseball double header between two visiting teams at the floodlit park. At the 5:00 P.M. general meeting, George Black had asked all men not on picket duty that evening to attend the downtown rally. But they already knew about the failed negotiations and had been spooked by Black's warning that they might be evicted. Several hundred men consequently chose to stay put that evening, including Phil Klein, the father of Alberta premier Ralph Klein.[14]

The Market Square meeting got underway shortly after eight; at the same time, ironically, that the Saskatchewan cabinet met to decide whether to help the trekkers disband. A white flat-bed truck, provided by Jack's Messenger Service and parked in front of the city weigh scales, served as a makeshift dais; there were four chairs on the back of the truck and two large speakers powered by electricity from the city scales. George Black chaired the meeting and was joined by fellow trekker Gerry Winters, whose real last name was Tellier, and John Toothill, a CNR clerk and Cooperative Commonwealth Federation party worker who would win an aldermanic seat in the Regina civic election later that fall. The fourth chair was for Evans, who was still mingling among the crowd, smoking a cigarette, at the start of the rally.[15] Climbing onto the truck and taking his seat, Evans was probably pleased as he surveyed the audience. The turnout was much larger than two nights earlier. But it is doubtful how much support the people could offer. Many had come to see what would happen next as part of the trekkers' continuing saga in Regina. Others were there simply because it was a holiday and there was not much else to do. The meeting was a cheap form of entertainment on a pleasant summer evening. The curious included young men, couples with children, and the elderly. There was labourer Chris Kostichuk and his two kids, ten and seven. Steve Pustas also brought his young family, and put his daughter on the truck platform to sit while he held his baby in his arms. Mrs. Christina Metcalfe went with her "lady friend," Mrs. Wray, while Pastor Harry Upton from Regina's Baptist Church walked over to the meeting with decorator Bill MacDonald. John Cheers, a barber, was on his way to the movies with his wife, but stopped to hear the speeches. Then there was elderly John McCarthy—he had lived in Regina since the early 1880s—who took up his "favourite position" on the square with his trademark shillelagh in hand. He would write a poem about his experience that night.[16]

Toothill was the first speaker on the programme. As he talked about the urgent need to support the trekkers who were out of funds, the RCMP vans pulled up along three sides of the square. Bill Neuert, a bricklayer who was on a ladder at the weigh scales holding the wires for the speakers, was among the first to see them. Before leaving the barracks at 7:45, Inspector Jones had addressed the men assigned to the vans, reviewing their assignment and the need to remain calm and follow instructions. The Jones and Brunet groups then headed downtown via Halifax Street, while Marsom went along Tenth Avenue. Not wanting to arrive too early, all three van drivers had to pull over a few blocks from the square and wait several minutes before taking up their positions around 8:13: van one (Marsom) on Osler Street, in front of the Regina Hotel and directly behind or west of the city scales and speaker's platform; van two (Jones) on the north side of the square, in front of the Metropole Hotel on Tenth Avenue; and van three (Brunet) on Halifax Street, outside the City Forge and facing the speaker's platform. The two backup units were dispatched at 8:00. Sergeant Charles Clarke left for the Town Station with twenty men in a van, while Inspector Cooper led his mounted troop at a slow trot along Twelfth Avenue to the corner of Osler.[17]

Toothill was still speaking when a trekker named Cunningham, in charge of the downtown patrol that evening, slipped Black a note about the vans. Black looked around the square and saw three red Peacock-Pounder and Smeed's Security Storage trucks, the same kind of vehicles the Mounties had used the night the trekkers had tried to run the blockade. Black leaned over to Evans, nodded in the direction of the vans and asked what they should do. Evans, apparently fearing a stampede if something was announced, decided to go on with the programme. But many in the crowd already knew something was terribly wrong. Inspector Jones, thinking he had heard the whistle and not able to see out the back of the van, ordered his men to get out and form a line along Tenth Avenue, facing the square. Brunet did the same thing on Halifax. The sight of the Mounties, in their brown tunics and riot gear, sent a ripple of fear along the edge of the crowd, and several people began to move away as quickly as they could walk. Reverend J. F. Stewart was heard to mutter as he left the square, "I think there is going to be difficulty here."

It was too late, though, for those standing closer to the speaker's platform. After Toothill had finished his remarks, Inspector Mortimer took one last look around the square to ensure that the vans and his plain-clothes men were all in place. He then checked his watch—it was exactly 8:17. Just as Gerry Winters began to ask for donations, jokingly suggesting that ten-dollar bills would not be accepted, Mortimer put his whistle to his mouth, took a deep breath, and sounded two loud blasts.[18]

The city police sprang from their hiding place like a jack-in-the-box. But it was no child's game. Four abreast, they charged the speaker's platform, driving into the crowd. The only warning—if it could be called that—came from Staff Inspector McDougall, who led the police from the garage on the double. Waving his baton in a sweeping motion, he shouted at the people to step aside. Many were too shocked to move. "I looked in their faces," John McCarthy recalled, "and I never saw such fear depicted on human beings as on those faces." Others remembered the two-foot long "white" clubs the police wielded. The constables reached their objective in less than a minute, apparently without striking a blow. Every single member of the squad that evening denied hitting anyone on the way to the platform—even though Sergeant Tom Logan called it an "attack." Those standing in the way of the police told a different story. "The policemen went slam bang into the crowd ... I saw people being knocked over," reported Allen Miller, who was standing beside the truck. "They would knock down any that was in the way," agreed James Davidson. "If you were in the road you were knocked over. If you got out of the way you was all right."[19]

Inspector Fred Toop watched the frenzied action from the windows of the city police station. As the constables rushed the platform, most people were pushed westward into the row of cars parked along Osler Street. Others fled south, running between the police station and the fire hall, or north to Tenth Avenue. In the mad scramble to escape, many fell or tripped over those already on the ground. Others were knocked over in the crush and trampled. Steve Pustas started to cry when he realized to his horror that his daughter had been left behind on the truck. It was only later he would learn that his wife had grabbed the girl during the chaos and hurried home. Mrs. S. Hungal, a short, stout woman in her mid-fifties, was not so lucky. Henry Lorenzen found her moaning in pain on the ground near the city scales. He and another man helped her across Osler Street and tried to prop her up against the wall of the Regina Hotel, but she collapsed. It was only then that they realized her leg was broken. She was taken inside the hotel to rest on a couch until an ambulance arrived. Agatha Sentes stopped to help another older woman who had fallen, only to be clubbed on the back and hurried along. Even a baby carriage was bumped in the melee.[20] The city police had a job to do, and no one was spared in their rush towards the platform.

When Mortimer blew his whistle, Evans and Black set off in different directions. Evans leapt down behind the truck platform, where he was immediately tackled by Constable Bailey, who had been waiting for the signal with one foot resting on the running board. Lovock ran to his partner's aid and grabbed the trek leader by the neck, with the warning, "Do nothing, Evans." The pair then marched their prisoner, surrounded by other plain-clothes Mounties, straight east to Halifax Street and into the back of a van. It had been only a matter of minutes before Evans was on his way to a cell at the RCMP town station. Black, meanwhile, had jumped to the north of the truck platform and tried to escape into the stampeding crowd. But he was caught by the back of his sweater by Corporal McFarlane and subdued with the help of another plain-clothes man. While Black was being led off the square, Clarence Mason, a nineteen-year-old who had joined the trek in Regina, lunged at Black's escort, but was pushed aside by Mortimer. When Mason fought back with his fists, he was arrested and hauled into the city police station with Black. None of the other five wanted men were found on the square that evening, let alone apprehended. In fact, at the very time the police operation was under way, Matt Shaw was boarding a CPR passenger train for Toronto. Colonel Wood would later brush off the failure to make more than two arrests as "our hard luck." At the same time, in a perverse kind of logic, he insisted that the city police moved onto the square at "an opportune time"; if they had moved any later, Evans and Black might have been rescued.[21]

When the city police charged from the station garage, they met with no resistance as they hustled over to the truck platform. Nor did Inspector Mortimer's men have any trouble collaring Evans and Black. But two of the Mountie units around the square did not wait—as per their instructions—to see whether they were needed. At the sound of the whistle, Inspector Jones ordered his men forward, four abreast, into the frightened crowd. The troop acted like a wedge, sending people to the northeast and northwest corners of the square along Tenth Avenue. Inspector Brunet's men, on Halifax Street, also advanced on the double, swinging their batons and striking anyone in their path. A member of the troop, Lance Corporal Lemieux, would later confess that they were sent into the crowd on the whistle, not knowing even who the plain-clothes men were, let alone if they had encountered any trouble in making the arrests. Brunet seemed to think, though, that his job was to clear the square and yelled at the panicking people to get going, to get home. One of the first victims was Pastor Upton. He was whacked on the thumb when he brought his arms up to shield his body from a baton blow. Only Inspector Marsom's group on Osler Street stayed in its van until the whistle blast. By the time they lined up outside, according to one constable, there was "considerable confusion"—screaming people running at them, driven west by the city police. Marsom, not knowing what was happening, ordered his men to walk forward to break up the crowd. Given the circumstances, his decision was understandable, but the troop's advance only aggravated an already ugly situation—for everyone on the square. As Wood later admitted, "More than one of our plainclothesmen was struck by our uniform men in the excitement."[22]

The advance of the four police groups effectively emptied the square. The commotion died down after a few minutes and for a short time, it seemed that nothing more was going to happen; everything was remarkably quiet, and some of the police enjoyed a much-needed smoke. Chief Constable Bruton and Assistant Commissioner Wood took this opportunity to leave the safety of the police garage and walk out onto the square to take a look around. But the greeting they got was "rocks, stones, and irons, pretty nearly everything imaginable." In fact, the counter-attack was so swift and so fierce that Bruton, among others, concluded that the trekkers had come to the meeting armed and ready to do battle with the police. It was "not a mob," he remembered, "but an organized gang."[23]

The first reprisal came from the northeast corner, at Halifax and Tenth, where about one hundred and fifty agitated people, a mix of trekkers and local residents, returned to the edge of the square and hurled whatever they could get their hands on in nearby alleys, back yards, and empty lots. "It was just like a hailstorm," remembered Regina citizen Daniel Ehman, "but they did not rain from Heaven." McDougall's men, along with Mounties from the Jones and Marsom units, responded to the shower of missiles by charging the corner with their batons and chasing the group north on Halifax or east on Tenth.

But no sooner had the police withdrawn to the square than a second punishing barrage rained down on them. The Mounties tried to dislodge the group through a series of coordinated sallies. At the sound of a whistle, several men would rush the corner and retreat when the whistle sounded again. They would then be replaced by a batch of fresh men. These tactics, however, proved futile, and several Mounties broke away from their units to join the city police in hunting down those throwing projectiles. Eventually, tear gas was used to try to clear the area.[24]

The skirmishing quickly spread, as other groups started to stone the police from around the square. One of the constables in Marsom's troop recounted, "We had to watch for missiles coming from all over the place." Nor were the trekkers, generally distinguishable by their camp sweaters, wholly responsible for the aerial assault. RCMP sergeant W. W. Hinton reported that Regina citizens, including women, were equally guilty, if not more so. A clutch of people would run out onto the square a few yards, fling a few projectiles, and then scurry into their hiding places until it was safe to do it again. They always tried to keep a certain distance between themselves and the police, so they could not be caught.[25] Others, armed with pieces of wood or metal, went looking for a fight. Young trekkers were seeking revenge after weeks and months of frustration, topped off by a shocking police raid on a peaceful meeting. Local Regina boys, on the other hand, seemed to be lashing out in frustration at their lot in life. At least in taking on a city policeman or Mountie, they could prove their manhood.[26]

The toll on both sides was a heavy one. Without the benefit of shields, several police were bloodied and bruised, some of them seriously, by flying rocks, bricks, wood, even bottles and horseshoes. Inspector Jones's steel helmet was dented during a missile barrage. An unfortunate few became separated from their troops as they tried to chase down their assailants away from the square, and were surrounded by angry mobs. Constable Bligh of the city police was knocked out by a large man wielding a post, while RCMP constable A. W. Francis was hit in the stomach by a large rock and then struck in the back of the head while he was doubled over in pain. By the time Francis was rescued, trekkers Joe Mottl and Sidney Stevens had him helplessly pinned to the ground and were viciously punching and kicking him about the head and torso. Another Mountie, D. W. Parsons, was so badly injured—blinded in one eye—that he retired from the force four months later.

The police, in turn, were equally brutal. Enraged by the stoning, they assumed that anyone found on or near the square that evening was "a danger" and used their batons freely about the bodies and heads of those they managed to run down or corner. One witness vividly recounted a savage beating. "Two mounted police bludgeon[ed] down a striker who had nothing in his hands," he explained, "and the striker attempted to stop the force of their clubs with his bare hands, but they clubbed and beat him down to his knees, and he fell to the ground where he lay apparently unconscious, and they continued to beat him across the head." RCMP constable Welliver, meanwhile, arrested trekker R. A. Ellis with a crack to the head, even though his matted hair and face were already covered in blood. "He appeared to be slightly dazed," Welliver reported in court, "and I thought probably he would not be interested in a riot any further." Some of the police did things they would later deny, if not regret. Sergeant Tom Logan of the city police, for example, steadfastly maintained that he never struck anyone at any time on

Market Square, even though several citizens identified him as one of three policemen they saw beating a man. Indeed, many citizens were appalled by the behaviour of the city police and held them responsible for provoking the riot.

Exactly who did what to whom on the square, however, will never be known. There is too much conflicting evidence. The photographic record is also limited. Ken Liddell, a *Leader-Post* photographer who had been assigned to cover the meeting, fled to Osler when the city police charged the platform. But he returned by the north side of the fire hall and climbed the twelve-foot drill tower, where he snapped three photographs of the skirmishing on the square with his Kodak Volenda camera. Another photographer, Dick Bird, took pictures of the fighting, but regrettably, his film did not turn out.[27]

It was during the hand-to-hand fighting on the square that tragedy struck. Detective Charles Millar of the Regina Police Department had remained behind in the station to assist Inspector Toop and was watching the police battle the trekkers and citizens from a window. Some five minutes after the raid had started, he spotted two city police constables in trouble—men he likely knew—and raced down the stairs and out the garage door. In his hurry, he nearly knocked over Ernest Doran's eight-year-old son. When Millar, dressed in a grey business suit and summer fedora, reached the square, he saw several people trying to break into the toolbox of some street-repair equipment parked near the drill tower. Armed with his revolver and a leather billy in his jacket side pocket, Millar tried to prevent one of the men from getting a shovel from the back of the roller. "There seemed to be a rumpus over near that steam roller," RCMP constable Macara later reported, "something similar to a rugby match ... men piled up on the top of another." During the brawl, Millar was struck on the shoulder and forehead by blows from a shovel and dropped to his knees. Someone then came up from behind, wielding a length of cordwood, and smashed the front of his head, fracturing his skull, almost from ear to ear, and causing a massive brain hemorrhage.[28]

RCMP plain-clothes man E. A. Wakefield, who had been assigned to arrest Matt Shaw, was standing at the edge of the fire hall when he saw Millar go down. He rushed to his side, only to be knocked unconscious, perhaps by the same assailant. City constable Alex Hill also hurried to Millar's assistance. He was photographed by Liddell bending over and trying to lift Millar to his feet by the armpits. But Hill would also be momentarily stunned by a blow and had to get help from fellow constable R. Anderson to drag a lifeless Millar into the police station garage. Here, the detective was temporarily slumped against the wall with other casualties until he could be laid in the back of a patrol wagon and driven to the hospital. As the car headed south on Halifax Street, a single shot was fired into the driver's front door. It made little difference to Millar. He was already dead.[29]

Chief Bruton examined the unconscious Millar in the garage before heading up to his office, where an agitated Colonel Wood had already called in reinforcements. The reserve troop from the Town Station arrived by van just before 8:30 and lined up, ducking rocks and other missiles, on the west side of the square facing the buildings on Osler Street. Sergeant Clarke and his men immediately jumped into the fray by breaking up a large crowd of onlookers anxiously watching the fighting from the sidewalk. These were the same people the city police had chased westward. Many stayed behind out of curiosity to see what would happen next. As Clarke's unit worked its way up Osler towards Tenth Avenue, it was pelted with debris, including a car shock absorber, probably from the Western Spring Company on the corner. The Mounties responded with a baton charge, followed by gas grenades, and then pursued some of the men who were too slow getting away. They caught twenty-eight-year-old labourer John Wedin, a trekker originally from Alberta, armed with a steel pipe behind Isman's Furriers. A camp organizer who had been blacklisted, Wedin tried to resist arrest by grabbing at the legs of his captors and kicking furiously while being dragged away. Another trekker, Sidney Stevens, from the Dundurn relief camp, was brought down with a baton blow. "I was knocked cold," he admitted, "cold as a kipper."[30]

The reserve troop was still trying to dislodge the stone throwers on the northwest corner when the mounted troop galloped up Halifax to Eleventh Avenue. Summoned by a messenger, Inspector Cooper had initially rode off in the wrong direction and had to double back with his troop to the square, where Superintendent Hill, waiting on the front step of city police headquarters, told him to disperse the crowd. Cooper ordered his men to unsheathe the leather truncheons strapped to the left side of their saddles, and then led them at a slow trot west on Eleventh to Osler, where the troop divided in two. Sergeant Major Griffin and his unit rode their horses into the crowd gathered at the BA service station on the corner and drove them west, yelling all the while as if they were pushing cattle. Anyone who refused to budge was deliberately pinned against a wall and clubbed on the head or shoulders. Cooper's men, meanwhile, swept north on Osler in fours and bulldozed before them the people lining the sidewalk. Some foolhardy individuals tried to squeeze as far back as they could into doorways, but could not escape the long reach of the truncheons the men carried like swords resting on their shoulders. Most people simply fled. Garage man William Curtis, for example, had already been knocked down by the city police on Market Square and took refuge in the St. Regis beer parlour as soon as the Mounties appeared on horseback. Once the crowds around the square had been routed, the mounted men went after several stubborn pockets of resistance along Tenth Avenue. They tried to chase down anyone throwing projectiles, pursuing them on their horses down lanes or through backyards, whacking into submission those they caught. Cooper would later brag his troop had no difficulty clearing the square. "No, none at all," he reported. But he added, "The civilians didn't move so quickly."[31]

By 8:50 P.M. Market Square was firmly under mounted police control. While the men on horseback patrolled the streets, riding four abreast along the sidewalks, the van units were lined up in a long double row in front of the city police station and fire hall.[32] Before them, through a lingering haze of tear gas, lay the battlefield, strewn with enough debris to fill five trucks the next day. The operation, from a blinkered perspective, had been a success—two of the most influential trek leaders were in custody. But in making the arrests at a peaceful rally, and in such a ruthless fashion, Wood and Mortimer had incited an equally violent backlash from both trekkers and Regina citizens. Nor was the trouble over. The police may have secured Market Square, but they did so by pushing the crowd into the downtown core. Here, a fiercer, bloodier guerilla war would be fought over the next few hours as darkness descended on Regina. The city and mounted police, reeling from the death of one of their own, were prepared to crush any resistance with their full might.

The trekkers, having kept their emotions in check for so long, wanted a crack at the forces of suppression and what they stood for. From the beginning, Colonel Wood had suggested the trek would eventually become violent. He had made his prediction come true.

CHAPTER TEN

Beaten Off the Streets

Joe Mynnie had his supper at the Clayton Cafe the night of the Market Square meeting. The twenty-three-year-old trekker from Calgary had taken a shine to waitress Maxine Millar and ate virtually every meal there. When Millar finished her shift at seven, Mynnie and his buddy, fellow trekker Ed Amyott, slowly walked her home to her one-room apartment on Rose Street. While Amyott had a nap, Mynnie and Millar listened to the radio and talked. They planned to go later that evening to a dance being held at the Arcadia to raise funds for the trekkers. Shortly after nine, Mynnie fiddled with the radio dial to find some better music. But he tuned in the broadcast of a riot—sounding just like the play-by-play of a hockey game. An incredulous Mynnie insisted that it could not be Regina, that it had to be some other city. But Maxine told him the announcer was naming local streets, not far from where they were. Mynnie woke Amyott, and the pair hurried off, heading south on Rose and then west along Twelfth Avenue towards Scarth Street. Within minutes, they reached the edge of a large crowd, anxiously watching as the trekkers and police battled on downtown streets.[1] Regina might have been a city on holiday, but in the early evening darkness of 1 July, it could easily have been mistaken for an urban war zone. And willingly or not, Mynnie, like many others that night, was swept into the conflagration.

❖ ❖ ❖

The Royal Canadian Mounted Police arrest of Slim Evans and George Black was to be carried out in conjunction with a series of searches for incriminating documents in other parts of Regina.[2] But the fierce fighting in and around Market Square had prevented the Mounties from raiding one important place, the Unity Centre. It was not until almost 9:00 P.M., when some order had been restored on the square, that Detective Inspector Mortimer could execute the search warrants. The way to the hall, one block east of the square on Tenth Avenue, was first cleared of people by Inspector Cooper's mounted troop. They met little resistance as they drove the crowd east with their horses. Pete Mikkelson, president of the Regina Union of Unemployed, watching from inside the centre, saw a Mountie break the front window with his truncheon when he took a wild swing at a fleeing trekker and missed. Inspector Jones's men followed on foot and stood in formation outside as Mortimer, with three RCMP plain-clothes men and two city police detectives, entered the building. The police asked those inside to identify themselves and state their business before they headed downstairs to the basement office. They emerged less than ten minutes later carrying a cardboard box of papers and sped away in a waiting car.[3]

While the raid was underway, RCMP assistant commissioner Wood and Regina chief constable Bruton, holed up in the city police station, tried to anticipate what might happen next. Wood had already sent constables Lovock and Bailey downtown by car to look for any of the other wanted men, in addition to checking on the movements of the trekkers who had been flushed from the square. But before they could report, the calls started to come in. First came the tragic news that Detective Millar had been pronounced dead on arrival at Regina's General Hospital. A pall fell over the station as word of his violent death was quickly passed to the men lining the corridors, gathering in offices, or waiting outside the building for fresh orders. Several anonymous calls followed, each reporting angry mobs of people moving along Eleventh Avenue, west of the square. Just how angry was discovered by four startled Mounties when twenty-five-year-old trekker Casper Blum hurled a brick through the windshield of their squad car near Tenth Avenue and Broad Street. Fortunately, Constable J. I. Mallow sustained only a bruised thigh.

City police constable Archie Apps, walking his beat in the downtown core, was not so lucky. At eight, Apps made his customary call to the desk sergeant and was told to report immediately to the station. He started east on Eleventh, rushing past shops and businesses decorated with flags and bunting in honour of the holiday. Just beyond Rose, he came face-to-face with a frenzied mob, pouring from the lane that ran behind the Army and Navy department store on the other side of the street. Two of the men were later identified by an eyewitness as trekkers Jack Kyle and Sam Coury. Someone in the group yelled, "There's one of the sons of bitches," and they started to pelt Apps with rocks and bricks, bringing him down. Somehow, the injured Apps staggered to his feet and made a desperate race for the station, trailed by several members of the hostile crowd. As he crossed Broad Street, he ran into the bumper of a car headed north. Falling to one knee, Apps was grabbed by the shoulder by one of his pursuers, but managed to break away when his tunic ripped. He reached the safety of the station, bloodied and hobbling, only to be sent out onto the square to help quell the skirmishing.[4]

Apps's assailants were probably some of the first people to flee the square following the initial charge on the speaker's platform. The crowd on Eleventh would quickly grow though, especially after the mounted troop started to clear Osler Street and Tenth Avenue. Many of the trekkers who had been harassing the police from the northwest corner of the square ran westward along Tenth to South Railway Street, where they encountered a gang of Canadian Pacific Railway police patrolling the yards and station. Believing their way to the stadium was blocked, they threw a volley of stones at the police and then made their way south to Eleventh Avenue. Here, they merged with another larger group that had been pushed from the southwest corner of the square by Sergeant Major Griffin's mounted men. In fact, there were so many converging on Eleventh Avenue from nearby streets and lanes that one witness, postal worker George Campbell, described it as "clogged with people."[5]

The commotion on Eleventh Avenue quickly brought out the curious from stores, businesses, and dwellings. People eating in restaurants made for the streets, while small shop owners locked up and stood anxiously outside. Others headed downtown—as if they were going to a parade—when they heard about the trouble on the square. J. A. Cross, a former Saskatchewan attorney-general, was astounded by how many citizens were on the streets that evening. Harold Kritzwiser, a *Leader-Post* reporter who spent two hours on Eleventh between 9:00 and 11:00 P.M., estimated there were literally thousands of civilians lining the sidewalks and intersections in the eight-block area between Osler and Albert streets. All of them would have their stories to tell about that evening.[6]

Few of the citizens had any intention or desire to join the fight. But they were equally determined to stay and watch the next act in the unfolding drama, despite the personal danger they faced on the streets. "I must say," Colonel Wood later told General MacBrien in Ottawa, "that spectators were the greatest hindrance to us in the course of our operations." This was war for the RCMP, and the people had no business being there. The trekkers felt much the same way. Throughout the evening, they would caution citizens not to get involved—this was not their battle—but to go home. Some even temporarily assumed the duties of traffic cop and could be found in the middle of the road directing drivers away from trouble. Clearly, though, many people on the streets supported the trekkers, even going as far as to provide them with weapons. Mike McAuley, who assumed command of the trek following Evans's arrest, later told a Vancouver meeting that two bicycle riders brought a steady supply of rocks in their carriers. Others tried to shield the men from the police or helped the injured from the street. There were also those, like Peter Waltz of the Ritz Cafe, who refused to take sides; Waltz happily escaped the trouble on Eleventh by buying a ticket and watching a movie at the Metropolitan Theatre.[7]

The trekkers, for their part, armed themselves with whatever they chanced upon as they retreated from the square. Many grabbed bricks piled behind businesses or dislodged chunks of concrete and smashed them against the sidewalk to make smaller projectiles. They also helped themselves to construction materials in front of the Army and Navy store and elsewhere. Many could not resist the temptation to break store windows or rip down holiday decorations as they fled from the square. Who could blame them? The police had done more than attack a peaceful meeting—they had struck at the very heart of the trek and what it was about. The men were going to

Ottawa to try to improve their lot in life and that of thousands of other Canadians like them. But the government's response was an iron fist. There would be no jobs, no work and wages. There would be no marriages, homes or children. There would be no hope—just an empty future. It was either back to the camps or back to a life on the road with no end. The bitterness and frustration that many had put behind them when they climbed aboard the freight to head east had all come rushing back, only this time mixed with a new-found rage. And it was the fear of these marauding men and what they were doing that prompted the calls to the police station.[8]

Colonel Wood responded to the news of the trouble downtown by sending half of the mounted troop, under Sergeant Major Griffin, to clear Eleventh Avenue. Inspector Brunet's group was to follow them on foot, ostensibly to deal with any stragglers. None of the Mounties had loaded revolvers. There was one man in each group, however, detailed to carry 250 rounds of ammunition in a haversack. Many of the dismounted men also sported new batons. During the skirmishing on the square, several of the leather-covered, steel-cored riot sticks were either bent out of shape or broken in two. Inspector Jones's baton, for example, snapped close to the head the first time he used it. In their place, the men were issued axe handles with leather straps to go around their wrist. Several witnesses that night, including a newspaper reporter, confirmed that the Mounties were armed with these weapons. There was also some consideration given to reading the Riot Act. Shortly after 9:00, Mayor Cornelius Rink, who was attending a banquet at the German-Canadian Hall, hurried over to the police station to talk to Chief Bruton about what was happening. Bruton and Wood immediately became embroiled in a debate over whether Rink should read the Riot Act that the mayor had been carrying with him in the event of just such trouble. Bruton maintained it was too late, that the fighting was now too dispersed. Wood reluctantly went along with the decision, but he would later claim the failure to use the Riot Act had severely hampered the mounted police and what they had been able to do that evening.[9]

Griffin marched westward along Eleventh Avenue, spreading his men and their horses across the width of the street like a bulldozer. As soon as the troop crossed Broad, according to Dr. Emil Sauer, who was watching from his second-storey office above the Metropolitan Theatre, a small gang of trekkers shouted profanities and threw a few missiles. But the Mounties remained in formation and kept moving forward, calling on people to disperse and shaking their truncheons at those who were slow to move along. "They were ... just riding their horses right up to the crowd, and shooing them like ... a herd of sheep or cattle," explained one observer, "and you had to move." The riders picked up the pace as they neared Rose Street to disperse a larger group yelling and milling around the front of City Hall. They pushed on another two blocks, first to Hamilton, where they chased a knot of people away from the intersection, and then towards Scarth, where a streetcar was stalled because of the growing congestion on the street. The mounted men swung to the left, or south, sidewalk, passing under the post office clock—it was around 9:20. When they came around the front of the streetcar, they were heavily bombarded by a group of trekkers lying in wait for them on the north side of the street. Griffin's troop scattered the crowd, but when Brunet's men reached the same corner minutes later, they too came under fierce attack. Bigger trouble lay just ahead at the next intersection.[10]

About a block and a half away, at 1739 Cornwall, on the east side of the street just north of Eleventh Avenue, was the RCMP Town Station, also known as Cornwall Station. The facility provided the Mounties with a downtown presence in Regina; there were a few offices and a basement guardroom with a row of six cells. The non-commissioned officer in charge of the station was Sergeant John "Dolly" Roberts of the Saskatoon RCMP. As part of the Mountie grand plan that evening, Roberts and a twenty-man unit had moved from the barracks to the station when Sergeant Clarke's reserve troop had been summoned to Market Square to help quell the rioting. Roberts's job was to guard the station and its prisoners, including Slim Evans, while the clerical staff, armed with rifles, protected the barracks.[11]

When Sergeant Roberts and his men climbed out of their van in front of the Town Station, they were welcomed with a missile shower. Roberts decided to give chase and ordered his unit south on Cornwall towards Eleventh Avenue. About the same time, a large group of trekkers came north on Lorne Street, one block west, and turned east on Eleventh. The clash was witnessed by Conductor Bill Norman who had stopped his street car just west of the intersection in front of the Grand Theatre. It was also watched by a crew from Regina radio station CJRM, who, on hearing of the trouble on the square, had scrambled to set up its broadcasting equipment on the roof of the Bank of Montreal building on the southwest corner of Eleventh and Scarth. Announcer Wilfrid Woodill went on the air at 8:50 and had to shout into the microphone to be heard over the clamour from the streets below; it was his blow-by-blow description of the brawling that Joe Mynnie had heard on the radio in his girlfriend's apartment.[12]

As soon as Roberts and his men rounded the corner at Eleventh and Cornwall, they were battered with rocks, bricks, and other debris from the irate trekkers headed towards them. The ferocity of the barrage likely shocked the Mounties, who had not been on the square earlier that evening. For their own safety, Roberts's men withdrew north towards the Town Station, while the trekkers went on a rampage, madly breaking windows along the north side of Eleventh between Lorne and Cornwall. Some of the rocks shattered windows in the streetcar, prompting Norman to tell his passengers to get down on the floor, while he watched nervously from his knees. Roberts decided to charge the intersection a second time, but his men were once again repulsed by a large gang who had gathered in front of the Grand Theatre. This time, though, the trekkers continued to advance on the Mounties, forcing them to retreat all the way back to the Town Station. As one of the trekkers later explained, "The police had us on the run before, and it was the opposite then." A frightened Bill Norman did not want to stick around to see what would happen next and backed his streetcar up to Scarth.[13]

Roberts formed his men in a line across Cornwall Street, in front of the station, determined to hold his ground. The Mounties, however, were like targets in a carnival sideshow, and the trekkers stoned them at will, seemingly from all directions. With bricks and rocks bouncing off his men and the front of the building, Roberts and his corporal lobbed tear gas grenades in the direction of their attackers. But the trekkers simply hurled many of the red canisters back. Badly outnumbered and reeling from the intensity of the assault, Roberts loaded his service revolver and fired a single shot over the heads of the trekkers. The trekkers briefly hesitated, then resumed their offensive. Roberts responded with five more shots, in rapid succession, directly south through the rising tear gas haze. He then went inside the station to call Colonel Wood for reinforcements. "I advised him that we were very hard pressed," he later recounted, "and didn't think that we would be able to hold out much longer." The next morning, the superintendent of the Canada Life Building found a 45-calibre slug on the floor of the Huron and Erie office.[14]

Wood assumed that the attack on Cornwall Station was an attempt by the trekkers to rescue the prisoners being held inside. Why else would they be shelling Roberts and his men? He consequently put out the order shortly before 9:30 for all men to be issued ammunition. He then sent Inspector Cooper and his mounted troop down Eleventh Avenue—about fifteen to twenty minutes behind Griffin and Brunet—while the Marsom and Clarke units got back into their moving vans and headed for the Town Station. Inspector Marsom was detailed to transfer the prisoners from the station to the barracks, where they would presumably be out of the trekkers' reach; Sergeant Clarke, on the other hand, was to work with Roberts and other RCMP units in securing the area around the station. Wood's decision to send armed men into such a volatile situation threatened to turn the conflict into a bloodbath, especially since some of the constables had been on the force for less than a year and had little experience. But he seemed more than justified when another telephone message was received right after Roberts's call. A frantic Wilfred McCubbin reported that a group of trekkers was breaking into his hardware store in the Somerset Block, at Eleventh Avenue and Smith Street, to get at the guns and ammunition. Staff Inspector McDougall of the city police rounded up sixteen constables who were not too badly injured, including Archie Apps, and sped off west in a patrol wagon and a private vehicle. RCMP Inspector Jones and his men, together with a handful of city constables under Sergeant Tom Logan, remained behind at the square to defend the station until they were needed elsewhere.[15]

Sergeant Roberts's warning shots persuaded his attackers to pull back to Eleventh Avenue. Here, they were joined by another group of trekkers being pushed westward by Griffin's mounted troop. Some of the cooler heads yelled at the men to get into fours to march back to the stadium. Alex Steuart, who was working at the United Cigar Store on the northeast corner of Eleventh and Cornwall, watched as a ragtag column of about 100 to 150 men, many of them with bloodied faces, formed up and started to march west. Several had the words On-to-Ottawa scrawled on the back of sweaters, overalls, and hats; others wore the fund-raising badges that had been prepared by the Citizens' Emergency Committee. Once in line, they started to sing "Hold the Fort." RCMP constable F. M. Murray remembered hearing the song as he stood outside the Town Station. Sergeant Major Griffin, about a block behind the trekker column, might have too. But it was the sound of Roberts's shots, plainly audible to those outside the Bank of Montreal at Scarth, that prompted Griffin to order his mounted troop to halt—it was not clear who was doing the shooting and whether there was more to come. After waiting for at least five minutes, the mounted troop resumed its street-clearing activities. Its approach, however, alarmed the marching trekkers. Someone in the column yelled, "Hold, here they come." The men swung around to face the mounted troop, while several near the back of the column pushed parked cars across the intersection, from the northwest corner to the southeast, to form a barricade.[16]

As the barrier was being erected, Griffin stopped his men again, about halfway between Scarth and Cornwall. He then ordered his troop forward—effectively into battle. The trekkers responded with a punishing shower of missiles, much like archers in medieval times. The intensity of the stoning forced the Mounties to ride north through a lane behind the Town Station and then swoop down, at full gallop with truncheons raised, from Cornwall. The trekkers behind the barricade tried to withstand the charge, desperately chucking whatever they had in their hands and pockets. But they were quickly overrun and routed by the men on horseback. Most escaped south on Cornwall, while others, like Fred Nogami, the only known Asian member of the trek, disappeared into alleys or empty lots. Those who remained behind were chased down like animals. Nick Schaack, originally from South Dakota, was one of those apprehended. The fifty-two-year-old trekker, with greying hair and beard and horn-rimmed glasses, was nabbed with a stone in each hand in a vacant lot near Cornwall Station and struck senseless. "They had absolutely no chance," recalled Edward Powell of the Saskatchewan Wheat

Pool. "They were unmercifully beaten off the streets." Allan Miller was even more damning: "I was pretty much incensed by the terrorism and brutality exhibited by the police.... They charged, it did not matter who was there, citizens, strikers or anybody else."[17]

Nor did the mounted police let up once the worst of the fighting was over. Up to then, the Mounties had concentrated on clearing the streets and arresting those who offered any resistance. But once the apparent siege of Cornwall Station had been ended, the RCMP decided to pick up any trekker they could get their hands on. They seemed to believe the trouble on the streets would not be over until the trekkers were off the streets, and they did not care how they accomplished it. Once the reinforcement units consequently arrived in the area, the mounted police went hunting for trekkers. While Griffin's troop ranged over several blocks, the Roberts, Brunet, and Clarke units patrolled the nearby streets and lanes on foot. They were assisted by several plainclothes men, including Inspector Mortimer, who had taken the seized materials from the Unity Centre to the Town Station by ambulance.[18]

Many of the trekkers, driven from Cornwall and Eleventh, decided to try to return to the stadium. They realized they were no match for the Mounties on horseback. But as they worked their way westward along streets or through lanes, in twos and threes, or formed up into larger groups, they were repeatedly intercepted by Griffin's troop and turned back. Ken Forsyth, a trekker from Regina, for example, was part of a gang of about twenty-five marching men on its way to the stadium that was ambushed twice by the Mounties—first on Tenth and then on Eleventh. Regina citizen Robert Scott might have witnessed one of these incidents. "When they [trekkers] got to the lane ... a number of police came out on horseback and rode in amongst them, striking at them and knocking some of them down," he vividly remembered. "They seemed to be determined on breaking them up, and not letting them get to the stadium." This determination to mete out some punishment to the trekkers led to some interesting incidents on the downtown streets. On Scarth, an overzealous Mountie reportedly chased some men into Ryan's Cafe, but got his horse stuck in the vestibule. One block east, on Hamilton, another Mountie apparently drove a trekker through the plate glass window of Lorne Electric with his horse. And on Eleventh, Constable R. S. Edge crashed headlong into a lamp-post and fell to the ground; he managed to get back on his horse, but only after being stoned by the men he was pursuing. While the credibility of some of these stories is debatable, they serve to underscore how the mounted men roamed the streets that evening as a law unto themselves.[19]

The blockade may have seemed the right thing to do at the time, but ironically, it prolonged the fighting on the streets. As word quickly passed among the trekkers that the way to the stadium was closed, they squeezed between buildings, hid in back yards, or slipped down alleys. A few took to rooftops, joining dozens of spectators already there watching the action. Whenever a police patrol passed below, the trekkers would bomb them with rocks and bricks. The Griffin troop sustained some of its heaviest shelling from the top of the Crescent Furniture Store at the corner of Lorne and Eleventh. Those concealed in lanes, meanwhile, played a kind of peekaboo with the police. They would wait until the Mounties had passed, run out and throw a few stones, and then scurry back into the darkness. A few became quite bold, like trekker Kellet Cole, who donned a Mountie's steel helmet and waged his own little war with rocks and stones. Others paid a stiff price for their resistance. Gordon Phillips, an unemployed lumber worker who had come east with the trek, and another, unknown man stepped out from an unlit alley just west of the Canada Life Building and hurled some rocks at a group of mounted policemen at the corner of Eleventh and Cornwall. A pair of Mounties rushed to the head of the lane, fired several shots in the direction of the fleeing men, and then returned to their unit. Phillips was struck three times, once in the left leg and twice below the right knee. Momentarily paralyzed, he was carried by fellow trekker Casper Blum and several others into the back of the Silver Dollar Cafe before being taken to hospital. He would require months of medical treatment.[20]

Some trekkers, like Joe Mynnie, kept on the move. He and his friend Amyott went west on Twelfth, north on Scarth to the post office, and then back along Eleventh to Rose and the safety of his girlfriend's apartment. Still others tried to elude capture by hiding in doorways behind the spectators who stood several rows deep on the sidewalks. In fact, many citizens flatly refused to leave the streets, often arguing with the Mounties about their right to be there. At other times, whenever a patrol went by, there would be a chorus of loud boos and catcalls from the crowd. One indignant woman called RCMP constable A. J. Lilly of the Roberts unit a "yellow-striped bastard" and other nasty names. These insults did little to deflect the police from their work. Scanning over the heads of the crowd, they would spot a trekker at the back, drag him out by the scruff of the neck, and haul him away to the station—usually clubbing him several times. Trekker John Smith, a former bank clerk from England, was grabbed from behind on Cornwall by Inspector Mortimer. Smith evidently matched the description of Detective Millar's murderer, and he was unceremoniously dragged by one arm down the stairs at the Town Station.[21]

It took the mounted police about half an hour from the time of Roberts's call to secure the area around the Town Station and as far north as Railway Avenue. But in driving the trekkers away from Eleventh and Cornwall, while at the same time preventing them from returning to the stadium, the RCMP created a new trouble spot one block southeast at Twelfth and Scarth. Indeed, the second major downtown battle of the evening was largely the Mounties' doing—albeit unintentionally. When Inspector Cooper led his mounted troop west on Eleventh around 9:30, on the heels of the Griffin unit, he encountered his first large group of stone-throwing trekkers just beyond Rose, around the grounds of City Hall. The troop wheeled around and jumped over the small railing in front of the building, easily scattering the men. "They ran for all they were worth," recounted Cooper. The troop then continued west to Scarth, where another gang of trekkers, including several driven from the Town Station area, had erected another car barricade. Cooper was reluctant to send his troop "into the crowd . . . because there were too many civilians, too many women and children." But his mounted men still managed to push most of the trekkers south on Scarth to Twelfth Avenue, where they joined those who had bolted in that direction during the Town Station battle. Cooper's men dispersed yet another gang just west of Cornwall—once again sending many of them south to Twelfth—before riding on to the Albert Street subway, four blocks away, where they turned around and headed back east on Eleventh. At Cornwall, because of lingering tear gas in the area, the troop turned south and unwittingly headed into the eye of a new storm on Twelfth Avenue. But as in the case of Market Square, it was the Regina city police who found themselves once again on the front line that evening.[22]

The squad of city policemen that responded to the call from McCubbin's Hardware left the station with a grim resolve—and memories of their late comrade, Charles Millar. The Scottish-born Millar had fought in the Great War before joining the Regina force in 1920 and becoming a detective nine years later. He was a respected cop, but even more so because of his personal circumstances. Millar's wife died giving birth to their daughter in 1927, and he had been raising Margaret with the help of a hired woman. The little girl was now an orphan. When Chief Bruton sent his constables back into battle, then, it seemed to be understood there had to be some kind of reckoning. Ed Stern, a prominent local coal merchant who was inside the station after the raid on the platform, said as much when it was learned that Millar had been killed. "Somebody is going to pay for this," he told another citizen in the corridor. This need for retribution was reinforced when the patrol wagon carrying the city constables was pelted with rocks and other missiles as it raced along Eleventh to the hardware store. Staff Inspector McDougall and his men were already distraught because of what had happened on the square. The stoning of their vehicle only inflamed their sense of grievance.[23]

When the Regina city police reached McCubbin's store, they found no signs of any forced entry or any trekkers. Believing that rioters might still be in the area, McDougall led his eighteen men east from Smith along Eleventh towards the Cornwall Station. They had travelled only a block when a civilian came running up, claiming that a large body of trekkers had headed south on Lorne, apparently intending to seize the Hotel Saskatchewan on Victoria Avenue. The city police marched at double time down Lorne to Twelfth and then turned east, past Cornwall, to confront a huge crowd, numbering several hundred, outside the Capitol Theatre at the corner of Scarth. As McDougall's men approached, dozens of trekkers ran into the bushes in Victoria Park on the south side of Twelfth, while others took up positions behind a barricade of cars thrown across the intersection. A third group secretly waited in a lane between Cornwall and Scarth, behind the McCallum-Hill building on the north side of Twelfth. Once the police were in the trap, the trekkers launched a withering missile attack from three sides. What made things worse was that it was impossible to see the rocks coming in the darkness. The constables desperately tried to shield their heads with their arms, but several were knocked down. "Nobody could realize it unless he was there," related Patrol Sergeant J. A. Lynch. "They were coming over just like hail stones ... and the situation was getting very dangerous. For a minute I didn't know what we were going to do." Constable Archie Apps believed they were "all in danger of being killed."[24]

Seeing no other way out, McDougall ordered his men to fall back a few paces and draw their revolvers. He then gave the command to shoot over the heads of the crowd. The constables fired several rounds in the air, sending people fleeing east on Twelfth or north on Scarth towards Eleventh. At least a hundred ran screaming into the lobby of the McCallum-Hill Building seeking shelter. As the panic subsided, a plain-clothes Mountie, Constable Walter Hutchinson, pulled up in a car and asked if the city police needed any assistance. Since several members of his squad were out of bullets—they had only six rounds each—McDougall asked Hutchinson to drive Constable W. G. Wilson to the city police station to retrieve more ammunition. He then went inside nearby Fell's Cafe, where he called Chief Bruton to report the shooting and the dispatch of Wilson. When McDougall emerged from the restaurant, Cooper's mounted troop had arrived and was busy clearing any remaining people away from the intersection, driving many of them north on Scarth. The Mounties then proceeded south to the Hotel Saskatchewan, where they patrolled around Victoria Park searching for any trekkers hiding in the bushes.[25]

McDougall expected to hold his men at the corner of Twelfth and Scarth for at least fifteen minutes. But Sergeant J. McPhee, who had just returned to the station after being treated at the hospital, was immediately dispatched with ammunition when McDougall's call came. It was just before 10:00 P.M. Once the shells McPhee brought were distributed, McDougall led his squad, walking in fours and swinging their batons, north on Scarth, on the west sidewalk. One block ahead at Eleventh were three stalled streetcars and another large crowd of trekkers and citizens. When the city police reached the Monico Cafe, just south of the intersection, a trekker climbed atop the middle streetcar and waved to a group on the other side. Stones and other debris started to fly at the police, but fell short of their intended target. The trekkers then moved to the northeast corner, by the Imperial Bank and the adjoining Bank of Nova Scotia, and unleashed a terrific bombardment. The police, who had advanced to the opposite corner, were, in the words of McDougall, "right in among the rocks again." As missiles struck the Bank of Montreal building to their backs, McDougall shouted at his men to spread out, draw their revolvers, and fire at will. This time, though, there would be no warning shots. The constables discharged volley after volley into the crowd. "When one or two of them started to tumble over," McDougall half-jokingly recalled, "they took to their heels."[26]

Miraculously, no one was killed by the shooting spree. But the street was littered with the wounded, and the call quickly went out for ambulances. Ernest Baugh, an assistant undertaker, picked up two people at Ryan's Cafe on Scarth and three at the Unique Cafe on Eleventh and took them to Grey Nuns' Hospital in his hearse. Citizens also brought around their cars to help ferry the wounded who lay bleeding on the sidewalk or hunched over against buildings.

According to hospital records, more than a dozen trekkers were injured by gunfire, but only a few of them seriously. Tom McMurray of Vancouver suffered a broken femur and spent several months recuperating. So too did David Lyons who was shot in the abdomen and suffered a punctured intestine. Phillip Duignan had a bullet lodged next to his spine, but had it safely removed. The actual toll was probably higher than the records show, because some of the wounded trekkers went into hiding rather than risk possible arrest. Tony Tom, hit in the leg, crawled under one of the streetcars and had to be fished out, crying in pain, by the Regina city police. But there is no hospital record for him. It was also rumoured that Bill Hammill, one of the trek advance men, had been shot. The *Leader-Post* reported that he had been felled by a bullet to the stomach and then whisked away in a private car. But at the time of the shooting, Hammill was sitting in a cell at the Town Station, having been picked up two hours earlier by the RCMP during a raid on a private home.[27]

A number of spectators were also injured. Railway section foreman

Joseph Slabick, standing with his hands in his pockets on the corner, was shot in the right hand and leg; a doctor removed the bullet in the lobby of the Champlain Hotel. Bill Rogers of Purity Dairy was watching from the doorway of the Apostolic Mission, about halfway up Scarth, when he was wounded in the chest. Jimmie Cross, a shipper for Chrysler Motors, was hit in the groin. One of the most surprised victims was Joe Rothecker, who had been drinking beer that evening. Rothecker was standing three full city blocks away at Broad when one of the constables fired down Eleventh Avenue. He suddenly fell to the sidewalk, thinking that it was a stroke, only to discover that he been shot in the neck. There was at least one other wounding on Eleventh—but not from the shooting at Scarth. During his trip to the city police station to retrieve more ammunition, Constable Wilson fired wildly into the crowd from the passenger window of the sedan as it sped recklessly east on Eleventh. Several witnesses reported seeing flashes from a dark car and then hearing the breaking of the window of the Glasgow House on the southeast corner of Hamilton. Wilson did the same thing on the return trip along Eleventh, but this time, leaning out the window, shot an unknown trekker in the shoulder at Rose. He may also have hit another man further down the street.[28] He would never be disciplined.

When Wilson rejoined McDougall's unit at Scarth, the city constables reloaded their guns for a second time and then stood guard in the immediate area for at least the next half hour; it was only after McDougall was convinced there would be no more trouble that he split his men into pairs and sent them to patrol the nearby streets. This mopping-up operation was performed in concert with the RCMP. The sound of the shooting had brought the two mounted units trotting to the corner—one from the south, the other from the west—where they were united for the first time since leaving the square. Cooper, nursing a fractured clavicle, put a solid row of armed horsemen across the intersection from the Bank of Montreal to the post office, in addition to sending out riders to encourage citizens to go home or at least get off the streets. Inspector Brunet was also drawn to the corner and, after conferring with McDougall about the clash, ordered twelve rounds of ammunition to be issued to each unmounted man in his unit. It may have been an unnecessary show of force—a kind of exclamation point—but the message was brutally simple. If the trekkers offered any more resistance, the combined police forces were ready to end it at gunpoint.[29]

Few of the trekkers, though, had much fight left in them. They were tired, hungry, and beaten—more than ready to return to the stadium. In fact, the only remaining problem area was around Regina's City Hall, where trekkers had been repeatedly scattered, but never cleaned out. This job fell to RCMP Inspector Jones and his unit, which had been held in reserve at Market Square for just such an eventuality. Arriving by van at the intersection of Eleventh and Hamilton, the Mounties found a gang of trekkers, some of them fresh from the shooting at Scarth, throwing rocks from behind three cars strung north-south from the United Cigar Store to the Royal Bank. The Jones troop rushed the men three times, but was able to dislodge them and secure the area only with the use of tear gas. Those arrested included Morris Dean, one of the trek Red Cross men, who tripped and fell as he tried to escape. When the lunch pail that served him as a first-aid kit was opened, two rocks fell on the ground. As one of the policemen summed up the outcome: "And that practically seemed to finish the fighting all night."[30]

The city police remained downtown until just past midnight, when they returned to the station for new orders. Most of the constables were told to get some sleep, while the sergeants were paired with detectives and sent out by car to patrol the streets through the night. Any trekker found, even if he was just sitting half asleep on a curb or step, was arrested and charged with vagrancy. Anyone who seemed the least bit suspicious was also picked up. Alex Theodor of the Regina Union of Unemployed had just left the Olympia Cafe when he was stopped and taken into custody for rioting. Even Joe Mynnie's luck ran out. He and two other trekkers were spotted drinking bottled milk that they had just bummed for breakfast and were apprehended in a nearby garage. The arrests brought the number being held to forty-two—well beyond the capacity of the seventeen single cells at the city station. The situation was even worse at the RCMP Town Station, where there were only six cells. During the night, Corporal J. E. Wright registered fifty-seven prisoners in his log book.[31]

The RCMP tried to relieve some of the congestion in the Town Station cells by transferring prisoners to the guard room at the barracks. Colonel

Wood had initially ordered the movement of trek leader Slim Evans and others when Sergeant Roberts had made his desperate call from the station for help. But it was subsequently decided to wait until the riot had subsided before attempting to move the men. It was not until 10:30, then, that the first batch of prisoners arrived at the barracks. A second group followed just before midnight. That left twenty-three men in the town cells. But in reducing one problem, the Mounties created another. The barracks guard room had been built for only ten prisoners, and some of the men had to be held in handcuffs in the corridor.[32]

Evans was among the second shipment of prisoners. He had to remove his jacket, vest, pants, and boots so that they could be searched before he was placed in a cell with Nick Schaack, who was moaning in a semi-conscious state in the lower bunk. Schaack's transfer to the barracks jail seems to have been a mistake—one that the Mounties later tried to cover up and deny. While the fighting was raging outside the Town Station, Doctors J. M. Le Boldus and D. S. Johnstone had been summoned to attend to the incoming injured. They did an initial assessment of Constable Walter McDonald's flattened nose and Constable R. J. Gammie's broken collarbone. They also examined trekker John Wedin's bloodied head; he was evidently considered so critical that it was decided not to place him in a cell. All three men were sent to hospital, but not Schaack, even though he was later remembered by Corporal J. E. Wright, provost at the station, as having severe head injuries. It is not even clear whether either doctor had a look at him. Schaack, according to Evans, was in "a very bad way." He had a swollen face, two split lips, and blood oozing from one ear. Corporal James Lyons, the provost in charge of the barracks cells, summoned the RCMP surgeon, Dr. Samuel Moore, who diagnosed a mild concussion and recommended the application of cold compresses. Moore visited Schaack several times throughout the night, between attending to the injured Mounties in the base hospital. By morning, Schaack had reportedly recovered. "He was not quite right," Corporal Lyons observed, "but he could get around. He didn't eat anything, but he had—he had some coffee." Schaack made a brief court appearance later that day and was then taken to the Regina jail.[33]

Most of the seriously injured were sent to one of Regina's two hospitals—

either the General or Grey Nuns'—where doctors and nurses started to report for duty as soon as word of the riot spread. In fact, Regina police chief Bruton was so alarmed by the number and apparent severity of the casualties that he sent Inspector Toop to Regina General Hospital at 9:00 P.M. to help coordinate triage. Those admitted—fifty-five in total—came in two waves: first from the skirmishing at Market Square and then from the shooting at Eleventh and Scarth. But for the doctors and nurses dealing with the wounded, the evening's chaos all ran together. No sooner had they dealt with the first large group of injuries then the second large group started to arrive. In retrospect, it is astounding that no one else was killed. But the lack of fatalities does not lessen the extent and nature of the injuries—to trekkers, policemen, and citizens. There were broken bones to be set, cuts to be stitched, deep contusions to be treated, and bullets to be extracted. Many also suffered from shock. One of the worst cases was that of RCMP constable Edward Wakefield, who had been knocked unconscious on the square, perhaps by the same person who had killed Millar. Wakefield's blood pressure was dangerously low, and at one point it was feared he might die.[34]

Those trekkers who were taken to hospital for treatment were placed under guard by the RCMP. All of them faced charges of rioting. The mounted police also surrounded and held captive the hundreds of trekkers who had remained at the stadium instead of attending the Market Square meeting. Just after midnight, eighty men from the unmounted units returned to the barracks, ate a hot lunch, and two hours later went back on duty at the exhibition grounds—only this time, with rifles and .303 ammunition. The Mounties were placed in a cordon around the stadium, while a huge spotlight atop nearby Grey Nuns' Hospital was focused on the front doors. A dummy machine gun was also mounted on the roof. The police later claimed they took the men hostage to prevent further fighting during the night. But by this time, many of the trekkers just wanted to get away. News of the riot at Market Square did not reach the men back at the stadium watching the ball game until after 9:00 P.M. Some talked about heading downtown—if they could break through the mounted police blockade—but were held back by cooler heads. Several others were worried about what lay ahead for them, especially after the police raid on the meeting, and had quietly slipped out of Regina as quickly as they could. They did not want to wait around and be saddled with the blame.[35]

What the fallout from the riot might be no one could predict that night; there had been little time to sort out all that had happened on the square and downtown. The *Regina Leader-Post*, for example, printed a series of extras through the evening that constantly adjusted the number of dead, from one trekker, to Detective Millar and a trekker, to Millar and "two others reportedly dying." CFCN, the voice of Calgary, meanwhile, sent an urgent appeal to its Regina correspondent for information: "Understand police shooting down strikers send full particulars." Even Colonel Wood, the architect of the botched police raid, had only a vague idea of what his men had faced and how they responded—he did not even know they had used their guns. The saddest part of the evening came later that night when a CNR passenger train returned from a holiday excursion to nearby Lumsden. The train had been deliberately held on the outskirts of the city while the riot raged downtown. By the time it finally pulled into the station, several hours late, news boys were hawking their extras. A sleepy Margaret Millar was startled to hear that Detective Millar had been killed. "That is my daddy," she shouted. Then she started to cry.[36]

CHAPTER ELEVEN

Decency and Tact

Jimmy Gardiner blamed the Bennett Conservatives for what had happened during the Market Square meeting. After all, when the Saskatchewan premier first learned the Royal Canadian Mounted Police had been ordered to stop the On-to-Ottawa Trek in Regina—by force, if necessary—he had publicly warned Prime Minister R. B. Bennett that a riot would be the only outcome. But instead of trying to score some easy political points at the expense of the prime minister, Gardiner's more immediate concern in the first few days of July was to get the On-to-Ottawa trekkers out of Saskatchewan as soon as possible. He had never wanted the men there and regarded their continued presence in the capital as a nagging reminder of how the Bennett government had usurped provincial authority. He also seemed to believe that Regina could not begin to recover from the Dominion Day debacle until the trekkers were on their way, and with them, the possibility of any further trouble. Gardiner's intervention, though, did little to lessen the tension and mistrust of the past few weeks. In fact, no sooner had the fighting stopped than the finger-pointing started. The trekkers denounced the police for attacking a peaceful rally, while the police accused the trekkers of coming to the meeting armed and ready for battle. The federal and provincial governments, meanwhile, opened a new front in their continuing war of words, this time over Saskatchewan's decision to disband the trekkers as a group from Regina. No one seemed ready to set aside their differences and begin the search for answers, preferring instead to cling to their own version of the events, regardless of the cost to the truth.

❖ ❖ ❖

Dawn on Tuesday, 2 July could not come soon enough for the hundreds of downtown workers anxious to survey the damage from the riot. Inspector Fred Toop of the Regina City Police drove around the centre of the city shortly after sunrise and counted 120 broken plate glass windows. This figure would almost double once people had the chance to inspect buildings and tally up the damage. There were entire blocks between Eleventh and Twelfth Avenues, and a six-block stretch along Eleventh, where nearly every glass pane had been smashed or cracked. All ten showcase windows of the Crescent Furniture Store at Eleventh and Lorne Street, for example, had been damaged during the fierce fighting near the RCMP Town Station. Broken glass, several inches deep in places, lay mixed on the streets with rocks, bricks, wood, and other debris. Civic cleaning gangs, sent into action early with brooms, shovels, and wheelbarrows, would gather by late afternoon "enough stones to build a cobble road and enough wood to build a barn." They might also have been able to build a small house: three thousand bricks were reported missing from a pile behind Central Auto Body on Lorne. Other damage was not so easily cleaned up or repaired. The Imperial Bank and the Canada Permanent buildings, at the corner of Eleventh and Scarth Street, bore the tell-tale white pock marks of bullets, while the sidewalks had been stained by pooling blood. The carnage fed the imagination of local children, who found a new game to play during their summer holidays: police and strikers.[1]

Colonel Wood was also up early that morning—if he had slept at all—and telephoned the RCMP commissioner at 6:00 A.M. to report that the riot had been successfully quelled. He also assured General MacBrien that no member of the force had fired a shot at any time. Two hours later, Wood called Premier Gardiner and Attorney-General Tommy Davis to discuss the events of the previous evening, including his decision to arrest the trek leaders at the Market Square meeting. It was then—and only then, Wood would later claim—that he learned that a trek delegation had met with Gardiner late Monday afternoon to find a way out of the impasse and that the Saskatchewan cabinet had just begun to consider the trekkers' request when someone called the legislature with news of the outbreak of the riot. Colonel Wood's recollection of these conversations was quite matter-of-fact, but it is readily apparent from the telegrams Gardiner exchanged with Prime Minister Bennett that the premier was seething with rage and was not going to watch events from the sidelines anymore. In a telegraph dated 1 July, but not sent until early the following morning, Gardiner angrily complained about the police operation, especially at a time when such trouble could have been avoided if he had been consulted. He then offered the prime minister a way out of the mess. "We are nevertheless prepared," he declared, "to undertake this work of disbanding the men without sending them to Lumsden." Bennett responded by simply asking for more details "in order that there may be no misunderstanding."[2]

Gardiner seized upon the prime minister's reply as the opening he needed and instructed Tommy Davis to get a trekker delegation to his office as soon as possible so that the negotiations from the day before could continue. Colonel Wood, when contacted about the request, offered no objection and allowed a small group, headed by Mike McAuley, to go to the legislature around 10:00 A.M. on the understanding that none of the men would be arrested. The premier asked the five-man delegation whether they were still interested in disbanding under provincial direction. McAuley said yes, but at the same time refused to enter into any agreement unless it was witnessed by the mounted police, particularly in light of what had happened the night before. Gardiner sent immediately for Wood, who revealed that his latest orders from Ottawa were to feed the trekkers, now under armed guard at the stadium, only at the Lumsden camp. The delegation countered they would never be forced into the camp. At this point, the premier interceded and announced in front of everyone that the men were going to be fed that day at the stadium—either by the federal government or by the provincial one, but they were going to be fed. He also bluntly told Wood that Saskatchewan was prepared to assert its authority over the mounted police. He reminded the assistant commissioner how the province had been without a police force for the past few weeks and warned that if the Mounties were not placed under his direction in the next twenty-four hours, he would organize another force.[3]

Gardiner's tough words were backed up by two forceful telegrams, which made no attempt to mask the premier's fury in the aftermath of the riot. In a wire to the federal minister of Justice, Tommy Davis challenged the federal government's authority to interfere in the administration of justice in the province and condemned the decision to arrest the trek leaders—"without our knowledge or concurrence"—as reckless. "This action on your part has gone too far now," Davis admonished his federal counterpart, "and I demand that you forthwith instruct the police to take orders from me and me alone." In the other telegram, Gardiner chided the prime minister for trying to precipitate "a riot worse than last night" by starving the trekkers into submission. And the premier was not going to allow it. "These men should be fed where they are," he scolded Bennett, "and immediately disbanded and sent back to camps and homes as they request." He also maintained that the province had a responsibility to protect its citizens from "this imported trouble" and was going to exercise this duty despite any federal orders. To this end, Gardiner gave the federal government two hours to feed the trekkers or Saskatchewan would act on its own.[4]

While Bennett chewed on Gardiner's ultimatum, the men in the stadium had gone at least eighteen hours without eating. At first light, a lone trekker slipped out the front door and headed towards town and the promise of breakfast. But he was quickly escorted back to his temporary prison by a rifle-toting Mountie. Over the next hour, groups of two or three tested the police blockade with the same disappointing result. Only Sam Anderson, whose head had been grazed by a bullet, was allowed to leave to go the hospital for treatment. The remainder of the men were forced to wait out the morning, not knowing if and when they were to be fed, let alone what the future held for them. Several of the more adventurous climbed out on the roof of the stadium and, stretching out in the sun, watched the police patrolling the exhibition grounds or waved to the newspapermen keeping a vigil on the roof of Grey Nuns' Hospital. Others smoked and talked about their situation or tried to catch up on some sleep after their anxious night. But as the day wore on, the boredom and frustration only magnified the men's hunger, and they became restless. No one, though, was prepared to confront the heavy police guard. For Ron Liversedge and his fellow trekkers, the stadium had become "the first Canadian concentration camp.[5]

At 1:30 P.M., Gardiner's two-hour deadline had elapsed, and he summoned Colonel Wood to his office again. The premier indicated that the province intended to feed the trekkers and that he wanted to meet with them at the stadium to discuss the arrangements. Wood agreed to take Gardiner and Attorney-General Davis to the exhibition grounds and, during the drive, tried to convince the Saskatchewan officials that it would be best, given the mood of the city, if the men were kept confined to the stadium and fed there over the next few days. The premier, however, had more ambitious plans. He wanted the trekkers out of the city by the next morning and had already contacted the Canadian Pacific Railway about the possibility of chartering a special train made up of colonist cars. To his surprise, the railway now seemed ready to cooperate with the province, but the details still had to be worked out.[6]

At the stadium, Gardiner and Davis had a frank and amicable discussion with the trekkers' strategy committee—in the absence of Wood. They offered to feed the men three meals a day, demobilize them from Regina as a group, and transport them to their point of origin, whether it be their home or the community nearest to their relief camp. They also gave their assurance that any man under arrest would be tried in a provincial court and receive a fair trial.

The province's proposal met with the general approval of the committee. And why not? The trekkers were to be disbanded based on essentially the same plan that had been put forward to the federal government only a day earlier. But when Gardiner, anxious to see the men on their way, suggested that travel registration begin almost immediately, Mike McAuley pleaded for more time. He disclosed there were as many as two hundred men who had not made it back to the stadium the night of the riot, and he wanted to wait at least a day to see whether any of the missing rejoined the trek. Four trekkers had hid the night of the riot in the home of social activists Ed and Marjorie Cooper and were safely helped out of the city the following day. McAuley also wanted to know if the men were to be fed downtown at restaurants. Gardiner replied that he hoped to secure equipment from the near-empty Lumsden camp so that food could be prepared at the stadium. Until then, the men would have to make do with coffee and sandwiches, which the province supplied at 5:00 P.M. It was the first meal for most of the trekkers in twenty-four hours.[7]

While the negotiations were underway, Prime Minister Bennett finally responded to the province's offer to disband the trekkers. In a mid-afternoon telegram, he stated that Ottawa was "ready and willing" to feed the men at Lumsden, but was opposed to returning them to Vancouver as a group "in view of the illegal character of their organization and avowed purposes of their leaders." But, he continued, if the Saskatchewan government wanted to assume responsibility for the trekkers, "we have no intention of interfering with any action you may decide to take that does not involve these men in violation of the laws of the country." Despite their patronizing tone, Bennett's comments were seen by Gardiner as a victory. The federal government was finally surrendering some ground. But the comments did not in any way represent a capitulation. If Saskatchewan wanted to attend to the trekkers, then it would have to do so on its own—as Gardiner quickly discovered. Following his return to his office in the late afternoon, the premier called the minister of National Defence to see whether the Lumsden equipment could be transferred to the Regina exhibition grounds. The minister turned him down flatly. There was also some question as to who was going to pay the hospital expenses of the injured trekkers. The federal Department of Labour wanted nothing to do with the men now that the province was handling their demobilization.[8]

This ongoing feud between Saskatchewan and Ottawa spilled over into the House of Commons debate on the riot. That afternoon, Hugh Guthrie, the minister of Justice, rose in his seat to defend the federal government's action. He recounted how Ottawa had been prepared to disband the trekkers, but they had insisted on returning to Vancouver, in his words, "as an organized revolutionary body." He also claimed that the mounted police were executing warrants at a "Communist gathering" when they were attacked by the trekkers. "The government is just as determined to maintain peace and order in Regina or any other part of Canada where disorder may break out," he vowed in a thinly veiled swipe at Gardiner. J. S. Woodsworth, the leader of the Co-operative Commonwealth Federation (CCF), spoke in response from the Opposition benches. He began on a note of caution, reminding Guthrie that the government had been repeatedly told there would be a violent clash in Regina and warning of future clashes if the government persisted in its heavy-handed treatment of the unemployed. "There is no doubt of that," he observed. Woodsworth then took issue with Guthrie's portrayal of the Market Square meeting, suggesting instead that it was a peaceful gathering until brutally raided by the police. "Communists may be a menace to democracy," he argued, "but ... the arbitrary action of government is a greater menace.... The people of Canada have a right not merely to freedom of movement, freedom of action, and freedom of association, but they have a right to live—and to live decently."[9]

Liberal leader Mackenzie King spoke next. Normally, as leader of the Opposition, he would have been expected to lead the debate against the government. In fact, King was well-versed on the situation, since Gardiner had been feeding him information from the time the trekkers arrived in Regina. But the cowardly King had been reluctant to take a stand on the trek or its stoppage. When the matter was raised in caucus on 26 June, King reminded his fellow Liberals there was no need for an official position since they were not in office. This wariness carried over to 2 July. King was genuinely worried that the Conservatives might accuse the Liberals of being soft on communism if they were too outspoken in their criticism of the handling of the trek. It was a perception he wanted to avoid at all costs, especially in conservative Quebec. King consequently decided to let Woodsworth speak first about the riot during the emergency debate. And when it came to his turn, he chose to limit his comments to reading the Gardiner telegrams into Hansard in an effort to counter the government version of events and then asking for copies of all mounted police instructions. It was typical King: no passion, no anger, no sense of the moment.[10]

Bennett, one day shy of his sixty-fifth birthday, was at his anti-Communist best in comparison, even if he was less than truthful and had some of the facts wrong. "One cannot read what took place," he gravely began, "without a feeling of deep regret." He then suggested that the Mounties were the real victims of the riot. "I desire this house and this country to understand," he continued, "that not a mounted policeman last night had a bullet in his holster, not one.... There were no cartridges in the hands of any members of the mounted police last night. Yet this afternoon there are mounted policemen lying in the hospital shot with bullets." The prime minister then reviewed the history of the Vancouver relief camp strike and the trek: that the men in the camps were "happy and content"; that "emissaries of a destructive and subversive force" corrupted them; that Ottawa had "no idea" that the striking men were going to leave Vancouver; that there was "no force" to cope with the trek until Regina; and that he had been a model of "moderation" in trying to defuse the situation. It was the trek leaders, according to Bennett, who refused to co-operate, refused to accept the helping hand that was being extended through the Lumsden camp. "This movement," he advised the House, "is ... not a mere uprising against law and order but a revolutionary effort ... the monster, the Frankenstein." The prime minister concluded by declaring that Ottawa was still prepared to demobilize the men. But if Saskatchewan wanted to assume this task, the federal government had one condition: the disbandment was not to be done at the expense of swelling the ranks of the Communists in Vancouver by allowing the men to return to the West Coast en masse. "We are faced with an organized attempt against the national life of Canada," Bennett intoned. "We are not prepared to yield to it; and what is more, we believe that it is not a matter of a province; it is a matter of the whole nation.... We are still convinced that the people of Canada are not prepared to substitute the rule of the commune and the guidance of the soviet."[11]

The reaction to the prime minister's remarks divided along partisan lines. When the debate in the Commons resumed that evening, Agnes MacPhail of the CCF denounced the police attack on the Market Square meeting: "It is altogether too simple to say that this was a Communist uprising. The government has played that little trick too often." Conservative Bernard Stitt from northern Manitoba, on the other hand, congratulated the prime minister for his stance. "We cannot let mob rule run riot in this country," he told the House. These differences were also reflected in letters to Bennett. J. Hone of The Pas, Manitoba, observed, "the quicker they [Communists] are stopped the better," while W. L. Woodger of Drinkwater, Saskatchewan, held that the police action "should be approved by every right thinking person regardless of politics." But Reverend S. H. Soper of Brampton, Ontario, regarded the use of force as "childish and silly," and Norman Priestly of Calgary suggested that "we are in the incipient stages of a movement towards Fascism." This competing tension between authority and civil liberties was perhaps best revealed when a *Toronto Globe* reporter took to the streets after the riot and randomly asked people for their opinions; although many sympathized with the plight of the trekkers, many also questioned their tactics and supported the need for law and order.[12]

What several people could not understand, though, is why the mounted police chose to seize the trek leaders at a public rally on a holiday evening in a downtown setting, especially when negotiations were underway with the provincial government. In a story filed from Regina the next day, veteran *Toronto Star* reporter Frederick Griffin questioned police motives. "The strikers had abandoned all hope of moving one step nearer to Ottawa," he told his readers, "and would only have been too glad to get out of Saskatchewan and Regina with any kind of grace." Arthur Roebuck, the attorney-general of Ontario, was not fooled by the timing of the police action and alleged that the riot was political opportunism at its worst. "Mr. Bennett's is not the first tottering government which has instigated a war to win an election," he informed the *Toronto Globe.* "Blood has flowed in the streets of Regina in order that the Conservative press may declare that our national life is at peril, and that Mr. Bennett is the saviour of the nation." Not unexpectedly, the Communist Party of Canada attributed the riot to the prime minister's infamous "iron heel" and savaged him in a series of devastating political cartoons in *The Worker.* In one, Bennett, wearing a Mountie's dress uniform, carves a second notch in the stock of a smoking rifle, next to the first notch from the 1931 Estevan riot. In another, entitled Regina Spotlight, a startled Bennett is caught in the beam of a flashlight, trying, without much success, to wash his bloodstained hands.[13]

Many people in Regina had mixed feelings about what had happened, as evidenced by the editorial page in the *Leader-Post* on 2 July. The lead editorial sarcastically observed: "The Dominion Government ... has now given Saskatchewan three weeks of long distance administration of justice. The results are not gratifying." In a similar vein, the second editorial noted that "Bennett and his cabinet are so vulnerable that it is surprising that more fur has not been knocked off them." But in the very next sentence, it called on "all persons interested in the maintenance of constitutional government ... to stand by law and order, overlooking the bungling at the seat of authority at Ottawa." This sense of seeing both sides of the riot was captured in a letter by federal civil servant James Paul to his Ottawa supervisor. "I find it very hard to conclude just what the general feeling is in the city today," he confessed the morning after the riot. "There is no doubt, I think, that the better thinking class of people are thoroughly disgusted and entirely out of sympathy with the strikers. It cannot be denied, however, that other sentiment seems to exist and what the outcome of the whole matter will be ... no one yet can tell."[14]

There were also those who blamed either the trekkers or the police for the trouble. The day after the riot, civic officials evidently contacted Brigadier Boak, the commander of Military District 12, about the possibility of declaring martial law and removing the men from the city under armed escort. Everett Leslie, one of the two federally appointed lawyers who had been advising the mounted police, believed that the public had not "got to the plain issue"—that the city and mounted police were performing their bound duty and executing arrest warrants when they were assaulted. Jack Flavelle, a stereotyper with the *Regina Daily Star*, meanwhile, helped organize a vigilante committee "to try to help the police or anyone else to keep peace and order."[15]

On the other side of the fault line was the Citizens' Emergency Committee (CEC), which had been actively assisting the trekkers for the past three weeks. The committee called a protest meeting on Market Square the night after the riot and drew about one thousand people, who kept nervously looking towards the city police station. "There was a tense feeling in the atmosphere," reported an undercover Mountie, "and the members of the audience in a state of jumpiness." Both Alderman C. M. Fines and Pete Mikkelson, who would be elected to city council as a Labour candidate later that fall, declared Monday's chaos the darkest day in the history of the city and censured the Regina city police for precipitating the riot. George Williams, a member of the provincial CCF and chair of the meeting, shared this conviction and called on the crowd to sign a petition demanding answers from Mayor Rink. "The greatest damage was not to property or to human flesh, but to the spirit of democracy," he observed. "Law and order must be maintained but in the interests of the people." Interestingly, the RCMP dismissed the crowd as

"Quarters of the Relief Camp Strikers in the Stadium. Regina, Saskatchewan, June 26–1935." LLOYD SCOTT SKETCH, NATIONAL ARCHIVES OF CANADA C150661

"Relief Camp Strikers' Quarters in the Stadium. Regina, Saskatchewan, June 26–1935." LLOYD SCOTT SKETCH, NATIONAL ARCHIVES OF CANADA C150660

"'On to Ottawa'—Evans addressing strikers in front of Union Station, Regina, on his return from meeting at Ottawa. June 26 – 1935." LLOYD SCOTT SKETCH, NATIONAL ARCHIVES OF CANADA C147320

"British Columbia unemployed at the stadium. Regina, Saskatchewan, June 23–1935." LLOYD SCOTT SKETCH, NATIONAL ARCHIVES OF CANADA C150690

"'Comrade' Matt Shaw addressing the relief camp strikers in the Market Square. Regina, Saskatchewan, June 24–1935." LLOYD SCOTT SKETCH, NATIONAL ARCHIVES OF CANADA C147319

"Mass meeting at Stadium. Relief Camp Strikers. Regina, Saskatchewan, June 26– 1935." LLOYD SCOTT SKETCH, NATIONAL ARCHIVES OF CANADA C150662

"Strikers picketing the Lumsden Camp registration bureau in the World's Grain Show building. Steel helmeted RCMP at door. Regina, Saskatchewan, June–1935." LLOYD SCOTT SKETCH, NATIONAL ARCHIVES OF CANADA C150663

"Relief Camp Strikers at the Stadium receiving word of RCMP blockade on No. 1 Highway and arrest of truck-load of strikers." LLOYD SCOTT SKETCH, NATIONAL ARCHIVES OF CANADA C147321

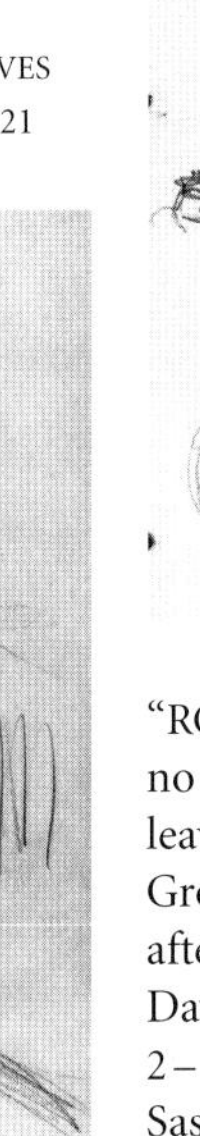

"RCMP allowing no one to enter or leave Exhibition Grounds—night after Dominion Day Riots. July 2 – 1935, Regina, Saskatchewan." LLOYD SCOTT SKETCH, NATIONAL ARCHIVES OF CANADA C147322

The new Regina city police headquarters was built as a relief project; the police column moved onto Market Square from a rear garage door.
SASKATCHEWAN ARCHIVES BOARD R-B9906-1

Hear the Reply of the authorities to Strikers' Delegation requesting immediate Relief and opening of negotiations on counter-proposals to Bennett Government's offer of Concentration Camps

MASS MEETING TONIGHT

Market Square 8 p.m.

(If wet will be held in Stadium)

Several Speakers representing local organizations will address the crowd

Winnipeg Strike Camp situation will be outlined. Latest developments will be given

Strikers' Funds are Completely Depleted

Support the Strikers and Force the authorities to grant immediate Relief

By 1 July 1935, trek leaders were prepared to negotiate an end to the Regina stalemate.
SASKATCHEWAN ARCHIVES BOARD R-A7865

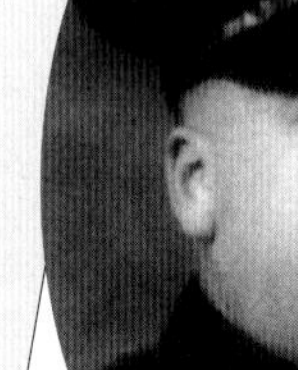

Inspector Duncan McDougall ordered his squad of Regina city policemen to fire their guns into a crowd of rock-throwing rioters at Scarth and Cornwall.
SASKATCHEWAN ARCHIVES BOARD R-B4032 DETAIL

Market Square was cleared by a column of club-wielding Regina city policemen and three mounted police units. The speaker's platform is on the far left. Saskatchewan Archives Board R-B171-3

No sooner had the square been cleared than small groups of trekkers and citizens returned, armed with stones, bricks and other missiles. Saskatchewan Archives Board R-B171-2

City police constable Alex Hill attempts to lift a lifeless Charles Millar, who had been savagely clubbed during the fighting in the square. Saskatchewan Archives Board R-B171-1

Many of the windows in downtown Regina were broken the night of the riot. *Regina Leader-Post*, 3 July 1935

An angry mob of trekkers attacked the RCMP Town Station on Cornwall Street during the riot downtown. Saskatchewan Archives Board R-B3096

Above: Rioters hidden in Victoria Park near Twelfth Avenue and Scarth Street attacked the Regina City Police with a barrage of missiles. NATIONAL ARCHIVES OF CANADA PA119921

Below: Regina's Eleventh Avenue, with City Hall as the backdrop, was turned into a battlefield the night of the riot. Many of the trekkers driven from Market Square moved west on Eleventh Avenue. Thousands of spectators lined Eleventh Avenue the night of the riot, watching the police and trekkers battle one another. NATIONAL ARCHIVES OF CANADA PA44614

Riot victim Detective Charles Millar was a fifteen-year veteran of the Regina police force. *Regina Leader-Post*, 2 July 1935

Eight-year-old Margaret Millar first learned of her father's death from newsboys selling papers at the Regina train station. *Regina Leader-Post*, 2 July 1935

The funeral for murdered city police detective Charles Millar was one of the largest in Regina history. *Regina Daily Star*, 6 July 1935

Trekker Nick Schaack was arrested for throwing stones near the RCMP Town Station. He would later die of his head injury. LORI KREI

The 3 July identification parade at the barracks for all of the men detained by the RCMP and Regina city police after the riot. NATIONAL ARCHIVES OF CANADA. PA204459

Trekkers atop Exhibition Stadium, their temporary prison after the riot. Premier Gardiner personally intervened to see that the men were provided with food and eventually released. *REGINA DAILY STAR*, 3 JULY 1935

Trekker Marsh (centre) played his concertina as the trekkers marched for their last time in Regina. The trekkers were happy to leave Regina after their three-week forced stay in the city. SASKATCHEWAN ARCHIVES BOARD R-A21749-2

Hundreds of Regina citizens turned out to bid farewell to the trekkers. One thousand three hundred and fifty-eight trekkers registered with the Saskatchewan government for a ticket home or to their former relief camp. The Saskatchewan government paid almost forty thousand dollars to have the trekkers transported by the two national railways from Regina. *REGINA LEADER-POST*, 5 JULY 1935

City of Regina---Police Department

PROVINCE OF SASKATCHEWAN

CANADA

WANTED FOR MURDER

$2000.00 REWARD

The Province of Saskatchewan and the City of Regina each offer a REWARD of $1000.00, making a total sum of $2000.00 for information leading to the conviction of any person or persons responsible for the murder of DETECTIVE CHARLES MILLAR of the Regina City Police Department, who was killed about 8.30 p.m. on July 1st, 1935, when assisting in suppressing a riot of Relief Camp Strikers in this City.

According to witnesses Detective Millar was attacked by three men with clubs, receiving a fractured skull, from the effects of which he died within a few minutes.

DESCRIPTION OF SUSPECTS

No. 1. About 5 ft. 10 inches; slender, with tapering shoulders; medium complexion; 165 or 170 lbs.; clean shaven; wore a dirty white or fawn colored shirt; no braces, vest or coat; peaked cap.

No. 2. Young man; fat face; mouse colored hair which was rather long; wore grey suit and khaki shirt.

No. 3. About 5 ft. 10 inches; 155 lbs.; clean shaven; dark red hair; fair complexion; wore a dark shirt and grey and black tweed trousers.

Referring to our CIRCULARS of AUGUST 9th and SEPTEMBER 1st, 1933, regarding the MURDER of CONSTABLE GEORGE A. LENHARD of this Department. The murderers of Constable Lenhard have not yet been brought to justice. The Province of Saskatchewan and the City of Regina are still prepared to pay the REWARDS of $1000.00 each (total of $2000.00) offered in this case.

In each of these cases the Board of Police Commissioners for the City of Regina reserves the right to apportion the reward should there be more than one claimant.

Any information obtained should be forwarded without delay to the undersigned.

Regina, Saskatchewan,
October 18th, 1935.

MARTIN BRUTON,
Chief Constable.

The Regina City Police offered a two-thousand-dollar reward for information leading to the conviction of the persons responsible for the murder of Detective Charles Millar. SASKATCHEWAN ARCHIVES BOARD R-B83336

The three members of the Regina Riot Inquiry Commission (left to right): William Melville Martin, James Thomas Brown (chair), and Algernon Ernest Doak. SASKATCHEWAN ARCHIVES BOARD R-B2800

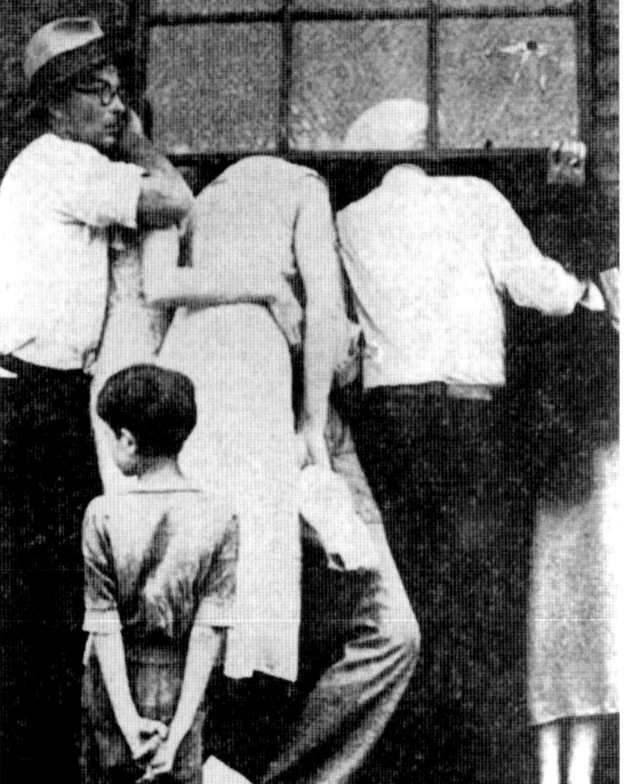

People listening outside the Regina courtroom the first day (19 July 1935) of the preliminary hearing of the six trekkers charged under Section 98 of the Criminal Code. *REGINA LEADER-POST*, 19 JULY 1935

The University of Saskatchewan student newspaper, *The Sheaf*, ran a cartoon suggesting the scales of justice were tipped against the trekkers. Leopold, the former RCMP undercover agent and Crown star witness, was portrayed as a drunk.
UNIVERSITY OF SASKATCHEWAN ARCHIVES 4797

"He's Heavy on Her Feet."
HALIFAX CHRONICLE, 18 SEPTEMBER 1935

“First Notch—Estevan 1931: Second Notch—Regina 1935.” *The Worker*, 9 July 1935

RCMP Sergeant John Leopold, a former undercover agent, as portrayed in the *Relief Camp Workers* newspaper, 5 September 1935.

Fifteen-year-old trekker Joe Balebeck faced trial in adult court until the defence was able to confirm his age.
SASKATCHEWAN ARCHIVES BOARD R-B9020 DETAIL

The Citizens' Defence Committee sponsored a national campaign to raise funds for the defence of the trekkers facing trial.
SASKATCHEWAN ARCHIVES BOARD R-B9020

ON-TO-OTTAWA TREKKERS ARRESTED ON JULY 1st, 1935

FOR YOUTH AND DEMOCRACY

SECTION 98

"overwhelmingly ... foreign" and recommended that rallies be banned "until such time as the public mind has had an opportunity to weigh the situation and arrive at a true estimate of the forces at work."[16]

Getting at the truth, though, remained a problem, as the different players jockeyed for position. At 10:00 on Wednesday morning, the trekkers held a mass meeting at the stadium to consider the offer of the Saskatchewan government. According to the CPR secret agent, some of the diehard members of the trek spoke against leaving Regina, insisting they had a duty to support their comrades who had been arrested and were facing trial. But the strategy committee recommended acceptance: the deal not only meant three meals a day; it meant the trek could be kept intact, especially if the men reported their home as Vancouver. In the end, the trekkers embraced Gardiner's proposal, but not without explaining their case to the public. In an official statement issued that same morning, the strike committee recounted the events of the past forty-eight hours, in particular how the men had been prepared to disband on 1 July and were seeking help to do so at the time of the Market Square meeting. "The relief camp trekkers disclaim all responsibility for Monday night's riot," the statement concluded. "The camp trekkers merely defended themselves when attacked."[17]

Premier Gardiner also spoke publicly on Wednesday morning for the first time since the riot. In announcing the terms of the deal with the trekkers, he ascribed the recent trouble to the "long distance control" by Ottawa. He also reported that the agreement with the trekkers was similar to the one the cabinet was considering the night of the riot. "If the police had communicated with us it need never have happened," Gardiner observed. But the premier was not prepared to point a finger at Colonel Wood and the RCMP, choosing instead to lay the blame at Bennett's doorstep. "Wood is not to blame," he contended. "He followed instructions." This simple assessment of police behaviour was certainly generous, if not blinkered. It served to demonstrate, though, that there was only one monster under Gardiner's bed and that was the prime minister. It might also have been intended to repair relations with the Mounties, especially after the premier had threatened to form his own force. But the gesture seemed to make little difference to Wood, who remained determined to put mounted police matters ahead of the interests of the province. That same day, in a formal note to Tommy Davis, the assistant commissioner insisted that the five trekkers for whom the police still had arrest warrants from late Monday afternoon turn themselves in. He also suggested that all trekkers be searched for weapons, especially guns, and that their organization be broken up before they left Regina and the men sent out singly or in small parties.[18]

The Saskatchewan government also experienced problems making travel arrangements for the men. Once an agreement had been reached with the trekkers, provincial authorities asked the CPR to provide a special train free of charge. They argued that the company was morally bound to remove the men from Saskatchewan since it had willingly brought them to Regina against the wishes of the Gardiner government and had refused to carry them any further. The railway, however, was not about to give the province a break, even if it meant distorting or ignoring what had happened in early- to mid-June. "Since these men in their movement east practically commandeered our trains and put us in a position where we could not cope with the movement," W. A. Mather, head of the CPR's western division, bluntly advised the regional superintendent, "we recognize no obligation to bear any part of the expense of their return movement and cannot allow ourselves to be put in a position of being a party to dumping a large number of these men in any province." The best deal the province could get was one-and-a-half cents per man per mile or approximately forty thousand dollars to transport the trekkers by special trains. It was a price that Gardiner was willing to pay in the interests of buying some peace for Regina and his government. But there was soon a new wrinkle. In making plans for the demobilization of the trekkers, Tommy Davis had gone to see Brigadier Boak to ask whether any closed Department of National Defence (DND) camps in British Columbia could be reopened, and to secure the location of the detraining points for the various camps. He also made a special plea for clothing for the men, especially socks and underwear. Boak, however, had been instructed by Ottawa "to have no dealings with the Attorney General in this matter" and refused to cooperate, beyond agreeing to take back all the men who had left Saskatchewan's Dundurn project.[19]

These difficulties frustrated Gardiner and Davis, but did not distract them from their ultimate goal—seeing the trekkers on their way out of the province as soon as possible. But they did not count on the continued resistance of the men. The first rumblings started Wednesday afternoon when the trekkers balked at another meal of coffee and sandwiches. They wanted to eat in city restaurants. Davis responded by issuing meal tickets Thursday morning and ordering Colonel Wood to remove the police picket from around the stadium so that the men could walk to downtown cafes. One of the more popular stops for dozens of freed trekkers was the post office, where they could be found writing postcards to worried family and friends. The other, more serious problem was getting the men to register for the trip home or back to their camps. Some of the trekkers were still opposed to leaving Regina, and the province reluctantly agreed to delay their departure until Friday on the understanding that registration would get underway at 9:00 on Thursday morning. The time had to be pushed back, though, until the early afternoon—again at the request of the trekkers. One of the reasons for the delay continued to be missing men; McAuley wanted more time to locate them. It was also rumoured that at least 150 men were being detained at the Lumsden camp against their will, and the trek leadership wanted the story investigated. But the real sticking point was that demobilization effectively meant an end to the three-month strike, to the trek, and to the campaign for work and wages. Several men refused to abandon the cause. They looked upon disbandment as an ignoble defeat at the hands of the Bennett government and the RCMP—something they could not swallow after they had come this far. The trek had given special meaning to their empty lives, and some stubbornly wanted to push on and finish what they had started. In fact, these emotions created the first real dissension in trekker ranks since they had left Vancouver.[20]

Colonel Wood, Brigadier Boak, and CPR officials watched the deadlock with great interest, if not smug delight. It seemed that the deal was about to come apart and Gardiner was going to learn about the kind of men he was trying to help. But Tommy Davis, who now seemed to spend all of his time at the stadium with the trekkers, was prepared to do what he had to to save the agreement. He met with a five-man delegation at the nearby Grain Show Building—where registration was supposed to commence—early Thursday afternoon and tried to ease a number of outstanding concerns. He affirmed that the trekkers in hospital would receive adequate treatment and be sent home at provincial expense once discharged. He also indicated that some sixty men currently under arrest for vagrancy would be released and sent home as well, while those facing criminal charges would be provided with limited assistance if necessary. The most important item, though, was his pledge that the men as a group would be transported to their desired destination and "will be carried to that destination and will not be prevented from going there." The delegation took these promises—which Davis provided in writing—to a mass meeting at the stadium. There the men agreed to register starting at 3:00 P.M., but not before a motion was adopted urging the trekkers to keep the organization intact to fight another day by coming together again in Vancouver under the auspices of the Workers' Unity League, an affiliate of the Communist Party of Canada.[21]

With registration finally underway, Colonel Wood wired Ottawa that the trekkers would definitely be leaving Regina on the morning of Friday, 5 July. The Bennett government had no intention of interfering with the men's departure—despite noises to the contrary—but remained concerned that the Gardiner government had made no effort to disband the trek beforehand. The RCMP commissioner consequently spoke to senior CPR officials about the possibility of placing railway police on the cars and breaking the trains into sections once they had left Regina so that the men did not descend on Vancouver all at once. He also had to deal with a potentially embarrassing problem of his own. Despite Colonel Wood's claim that the Mounties went into action with empty holsters, it soon became apparent that he had misinformed Ottawa the morning after the riot. That same day, a reporter for the *Regina Daily Star* had called Wood with the news that several citizens had reportedly seen a mounted police fire his gun down a lane near the Town Station and that a .45 calibre slug had been removed from one of the wounded trekkers. Although Wood was reluctant to admit any police shooting until the incident had been investigated, Commissioner MacBrien knew that his senior officer in Regina had to provide some kind of public explanation or the prime minister would be accused of misleading the House of Commons or, worse, engaging in a cover-up. Wood's way of setting the record straight, however, was devious at best. He told the *Leader-Post* that "no denial is being made that the RCMP fired their guns during the rioting," but admitted he knew nothing about it and would welcome any information from the public. He also maintained—in what would become his standard line in the coming months—that his men intended only to arrest the trek leaders and did not anticipate the break-up of the meeting or a clash with the trekkers.[22]

Wood's statement was the second time in the last few days that he had had to clarify what he had said, the first being his 28 June declaration that Ottawa had passed a government order forbidding any kind of assistance to the trekkers. He did not care to learn from the experience, though. With the trekkers set to leave the next morning, he prepared a report on the riot for Commissioner MacBrien late Thursday, covering a number of controversial issues. In defending the decision to arrest the leaders at Market Square, he claimed that the warrants were issued only an hour before the meeting, instead of the actual three, and that he had had little time to come up with a plan. He lied again when he said that ammunition was issued to all ranks only after the city police had discharged their guns at Scarth and Twelfth, when in fact the order to that effect had been given half an hour earlier, before several of the RCMP units had left the square. Wood had no qualms about bending the truth to suit his purposes—it was all part of defending the integrity of the force in the nasty battle with communism. But his dishonesty came at the expense at the Regina city police, who were already being publicly skewered for provoking the melee. Indeed, an embattled Chief Bruton spent the first few days after the riot on the defensive. When asked to comment about the force's behaviour by one of the city's newspapers, he said little except that his men were simply assisting a mounted police operation and that they had reached the platform ahead of the other units only because they had been situated closer. Although several groups and individuals, such as Frank Turnbull, the Conservative MP for Regina, spoke up in support of the city police, the criticism became more pointed after the trekkers left Regina.[23]

Once the registration of the trekkers started late Thursday afternoon, it took twelve provincial clerks, working all night, to register the men and ensure that each one of them had a ticket. In all, 1,358 men came forward—

up from the 1,104 the RCMP had counted a day earlier when the trekkers were finally allowed out of the stadium for breakfast. Men were headed home to every province, including one to Prince Edward Island. The majority—857, or two-thirds—registered for British Columbia. Of these, 650 claimed to be from Vancouver. The trekkers returning westward were scheduled to leave as a group on one train at 10:30 A.M.—that's what the men wanted, and it was the cheapest way for the province to transport them. But Friday morning, the CPR balked at the arrangement and recommended that half the men be carried by the Canadian National Railway. This last-minute hitch prompted yet another meeting between a trek delegation and an exhausted Tommy Davis, who eventually persuaded the men to leave in two detachments by promising there would be no railway police escort. Those going to southern Alberta and Vancouver would travel by CPR train, while the remainder would ride on the CNR, north to Saskatoon and then west to Edmonton and Vancouver. Men destined for points east would leave on a regularly scheduled CPR passenger train later that night. Another three men—Winters, Young, and Hellind—would remain behind at provincial expense to look for trekkers still hiding in the city after the riot.[24]

Back at the stadium, as the time of departure drew closer, there was an air of excitement as the trekkers packed their belongings and said goodbye to girlfriends, other new acquaintances, and supporters, who were there to bid them farewell. Two reporters likened the scene to men heading off to war. Had it been a generation earlier, these young men could have been bound for the Great War. Calls soon rang out for the trekkers to form in their divisions. On a signal, they started to march, in fours, to two twelve-coach trains idling nearby. Comrade Marsh pumped his concertina, while the men broke into their trademark song, "Hold the Fort, For We Are Coming." It was quite a contrast from the morning of 14 June, when they had arrived wet and weary, just happy to have reached Regina. This time, there were smiles, laughter, and joking—the tension of the past few weeks was now gone. But the fire still burned in many of them. Some chalked slogans, such as Abolish Slave Camps and The Battle Must Go On, on the sides of the waiting coaches, while one trekker cut down the tired effigy of R. B. Bennett that had hung for days from a telephone pole outside the stadium and suspended it from one of the coach windows. It was the only semblance of a federal official to be seen that morning. The heavily armed mounted police had finally been withdrawn from the exhibition grounds, except for those hiding in the nearby armouries.[25]

Tommy Davis, his hat askew, was there attending to any remaining details, such as the loading of crates and boxes of food and supplies into the baggage cars. Over the past few days, he had come to know several of the trekkers. They stopped to shake his hand heartily and thank him. One reporter, watching the exchanges, wondered what Davis thought of the men. "Are they hoodlums and foreigners, as has been alleged?" he asked. "You can't beat them as a bunch of boys," Davis answered. "I wouldn't want to meet better." On a signal, the men climbed aboard the maroon-coloured coaches, stowed their gear, and then lifted up the windows and stuck out their heads to talk to and shout at the crowd. At 11:50, following two short whistle blasts, the CNR train slowly pulled away, followed about five minutes later by the CPR train. The hundreds of people who had gathered to see the trekkers on their way waved back and cheered, while photographers snapped pictures. And then they were gone, ending what one Regina reporter called "three weeks of suspense unequaled ... in the city's history."[26]

It had been a draining week for Gardiner and Davis. No sooner had the trekkers departed than the two men went on vacation. Gardiner and his family left early that afternoon by car to visit relatives in southwestern Ontario for several weeks, while Davis headed north for a few days of rest in Prince Albert National Park. They could both look back with considerable satisfaction at what they had accomplished. "The fact is," wrote one reporter about the premier's handling of the trekkers, "he showed that he could do more in twenty-four hours by decency and tact than massed police could do in three weeks." But many of the issues underlying the trek and riot were not so easily or so quickly resolved. One of the first problems to rear its head—even before the chartered trains had left Regina—was British Columbia's attempt to prevent the trekkers from returning to Vancouver. On Thursday afternoon, John Hart, the acting premier of British Columbia, appealed to Gardiner to send only those men to his province who had homes there, to provide transportation only as far as Kamloops, and to ship only small groups of men, with groups arriving at two-day intervals. Gardiner, however, doggedly pushed ahead with his plans, leaving British Columbia no choice but to ask the Bennett government to intervene—the province wanted all men to be detrained at Kamloops and placed in a special holding camp. But the prime minister dodged the request by stating that the responsibility for moving the trekkers had been assumed by the Saskatchewan government. Ottawa's response stunned British Columbia officials, who believed that Bennett was now betraying all that he had said about the men and the danger they posed. This disbelief turned to anger when the two westbound trains, carrying over one thousand men, were reported to have left Regina for the coast. "Does this mean that any government in Canada can ship undesirables into cities outside the province," a nearly apoplectic Mayor Gerry McGeer of Vancouver wired Bennett. "If so we can ship these men back to Ottawa." But there was little that could be done since the men carried tickets for their destination. The province had to work with the DND authorities to see that as many men as possible were taken back into camps.[27]

There were also nagging questions about the role of the police in the riot—and the reasons for Detective Millar's death. Dr. R. C. Ryley, a pathologist at Regina's General Hospital, conducted the post-mortem the morning after the riot and concluded that Millar had been killed by a single blow—of "considerable force, immense force"—to the top of the head. But identifying his assailant and the weapon was another matter. At the inquest into Millar's death on 11 July, eyewitnesses described three likely suspects and several possible weapons, from a broom to a shovel to a piece of cordwood. Millar's funeral, one of the largest in city history, was held Friday afternoon, just two hours after the trekkers had left the Saskatchewan capital. All downtown stores and businesses were closed during the service, while thousands of mourners lined the streets in the afternoon heat from the First Presbyterian Church to the Regina Cemetery. Reverend Samuel Farley, who had buried Millar's wife eight years earlier, could not contain his grief and lashed out at those who had struck down his courageous friend in a "cowardly and cold blooded" attack. "Detective Millar gave his life for the constitution of our land," Farley solemnly declared. "Mob law cannot and must not be permitted to run riot."[28]

But the real tragedy was that the death was unnecessary. The riot might never have occurred had the RCMP chosen to handle the arrest of the trek leaders differently. The police could have easily served the warrants at the end of the meeting or picked up Evans, Black, and the other leaders at some other place at some other time instead of forcing their way onto Market Square. Or, they could have surrounded the stadium in the middle of the night and effectively starved the men into submission. A public rally in the heart of downtown Regina should have been the last place to launch an offensive against the trekkers.

The Citizens' Emergency Committee wondered about these very questions and wanted answers. At an animated meeting on Wednesday, the committee called for an investigation into Monday night's riot: why had the Riot Act not been read, and why had the meeting not been told to disperse? Two days later, the committee, renamed the Citizens' Defence Committee (CDC), held a spirited rally on Market Square at which it demanded the release of all trekkers held in police custody. Speaker after speaker slammed the city and mounted police for attacking a peaceful meeting. "The slaughter was a provoked and prearranged proposition," shouted Fred Donner, "in order to bust up the boys."[29]

This sentiment was echoed by Regina lawyer J. J. Stapleton, who had watched in disbelief as the city police turned their guns on trekkers and citizens Monday night. In a 5 July letter to the city clerk, written on behalf of seventeen unidentified businessmen, Stapleton asked that Chief Bruton be suspended pending an inquiry into the riot. He sent a similar letter to Prime Minister Bennett, in which he provided a searing ten-point critique of Colonel Wood's actions and his subsequent explanations. "The Mounted Police, in conjunction with the City Police, intended to crush the strikers' organization, not to arrest the leaders as they now state," he charged: "They came armed for such purpose." He added, "These strikers held a number of meetings in Regina and no trouble arose, nor did the strikers want trouble. They were compelled to fight here in self-defence."[30]

Stapleton's letter found its way into Colonel Wood's hands. He responded at length to RCMP commissioner MacBrien, contradicting every accusation and insisting that the trekkers were the aggressors, determined, in his words, "to exterminate the police" during the fighting on the square and downtown.

He also questioned Stapleton's motives, noting his "complaints ... show a great similarity to those appearing in the Communist press." But when Wood claimed, in justification of his actions, that he was simply following the commissioner's instructions to arrest the trek leaders as soon as possible, MacBrien penned in the margin of his copy of the secret memo: "at an opportune time." It was the only indication that the commissioner might be displeased by how the arrest warrants had been handled. Otherwise, he stood by Wood and even requested an assessment of how the Mountie response to a similar situation might be improved. Wood gladly complied in a chilling, nineteen-page memo entitled, simply, "Training." Reviewing mounted police operations the night of the riot, Wood recommended that in the future the men be issued protective shields, steel helmets which came down over the ears and neck, gas grenades which exploded upon release, and "a baton which will disable a man at one blow." He also believed that his men "should have used ... firearms and should have been equipped with sawed-off shot guns and Thompson machine guns." To this end, he proposed the creation of an "armed party" organized separately from the regular dismounted and mounted units. What was perhaps most disturbing about Wood's report, though, was that there was no sense that methods other than brute force could have been used in dealing with the trekkers once negotiations had broken down. In fact, the assistant commissioner regretted that the Saskatchewan government had stepped in to disband the trek the morning after the riot. "We were in full control of the situation," Wood reminded MacBrien, "and could have forced them, within six hours, to meet all our requirements."[31]

Wood's musings aside, Premier Gardiner would never have allowed the mounted police to have forcibly moved the trekkers to the Lumsden camp. The premier already believed that the Monday night riot was unwarranted—what with the provincial cabinet considering a proposal from the men—and would not have risked any more trouble. Nor was he prepared, once the trekkers had left Regina, to dismiss the riot as an unfortunate incident and try to put it behind him. The Bennett government had foisted the trek on Saskatchewan and had to be held accountable for what had happened. There had to be some kind of reckoning. As the premier headed east for Ontario with his family on Friday afternoon, shortly after the departure of the trekkers, it was announced in the Regina newspapers that the provincial government had appointed a commission of inquiry into the trek's three-week stay in the capital. Gardiner's timing could not have been better. That same day, the Bennett government had ended the parliamentary session, and with it any more questioning of its role in the trek and the riot. But with the provincial inquiry set to begin hearings as soon as mid-July and a general election to be held in a few months, there would be no escape for the prime minister. The federal government might have "dug a pit for Premier Gardiner at Regina," the *Moose Jaw Times-Herald* gleefully noted, "but Bennett fell into it himself."[32]

CHAPTER TWELVE

Much to Be Known

When the Saskatchewan government appointed the Regina Riot Inquiry Commission, many expected that the hearings would last only a few weeks and a report would be issued before the end of the summer. It was a naive hope. The Bennett government not only challenged the authority of the province to appoint federal judges to such an investigation, but insisted that the best way to secure answers was through the prosecution of the trek leaders and those who had been charged with rioting and assault. In fact, while the start of the provincial inquiry was delayed until the late fall, a series of preliminary hearings were quickly convened to determine which men should be sent to trial. At these proceedings, and later before the commission hearings, federal lawyers sought to portray the On-to-Ottawa trek as a revolutionary movement aimed at the throat of Canada: the leaders were die-hard Communist agitators bent on sowing dissent and fomenting chaos, while those who had committed violent crimes were little better than thugs who had no respect for the laws of the country. This blinkered depiction of the trek and riot discredited the campaign for work and wages and the improvement of relief camp conditions—the trekkers' very reason for going to Ottawa. It also made it difficult to unravel exactly what had happened in Regina. If the trek was Communist-inspired and Communist-led, then it naturally followed that the trekkers were to blame for the Dominion Day trouble on Market Square and the downtown streets. There was no room for any other explanation, let alone hard questions about the actions of the

Bennett government and the two police forces. It was a simple, convenient way of looking at the riot, and one that gained widespread currency in the months ahead.

❖ ❖ ❖

On 10 July 1935, just five days after the trekkers had finally left Regina, Saskatchewan attorney-general Tommy Davis formally established a three-person inquiry into the Regina riot. It was to be an ambitious undertaking. The commission was to examine every aspect of the month-long history of the trek from the time it left Vancouver until its disbandment. Put quite simply, in the words of the order-in-council, it was to be "the most complete and exhaustive inquiry possible." The justices who were to lead the investigation into "all facts and circumstances" surrounding the trek and riot were James Thomas Brown, William Melville Martin, and Algernon Ernest Doak. All three men were Liberal supporters. Brown ran unsuccessfully for a seat in the House of Commons in 1908, while Martin had spent eight years in Ottawa as the member of Parliament for Regina before resigning to serve as Saskatchewan's second premier from 1916 to 1922. They were also respected, experienced jurists. Brown, who would chair the commission, was chief justice of the Court of King's Bench in Saskatchewan, a position he held for a remarkable thirty-nine years. The other two commissioners were equally qualified: Justice Martin had sat on the Saskatchewan Court of Appeal since his resignation as premier, while Doak, an expert on practice and procedure, was a long-time district court judge for Prince Albert.[1]

The appointment of the provincial inquiry was widely applauded in Regina, both by those who had supported the trek and those had opposed it. Not only did citizens want to understand how a peaceful rally had degenerated into a riot, but there were all kinds of rumours circulating in the city that required investigation: that the mounted police had been drinking; that the city police had indiscriminately bowled over several baby carriages on Market Square; that one hundred fifty trekkers had been killed during the riot and secretly buried at the Royal Canadian Mounted Police barracks; that the bodies of several riot victims were being held by local undertakers; that the trekkers had been armed with guns; that sixty Mounties had refused duty in the city the night of the riot and an equal number had later laid down their weapons; that someone had used a machine gun; and that a Mountie had discovered the night of the riot that his son was a trekker. The *Regina Leader-Post* claimed that it was in the public interest to uncover the facts "so far as they are obtainable, and appraised by those competent to deal with evidence ... Certainly, there is much to be known." E. C. Leslie, one of the two Regina lawyers who had helped work up the arrest warrants for the trek leaders on 1 July, also welcomed the commission. "The public reaction is not as favourable as one would expect," he told a Conservative friend in Ottawa, "but in my opinion ... when all the evidence comes out I think public opinion will be changed." Even the RCMP appeared ready to cooperate and asked the Justice Department to arrange for legal representation at the hearings, scheduled to commence 17 July.[2]

The Bennett government, on the other hand, was extremely wary of washing its dirty laundry in public, especially when it would soon have to go before the electorate to renew its mandate. James Bryant, a former cabinet minister in the Anderson government, had warned Prime Minister Bennett about the danger ahead for the Conservative party when word of the commission first leaked out: "Dice loaded for political effect advisable to figure contra scheme before Gardiner announcement made." Coming up with an alternative, though, was secondary to stopping the provincial inquiry from going forward. Hugh Guthrie, the federal minister of Justice, consequently lost little time in throwing up an apparent constitutional roadblock. While insisting that Ottawa wanted answers too, Guthrie advised Davis that the appointment of federal judges to the riot commission required the prior approval of the Bennett government and that the hearings would have to be postponed until the province submitted the necessary request. He also wrote Chief Justice Brown and asked whether it was appropriate for a provincial inquiry to consider the actions of the dominion government in dealing with a national crisis. This federal intervention prompted the three commissioners to ask the Gardiner government to be released from their appointments. But Davis not only refused the request, but questioned Guthrie's motives, particularly when similar appointments to provincial commissions had never been contested by Ottawa in the past. "No objection whatsoever ... has ever been raised on this point," he rebuked his federal counterpart, "and we shall continue to assert this right." Guthrie was plainly wrong, and Davis knew it.[3]

While Davis and Guthrie shadow-boxed over the commission, the city and mounted police forces worked together to pin the responsibility for the riot on the trekkers. Chief Constable Martin Bruton, who privately blamed senior Mounties for placing the city police in an impossible situation during the Market Square raid, argued that the trekkers "were fully prepared to start a riot ... and would have done so sooner or later even if the leaders had not been arrested." Other city policemen recited a similar story. "[Inspector] Dunc McDougall, who is not panicky at all," related E. C. Leslie, "told me that if the city police had not been armed and had not shot, a number of them would have been killed." Colonel Wood, in the meantime, reported that only one mounted policeman—Sergeant Roberts at the Town Station—had discharged his revolver—in the air during a desperate attempt to hold off an attack. Commissioner MacBrien, who had avoided making any public comment in the aftermath of the riot, pushed this idea that the trekkers had initiated the violence. In the coming weeks, he steadfastly maintained that the mounted police were simply trying to execute arrest warrants when the trouble had unexpectedly erupted at the square and spread to the downtown streets. He also praised his subordinate's performance in what seemed to be a calculated effort to defuse any public criticism of the police strategy that evening. "Assistant Commissioner Wood," MacBrien advised Guthrie, "is regarded as one of the most efficient Officers in our Force who, under difficult conditions, performed his duties to the best of his ability, and I feel he should be protected from attacks as far as possible."[4]

This sense that the trekkers were the real culprits and had to be subdued—seemingly by any means—did not end in Regina. No sooner had the fighting on the streets come to an end than the mounted police prepared for new trouble from striking relief camp workers in other major cities across the country. What the Mounties feared most was a renewal of the strife in Vancouver, what with the injection of hundreds of trekkers fresh from the Regina battleground. But in a 12 July status report on the national situation, Vancouver was said to be "quiet." Authorities also feared the march to Ottawa would be taken up by the men who had been waiting in cities east of Regina. In Winnipeg, for example, where over a thousand single homeless unemployed gathered in anticipation of the arrival of the trek, there had been a huge protest rally on 3 July. But the anger over the Regina Riot never translated into support for a new trek. Less than a hundred men left the Manitoba capital for Ottawa on 15 July and managed to get only as far as Kenora. Support also quickly fizzled out in Sudbury and North Bay. Only Toronto managed to send a sizeable contingent to Ottawa—some three hundred marchers, including women, on foot—and it quietly withdrew after being rebuffed by the Bennett government. This outcome did not mean, though, that the unemployed, let alone the Communists, were no longer seen as a threat. In a meeting with former Conservative prime minister Sir Robert Borden in late July, Commissioner MacBrien resurrected the idea of camps of discipline where so-called troublemakers, like those in Regina, would be incarcerated. There was also talk of establishing a national registration of the unemployed and fingerprinting all Canadians.[5]

These ideas were evidently part of General MacBrien's larger strategy for dealing with the unemployed and unrest if the Depression continued for at least another year. The more urgent need, though, was punishing those trekkers who had been arrested in Regina. The Bennett government believed that the criminal trials should precede any provincial inquiry into the trek and riot, especially since the men would have to be tried in the Saskatchewan courts. And these trials could take weeks, if not months. On the afternoon of Wednesday, 3 July, an identification parade was held at the RCMP barracks. All of the men being detained by the two police forces—including those already formally charged—were lined up in two long rows and assigned numbers, while groups of policemen who were on duty that night and a few citizen witnesses took turns going from man to man and picking out anybody they recognized. RCMP constable R. C. Torrens quickly identified trekker Casper Blum, a twenty-year-old Hungarian-born baker with a crooked left eye, as the person who had hurled a brick through the windshield of his squad car. Reg Ellis, who had changed his name from Keeton after being blacklisted from the British Columbia camps, was also identified by two Mounties as one of the rioters.[6]

The lineup took the better part of the afternoon and brought the total number of arrests to 118. Most were trekkers, but a handful of Regina citizens were also charged. Because of the numbers involved, the men were taken in batches by van to the city court house over the next few days, where they briefly appeared before Magistrate R. E. Turnbull, nominally charged with vagrancy, and then remanded until the following week. Thomas Newlove, who had had a private law practice in the city since 1923, had been retained by the new Citizens' Defence Committee (CDC) to serve as defence counsel at the arraignment hearings. He had been on Market Square during the police raid and had watched the downtown fighting with his friend Pete Mikkelson. E. C. Leslie and F. B. Bagshaw, the two lawyers who had earlier advised the RCMP that there was enough evidence to proceed against the trek leaders, initially acted for the Crown. They were soon joined by veteran Crown prosecutor Herbert Sampson at the request of the provincial Attorney-General's Office. Sampson's appointment threatened to open up a new wound in the ongoing feud between the federal and provincial governments. "But we finally ironed it out and we are all acting together," reported Leslie a few days later. This cooperation was the only instance where Ottawa and Regina seemed to be able to work together on a trek-related matter. But the Bennett government really had no choice. Any trials resulting from charges laid by the two federal lawyers would fall under provincial jurisdiction. Besides, it was in Ottawa's interest to cooperate to ensure that the trials were held and the rioters convicted before any inquiry got underway.[7]

On Saturday, 6 July, after securing additional information from the police and assessing each case, the prosecution team withdrew sixty-one vagrancy charges. That still left more than fifty men in custody, thanks to the addition of several trekkers who had been released from hospital during the week only to be immediately arrested by the police. The preliminary hearings were held before Judge Turnbull the following week, from Tuesday to Friday, and resulted in thirty-eight men being committed to trial on charges of inciting to riot, assault, or both. All but three of the accused—Regina residents Carl Johnson, Stanley MacKinnon, and John Gallinger—were trekkers. One, Joe Belabeck, who had been found hiding under a car the morning after the riot, was a lame fifteen-year old from Manitoba. Most of the prosecution witnesses were either city or mounted policemen, who were given wide discretion in what they could report. But when defence counsel Newlove tried to ask about police violence, Turnbull ruled the question out of order and struck it from the record. He also denied Newlove extra time to prepare some of the cases. "We can't hold them up," countered crown prosecutor Sampson at one point, "because we have a lot of others to get rid of." This apparent bias carried over into the bail hearings the following week. The accused men were to stand trial in September and appeared before Judge A. G. Farrell in the district court to elect trial by judge or jury and apply for bail. At the first hearing, Sampson recommended that bail be set at fifteen hundred dollars for each of the men. But Farrell would not hear of it. Claiming they were all "wandering Jews and floaters" who might try to skip trial, he granted bail ranging from two thousand to four thousand dollars.[8]

The other trekkers waiting to learn their fate in early July were leaders Arthur Evans and George Black, who had been arrested at the Market Square meeting, and Ivan Bell, Ernest Edwards, and trek marshal Jack Cosgrove, who had been held since 27 June when they tried to break through the police blockade. Evans and Black made their first court appearance the morning after the riot. Arraigned before Police Magistrate Walter Scott in the RCMP court, while Mounties in riot gear stood guard around the building, the pair were remanded for a week. They made another brief court appearance on 9 July and then again three days later, only this time with the other three accused. Using section 98 of the Criminal Code, the Crown formally charged Evans, Black, and Cosgrove with being officers and members, and Bell and Edwards with being members, of an unlawful association—namely, the Relief Camp Workers' Union (RCWU). Magistrate Scott then agreed to adjourn the preliminary hearing for another week in order to give the lawyers a chance to clear the heavy load of riot-related cases they were also handling. The prosecution, however, had another reason for the delay. Bagshaw and Leslie wanted to try prominent trekker Matt Shaw, who had left for Ontario just before the Market Square meeting, as part of the same case. But at the time of the 12 July hearing he was sitting in a Toronto jail after being picked up on the warrant that had been issued just before the riot. Sampson, who had a remarkable grasp of the Criminal Code, questioned the decision to bring Shaw back to Regina. "There is not sufficient evidence," he concluded after reviewing the file, "upon which a case could reasonably be made out against Shaw ... in reference to acts or words committed or spoken by him in Saskatchewan." The prosecutor's assessment would prove prophetic.[9]

The preliminary hearing of the six trekkers was played out against a strong anti-Communist backdrop. Former Winnipeg mayor Ralph Webb, declaring that the Gardiner government had not been tough enough on communism, called for a group of "red-blooded citizens to drive the reds out.... We will have to take the law into our hands." The Orange Lodge of Silton, Saskatchewan, meanwhile, saw "no difference between what Louis Riel did in 1885 and those people in Regina last week"; one member accused the trek of "trying to destroy the Christian church, home life, law and order."[10]

The mood in Regina was one of anticipation, if not curiosity—people unable to find a place in the small courtroom lined up three-deep in the back alley and listened through the open windows. Even Tim Buck, the national leader of the Communist party, made a brief appearance in the court audience. The trial opened at 11:00 A.M. on Friday, 19 July, but was immediately adjourned for three hours to allow for the arrival of Shaw, who would not reach Regina until noon. When the court reconvened in the afternoon and the amended charges were read, Bagshaw explained that the Crown intended to show that the RCWU was an illegal organization with direct links to the Communist Party of Canada.[11]

Thirty witnesses, at least half of them mounted policemen, were called over the course of the six-day trial. Many gave evidence about the intimidation tactics of the trek and the damage caused by the riot. But it fell largely to the last witness, RCMP sergeant John Leopold, to connect the campers' union with the Communist party. Leopold had performed a similar function in Toronto in 1931 when he was the star witness against eight Communists, including Tim Buck. He had also cut his teeth as an undercover agent—disguised as a Communist organizer—in Regina in the 1920s. But that was the problem with his evidence. Defence counsel Newlove protested that the documents that Leopold tendered did not relate to the period covered by the charges against the six men. Magistrate Scott, however, seemed to be swayed by the prosecution argument that the Communist party was still an unlawful association, and on 1 August committed the accused—except for Bell—to trial in September. Four days later before Judge Farrell, Evans had his bail set at ten thousand dollars, Black, Cosgrove, and Shaw at seven thousand dollars, and Edwards at six thousand dollars.[12]

With the preliminary hearings out of the way, Saskatchewan considered going ahead with the inquiry into the riot, over the objections of Ottawa if necessary. The provincial government's frustration with the turn of events was certainly understandable, but it was also being hounded to do something by the CDC. On 22 July, a delegation had called on Tommy Davis to appoint a laypersons' commission and warned that if Premier Gardiner was not going to act, then the committee was ready to hold its own investigation. It was not a bluff. Since the reconstitution of the Citizens' Emergency Committee into a defence committee in the aftermath of the riot, the group had become a formidable advocate on behalf of the trekkers. Headquartered in downtown Regina at 406A and 409 Kerr Block, the committee featured several prominent local activists: M. J. Coldwell, future national leader of the Co-operative Commonwealth Federation (CCF); alderman Clarence Fines, a future Saskatchewan finance minister; A. C. Ellison, soon-to-be mayor of Regina; and John Gregory [Jack] King, editor of the *CCF Research Review* and a founder of the labour newspaper *Canadian Tribune*. But like its predecessor, the committee relied largely on a network of committed volunteers who had been angered by what had happened on Dominion Day and wanted to help the boys.[13]

Nor was the Regina branch alone in its efforts. Within weeks of the riot, there were supporting defence committees in Moose Jaw, Swift Current, Saskatoon, Winnipeg, Calgary, Vancouver, and Toronto. Even *The Sheaf*, the student newspaper at the University of Saskatchewan, added its voice in support of the trekkers.[14]

The defence committee had initially concentrated its energies on helping those men under arrest and facing possible trial. A legal committee assisted Newlove with the court proceedings, taking notes and interviewing potential witnesses, while a prisoners' welfare committee attended to the needs of the men in jail or hospital. Once the men were committed to trial, though, the Regina committee began a blitz to have the charges dropped or at the very least to have any further legal proceedings postponed until the proposed provincial commission had reported. Rallies were held on Market Square, delegations dispatched to see Tommy Davis, speakers sent out across the West, and thousands of leaflets, addressed to the prime minister or the premier, and with a space for signatures, distributed. The Regina committee refused to accept anything less than the release of every man and a full investigation of the riot. "It's time we found out," shouted Reverend East, now known as the "fighting preacher," at a public meeting on 5 August. But many of these activities cost money, and the eight defence committees began to sell "liberty bonds," ranging from ten cents to five dollars, to cover expenses and raise funds for bail and the pending trials. Some of the first contributions came indirectly from the province. In sending about 150 trekkers east to their homes after the riot, the Gardiner government had provided them $2.50 on average for meals. But instead of spending the money on food, the men donated it to the Regina defence committee.[15]

On 13 August, after yet another visit from a defence committee delegation, Tommy Davis wrote the minister of Justice and formally asked the Bennett government to withdraw its objection to the use of federal judges in the riot inquiry. But four days later, before the deadlock could be resolved, Prime Minister Bennett called a general election for 14 October. The prime minister's announcement meant that the Regina trials, scheduled to start 10 September, would become campaign fodder. And Bennett, fighting for his political survival, was ready to use the Evans trial and those of the other trekkers as part of a broader law and order message designed to put King's Liberals on the defensive. "I have been told that the police record of one of the leaders [Evans] is being made available," the prime minister's secretary confided to a Conservative candidate. "He is definitely a bad lot, and this will be very helpful when we are on the hustings." There was good political reason, then, for the Saskatchewan government to delay the trials, especially since Gardiner expected to jump to federal politics and a cabinet post once Bennett had been swept from office. Davis consequently announced on 2 September that all of the trials would be set over to the January sitting of the Court of King's Bench, on the pretext that the defence counsel required more time to prepare the cases. He also indicated, in a bald-faced attempt to make the Conservatives squirm a bit, that the riot commission would go forward. Less than three weeks later, Davis made good on this pledge and told a news conference that the inquiry would start on 12 November. Somewhat surprisingly, though, he suggested that the hearings would last no more than ten days.[16]

The Regina defence committee looked upon Davis's actions as a victory. There was other good news as well. In early September, Sampson dropped the charges against ten men alleged to have participated in the riot. That left twenty-four, including two Regina residents, still waiting for their day in court. The committee decided to build on this momentum by sending Reverend East and Arthur Evans, who was out of jail on bail, on a national speaking tour to tell the trekkers' side of the story. Their first appearance was in Regina on 12 September, only two days after Evans had been cautioned at his bail continuance hearing to be careful about what he said in public or he could be held in contempt of court. At a meeting of more than one thousand people at City Hall, East spoke in defence of the men facing trial—"Christ would have led the march if He had been on earth"—before calling for a thorough investigation into the riot. A feisty Evans picked up on this theme, arguing that he would continue to tell the truth about what had happened on Market Square, regardless of the court warning. He then explained how he could have easily been arrested at any time during the day of the fateful meeting and that the riot was a "vicious frame-up ... a savage premeditated attack" by the mounted police in concert with the Bennett government. In fact, Evans seemed determined to force the courts to try to silence him and over the next few weeks made no effort to disguise his Communist links and even accused the police of killing Detective Millar.[17]

The city and mounted police fought back in whatever way they could. On 11 September, city constables arrested a dozen trekkers who had remained behind in Regina and were posting bills advertising the Evans-East meeting at city hall. One had defiantly stuck a poster on the front door of the police station. Further arrests followed the next day when another batch of trekkers hit the streets, this time carrying boards for the meeting. Seventeen were subsequently convicted of vagrancy and given sentences from three weeks to sixty days in jail, all at hard labour. The RCMP, meanwhile, did their best to discredit Evans and his cause. They not only filed detailed reports on his speeches—reports that found their way into the hands of the Saskatchewan attorney-general—but chased down any leads and interviewed any witnesses that might provide incriminating information about the trek leader. Even the telegrams Evans sent to his wife, who lived in Vancouver with their daughter, were intercepted. Nor was the prime minister above a little intimidation, even though he was in the midst of an election campaign where his political career was on the line. In early September, Bennett wrote Tom Newlove, the lawyer for the trekkers, and advised him that the statements made in a defence committee appeal were "untrue" and that the appearance of his name on the pamphlet was "contrary to the ethics of the profession." When Newlove refused to disassociate himself from the pamphlet, the prime minister suggested that the provincial law society might be interested in the matter. Newlove took the hint and resigned as defence counsel.[18]

The loss of Newlove left the defence committee scrambling to find another lawyer, especially since it had petitioned Tommy Davis for trekker representation at the riot commission hearings. There was also a continuing need for money to sustain the speaking tour—so much so that the committee had to rely increasingly on volunteers for most of its Regina work. One of the more successful groups was a new mothers' committee, initiated by Florence Theodor. Adopting the slogan "a mother for every boy in jail and hospital," the committee paired women with the men awaiting trial or still recuperating in hospital and arranged for visits every Sunday, complete with food hampers. It was during their first trip to the Regina jail on 14 August that the women learned that Nick Schaack, who had shared a cell with Evans at the RCMP barracks the night of the riot, was seriously ill. Schaack had been committed for trial on 12 July based on the testimony of RCMP constable John Timmerman. At the preliminary hearing, the constable reported that he had found Schaack, with a rock in each hand, near the Town Station and that he had simply struck him with his riding crop across the shoulders. "He didn't have much chance to show resistance," Timmerman confessed to the court. "He went down almost immediately after I hit him." By 12 July, Schaack was too ill to attend his bail hearing. He had trouble eating and standing and spent his days confined to his cell bed. At the urging of the mothers' committee, he was eventually sent to the General Hospital on 25 August, the same day charges against him were dropped. Schaack's condition steadily worsened. He suffered a heart attack and then developed pneumonia. On 9 October, the hospital superintendent wrote Schaack's family in Watertown, South Dakota, that he was unlikely to recover and that if he did, he would be transferred to the Weyburn mental hospital. He died nine days later.[19]

Nick Schaack was the second fatality of the Regina riot—something that was denied at the time by his attending physician and later by the mounted police. Dr. E. K. Sauer, who had initially regarded Schaack's case as "purely a mental one," told the *Leader-Post* on 19 October that the trekker had died from pneumonia, precipitated by a heart disorder. Several months later, he offered a more convoluted explanation. "He was just getting over a scratch over his forehead," Sauer remembered, "there was nothing wrong with him." But when asked for the cause of death, the doctor responded: "Tumour of the brain." He added, though, that the tumour was not caused by any injury that Schaack had sustained on 1 July. The other curious thing about Schaack's death is that his hospital record has inexplicably been wiped clear. Every single trekker who was treated at one of the two Regina hospitals had a card detailing the period and nature of the illness and the cost of treatment. But in Schaack's case, all that appears on his record is his name. By coincidence, on the same day the trekker died, the Regina city police issued a circular offering a two thousand dollar reward for information leading to the conviction of those responsible for the murder of the other riot victim, Detective Charles Millar. A description of three suspects, provided by witnesses at the coroner's inquest, was included. Schaack was quietly buried three days later in the same cemetery as Millar. His family has always wondered about the circumstances behind his death.[20]

The other person whose fate was determined in October 1935 was Prime Minister Bennett. It was widely conceded that the Conservative government would go down to defeat in the federal election. The question was, by how great a margin? Many looked to Mackenzie King to propose new programmes or talk about new ideas during the campaign, but the wily federal Liberal leader remained non-committal. He did not want to give his opponents anything to criticize or attack and believed it best to hammer away at

Bennett's mismanagement of the unemployment crisis, while at the same time portraying the Liberals as the only viable and trustworthy alternative. In other words, the best policy was to have no policy, or as the Liberal campaign slogan aptly put it: "It's King or Chaos." The strategy worked, and the Liberals stormed back into office with the largest and most lopsided general election victory to date. Jimmy Gardiner resigned as premier and leader of the Saskatchewan Liberal party on 1 November and was named to the federal cabinet as minister of Agriculture three days later. Tommy Davis could have succeeded him—he was Gardiner's choice—but did not want the premiership and agreed to continue to serve as attorney-general under W. J. Patterson.[21]

The defeat of the Bennett government removed any federal objection to the provincial inquiry. The new Liberal minister of Justice, Ernest Lapointe, maintained that it was "our duty" to determine "what the facts are with regard to those unfortunate troubles." There was some confusion, though, over the scope of the commission. Tommy Davis, seemingly having second thoughts about the inquiry's broad mandate, said there was no need to hold sittings in other provinces. But he was contradicted by G. H. (Bert) Yule, one of two legal counsel for the commission, who indicated that the trek would be probed from start to finish.[22]

The Department of Justice also provoked a small tempest when Bagshaw, who had represented the federal government along with Leslie since late June, was replaced only days before the start of the inquiry by Bamm Hogarth, a distinguished local lawyer and president of the Regina Liberal Association. Defeated Conservative MP Frank Turnbull, knowing that Yule was also a Liberal organizer, immediately wired Bennett: "Looks like an attempt to convict your government." The former prime minister agreed and in an angry letter to Lapointe, damned the commission as not only "clearly political," but "prejudicial" to the upcoming trials. He also wondered how a province could appoint federal judges to investigate the actions of the federal government. The Justice minister simply replied that the appointment of two lawyers of different political colours to represent his department and the mounted police was "a guarantee of complete impartiality.... The ends of justice will be effectively served."[23]

But seeing justice served was precisely the concern of the CDC. At a huge public rally at Regina's city hall the night before the start of the inquiry, both Evans and East claimed that the truth about Ottawa's handling of the trek would never be known unless the inquiry was dominion-wide, with power to question members of the former government. A defence committee delegation headed by the tireless CCF worker Jack King took this demand, along with a request for a broader, more representative commission, to Ottawa in late November, but was sent home empty-handed by Lapointe.

After a four-month delay, the Regina Riot Inquiry Commission officially opened at the courthouse at 10:00 A.M. on Tuesday, 12 November. G. H. Yule and Lucien Tourigny, from Saskatoon and Shaunavon respectively, served as commission counsel, while Herbert Sampson represented the Regina city police. Frank J. G. Cunningham, who had practised law in the city since 1928, had been hired by the CDC to replace Newlove as counsel for the trekkers and been granted official standing before the commission; like many other Regina citizens, he had watched the downtown rioting from the relative safety of a rooftop. Chief Justice Brown began by instructing the secretary to read the provincial proclamation establishing the inquiry and then announced, to the surprise of many, that the hearings would be recessed a week in order to give the two federal lawyers more time to prepare—neither Hogarth nor Leslie were even in the courtroom at the time.

When the inquiry resumed a week later, Cunningham argued that the hearings should actually start in Vancouver—since the relief camp strike and trek had originated there—before considering evidence in Regina. But Yule, who had a reputation for seeing the entire case before him, suggested instead that the commission proceed as far as it could in Regina and leave the question of going to Vancouver to be resolved at some future date. He also proposed to deal with the evidence in two parts: first, the trek, from the time it left Vancouver up until the Market Square meeting on 1 July, and then the riot itself. All parties agreed.[24]

The first of 359 witnesses to appear before the commission was RCMP constable Frank Kusch of Vancouver. It was immediately apparent during his cross-examination how the lawyers for the trekkers and government intended to portray events. Cunningham sought to demonstrate that

Ottawa had made no attempt to stop the men from leaving Vancouver and that the Canadian Pacific Railway proved a cooperative carrier, while Hogarth tried to make a link between the RCWU and the Communist party and paint the trek as a revolutionary movement prepared to use force to get its way. Over the next few days, Cunningham, with Evans sitting at his side, worked at developing the idea that the men were orderly and well-behaved—even after they had been stopped in Regina—and that Ottawa was the intransigent party. Here, he got unexpected support from Yule and Brown, who both wondered why it made any difference if the trekkers disbanded from the stadium or the new Lumsden camp. Cyril Burgess, the federal representative in Regina, also testified that Evans had announced during their Dominion Day meeting, in the presence of Assistant Commissioner Wood of the RCMP, that he intended to take the same disbandment plan to the provincial government. This statement was potentially damaging, in that Wood appeared to order the arrest of the trek leaders at the same time that Saskatchewan was considering the trekker proposal. The government lawyers, however, did not see things as being so neat and simple. During his pointed questioning of Jimmy Gardiner, for example, Leslie insisted that Ottawa had every right to use the RCMP to stop the trekkers from trespassing and took issue with the former premier's statement that Saskatchewan could have resolved the matter if left alone. He also got Tommy Davis to admit that Colonel Wood was in an "impossible situation."[25]

Evans took the witness stand on 26 November, in what would be the first of five days of testimony. Cunningham wanted the trek leader to talk about the conditions in the camps that led to the strike and trek, but Chief Justice Brown ruled that such evidence was beyond the scope of the commission. They could deal only with the time the trek left Vancouver. Hogarth came up against this same wall when he attempted to show in his questioning of Evans that the Communists were behind the trek. "The whole idea," Brown lectured Hogarth, "is to investigate how these men left ... the facts and circumstances ... not their *reason!*" This narrow interpretation of the inquiry's mandate could do only harm to the federal government's case. But during his fourth day on the stand, against the wishes of Cunningham, Evans proudly admitted that he was a member of the Communist party and that the

On-to-Ottawa Trek had been his idea. Evans later claimed that there was no connection between the RCWU and the trekkers, but the damage had been done. At the start of a new day of testimony, Hogarth mockingly wondered whether Evans would take the oath of allegiance or sing the national anthem. Leslie also played up this link between the Communists and the trek during his examination of George Black, who had been arrested with Evans at the Market Square meeting. He accused the trekker of resorting to any means necessary, including using citizens as human shields, to see that the trek got to Ottawa. Black gamely responded that the real pawns were the RCMP.[26]

Despite Evans's declaration before the commission, the government lawyers were still worried about the strength of their case. In a letter to Bennett's private secretary in December, Leslie reported that there seemed to be "an undercurrent of feeling" that Ottawa had asked the railways to complain about the trekkers. "So far I have been afraid to probe it very deeply," he told Rod Finlayson, "Naturally I would prefer that the actual request did in fact come from the railways." Leslie also wanted access to the information that Bennett had used to declare the trek a Communist movement and even suggested that the former prime minister might want to appear before the inquiry to clarify a few issues, but Finlayson quickly rejected the idea.[27]

Hogarth experienced similar difficulties with the mounted police. While working up the case, he learned that the Mounties had decided to move against the trekkers largely because of the reports they were receiving from the CPR secret agent who had successfully infiltrated the trekker organization. The police, however, refused to divulge the identity of the agent, let alone allow him to give evidence at the commission, because he was still working undercover. Hogarth considered the man's evidence crucial, going as far as to advise the deputy minister of Justice: "I am a little fearful of the successful defence of the Mounted Police in this investigation should he not come forward as witness." But the Mounties would not give him up, and as a compromise, the agent's reports were placed confidentially before the commission.[28]

On 9 December, just before the lunch recess of the fifteenth day of the hearings, the commission finally heard its first evidence about the riot when Reverend Harry Upton was called to recount what he had seen on Market

Square. There followed dozens of witnesses, mostly Regina citizens, who described in graphic, at times shocking, detail how the city and mounted police had stormed a peaceful meeting, sending hundreds of people running for safety. Many also talked about how the combined police forces showed no restraint when the battle spilled downtown. Trekker George Phillips even showed off his gunshot wounds.

There were also those who challenged the prosecution version of the trek and riot. Harold Kritzwiser, a *Leader-Post* reporter, for example, spent two weeks with "the boys" and never heard them discussing communism, the overthrow of the government, or the kidnapping of the prime minister.[29]

This testimony, lasting several weeks, seemed to take Hogarth and Leslie by surprise, and they called on Colonel Wood to make available any mounted policeman who was there that night and could rebut some of the more damaging statements. It also made the assistant commissioner's appearance before the commission all that more important, since he would have to justify police action the night of the riot. As a precaution, Wood called on Chief Bruton at the Regina police station two days after Christmas and claimed that he "was not sure regarding time [that] certain events took place." He did suggest to Bruton, though, that the mounted police had come to the assistance of the city police at Market Square and that the Mountie units became involved in the fighting only after the crowd started to throw missiles. Wood also instructed his men to investigate any person who publicly claimed to have been hurt by the mounted police. In particular, Constable Henry Cooper, one of the two undercover policemen who had spent time with the trekkers, looked into George Phillips's story by visiting General Hospital and interviewing the doctors who attended to his wounded legs. Evidently, at least one of the extracted bullets—from a Mountie revolver—was given to Inspector Toop of the Regina city police.[30]

Assistant Commissioner Wood spent four days on the stand, starting on 20 January 1936. Resolute and self-assured, he testified that he suspected from the beginning that the trek was a revolutionary movement, organized and directed by the Communist party. He also maintained that his force had to move quickly against the trek leadership because of the disturbing reports provided by police agents. Cunningham tried to puncture Wood's version of events by challenging the reliability of his informants—had not Sergeant Leopold been recently demoted for drunkenness? He also sarcastically wondered whether Regina's senior Mountie had studied police methods in Germany or Russia. But Cunningham stepped over the line when he asked Wood to provide a copy of RCMP instructions on crowd control. Chief Justice Brown reacted as if some great indiscretion had been committed. "You have got to realize," he chastised the counsel for the trekkers, "that the Royal Canadian Mounted Police Force of Canada ... are a sacred thing not to be looked into and criticized or examined by the public generally."[31]

Perhaps the most anticipated testimony at the inquiry—at least for Regina citizens—was that of the city police. Many people wanted to know why the police attacked the Market Square meeting and later fired their guns into a crowd during the skirmishing downtown. Chief Martin Bruton appeared on the afternoon of 4 February and under questioning by Sampson told the commission that his instructions from the RCMP were to send his men onto the square at the sound of the whistle and clear a passage for the plain-clothes men making the arrests. Inspector Duncan McDougall, who headed the police column, offered the same explanation. What was curious, though, was that none of the constables claimed to have struck anyone on the way to the speaker's platform—the crowd apparently parted like the proverbial Red Sea. McDougall did, however, admit that his men had used their side arms in two locations, but only in self-defence. He also insisted that the shooting of people in other parts of the downtown was not done by his men. This evidence raised questions about the RCMP testimony, but Cunningham had little opportunity to exploit the inconsistencies. The inquiry had already sat for more than fifty days and Brown and his fellow commissioners were growing weary. When Hogarth, for example, recommended a day of hearings in Toronto, in addition to those now scheduled for Vancouver and Calgary, Brown cut him off: "I am afraid we cannot do that.... We cannot keep this commission open for ever." Cunningham was similarly treated when he asked that the RCMP commissioner, the former prime minister, and the former minister of Justice be called to give evidence. "I don't think we will waste our time on that," ruled Brown. The Regina hearings were recessed for ten days while Doak and Tourigny took testimony in Vancouver and Calgary in late February. The last witness in Regina was heard on 9 March, almost four months from the start of the inquiry and over eight thousand pages of testimony later.[32]

Closing arguments took the better part of four days. Working in tandem, Hogarth and Leslie zeroed in on Evans and his Communist allies, branding the leaders of the trek as "wolves in sheep's clothing." They also charged that Premier Gardiner had failed to appreciate the gravity of the situation—the railways had practically been forced to carry the trekkers—and that he had engaged in a kind of political gamesmanship by trying to shoo the men along to Ottawa. The Bennett government, on the other hand, had been right in stopping the trek in Regina and refusing to negotiate with known Communists. So too had the RCMP been correct in deciding to arrest the leaders at Market Square; it was the trekkers who initiated the violence and carried the fighting to the downtown streets.[33]

Sampson's closing address dovetailed nicely with the federal version of events. Insisting that the Regina city police were assisting a Mountie operation the night of the riot, he dismissed the stories of police beatings as "unbelievable" or "pure fiction," while defending the two shooting incidents as "entirely justifiable." For Sampson, the task of the commission was a simple one: choosing between the testimony of city constables who were simply doing their job and that of some "very prejudiced persons."[34]

Cunningham spoke last and at length. He challenged the federal contention that the trek was a revolutionary movement. If it was such a threat to law and order, then why were the men well behaved and well supported? He also accused the mounted police of overreacting. They were the ones who had moved into the crowd on the square even though there had been no sign of trouble. They were the ones who had terrorized people downtown, even using their revolvers, and then denied any wrongdoing. But the biggest tragedy, according to Cunningham, was that the trek could have been disbanded without incident, had the federal government not been so heavy-handed or so hard-hearted.[35]

The three commissioners were expected to need at least a month to wade through the fifty-three volumes of evidence and prepare their report. Some involved, though, seemed to believe that the judges had already made up their minds. "I am well satisfied with the course of the investigation," Colonel Wood advised Commissioner MacBrien, "and believe that we have effectively established in the minds of the Commissioners and the public that this trek was a revolutionary movement." Leslie agreed. "I do not see how they can quarrel with the actions of your Government," he wrote the former prime minister at the completion of the hearings. The federal minister of Justice also seemed to tip his hand in the House of Commons when Bennett continued to complain about the possible impact of the commission on the pending trials. "I believe that the evidence ... will rather be a justification of what the police did," Lapointe responded, "and will clarify certain issues which were perhaps dangerous." Although the minister was immediately accused of prejudicing the inquiry, the commissioners themselves had made no secret of their profound dislike of Evans and his methods. At one point during the hearings, after learning that the trek leader had written a public letter critical of the commission, an exasperated Brown had exploded: "Mr. Evans seems to have gone insane with the idea of his own importance.... I don't think it is gaol where Mr. Evans will go. I think perhaps one day he will go to asylum instead."[36]

Not all the signs, however, pointed in favour of the Bennett government and the RCMP. On 3 March, after consulting with Herbert Sampson and commission counsel Bert Yule, Tommy Davis formally withdrew the charges under section 98 against Evans and the other four men. Their trial, after two postponements, had been scheduled to go ahead on 11 March, around the same time that the commission was expected to draw to a close. But there was not enough Saskatchewan evidence to warrant proceeding with the charges—something that Wood had known in late June 1935 when he was being encouraged by Commissioner MacBrien to arrest the trek leaders as soon as possible. He had actually warned Ottawa that the trekkers had been cagey about what they said publicly in Regina and that it had been necessary to secure evidence against the men and the trek from outside the province. But the RCMP went ahead with the arrests anyway, ironically based on charges that would never be pursued.[37]

The significance of the dropping of the section 98 charges seemed to get lost in the fact that the commission still had to report. The CDC, meanwhile, knew that its work was only half-finished. There were still twenty-two trekkers and two Regina citizens awaiting trial. In the late winter, the committee launched a national publicity campaign—complete with biographies and portraits of the accused—to help fund a legal war chest. It also embarked on a new resolution drive directed at the Saskatchewan attorney-general to withdraw all charges against the men. But even though Tommy Davis publicly admitted that his office had been swamped with petitions, letters, and telegrams, he insisted that the courts would have to deal with those facing rioting and assault charges.[38]

The trials, delayed three times, finally opened on 14 April before Justice J. H. MacDonald. Sampson, occasionally spelled by Bagshaw, handled the prosecution, while Peter G. Makaroff, Canada's first Doukhobor lawyer, served as lead defence counsel. Makaroff, a prominent Saskatoon social and peace activist and failed CCF provincial candidate, had been contacted by the defence committee within days of the riot to see whether he would handle the trials. He shared the defence duties with his law school colleague Emmett Hall, a conservative with strong sympathies for the underdog who would go on to be a Supreme Court of Canada justice and the father of Canadian medicare. He had also coaxed Tom Newlove into lending a hand given his familiarity with the cases. All three would be vilified by the Regina legal community for representing the trekkers.[39]

Makaroff and Hall chose to defend their clients by pinning the blame for the riot on the city and mounted police forces. The Market Square meeting had been a peaceful gathering until the police moved to arrest the trek leaders. The strategy enjoyed some unexpected success during the first trial when Judge MacDonald ruled that the evidence did not justify the rioting charge against Joe Mottl and Sidney Stevens—the mere assembly of the crowd did not mean that they had a common purpose to disturb the peace. But MacDonald refused to accept the argument that the men were acting in self-defence when they fought with RCMP constable Francis and ordered the assault charges go forward to the jury. He also rejected the defence counsel's motion that jurors who were known to have given evidence before the riot commission be dismissed from hearing the case. "If we wait to get jurymen without human frailty," the judge snapped, "we will never have them."[40]

In subsequent trials, Makaroff and Hall continued to argue that the brutal police break-up of the meeting was the real crime. How long would the RCMP commissioner keep his job, Makaroff asked the jury, if one hundred policemen had attacked the shareholders' meeting of the Royal Bank of Canada in Toronto? But Judge MacDonald disputed the analogy, instructing the jury to consider whether people could take the law into their own hands and attack those sworn to defend the peace. The pair wrangled again when Makaroff called on Saskatchewan cabinet minister George Spence to describe how the provincial cabinet had been meeting when the riot erupted. MacDonald ruled the testimony irrelevant and told Spence to step down from the witness box over Makaroff's objections. The atmosphere in the court eventually became so caustic—with frequent interruptions from the bench and constant challenges in response—that MacDonald threatened Makaroff with "extreme measures."[41]

The behaviour of the defendants was little better. Indeed, their months languishing in jail, waiting to go to trial, had only aggravated their sense of persecution. When Joe Mynnie was asked to enter a plea, he shouted: "Not guilty and the whole Dominion knows it." John Wedin was equally adamant about his innocence. "More than two million words have been heard in the riot commission to prove the police started the riot" he announced to the applause of a fellow trekker seated in the courtroom. "I don't see any reason to be here at all." He also challenged the fairness of his trial after he was found guilty. "I think it very easy to find anyone guilty on perjured evidence. It's a cinch," he bluntly told the judge. "I can't expect any mercy. I'm proud of it." MacDonald coolly sentenced Wedin to eighteen months—the longest sentence for any of the convicted men. Eight others were handed sentences from six to twelve months, in addition to the time they had already spent in jail. One, Kenneth Forsyth, a freckle-faced young Scot, faced possible deportation. Nine other trekkers had their charges dropped, while five were acquitted. Joe Belabeck was granted a suspended sentence in juvenile court, but only after his age had been confirmed.[42]

Four days after the last trekker trial, on Saturday, 16 May, the provincial Department of Justice released the Regina Riot Inquiry Commission report. E. C. Leslie, relying on information from friends inside the government, had predicted: "it will be all right, except that it won't condemn Gardiner." It was an accurate assessment, but as it turned out, unnecessarily cautious—the 311-page report was much more one-sided. Bowing to the prerogatives of law and order, the commissioners declared that the federal government was entirely "justified" in stopping the trek in Regina, given that it was led by a notorious Communist agitator and dominated by a number of "vicious characters." They also maintained that the trekkers had been prepared for trouble that evening, as evidenced by the "speed" and "ferocity" of their attack on the square; in contrast, the police had acted with "courage" and "restraint," employing no more force than necessary. To support these conclusions, the commissioners found testimony about police brutality to be "unreliable" or "half-truths," as well as dismissing injuries as "trivial." They even attributed Millar's death to a blow from a trekker club. The federal government and the police, however, were not completely exonerated. The commissioners believed that Ottawa should have given Colonel Wood greater freedom to reach a disbandment arrangement with Evans and thereby avoid possible trouble. And in what amounted to little more than a slap on the wrist for the RCMP, they also wondered about the "expediency of effecting the arrests on the Market Square." In the end, though, it was the trekkers—and not the police—who showed bad judgment in placing their cause in the hands of Communists. "The leaders ... gave the whole movement a colour and character which condemned it from its inception," the report concluded, "and which caused it to be branded as dangerous by those in authority ... responsible for the preservation of the peace, order, and good government of the country."[43]

Coming almost a year after the trek and the riot and costing $27,600 (the equivalent of the monthly allowance for over fifty-five hundred relief camp workers), the commission report was expected to provide some much needed perspective on one of the ugliest incidents of the Depression. Certainly, there were those who contested the findings. Former prime minister Bennett, for example, scoffed at the suggestion that "long-distance negotiations" had aggravated the situation. "I never believed that those Judges should undertake this work," he ranted to a Regina colleague even before he had read the report. Peter Makaroff, on the other hand, countered that it was the utter hopelessness of the situation—not Evans and a handful of Communist organizers—that drove the men to walk out the federal relief camps in British Columbia and head to Ottawa with their grievances. "Men do not trek because they are agitated," he bluntly informed a Saskatoon press conference. "History proves that humanity does not move because of a few so-called agitators. The causes of treks go deeper into the economic forces of life." The general response to the report, though, was that the three judges had provided a realistic assessment of the trek and riot—as evidenced by the reaction of Regina's two competing daily newspapers. The *Daily Star* headlined the commission argument that the RCMP had prevented a "far worse riot" in Ottawa by stopping the trek in Regina. Similarly, the *Leader-Post* not only acknowledged that the trek was clearly the work of the Communists, but endorsed the finding that the city and mounted police were simply doing their duty. "The police forces acted under orders," the paper observed, "which is what police forces must do." This acceptance of the commission report, a willingness to embrace it as the final word, might seem short-sighted. But the spectre of communism seemed to blunt any desire to probe beneath the surface. So too did the memory of the fighting on the streets of Regina on Dominion Day when police battled trekkers and citizens. It was much easier to see the trek and riot as unfortunate, regrettable, even misguided—but most of all, thankfully over.[44]

EPILOGUE

Wiping Out the Stain

The On-to-Ottawa Trek had one simple goal: to force the Bennett government to do something about the miserable plight of Canada's relief camp workers. Since federal authorities had stubbornly refused for weeks to negotiate with the strikers in Vancouver, the men boldly decided to go to Ottawa and turn their campaign for work and wages into a national crusade. They wanted an end to their empty, seemingly hopeless lives and looked to the federal government to bring about a better deal for them and thousands of others who had been shunted to the margins of society by the Depression. But the fighting between the trekkers and the police effectively quashed any flickering hope that the men would get to Ottawa. In fact, the riot did more than kill the trek. It sullied the public image of the men, as well as throwing into doubt their purpose in setting off for Ottawa. It was a bitter, profoundly disappointing outcome, one that supporters of the trekkers were determined to set right by raising difficult questions about what had really happened in Regina. But even though the new Mackenzie King government was uneasy with the way the trek had been handled, it was not about to open old wounds once the trials were over and the commission had reported. Nor was it prepared to admit any misjudgment or wrongdoing that might weaken the integrity and reputation of the Royal Canadian Mounted Police. It was far easier for the Liberal government to do nothing, to let the On-to-Ottawa Trek and Regina Riot be remembered simply as the legacy of the Bennett years—albeit at the expense of the trekkers and their cause.

❖ ❖ ❖

Although the commission report was supposed to provide answers about what had happened during the Dominion Day riot in Regina, the Citizens' Defence Committee was far from satisfied with the explanation offered by the three Saskatchewan judges. It believed that the commissioners had deliberately side-stepped some of the hard issues associated with the trek and riot in favour of blaming the trouble on agitators. The committee, at the same time, had come to realize that the riot had coloured the Canadian public's perception of the trekkers and that it would be difficult to maintain support for the men's cause unless it widened its focus. In the late winter of 1936, then, under the direction of Jack King of the Regina national office, the committee had been reborn as a broad civil-rights body, the Citizens' Defence Movement (CDM), with three key objectives: the protection of democracy and civil liberties; the repeal of section 98 of the Criminal Code; and the defence of anyone arrested for political activities. King also sought to put the committee on a more permanent footing by establishing a national council, composed of more than two dozen leading civil-rights activists, and by creating separate provincial sections in Alberta and British Columbia. Many former trek leaders played a prominent role in the new defence organization. Bill Hammill, who had been an advance man for the trek, worked at the Regina headquarters, while Jack Cosgrove, and George Black, along with his wife Maggie, ran the Calgary and Vancouver offices, respectively. Matt Shaw, meanwhile, stormed the back roads of western Canada in an effort to raise money and form local affiliates.[1]

One of the first challenges of the new CDM was to try to reduce, if not overturn, the sentences of the eight trekkers who had been found guilty of rioting and assault. To help fund the men's appeals, it sponsored a liberty draw, selling tickets for a chesterfield suite valued at one hundred dollars. But the draw date, originally set for 30 May 1936, had to be repeatedly postponed because of the lack of sales. The Regina office also produced a six-page pamphlet, *Has Justice Been Served?*, which maintained that the RCMP were "the guilty ones" and that the trekkers had been "sentenced to jail terms for no other reason than to justify the police action on Dominion Day on Regina's

Market Square." Excerpts from several letters and telegrams—entered as exhibits at the commission hearings—confirmed that the mounted police had the trekkers by the jugular in late June 1935 and moved against them at the very time they were negotiating a way out of Regina with the Saskatchewan government. In fact, the pamphlet's findings stood in stark contrast to the commission report, even though they were based on the same evidence. "We appeal to you to support ... these cases," the pamphlet exhorted. "By wiping out the stain of Regina, July 1, 1935, upon the pages of Canadian history, you will be laying the foundations for your own security in the future.... Democracy and justice must be maintained in Canada!"[2]

The appeal hearings began Monday, 15 June, a year less a day from the time the trekkers had arrived in Regina. First to be heard were the cases of Joe Mottl and Sidney Stevens, who had each been sentenced to seven months at hard labour for assaulting a mounted policeman during the fighting on Market Square. Peter Makaroff, who continued to represent the men, took issue with the judge's instructions to the jury and asked that the convictions be overturned. But the court dismissed both appeals in the early afternoon. Chief Justice Frederick Haultain, the former territorial premier, considered Makaroff's objections to be "absolutely frivolous" and "without merit," even chiding him at one point for going through the evidence with a microscope, while Mr. Justice Gordon commented that the men had been given a "wonderful trial." This sense that the appeals were futile carried over into the next day's hearings. When court resumed Tuesday morning, Haultain announced that Jack Wedin's appeal had been rejected as well. A frustrated Makaroff immediately advised the court that he was abandoning his appeal against conviction in the remaining five cases, but intended to proceed with a plea for reduced sentences. The results were little different. Four trekkers—Jack Kyle, Kellett Cole, Fred Nogami, and John Gallinger—had their sentences upheld, while Kenneth Forsyth, who was awaiting deportation, had his sentence cut from six to three months, but only because he had already spent four months in jail before being bailed out. Chief Justice Haultain believed that the convicted trekkers had been treated leniently under the circumstances. "We have every sympathy for the men and the conditions they find themselves in," he told the court at the end of the two-day hearings, "but at the same time, it appears that they allowed themselves to be led away by leaders, agitators—I almost might say scoundrels.... Men will get nothing in this country by force and violence."[3]

The CDM was naturally disappointed by the appeal hearings and issued a public statement that came dangerously close to questioning the integrity of the court. But instead of continuing to push for the remission of the sentences in Saskatchewan, Makaroff, along with Jack King, hurriedly left for Ottawa, where they hoped to meet with the Justice minister before Parliament adjourned for the summer. Making a direct appeal to the new Liberal government had been contemplated by the defence movement for weeks—it was only a matter of timing. There was no guarantee, though, that Ernest Lapointe would see the men, let alone consider their request. Co-operative Commonwealth Federation (CCF) leader J. S. Woodsworth, trying to establish his party's pre-eminence on the left, thought it was fruitless. "From the Ottawa end this kind of thing has very little value," he warned. "The capital is every week crowded with delegations of all kinds. One more hardly attracts any attention." Woodsworth's reluctance was likely a result of his own party's frustration in getting Lapointe to pass judgment on the actions of the former Bennett government. For the past few months, M. J. Coldwell and Tommy Douglas, two of the new CCF members of Parliament from Saskatchewan, had been patiently waiting for the department estimates to be tabled so that they could raise the matter of the riot in the House of Commons. In the meantime, on 6 May, Douglas submitted a formal motion for copies of all mounted police and Department of Justice correspondence relating to the trekkers' three-week stay in Regina. Lapointe strenuously objected to the release of secret police communications, but reluctantly agreed to provide all nonconfidential Department of Justice material. The defence movement tried to fill in the gaps. In mid-May, Jack King sent Douglas the full transcript of the riot commission evidence of former Premier Jimmy Gardiner, Attorney-General Tommy Davis, and Assistant Commissioner Wood of the RCMP. "It might be well to put this Hon. Gentleman on the spot," King advised in reference to Gardiner, now the federal minister of Agriculture. "For at least if he has not changed his stripes, he most certainly has permitted them to fade out of sight." His most acerbic remarks, though, were reserved for "Sub-Fuhrer Wood" and "Big Chin MacBrien" and all their "Ducky" messages. "Light the fuse and let her go," he urged Douglas.[4]

The Opposition finally got its chance to discuss the circumstances behind the Regina Riot during a review of defence expenditures in the House on 19 June. But the debate was not between the government and the CCF, but with former prime minister R. B. Bennett, who continued to equate the trek with communism. When Coldwell attempted to pin the blame for the riot on a botched police raid, a thin-skinned Bennett countered that the Mounties were attacked when they attempted to serve arrest warrants for the trek leaders. The issue resurfaced the next day during a special Saturday sitting—but this time, Douglas, who had been in Regina the night of the riot, spoke on behalf of the trekkers. "The point we fail to see," he told the House during a discussion of federal relief support, "is that agitators do not stir up trouble. It is economic dissatisfaction and insecurity that provide the material which enables agitators to make trouble." He continued over Bennett's interjections: "The solution lies in giving these young men opportunities to live ... but unfortunately we do not do that; unfortunately we refuse to realize the urgency and dangerous nature of the situation until it is upon us. Then a catastrophe occurs for which no one wishes to accept the blame." Douglas concluded by calling on the King government "to be prepared to see the men's point of view ... the actual conditions under which these men are living.... I am asking that we attempt to spend money in trying to clean up the situation rather than to whitewash it."[5]

Makaroff and King met with Justice Minister Lapointe and Prime Minister King that same day. Armed with a two-page brief that attributed the riot to an "entirely unwarranted and inexcusable attack" on "a peaceful public meeting," they appealed for the immediate release of the eight convicted trekkers. "These young men are not criminals," the pair insisted, "and they should therefore be absolved from any further punishment." It is not known what the two Liberal ministers said at the meeting or whether they indicated how the government might respond to the request. But Lapointe had always been extremely wary of saying or doing anything that might be interpreted in Quebec as being sympathetic to communism. Nor was he prepared to tie the hands of the mounted police in responding to dissent, even though he had once complained that the RCMP were becoming too militaristic. He had insisted, for example, on personally screening all Justice Department documents about the trek and riot before they were to be released to Douglas.[6]

The prime minister's thinking about the trek and riot, on the other hand, had come full circle since returning to power. The day after the Dominion Day riot, King had confided to his diary that the Regina debacle was symbolic of Bennett's years in office: "This tragedy ... discloses the complete failure of his government to provide work and solve the unemployment problem." He repeated these remarks the next day at caucus, admonishing his members that unemployment, not communism, was the real issue behind the trek and that Bennett was trying to use the threat of subversion to divert attention away from his sorry record. In fact, two days later, King was now regretting that he had not spoken in defence of the trekkers during the Commons debate on the riot. "I should have made one of the great speeches of my life," he noted in his diary on 5 July 1935. "Had I been faithful to that end, I would have had a veritable crown of life." But once his return to office seemed a certainty, King had a change of heart. Just before the election was called, he confessed to Tommy Davis that the riot "has increased rather than lessened the problems with which a new Liberal government will be faced." And from King's perspective, it was preferable to ignore this particular problem by pretending that his government was hamstrung by the decisions of the provincial commission and the criminal courts. It was a political strategy identical to that pursued by Bennett in the spring of 1935 when he insisted that the Vancouver relief camp strikers were a provincial problem.[7]

Makaroff and King got an answer to their appeal—albeit indirectly—on Monday, the day before the parliamentary session came to an end. During the afternoon sitting, Woodsworth used the debate on Department of Justice estimates to shoehorn in a damning critique of the riot commission report, culminating in a call for an official investigation into the behaviour of the RCMP. As a kind of postscript, he suggested that the government recognize one of the old traditions associated with the king's birthday (to be celebrated the next day) and grant the imprisoned trekkers clemency. "The victims of those blunders are still in gaol," Woodsworth observed. "I suggest that we try to wipe out these blunders as far as is possible by a gesture of generosity towards those who have been the victims." Lapointe responded later that evening, reading selectively from those sections of the commission report that heralded the mounted police for their conduct and composure during the riot. He then added, almost sanctimoniously, "We must do our best to strengthen the hands of those who have, after all, to maintain peace and order in Canada.... I do not think the country has to be humiliated in any way by the part played by those who had to take responsibility at that time."[8]

The Lapointe statement ended any hope of seeing the men released—or for that matter, of seeing the riot investigated any further. Despite any misgivings about what had happened on the streets of Regina, the King government chose to stand by the mounted police and their use of force to break up the trek. The needs of the state—in other words, the Liberal party—took precedence over the plight of the men, no matter how justifiable their grievances might have been. Even the normally volatile Jimmy Gardiner, who was still irked by how his province had been treated, played along with the political game. When Bennett renewed his complaint about the legitimacy of the provincial investigation, in an apparent attempt to cross swords with the former Saskatchewan premier, Gardiner calmly explained to the House that the commission had been established "to clear up the whole matter. It has been cleared up ... fairly satisfactorily to all parties concerned. I have nothing further to say." The Liberal government could not be accused, though, of standing still. On the last day of the session, 23 June, it repealed section 98 of the Criminal Code—as it had promised during the 1935 election campaign. One week later, it accepted the recommendation of a Department of Labour committee and announced the closure of all federal relief camps.[9]

These actions removed some of the irritants from the Bennett years—irritants that had figured in the trek and riot. They also proved relatively noncontroversial. Several groups and organizations had been calling for the repeal of section 98, while Bennett himself had toyed with doing away with the camps in late 1934. But they did nothing to help the over one million Canadians still out of work, including the thousands of single homeless unemployed who continued to tramp the country. Indeed, the closure of the camps only exacerbated the transient problem. Prime Minister King, however, was reluctant to see his government do more to provide work; he was more interested in reducing federal relief spending and returning to the days of balanced budgets. It was as if the past six years of suffering and deprivation had been an aberration. King consequently ignored the recommendations of his own National Employment Commission—save for one proposal left over from the Bennett years. Beginning in the fall of 1936, Ottawa entered into agreements with all the provinces, except for Ontario and Nova Scotia, to share the cost of a national farm placement scheme. Participating farmers, and the single men and women they hired, would receive five dollars per month. This amount was identical to what relief workers had been paid in the federal camps. But the true appeal of the scheme for the King government was that it cost only a third as much per capita as the camps without the attendant unrest. "It would take Arthur Evans," remarked one observer, "a long time to organize another On-to-Ottawa Trek from … men scattered on farms the length and breadth of Canada." The introduction of a national unemployment insurance plan would have to wait until 1940 and the need for stability during the early years of World War II.[10]

R. B. Bennett, by this time, had left both federal politics and Canada. In March 1938, he grudgingly submitted his resignation as leader of the Conservative Party—now reduced to a small rump in the House of Commons—and was succeeded by Robert Manion, one of the two cabinet ministers who had been dispatched to Regina to meet with the trekkers. "I have no regrets, nor yet complaints to make," Bennett told Arthur Meighen, another former Conservative prime minister, after being shellacked in the 1935 election. "I gave the best I had to the country.… I am glad that I … did not evade punishment at the hands of the electorate." But these words belied his true feelings. Bennett felt abandoned by his party and unappreciated by Canadians for all that he had done during the Depression. He believed he had worked tirelessly—done all he humanly could—to bring the country through one of the bleakest periods in its history. And yet he and his Conservative government were tossed ignominiously from office for their efforts. The On-to-Ottawa Trek encapsulated this failure. The movement eastward was a kind of communication tool for all that was wrong with the federal government's relief policies. But Bennett could not accept the message, unless he was prepared to admit that he had failed the single homeless unemployed. It was far easier for the beleaguered prime minister to zero in on the Communist leadership of the trek, not the demands of its rank-and-file members. In the end, though, his gruff handling of the trek gave the Conservative government a black eye from which it never recovered. In January 1939, Bennett turned his back on Canada and left for England. He entered the House of Lords two years later as a viscount. He spent his remaining years on a country estate in Mickleham, Surrey, where he died alone in 1947. He is the only former prime minister not to be buried on Canadian soil.[11]

Jimmy Gardiner, Bennett's political foe during the trek stand-off in Saskatchewan, served as federal minister of Agriculture until 1958, when the Liberals were swept aside by the John Diefenbaker landslide. Gardiner would never forget how his home province had been treated by the Bennett government and took full partisan advantage of the incident to smear the Conservatives during his first few years in Ottawa. During a debate in the Commons in February 1938, for example, he noted that "on every one of three occasions [in Estevan 1931, in Saskatoon 1933, and in Regina 1935] in which the former federal government came into Saskatchewan to deal with labour questions the result was that certain members were taken to the graveyard, others to the hospital, and still others to gaol."[12]

But by the 1950s, when Gardiner was gathering information for his biography, he looked back upon the trek somewhat nostalgically. "When you and I," he reminisced with Tommy Davis, then Canadian ambassador to Japan, "acted as station agents and sold tickets ... on CPR and CNR trains which we forced the companies to run out of Regina would make quite an interesting story and I imagine most people would read it." These remarks would suggest that Gardiner was one of the few political figures in power at the time who understood why the trekkers were on the road to Ottawa. But it also needs to be remembered that the premier did not want the men stopping in Saskatchewan. His first and only priority during the crisis was to get them out of Regina before trouble erupted. This sense of urgency did not lessen even after Gardiner realized that the trek was not a revolution on wheels and that the leaders were not interested in a bloody showdown with the police. His efforts to secure a peaceful way out of the impasse were done primarily in the interests of the city, the province, and his government. At the same time, Gardiner was able to work with the trekkers in finding a solution because of the predicament they both found themselves in. They grudgingly trusted one another, and only the police raid on Market Square prevented the Gardiner cabinet from considering the trekker offer to disband under provincial supervision.[13]

The Saskatchewan government, for its part, wanted to put the entire episode behind it and get on with other matters. But no sooner had it moved beyond the trek and riot than it faced another difficult challenge in 1937—the driest year of the 1930s. The province would not emerge from the depths of the Depression until the start of World War II. The trek's legacy for Regina was more complicated. Citizens certainly took sides during the heady months of June and July 1935 and would continue to hold strong beliefs about what had happened during the night of the riot and who was to blame. These divisions were plainly evident when the Saskatchewan Federation of Labour hosted a sixtieth anniversary reunion for surviving trekkers in Regina in 1995. The city police countered with their own memorial service for officers who had died in the line of duty and invited Margaret [Millar] Grayling to unveil a monument in front of the new police building. These different responses might also explain why it took the Historic Sites and Monuments Board of Canada more than six decades to recognize the On-to-Ottawa Trek as an event of national historical significance. On 7 June 2001, two elderly trekkers unveiled a bronze tablet, with a simple, narrative text, near the corner of Eleventh Avenue and Scarth Street, the scene of some of the worst fighting.[14]

The fault line created by the riot also obscured the warm, if not enthusiastic, response of Regina citizens to the trekkers in the last two weeks of June 1935. Those on the political left, especially Christian socialists and labour radicals, welcomed the trek, because the men were saying many of the same things they had been voicing during the Depression. In fact, local activists looked to the trek to bring about some kind of reform breakthrough. But public sympathy was not confined to any one party, or any one group in

Regina. People were easily won over by the trekkers' behaviour, their youth, and their quixotic quest to ride halfway across the country atop boxcars to confront the prime minister. More than anything else, though, many Regina residents found common cause with the dissatisfaction and anger that propelled the march to Ottawa. It was as if the trek was articulating ordinary people's sense of crisis. Reverend East captured this feeling when he publicly claimed, "You're fighting the battle of everyone crushed by the depression." So too did two letter-writers to the *Regina Leader-Post.* Mrs. W. W. Allin encouraged Reginans to "go and sit down with these camps strikers ... share their life, hear them tell their story.... There is more Christianity in the cry of the strikers who stand for the people against the system." The second writer was even more pointed: "Something more than permission to ride the rods is at stake."[15]

It is debatable, though, whether the trek and riot radicalized Regina. In November 1935, for example, five trek sympathizers or Citizens' Emergency Committee supporters won half the seats in the civic election, including Alban Ellison, who defeated Mayor Cornelius Rink. But many of these Labour candidates not only had a popular following before the trek's arrival in the city, but offered an attractive reform programme. One Regina historian has suggested that the public simply voted for change. It is also apparent that local citizens generally looked upon the shooting by Regina city policemen during the downtown fighting as regrettable, but understandable in the circumstances. It seemed to be understood that the mounted police had placed its civic counterpart in an awkward position, but once in that position, the city police had a sworn duty to restore order and protect property. Any bitterness was quickly forgotten when it came to honouring Regina city policeman Charles Millar. A plaque commemorating the slain detective was unveiled at a public ceremony at police headquarters on 29 May 1936, while almost five thousand dollars was donated to a trust fund for his daughter Margaret. Solving the mystery of who killed Millar, however, was not so easy. The RCMP spent four years following up every lead or tip and interviewing supposed eyewitnesses to the assault, but was no closer to apprehending Millar's murderers when the file was closed in late 1939.[16]

The mounted police survived the fallout from the riot without a blemish on its record. It was nothing short of remarkable, especially since the police were largely responsible for the turmoil and destruction on the streets of downtown Regina because of their foolish insistence to wade into a volatile situation. But the lack of any official rebuke served to show how the RCMP were above the law in dealing with unrest and dissent during the Depression. When a Hollywood movie company, for example, asked permission in the fall of 1935 to use actual Mounties instead of extras in the film *Rose Marie*, Prime Minister Bennett responded, "I believe it would be a good opportunity for favourable publicity as against possible inaccurate representation of the greatest police force in the world." Under the Liberals, the RCMP continued to monitor the activities of the Communist Party of Canada, in particular its apparent efforts to organize another trek, and the political left in general. This police work was done without Commissioner J. H. MacBrien, who died suddenly in March 1938. His replacement was Assistant Commissioner Wood, the Mountie who had made the fateful decision to arrest the trek leaders at the Market Square meeting on Dominion Day. Wood's career was unaffected by events in Regina in 1935. After a four-month course at Britain's Scotland Yard, he was appointed director of the Criminal Investigation Branch in Ottawa and worked closely with the United States Federal Bureau of Investigation before being named commissioner. Nor had he changed his view that reds constituted the greatest threat to Canadian life. In fact, RCMP intelligence activities under Wood's leadership were so fixated on communism—to the exclusion of the new threat posed by fascism—that one government official remarked in 1940 that "one would scarcely realize that Canada was at war with Germany." Wood's obsession with reds appeared to be vindicated, however, by the coming of the Cold War in the immediate post-war period. By then, a 1954 *Maclean's* magazine article claimed that the trek and riot were one of the defining events in the Mounties' protracted "war with the Commies."[17]

Trek leader Slim Evans might have been somewhat amused by this assessment of the trek. After all, the Communist Party had initially disapproved of the idea of the striking relief camp workers heading to Ottawa. Nor did the party start to promote the march until after it had acquired some momentum and begun to fire the popular imagination. Even then, it was more than a simple Communist event—if it ever was. Granted, the leaders spoke the language of class conflict, when not trying to get under the skin of the authorities. But the men who deserted the relief camps in British Columbia and then set off to confront the prime minister were not shock troops intent on overthrowing the government. "All we ever wanted was work and wages," insisted ninety-two-year-old Harry Linsley during a Saskatoon interview in April 2001. Evans also stepped back from the brink in Regina—refused to engage the police like a good Communist—preferring instead to try to negotiate a peaceful retreat for his men. And when trouble did erupt at the Market Square meeting, the trekkers and citizens had not been whipped into an anti-capitalist frenzy but were shocked into action when attacked by the two police forces. Perhaps the final word on the revolutionary nature of the movement belongs to long-time Communist Party of Canada leader Tim Buck. It appears Buck either doubted the value of the trek or was jealous of its success or its leader, for he made no mention of the march from Vancouver to Regina in his reminiscences, *Yours in the Struggle*. For Buck, the trek never happened.[18]

Once the hearings, trials, and appeals associated with the riot were over, Evans returned to British Columbia and resumed his organizational work throughout the province. There were also new causes. In 1937, he helped raise medical funds for the Mackenzie-Papineau Battalion, an international brigade that had been recruited in Canada to fight for the Republican side in the Spanish Civil War. Evans's drinking, though, eventually got him into trouble with the Communist Party—he was sentenced to a week in jail in 1939 for being drunk in public—and he was released from his duties. After the start of the war, Evans found employment in Vancouver's West Coast Shipyards as a carpenter. Just after midnight on 22 January 1944, he left a union meeting and caught a streetcar home. Exiting by the back door at Joyce and Kingsway (now renamed Evansway), he went around the rear to cross the street and walked into the path of an oncoming car. He died three weeks later in hospital.[19]

The hundreds of men who had joined the trek went their different ways once the march to Ottawa had been officially disbanded. Several returned to the relief camps and then probably signed on with the new farm placement programme. Others continued to wander the country. A few, like Linsley, found the jobs that had eluded them for years. A good number—including four members of the trek delegation which had met with Prime Minister Bennett in June 1935—joined the so-called "Mac Paps" and fought General Franco's fascists in Spain. Paddy O'Neill and Peter Neilson died there, while Red Walsh and Tony Martin were captured and held in a prison camp. Many answered the call again when Canada went to war against Nazi Germany and another dictator in September 1939. As with other Canadians, volunteering to fight for king and country provided the first steady employment in almost a decade for many trekkers.[20]

Since the Depression, the trek has come to be a source of historical inspiration for western Canadians who are unhappy with the policies or inactivity of a distant, seemingly insensitive federal government. They want answers, or in some cases, action, and resurrect the idea of going to Ottawa, hoping to recapture the same sense of determination and momentum that energized the 1935 trek. The symbolism of the trek, for example, is currently being tapped into by those struggling to ease the agricultural crisis in western Canada. On 13 May 2002, Saskatchewan Premier Lorne Calvert announced that the provincial government wanted to organize its own Ottawa trek to highlight the problems that a new United States farm subsidy bill would create for prairie producers. A little more than two weeks later, Bryce Brodie, riding his tractor, set off on his own trek to the nation's capital, seeking to secure federal funds for a farm benefit concert.[21]

This trek legacy is somewhat ironic, especially since the men never did make it beyond Regina. But in retrospect, the idea of going to Ottawa was more important than actually getting there. Men who had come to know the depths of the Depression in their minds, their hearts, and their stomachs set off on a cross-country journey to draw attention to their situation in the hope of securing a better future. This purpose is something that seems to have been forgotten or overlooked in the intervening years: the men just wanted to live normal lives. Jean McWilliam of Calgary clearly understood this basic need. In a letter to Alice Millar, Prime Minister Bennett's personal secretary, dated two days after the Regina Riot, she provided a poignant reminder of what the men were seeking and what they faced in their young lives: "This is the third time I started to write you regarding the boys.... These boys who went thro Calgary seemed to be a very fine type of boys. I spoke to quite a few of them.... And you know Miss Millar, young men of that age like to have money to spend, like to take a girl out, like to get married, like to build their homes. Like to dress nice and go to a dance occasionally. Lack of these things drive them easy into discontented lines. And make them easy prey for agitators. So they are really tired of camp life. It is just like being in gaol. It is the oneness of it all, the monotony if you get what I mean. No outlook ... And I am heartily sorry for them. To me it is ... a lost generation. No one wants them. No one can understand the loneliness of their lives. You asked my opinion. You've got it.... P.S. I trust Mr. Bennett does not be too harsh on those lads. Some mother owns them."[22]

On-to-Ottawa Trekkers

The following names represent about 20 percent of the approximately two thousand On-to-Ottawa trekkers. Although the men had to register with the Saskatchewan government before leaving Regina, the list made at that time has not been located. These names have been collected from newspapers, police reports, hospital admittance files, court records, and the prisoner register for the Regina jail. Garnet Dishaw of the Saskatchewan Federation of Labour also provided a list of trekkers from the sixtieth anniversary celebration in Regina. In many instances, several names had different spellings; some are incomplete (last name only). Errors are unavoidable. There is likely some duplication, since trekkers often used aliases or had nicknames.

F. A. Acey
Alfred Allerud
Bruce Ames
Ed Amyott
George Anderson
Herbert Anderson
Ivor (Tiny) Anderson
L. A. Anderson
Sam Anderson
Metor Andruseak
Harry Arnold
Bill Austin
Ross Baker
Mike Jacob Balzer
Neil Bartlett
Reginald Bateman
Tom Bayne (Reid)
Joseph Bealene
Lester George Beaton
William Beaven
Joe Belaback
Joseph Beland
Alex Belger
Ivan Bell
John Bell
Albert Benson
George Black
Tom Black
Ed Blondren
Casper Blum
Frank Bobby
? Bradley
Treavers Bremner
T. Brennan
Thomas E. Brewer
Vern Brimacomb
Steve Brodie
George Brooks
Donald Brown
George Brown
Richard Brown
Leonard Brownstone
R. C. Brule
Robert Bruning
William A. Burro
Artie Burnell
S. B. Butt
Morris Carrel

Frank Carter
Ernest Chatten
Nick Chupa
Tom Clarke
Red Clarkson (Bob Prange)
Max Clem
Kellett Cole
John D. Connon
Roy Conroy
Jack Cosgrove
Tony Costello
Samuel Coury
George Crawford
George Creighton
James Cross
Clyde Crossley
? Cuff
Terry Cunningham
Owen D'arcy
Robert Daniels
Y. A. Daniels
William Davis
Harry (Tiny) Davies
William D. Davies
Alexander Dawson
Morris Deane
Stanley Delmage
Martin Dennis
Albert Dettman
Phillip Digman
Lyle Douglas
Fred Duncan
Maurice Dupuis
Joe Duquette
J. Eddy
Ernest Edwards
Reginald A. Ellis
Roger Ellis
Mike Enasiuk
Arthur (Slim) Evans
Rudy Fedorowich
James Fehr
Chris Fissel
George Fissel
Jimmy Fitzgerald
George F. Foley
Ken Forsyth
Dan Fraser
William Friebert

Eric Gable
Walter Gawrycki
Jack Geddes
Jack Gladhill
Gordon Glover
Andre Goessaert
Harold Goodson
A. Goodwin
Ed Goodwin
A. Goslin
Aitken Gossell
John Grainger
Louis Green
John Grimshaw
Harry Guilliman
Tolsen Habbe
Bill Hacket
William Hammill
George Hanks
James Harding
John Harding
Percy Harding
James Harland
R. Harper
Lindsay Harris
Norman Harris
Charles Harrison
Bruce Hart
David Hastings
Harry Herbert
Harry Hesketh
Frank Hess
George Hewitt
Seward Hicks
Perry Hilton (Perry Wellington)
William Hladey
B. Hodgson
Steve Holowey
? Houston
Henry Jackson
Robert Jackson
Sidney James
Douglas George Jewell (John Smith)
Henry Johns
Carl Johnson
John George Johnson
Mac Johnson

Russell Johnson
William Johnson
Griffith Jones
Hugh Jones
John Jones
Jack Jonkson
Fred Jonoisiuk
Steve Karapanski
David Karch
Robert Kearney
Elof Keller
J. Kennedy
Alfred Keyes
Alex G. Kilimchuk
Nick Kilostaff
Jim King
Phil Klein
Alex Klemchuk
Arne Knudson
Steve Koropatnisai
R. Kotilo
Jack Kyle
James Lacey
Armand Laframbois
Victor Lamframbois
James Lamb
Alex Lamont
G. Lang
Armand Lapointe
Alex La Rocque
A. Larsen
Einas Larsen
Jack Lawson
George Layton
Harry Linsley
John Linster
Peter Linteris
Fred Litwin
Ron Liversedge
Gene Llewellyn
Cameron Long
Jim Lucas
Scott Lumsden
Douglas Lycett
David Lyons
Frank Mabie
Ken Macaltery
G. MacKenzie
Mike Manetosky

Arthur March
Basil Marchand
Ed Martin
Jim Martin
Tony Martin
Clarence Mason
Mike Matiesh
Fred Mattersdorfer
Ken McCaffrey
J. McCarthy
J. McCauley
Butts McDonald
J. McDonald
John McElligott
William McGowan
Jim McHugh
Ted McKay
George McKenzie
Donald McLaren
Tom McMurray
Fred McNeil
Fred McPhee
William McTavish
Hugh J. McWatters
Robert Melville
Louis Metz
George Millar
John Miller
Jack Mitchell
Andrew Molyneaux
Leo Monette
F. Moorehouse
R. Morgan
Joe Mottl
Jack Myers
Joe Mynnie
John Napier
Peter Neilson
Fred Nogami
James Noone
Patick O'Grady
Barney Olness
Stewart O'Neill
Charles O'Rourke
George Pareles
Ed Parrell
Larry Patrick
Anker Peterson
George Phillips
Jack Phillips
John Pisactky
Eli Plavac
Dennis Porter
Wilfred W. Potter
John Powers
Fred Poznekoff
Thomas Reid
Harold Reynolds
Tony Ribell
Joseph Richards
George Ritchie
Nick Roback
John Robinson
R. Robson
W. Rodgers
James Rose
John Ross
Phil Ross
Ferdinand Roy
Wilfred Roy
Joe Ruginski
Jack Ryan
Nick Salemyk
Charles Sands
Peter Sanka
D. Saprunof
Robert Savage
Albert Savay
Nick Schaack
Irven P. Schwartz
Allen Scott
Charles Scott
James Scott
Willis Shaparla
Matt Shaw
William Shelton
Nat Sherlock
Victor Shero
Edward Silver
Alan Simpson
Joseph Slabick
Dan Slovay
Bob Smith
J. L. Smith
J. T. Smith
Leonard James Smith
Frank Smythe
Bill Snider
Charles Stanforth
James Stephens
Sidney Stevens
Mike Strijack
James Stuart
Gus Switzer
Joe Szedry
Henry Tarten
Gerry Tellier
Nick Tlatoff
Tony Tomachuk
Habbe Torsten
Jean Trahan
Walter J. Tully
Robert Edward Usher
Steve Valescak
John Vermeulan
William Wadsworth
Wayne Wainwright
Victor Walkow
Alfred Wallerud
Jim Walsh
Andrew Weber
John Wedin
Albert Weir
Allen Weir
Alfred Wells
Carl Whitney
Clinton Whyte
William Wilkes
Roy Williams
William Williams
William Evan Williams
Gerry Winters
George Wilson
Jim Wilson
Leornard Wilson
Ernest Woodley
Mike Yarmus
Andte Yerkotila
Mike Yonda
John W. Young
Joseph H. Young
Mike Zacharuk
Hans Zappe

NOTE ON SOURCES

All Hell Can't Stop Us is based on a number of new sources that have become available only in the last two decades. Previously closed Royal Canadian Mounted Police records are now under the control of the National Archives of Canada in the Government Archives Division (Record Group 146, Canadian Security and Intelligence Service). Although these confidential documents must first be reviewed by the Access to Information and Privacy Division before release, they constitute one of the best government sources on the trek and riot. The Mountie material is nicely complemented by Regina city police records for 1935. Long considered missing or destroyed, they were unexpectedly made available to the author for the first time during the research phase. The story also greatly benefited from the records of John Gregory (Jack) King, a Co-operative Commonwealth Federation activist who was one of the leading figures in the Regina Citizens' Emergency Committee and later defence committee. His papers were found in an attic in Nova Scotia following the death of his wife, Betty Hearn, in 1997; the documents (over fifteen hundred pages) were in such poor physical shape that they had to be photocopied by the Saskatchewan Archives Board and the originals destroyed.

A good deal of trek- and riot-related material is found in the papers of prime ministers Bennett and King, Saskatchewan premier Jimmy Gardiner, and General Andy McNaughton, who devised the federal relief camp scheme. Government department records, in particular those of the Departments of National Defence and Labour, were also consulted. Another key source proved to be the files of the vice president (western region) of the Canadian Pacific Railway, held by the CPR Archives in Montreal.

By far the most voluminous and comprehensive primary source are the records, including fifty-three volumes of testimony, of the provincial Regina Riot Inquiry Commission. No study of the trek and riot is possible without a close reading of this material. An unexpected bonus were the trial transcripts for those charged with rioting or related offences—most of these records have never been consulted since they were filed in 1936.

Readers interested in particular or detailed references should consult the endnotes.

NOTES

PREFACE (pages vii–xi)

1. Saskatchewan Archives Board [SAB], J. G. Gardiner papers, vii, 6, 46185, "1937 Ontario Provincial Election Speech."
2. SAB, Regina Riot Inquiry Commission, v. 5, 41.

INTRODUCTION (pages 1–7)

1. The exact number of trekkers is a matter of debate. At the Regina Riot Inquiry Commission, defence lawyer Frank Cunningham reported that either 2,014 or 2,016 men arrived in Regina that morning. The two Regina daily newspapers offered different estimates: 1,500 or 2,000. Saskatchewan Archives Board [SAB], Regina Riot Inquiry Commission [RRIC], v. 2, 148; v. 3, 50; *Regina Leader-Post*, 14 June 1935; *Regina Daily Star*, 14 June 1935. Since roughly 1,350 trekkers had been counted in Moose Jaw, it is possible that their numbers might have reached 1,500 by the time they reached Regina.
2. *Ottawa Journal*, 14 June 1935.
3. SAB, RRIC, v. 8, 87; v. 12, 56; *Regina Leader-Post*, 13 June 1935.
4. *Regina Leader-Post*, 14 June 1935.
5. National Archives of Canada [NAC], Government Archives Division, Canadian Security Intelligence Service, RG 146, f. 93-A-00086, pt. 3, S. T. Wood to J. H. MacBrien, 24 June 1935; RRIC, v. 35, 176; v. 36, 137.
6. *Regina Leader-Post*, 14 June 1935.
7. *Ibid.*
8. Reporter James Kingsbury of the *Toronto Star* rode with the trekkers from Swift Current to Regina. *Toronto Daily Star*, 17 June 1935; *Winnipeg Tribune*, 14 June 1935; *Regina Daily Star*, 14 June 1935; *Regina Leader-Post*, 14 June 1935; RRIC, v. 2, 122; v. 28, 30.
9. *Regina Leader-Post*, 14 June 1935.
10. *Regina Daily Star*, 14 June 1935.

CHAPTER ONE (pages 9–24)

1. Quoted in J. Petryshyn, "R. B. Bennett and the Communists: 1930–1935," *Journal of Canadian Studies* (November 1974), 51. For a discussion of the supposed threat that communism and unemployment poised to the morality of Canada during the 1930s, see Carolyn Strange and Tina Loo, *Making Good: Law and Moral Regulation in Canada, 1867–1939* (Toronto: 1997), 124–33.
2. For a listing of Bennett's major financial holdings and directorships, see Alvin Finkel, *Business and Social Reform in the Thirties* (Toronto: 1979), 11; P. B. Waite, *The Loner: Three Sketches of the Personal Life and Ideas of R. B. Bennett, 1870–1947* (Toronto: 1992), 34.
3. Quoted in C. A. Bowman, *Ottawa Editor* (Sidney, B.C.: 1966), 138; Blair Neatby, *The Politics of Chaos: Canada in the Thirties* (Toronto:1972), 70; *Toronto Daily Star*, 29 July 1930; J. H. Gray, *R. B. Bennett: The Calgary Years* (Toronto: 1991), 36, 89; Lord Beaverbrook, *Friends: Sixty Years of Intimate Personal Relations with R. B. Bennett* (London: 1959), 75; Ernest Watkins, *R. B. Bennett* (Toronto: 1963), 215; L. R. Betcherman, *The Little Band: The Clashes between the Communists and the Political and Legal Establishment in Canada, 1928–1932* (Ottawa: 1982), 140. The author wishes to thank Don Story of the University of Saskatchewan Political Studies Department for providing several good references to Bennett's character.
4. *Toronto Daily Star*, 29 July 1930.
5. Larry Glassford, *Reaction and Reform: The Politics of the Conservative Party under R. B. Bennett, 1927–1938* (Toronto: 1992), 110–12.
6. In 1928, total Canadian exports (on a crop year basis) amounted to $1,249.5 million; the total value of wheat exports was $321.67 million, or 25.74 percent of total Canadian exports. In 1930, total Canadian exports had dropped to $716.7 million, while the total value of wheat exports was $126.73 million, or 17.68 percent of total Canadian exports. These figures were kindly provided by Bill Martin, who is doing a major study of Canadian wheat marketing in the 1940s and 1950s.
7. J. H. Thompson with A. Seager, *Canada, 1922–1939: Decades of Discord* (Toronto: 1985), 193–221.
8. James Struthers, *No Fault of Their Own: Unemployment and the Canadian Welfare State, 1914–1941* (Toronto: 1983), 12–43.
9. T. Healey, "Prayers, Pamphlets, and Protest: Women and Relief in Saskatoon, 1929–1939," unpublished M.A. thesis, University of Saskatchewan (1989); Barry Broadfoot, *Ten Lost Years, 1929–1939: Memories of Canadians who Survived the Depression* (Toronto: 1973), 70; Strange and Loo, *Making Good*, 124–25.
10. The formal title was "An Act to confer certain powers upon the Governor in Council in respect to unemployment and farm relief, and the maintenance of peace, order, and good government in Canada." *Statutes of Canada*, 21–22 George V, c. 58.
11. *House of Commons Debates*, 29 July 1931, 4278, 4286.
12. Quoted in J. Torrance, *Public Violence in Canada, 1867–1982* (Kingston:1986), 20; *Saskatoon Daily Star*, 7 February 1920.
13. See D. De Brou and B. Waiser, eds., *Documenting Canada: A History of Modern Canada in*

Documents (Saskatoon: 1992), 272–74; G. S. Kealey, "The RCMP, the Special Branch, and the Early Days of the Communist Party of Canada: A Documentary Article," *Labour/Le Travail*, no. 30 (Fall 1992), 171; G. S. Kealey, "The Early Years of State Surveillance of Labour and the Left in Canada: The Institutional Framework of the Royal Canadian Mounted Police Security and Intelligence Apparatus, 1918–26," *Intelligence and National Security* 8, no. 3 (1993), 129–48.

14. See G. S. Kealey and Reg Whitaker, eds., *RCMP Security Bulletins: The Early Years, 1919–1929* (St. John's: 1994); Betcherman, *The Little Band*, 7, 19, 28, 53. The January 1929 police order forbidding the use of a hall for a Communist meeting served as the basis for Quebec's infamous padlock law.
15. Quoted in J. Manley, " 'Starve, Be Damned': Communists and Canada's Unemployed," *Canadian Historical Review* 79, no. 3 (September 1998), 469; Betcherman, *The Little Band*, 88; L. Brown, "Some Responses to the Canadian Unemployed as a Political and Occupational Constituency, 1930–35," unpublished paper presented before Canadian Historical Association (1989).
16. Quoted in Betcherman, *The Little Band*, 44–45, 147–48, 154.
17. Bennett apparently made his now famous remark at the November 1932 meeting of the Ontario Conservative Association. Quoted in S. M. Jamieson, *Times of Trouble: Labour Unrest and Industrial Conflict, 1900–66* (Ottawa: 1968), 217; J. H. Thomas, *My Story* (London: 1937), 210.
18. Betcherman, *The Little Band*, 151.
19. D. Macgillivray, "Military Aid to Civil Power: The Cape Breton Experience in the 1920s," *Acadiensis* (Spring 1974), 46; V. Kemp, *Without Fear, Favour or Affection* (Toronto: 1958), 156; Quoted in Betcherman, *The Little Band*, 4. MacBrien's Great War honours were the Commander of the Order of the Bath (CB), the Companion of the Order of St. Michael and St. George (CMG), and the Distinguished Service Order and Bar (DSO). Information about MacBrien's honours was provided by Christopher McCreery of Queen's University.
20. Quoted in Petryshyn, "Bennett and the Communists," 45; R. A. Adams, "The 1931 Arrest and Trial of the Leaders of the Communist Party of Canada," unpublished paper presented before the Canadian Historical Association (1977).
21. Kemp, *Without Fear*, 150; P.C. 3087, 16 December 1931; *House of Commons Debates*, 23 February 1932, 450.
22. *House of Commons Debates*, 10 March 1932, 979.
23. *Ibid.*, 17 March 1932, 1224; 23 March 1932, 1413.
24. See Bill Waiser, *Park Prisoners: The Untold Story of Western Canada's National Parks, 1915–1946* (Saskatoon: 1995), chapters 2–3; Thompson, *Canada 1922–1939*, 216–18.
25. *Statutes of Canada*, 22–23 George V, c. 37.
26. *House of Commons Debates*, 3 May 1932, 2591–94, 2601.
27. Betcherman, *The Little Band*, 93.

CHAPTER TWO (pages 25–40)

1. James Eayrs, *In Defence of Canada: From the Great War to the Great Depression* (Toronto: 1964), 125.
2. A. Roddan, *Canada's Untouchables* (Vancouver: 1932), 14.
3. The author had two uncles who left home, in southwestern Manitoba, at the age of twelve and fourteen and crossed into the United States; they never returned to Canada. The author's father, the second eldest of eleven children, "rode the rods" in the early 1930s and eventually spent time in a B.C. relief camp.
4. National Archives of Canada [NAC], Manuscript Division, R. B. Bennett papers, 49366–72, W. A. Gordon to R. B. Bennett, 14 June 1932; J. Struthers, *No Fault of Their Own: Unemployment and the Canadian Welfare State, 1914–1941* (Toronto: 1983), 55–56.
5. In 1934, the residency qualification was changed to twelve consecutive months. R. Liversedge, *Recollections of the On To Ottawa Trek* (Toronto: 1973), 10.
6. NAC, Bennett papers, 49366–72, Gordon to Bennett, 14 June 1932; Struthers, *No Fault*, 52–53.
7. Bennett papers, 491438, W. A. Coulter to Bennett, Spring 1934. See L. M. Grayson and Michael Bliss, eds., *The Wretched of Canada: Letters to R. B, Bennett, 1930–1935* (Toronto: 1971); B. Waiser, *Park Prisoners: The Untold Story of Western Canada's National Parks, 1915–1946* (Saskatoon: 1995), chapter 2; B. Roberts, *Whence They Came: Deportation from Canada, 1900–1935* (Ottawa: 1988), 159–94. Roberts suggests that Immigration officials during the Depression were "dishonest and malevolent" in enforcing the law. There were 17,229 public charge deportations between 1929–30 and 1934–35. Since British-born immigrants at the time did not have to become naturalized to enjoy Canadian citizenship, they were technically subject to deportation. L. R. Betcherman, *The Little Band: The Clashes Between the Communists and the Political and Legal Establishment in Canada, 1928–1932* (Ottawa: 1982), 144.
8. Struthers, *No Fault*, 77–80; G. Marquis, *Policing Canada's Century* (Toronto: 1993), 162. In Saskatchewan in 1934–35, for example, only 78 of the 16,847 transients removed from trains were prosecuted. Saskatchewan Archives Board [SAB], Regina Riot Inquiry Commission [RRIC], v. 36, 130.
9. Eayrs, *In Defence of Canada*, 257–58.
10. *Ibid.*, 125.
11. Quoted in *ibid.*, 129.
12. Struthers, *No Fault*, 81–82.
13. A. Prentice et al., *Canadian Women: A History* (Toronto: 1988); N. Christie, *Engendering the State: Family, Work, and Welfare in Canada* (Toronto: 2000); T. Healey, "Prayers, Pamphlets and Protest: Women and Relief in Saskatoon, 1929–1939," unpublished M.A. thesis, University of Saskatchewan (1990), 33; M. Hobbs, "Equality and Difference: Feminism and the Defence of Women Workers During the Great Depression," *Labour/Le Travail* 32 (Fall 1993), 215; M. Martin, "Go Home, Young Woman!," *Chatelaine* (September 1933), 10; see response in November 1933 issue. A job during the Depression, according to David Bright, was a "qualified" female right. D. Bright, "Conflicts Between

the State, the Unemployed, and the Communist Party in Calgary, 1930–1935," *Canadian Historical Review* 78, no. 4 (December 1997), 544.

14. For a description of relief activities in western Canada's national parks, see Waiser, *Park Prisoners*, chapters 2–3.
15. Struthers, *No Fault*, 82–83.
16. McNaughton tried repeatedly, without success, to close the relief camps in national parks; he did not believe that there should be two separate programmes for transients.
17. NAC, Government Archives Division, National Defence, RG 27, v. 2245, "Report on the Department of National Defence Unemployment Relief Scheme," August 1936. For a decription of relief camp activities in Ontario, see L. S. MacDowell, "Relief Camp Workers in Ontario during the Great Depression of the 1930s," *Canadian Historical Review* 76, no. 2, June 1995, 205–28. By the time the programme was finally wrapped up in early 1936, 167,171 men had provided over 18 million man-days of relief work on 144 projects at a cost of $22.5 million. These numbers suggest a high turn-over rate, especially in the spring, when men left the camps in search of other work.
18. L. S. MacDowell, "Canada's Gulag: Project #51 Lac Seul (A Tale from the Great Depression)," *Journal of Canadian Studies* 28, no. 2 (Summer 1993), 130–58; James H. Gray, *The Winter Years* (Toronto: 1966), 148.
19. B. Broadfoot, *Ten Lost Years, 1929–1939: Memories of Canadians Who Survived the Depression* (Toronto: 1973), 96; *House of Commons Debates*, 13 February 1936, 185.
20. John Swettenham, *McNaughton, Volume One: 1887–1939* (Toronto 1968), 270–71.
21. S. M. Jamieson, *Times of Trouble: Labour Unrest and Industrial Conflict 1900–66* (Ottawa; 1968), 242–43.
22. Betcherman, *The Little Band*, 90–91; "Report on the DND Unemployment Relief Scheme," 55–60.
23. Lorne Brown, *When Freedom was Lost: The Unemployed, the Agitator, and the State* (Montreal: 1987), 73–76.
24. Broadfoot, *Ten Lost Years*, 364; Eayrs, *In Defence of Canada*, 130–32.
25. Betcherman, *The Little Band*, 136–37.
26. Justice Minister Hugh Guthrie denied the existence of the squad when questioned about the matter in the House of Commons—even though a senior mounted police source was quoted. *House of Commons Debates*, 3 May 1932, 2602.
27. The use of the military to quell civil disturbances after the creation of the RCMP in 1920 declined considerably. S. R. Hewitt, "Old Myths Die Hard: The Transformation of the Mounted Police in Alberta and Saskatchewan," unpublished Ph.D. dissertation, University of Saskatchewan (1997), 141, 210–19, 246.
28. *House of Commons Debates*, 3 April 1933, 3636, 3638; 11 May 1934, 2987.

CHAPTER THREE (pages 41–55)

1. Victor Howard, *"We Were the Salt of the Earth!" The On-to-Ottawa Trek and the Regina Riot* (Regina: 1985), 14–15; National Archives of Canada [NAC], Government Archives Division, Department of National Defence, RG 24, v. 3034, f. "Rod Riders," Alberta Unemployment Relief Commission to Commander, Military District 13, 17 November

1933; Department of Labour, RG 27, v. 2140, f. "DND Correspondence Camps, 1933–36," A. L. McNaughton to J. H. MacBrien, 1 November 1934; W. A. Dickson to A. MacNamara, 20 September 1934.

2. Howard, *Salt of the Earth*, 13–14.
3. NAC, RG 27, v. 2255, A. L. McNaughton to W. A. Dickson, 18 February 1935.
4. Howard, *Salt of the Earth*, 18–19.
5. James Eayrs, *In the Defence of Canada: From the Great War to the Great Depression* (Toronto: 1967), 136–42.
6. NAC, RG 27, v. 2140, f. "DND Correspondence Camps, 1933–36," A. L. McNaughton to W. A. Dickson, 7 March 1935, draft telegram appended.
7. R. Liversedge, *Recollections of the On To Ottawa Trek* (Toronto: 1973), 59; J. E. Shiels and B. Swankey, *"Work and Wages!": A Semi-Documentary Account of the Life and Times of Arthur H. (Slim) Evans* (Vancouver: 1977), 31
8. NAC, Government Archives Division, Canadian Security Intelligence Service, RG 146, f. 94-A-00006, pt. 1, F. J. Culverhouse to S. T. Wood, 5 September 1932; J. H. McMullin to S. T. Wood, 24 November 1932.
9. *Ibid.*, A. H. Evans circular letters, 4 October 1932; 28 October 1932.
10. Howard, *Salt of the Earth*, 26–27.
11. Eayrs, *In Defence of Canada*, 141–44.
12. Quoted in Shiels and Swankey, *Work and Wages*, 106.
13. Quoted in V. Howard, "Citizen Support of the On-to-Ottawa Trek," in R. D. Francis and H. Ganzevoort, eds., *The Dirty Thirties in Prairie Canada* (Vancouver: 1980), 33; J. M. Torrance, *Public Violence in Canada* (Montreal: 1986), 194–7; Howard, *Salt of the Earth*, 43–44.
14. McNaughton warned the government that there were thousands of single homeless unemployed in other cities watching what happened in Vancouver. J. Swettenham, *McNaughton, Volume One: 1887–1939* (Toronto: 1968), 280; Eayrs, *In Defence of Canada*, 145–46.
15. Howard, *Salt of the Earth*", 37; Irene Howard, "The Mothers' Council of Vancouver: Holding the Fort for the Unemployed, 1935–1938," in R. A. J. McDonald and J. Barman, eds., *Vancouver Past: Essays in Social History* (Vancouver: 1986), 269–71; P. Knight, *A Very Ordinary Life* (Vancouver: 1974).
16. Howard, *Salt of the Earth*, 49–52, 72, 74–76; Shiels and Swankey, *Work and Wages*, 106.
17. NAC, Manuscript Division, R. B. Bennett papers, 496383–5, H. H. Stevens to G. H. Perley, 30 April 1935.
18. *Toronto Star*, 13 May 1935.
19. Bennett papers, 496509-11, G. G. McGeer to R. B. Bennett, 21 May 1935; Lorne Brown, *When Freedom Was Lost: The Unemployed, the Agitator, and the State* (Montreal: 1987), 133; R. C. McCandless, "Vancouver's 'Red Menace' of 1935: The Waterfront Situation," *BC Studies*, no. 22 (Summer 1974), 60.
20. See McCandless, "Vancouver's 'Red Menace'"; J. Struthers, *No Fault of Their Own: Unemployment and the Canadian Welfare State, 1914–41* (Toronto: 1983), 136.
21. Howard, *Salt of the Earth*, 79; Swettenham, *McNaughton*, 280; Eayrs, *In Defence of Canada*, 136.

22. Saskatchewan Archives Board [SAB], Regina Riot Inquiry Commission [RRIC], v. 8, 32; Liversedge, *Recollections*, 83.
23. NAC, RG 24, v. 3047, f. C18-34-1B, v. 1, W. W. Foster to E. C. Ashton, undated.
24. *The Worker*, 1 June 1935.
25. Howard, *Salt of the Earth*, 82–84.
26. *Report in the Matter of the Commission on Relief Camps British Columbia* (Ottawa: 1935), 12, 15: SAB, RRIC, v. 8, 35–9, 41; v. 13, 10.
27. Liversedge, *Recollections*, 328; NAC, RG 24, v. 3047, f. "Unemployment Relief Diary B.C. to Ottawa."

CHAPTER FOUR (pages 57–79)

1. J. Struthers, *No Fault of Their Own: Unemployment and the Canadian Welfare State, 1914–1941* (Toronto 1983), 137.
2. *Toronto Star*, 4 June 1935; *The Worker*, 6 June 1935; *House of Commons Debates*, 5 June 1935, 3317; Canadian Pacific Railway Archives [CPR], Vice President papers, f. 15989, D. C. Coleman memo, 4 June 1935; R. J. Manion to D. C. Coleman, 5 June 1935. A history of the RCMP Security Service claims that Constable L. H. Graham, who had been working undercover in Vancouver since 1932, joined the trek in Vancouver, but this is contradicted by Assistant Commissioner Wood's correspondence and Graham's own testimony at the preliminary hearing of *R. v. Bell et al.* C. Betke and S. W. Horrall, *Canada's Security Service: An Historical Outline, 1864–1966, Volume 2*, unpublished RCMP Security Service Report (1978), 448.
3. *The Worker*, 4 June 1935; National Archives of Canada [NAC], Canadian Security Intelligence Service, RG 146, f. 93-A-00086, pt. 3, "Relief Camp Strikers—March from Vancouver to Ottawa," 7 June 1935.
4. V. Howard, *"We Were the Salt of the Earth!" The On-to-Ottawa Trek and the Regina Riot* (Regina: 1985), 87–8; RG 146, f. 94-A-00006, pt. 1, C.I.B. memorandum, 5 June 1935.
5. R. Liversedge, *Recollections of the On To Ottawa Trek* (Toronto: 1973), 87, 89–90. The lyrics are taken from the song sheets distributed at the trek rallies. See Saskatchewan Archives Board [SAB], Regina Riot Inquiry Commission [RRIC], v. 5, 39.
6. Liversedge, *Recollections*, 90; Howard, *Salt of the Earth*, 89.
7. Quoted in G. Montero, *We Stood Together* (Toronto 1979), 39. See also Liversedge, *Recollections*, 91–3 and Howard, *Salt of the Earth*, 89–90.
8. SAB, RRIC, v. 8, 87.
9. Howard, *Salt of the Earth*, 90.
10. *Ibid.*, 90–91.
11. *Ottawa Citizen*, 5 June 1935; 8 June 1935; *The Worker*, 8 June 1935.
12. Premier R. G. Reid of Alberta telegraphed Bennett twice (4 and 6 June) about the impending arrival of the trekkers in his province; both times, he urged the federal government to stop them. National Archives of Canada [NAC], Manuscript Division, R. B. Bennett papers, 496539–40, 496547; *House of Commons Debates*, 21 May 1935, 2922; 7 June 1935, 3396–7. Bennett's comments would become an issue at the Regina Riot Inquiry Commission when excerpts from Hansard were read into the record: SAB, RRIC, v. 6,

154–55; Struthers, *No Fault of Their Own*, 137.

13. SAB, J. G. King papers, f. 9, "John C. Cosgrove."
14. *Calgary Herald*, 7 June 1935; 8 June 1935.
15. *Calgary Herald*, 7 June 1935; *Toronto Daily Star*, 10 June 1935; Howard, *Salt of the Earth*, 95.
16. *Toronto Daily Star*, 10 June 1935; David Bright, "Conflict Between the State, the Unemployed, and the Communist Party in Calgary, 1930–1935," *Canadian Historical Review*, 78, no. 4 (December 1997), 565; *Calgary Albertan*, 13 June 1935.
17. CPR, Vice President papers, f. 15989, W. J. Stevens to A. H. Cadieux, 14 June 1935.
18. SAB, King papers, f. 9, "Matt Shaw"; Howard, *Salt of the Earth*, 36–37; *Toronto Daily Star*, 10 June 1935.
19. This incident is described by both Liversedge (*Recollections*, 101) and Walsh (*We Stood Together*, 40), but Liversedge has the day wrong (Monday night) and Walsh has both the day and place wrong (the Saturday night public rally). That the incident happened is confirmed by James Kingsbury, the *Toronto Star* reporter who was covering the trek: *Toronto Daily Star*, 10 June 1935.
20. Military District 13 reported that 58 men left DND Relief Projects 120 and 155 for Calgary and that men in the Crowsnest Pass area were planning to join the trek at Medicine Hat: NAC, Government Archives Division, National Defence, RG 24, v. 3047, f. "U.R. Diary B.C. to Ottawa," 29; O'Neill quoted in Liversedge, *Recollections*, 102.
21. NAC, Department of National Defence, RG 24, v. 3047, f. "U.R. Diary B.C. to Ottawa," 29; *Toronto Daily Star*, 11 June 1935; Liversedge, *Recollections*, 122.
22. NAC, RG 24, v. 3047, f. "U.R. Diary B.C. to Ottawa," Officer Commanding M.D. 13 to Chief of the General Staff, 14 June 1935; NAC, Manuscript Division, A. G. L. McNaughton papers, v. 60, f. 378, Officer Commanding M.D. 13 to Chief of the General Staff, 8 June 1935; RRIC, v. 36, 110.
23. McNaughton papers, v. 60, f. 378, Officer Commanding M.D. 13 to National Defence Headquarters, 9 June 1935; Bennett papers, 496566, A. A. Mackenzie to W. A. Gordon, 11 June 1935; 496647, A. A. Mackenzie to R. Weir, 17 June 1935.
24. CPR, Vice President papers, f. 15989, D. C. Coleman to R. J. Manion, 6 June 1935; Bennett papers, 496548, R. B. Bennett to R. G. Reid, 11 June 1935.
25. *Calgary Herald*, 10 June 1935; Bennett papers, 236364–71, R. B. Bennett to C. Wigram, 3 May 1931; 236519, J. H. MacBrien to R. B. Bennett, 4 June 1935.
26. *Toronto Daily Star*, 11 June 1935.
27. Montero, *We Stood Together*, 40; Howard, *Salt of the Earth*, 88, 96.
28. Swankey and Sheils, *"Work and Wages!": A Semi-Documentary Account of the Life and Times of Arthur H. (Slim) Evans* (Vancouver: 1977), 113.
29. Prime Minister Bennett told the House of Commons on 2 July 1935 that the decision had been made the next day—when the trekkers were between Swift Current and Moose Jaw. SAB, RRIC, v. 36, 114, exhibit 158, J. H. MacBrien to S. T. Wood, 11 June 1935; G. T. Hann, "Stuart Taylor Wood," *RCMP Quarterly* 17, 4–9; V. Kemp, *Without Fear, Favour, or Affection* (Toronto: 1958); S. R. Hewitt, "Old Myths Die Hard: The Transformation of the Mounted Police in Alberta and Saskatchewan," unpublished Ph.D. dissertation, University of Saskatchewan (1997), 177.

30. S. D. Hanson, "The 1931 Estevan Strike and Riot" in I. Abella, ed., *On Strike* (Toronto: 1975), 33–78; G. Makahonuk, "The Saskatoon Relief Camp Workers' Riot," *Saskatchewan History* 37, no. 2 (1984), 55–72; P. Berton, *The Great Depression* (Toronto: 1990), 119; Hewitt, "Old Myths Die Hard," 141, 215, 249.
31. NAC, RG 146, f. 93-A-00086, pt. 3, S. T. Wood to Officer Commanding Regina Subdivision, 6 June 1935; W. Munday to S. T. Wood, 13 June 1935; SAB, RRIC, exhibit 157, S. T. Wood to Dann, 10 June 1935. Wood reported that 76 officers and men had been sent from F Division and the Regina Depot to Vancouver in early May. The Saskatoon RCMP arrested twenty-two men, travelling illegally by train, on 12 June 1935: *Toronto Daily Star*, 13 June 1935.
32. J. E. Shiels and B. Swankey, *Work and Wages*, 31.
33. *Winnipeg Tribune*, 13 June 1935.
34. SAB, RRIC, v. 8, 87; v. 12, 56; *Winnipeg Tribune*, 13 June 1935.
35. NAC, RG 146, f. 93-A-00086, pt. 3, S. T. Wood to J. H. MacBrien, 15 June 1935; G. C. P Montizmabert to S. T. Wood, 15 June 1935; SAB, RRIC, exhibit 166, W. A. Mather to S. T. Wood, 11 June 1935; exhibit 150, RCMP Memo, S. T. Wood to Inspectors and Sergeants, 12 June 1935.
36. NAC, RG 146, f. 93-A-00086, pt. 2, G. C. P. Montizambert, "Relief Camp Strikers," 15 June 1935; CPR, Vice President papers, f. 15989, W. M. Neal, "10K Report–Eastern Standard Time," undated.; *Winnipeg Evening Tribune*, 14 June 1935. The trek, as a media sensation, had direct parallels with other unique events of the decade, such as the marketing of the Dionne quintuplets, Grey Owl's beaver project in Prince Albert National Park, and the Great Stork Derby in Toronto.
37. See, for example, "While Rome Burns," *The Worker*, 11 June 1935.
38. *House of Commons Debates*, 13 June 1935, 3585–88.
39. *Ibid.*, 13 June 1935, 3592–93.
40. *Regina Leader-Post*, 13 June 1935; *Winnipeg Tribune*, 13 June 1935.
41. *Regina Leader-Post*, 14 June 1935. The RCMP interpreted Shaw's remarks to mean that the trekkers would resist any obstruction.
42. *Regina Leader-Post*, 14 June 1935; 20 July 1935.
43. SAB, RRIC, v. 3, 50.

CHAPTER FIVE (pages 81–98)

1. Just three years earlier, total net farm income had been $178.5 million. Alma Lawton, "Urban Relief in Saskatchewan During the Years of the Depression, 1930–1939," unpublished M.A. thesis, University of Saskatchewan (1969), 37.
2. B. Neatby, "The Saskatchewan Relief Commission," *Saskatchewan History* 3, no. 2, (Spring 1950), 41–56; Province of Saskatchewan, *A Submission by the Government of Saskatchewan to the Royal Commission on Dominion-Provincial Relations* (Ottawa: 1937), 181–84.
3. For a first-hand contemporary account of life in the Saskatchewan dust bowl, see D. B. MacRae and R. M. Scott, *In the South Country* (Saskatoon: 1934).
4. A. J. Artibise, "Patterns of Prairie Urban Development, 1871–1950," in D. J. Bercuson and

P. Buckner, eds., *Eastern and Western Perspectives* (Toronto: 1981), 124–32.

5. D. Bowen, "Forward to a Farm: Land Settlement as Unemployment Relief in the 1930s," *Prairie Forum* 20, no. 2 (Fall 1995), 207–30; C. Danysk, "No Help for Farm Help: The Farm Employment Plans of the 1930s in Western Canada," unpublished paper presented before Canadian Historical Association (1993). Saskatchewan became the most heavily indebted province in the country in the 1930s, an almost complete reversal of the situation at the start of the decade: Lawton, "Urban Relief in Saskatchewan," 43–50.
6. J. W. Brennan, *Regina: An Illustrated City* (Toronto: 1989), 31.
7. *Ibid.* 119,128.
8. *Ibid.* 117,137–43.
9. *Regina Leader-Post,* 2 May 1931.
10. N. Ward and D. Smith, *Jimmy Gardiner: Relentless Liberal* (Toronto: 1990), 130, 143–45; R. A. Wardhaugh, *Mackenzie King and the Prairie West* (Toronto: 2000), 166.
11. Quoted in *Saskatoon Star Phoenix,* 1 June 1931.
12. Quoted in *Alameda Dispatch,* 8 March 1935.
13. Wardhaugh, *Mackenzie King and the Prairie West,* 181.
14. Saskatchewan, *Submission,* 148; National Archives of Canada [NAC], Manuscript Division, R. B. Bennett papers, 491515, "Memo on Direct Relief Figures," 9 September 1935; Brennan, *Regina,* 136; Saskatchewan Archives Board [SAB], J. G. Gardiner papers, vi, f. 31, "Relief," M. Bichel to J. G. Gardiner, undated.
15. *Regina Daily Star,* 23 October 1934.
16. L. Glassford, *Reaction and Reform: The Politics of the Conservative Government Under R. B. Bennett, 1927–1938* (Toronto: 1992), 69.
17. SAB, Gardiner papers, f. 33–1, "Relief," J. G. Gardiner to E. N. Rhodes, 7 September 1934; memorandum to file, J. G. Gardiner, 5 November 1934.
18. *Ibid.*, J. G. Gardiner to E. N. Rhodes, 7 September 1934; memorandum to file, J. G. Gardiner, 5 November 1934; E. N. Rhodes to J. G. Gardiner, 30 April 1935.
19. Quoted in *Regina Leader-Post,* 4 June 1935; SAB, Regina Riot Inquiry Commission [RRIC], v. 2, 138; v. 4, 48.
20. SAB, Gardiner papers, f. 46, "Unemployed On-to-Ottawa Trek," W. A. Mather to J. G. Gardiner, 11 June 1935; RRIC, v. 2, 120, 137; v. 4, 48–50; v. 36, 111; exhibit 168, S. T. Wood to J. H. MacBrien, 13 June 1935.
21. Anyone associated with the trek reported that the CPR did whatever it could to facilitate the movement of the men eastward: SAB, Gardiner papers, f. 46, "Unemployed On-to-Ottawa Trek," J. G. Gardiner to R. B. Bennett, 12 June 1935; R. B. Bennett to J. G. Gardiner, 12 June 1935; J. G. Gardiner to R. B. Bennett, 12 June 1935; J. G. Gardiner to W. A. Mather, 12 June 1935; J. G. Gardiner press release, 12 June 1935. The release was published almost verbatim in the *Regina Leader-Post* that same day.
22. P. B. Waite, *The Loner: Three Sketches of the Personal Life and Ideas of R. B. Bennett, 1870–1947* (Toronto: 1992), 85; E. Watkins, *R. B. Bennett: A Biography* (Toronto: 1963), 217; Glassford, *Reaction and Reform,* 169.
23. NAC, Bennett papers, 496515–6, R. B. Bennett to G. G. Webber, 4 June 1935.
24. Glassford, *Reaction and Reform,* 170. Bennett's feud with Stevens shared front-page news with the trek. See, for example, *Toronto Daily Star,* 11 June 1935.

25. SAB, RRIC, v. 36, 110; G. M. Stone, "The Regina Riot: 1935," unpublished M.A. thesis, University of Saskatchewan (1967), 45, 124–25.
26. Although the author has not found any minutes of the 11 June Ottawa meeting, the Gardiner papers confirm that such a meeting took place, as does his interview with a *Toronto Daily Star* reporter on June 13. See SAB, Gardiner papers, f. 46, "Unemployed On-to-Ottawa Trek," J. G. Gardiner to R. B. Bennett, 13 June 1935; *Toronto Daily Star*, 13 June 1935.
27. SAB, Gardiner papers, f. 46, "Unemployed On-to-Ottawa Trek," R. B. Bennett to J. G. Gardiner, 13 June 1935; S. J. Hungerford to J. G. Gardiner, 12 June 1935; W. A. Mather to J. G. Gardiner, 13 June 1935. In a telegram to Prime Minister Bennett that same day, Edward Beatty, President of the CPR, reported that "the Company had not done anything" to assist the trekkers: NAC, Bennett papers, 496584, E. W. Beatty to R. B. Bennett, 13 June 1935.
28. NAC, Manuscript Division, A. G. L. McNaughton papers, series 2, v. 60, f. 380, "Memorandum of a Conference in the office of the deputy minister of Justice," 12 June 1935. McNaughton's last official act as chief of the general staff was on May 29, when he appeared before cabinet to discuss the preparedness of Canada's armed forces. J. Eayrs, *In Defence of Canada: From the Great War to the Great Depression* (Toronto: 1964), 319.
29. *House of Commons Debates*, 13 June 1935, 3592; SAB, RRIC, exhibit 168, S. T. Wood to J. H. MacBrien, 13 June 1935.
30. *Toronto Daily Star*, 13 June 1935; Gardiner papers, f. 46, "Unemployed On-to-Ottawa Trek," J. G. Gardiner to R. B. Bennett, 13 June 1935. Gardiner dutifully sent copies of all telegrams to federal Liberal Opposition leader Mackenzie King.
31. *Ottawa Journal*, 11 June 1935, 14 June 1935; *Saskatoon Star Phoenix*, 11 June 1935, 14 June 1935; *Moose Jaw Times-Herald*, 14 June 1935; *Regina Leader-Post*, 14 June 1935.
32. SAB, RRIC, v. 8, 137; v. 4, 59; *Toronto Daily Star*, 13 June 1935. W. Lawson of Regina told Prime Minister Bennett that Premier Gardiner had secretly sent a $600 cheque to the trekkers before they entered Saskatchewan to facilitate their travel through the province: NAC, Bennett papers, 496880, W. Lawson to R. B. Bennett, 21 August 1935.

CHAPTER SIX (pages 99–122)

1. *Regina Leader-Post*, 8 June 1935, 14 June 1935; Saskatchewan Archives Board [SAB], Regina Riot Inquiry Commission [RRIC], v. 14, 158–59; v. 15, 76. The Rotary, Kiwanis, and Lions clubs refused to support the CEC or its activities.
2. SAB, RRIC, exhibit 59, Citizens' Emergency Committee minutes, 13 June 1935; exhibit 60, CEC Minutes, 14 June 1935; v. 6, 21; v. 14, 161–62; *Regina Leader-Post*, 14 June 1935; *Regina Daily Star*, 14 July 1935.
3. C. Betke and S. W. Horrall, *Canada's Security Service: An Historical Outline, 1864–1966, Volume 2*, unpublished RCMP Security Service Report (1978), 397–98; Regina city police records [RCP], S. T. Wood to M. J. Bruton, 12 June 1935; "Police Notice," 14 June 1935; M. J. Bruton to S. T. Wood, 16 June 1935; SAB, RRIC, v. 36, 141, 143–44; v. 37, 39; SAB, J. G. King Papers, f. 2, J. H. MacBrien to S. T. Wood, 14 June 1935.

4. *Regina Leader-Post*, 14 June 1935; 15 June 1935; *Regina Daily Star*, 14 June 1935; SAB, RRIC, v. 22, 75.
5. SAB, J. G. Gardiner papers, f. 46, "Unemployed On-to-Ottawa Trek," press statement, 14 June 1935; *Regina Leader-Post*, 14 June 1935; SAB, RRIC, exhibit 173, J. W. Estey to S. T. Wood, 14 June 1935.
6. National Archives of Canada [NAC], Manuscript Division, R. B. Bennett papers, 496594–95, F. B. Bagshaw et al to R. B. Bennett, 14 June 1935; NAC, Government Archives Division, Canadian Security Intelligence Service, RG 146, f. 93-A-00086, pt. 2, S. T. Wood to J. H. MacBrien, 19 July 1935.
7. Mikkelson also headed the Saskatchewan Union of Unemployed and had spent much of the past year fighting for improved relief benefits. See SAB, Gardiner papers, f. 47, "Saskatchewan Union of Unemployed," 15 April 1935 conference notes.
8. *Regina Leader-Post*, 15 June 1935; *Regina Daily Star*, 15 June 1935; *Winnipeg Tribune*, 15 June 1935; *Toronto Daily Star*, 15 June 1935.
9. SAB, Gardiner papers, f. 46, "Unemployed On-to-Ottawa Trek", J. G. Gardiner to R. B. Bennett, 15 June 1935. The May 1932 Guthrie letter was entered as exhibit 34 at the Regina Riot Inquiry Commission: SAB, RRIC, v. 4, 71–72.
10. SAB, RRIC, exhibit 204, S. T. Wood to J. H. MacBrien, 24 June 1935; v. 35, 33; v. 36, 142; NAC, RG 146, f. 98-A-00230, "Regina Riot 1935," S. T. Wood to J. H. MacBrien, 15 June 1935; J. H. MacBrien to S. T. Wood, 15 June 1935; *Regina Daily Star*, 15 June 1935.
11. For an examination of Rink's early career, see J. W. Brennan, "A Populist in Municipal Politics: Cornelius Rink, 1909–1914" *Prairie Forum* 20, no. 1 (Spring 1995), 63–86.
12. When City Clerk George Beach testified before the Regina Riot Inquiry Commission, he never gave a reason for the city's refusal to grant a tagging permit to the trekkers. SAB, RRIC, v. 3, 162; v. 15, 94–96; v. 46, 124; exhibit 6, M. Shaw to E. Cumber, 17 June 1935; J. W. Brennan, "The 1935 On-to-Ottawa Trek and the Regina Riot: A Local Perspective," unpublished paper presented before the Northern Great Plains History Conference (September 1997).
13. *Regina Leader-Post*, 15 June 1935; *Toronto Daily Star*, 17 June 1935.
14. SAB, RRIC, v. 4, 103. Premier Gardiner reported that Manion and Weir believed that the ministers of Labour and National Defence should have been sent to Regina instead. R. J. Manion, *Life is an Adventure* (Toronto: 1936), 354.
15. *Regina Leader-Post*, 7 March 1939.
16. *Toronto Globe*, 17 June 1935; *Montreal Gazette*, 15 June 1935; *Regina Daily Star*, 15 June 1935; *Regina Leader-Post*, 15 June 1935.
17. *Toronto Daily Star*, 15 June 1935.
18. SAB, RRIC, exhibit 6, M. Shaw to E. Cumber, 17 June 1935.
19. *Regina Leader-Post*, 17 June 1935. The Regina Council of Women supported "the trekkers as part of their duty to meet the extreme economic conditions created by the depression, but that support would not be universal among the members nor would it necessarily have been unconditional or complete." J. Harvey to B. Waiser (e-mail), 16 October 2002.
20. SAB, RRIC, exhibit 61, CEC Minutes, 15 June 1935; exhibit 62, CEC Minutes, 16 June 1935; v. 15, 118; *Regina Leader-Post*, 17 June 1935; *Toronto Daily Star*, 17 June 1935.

21. The newspapers reported that the RCMP originally planned to nab the trekkers when they arrived in Regina and put them in a special camp, but the orders were changed. See *Toronto Daily Star*, 13 June 1935; *Ottawa Journal*, 13 June 1935.
22. Canadian Pacific Railway Archives [CPR], Vice President papers, f. 15989, W. A. Mather memorandum, 16 June 1935; RRIC, v. 36, 142; v. 37, 4, 40, 117–8; exhibit 180, S. T. Wood to Chesser, 16 June 1935; exhibit 182, S. T. Wood to M. J. Bruton 16 June 1935; exhibit 183, M. J. Bruton to S. T. Wood, 16 June 1935; exhibit 193, S. T. Wood to J. H. MacBrien, 18 June 1935; SAB, King papers, f. 2, J. H. MacBrien to S. T. Wood, n.d.
23. SAB, Gardiner papers, f. 46, "Unemployed On-to-Ottawa Trek," H. Guthrie to J. G. Gardiner, 16 June 1935; J. G. Gardiner to W. A. Mather, 16 June 1935; NAC, Bennett papers, 496607–9, J. G. Gardiner to H. Guthrie, 17 June 1935; SAB, RRIC, v. 6, 28.
24. SAB, RRIC, v. 6, 28; v. 39, 24; exhibit 72, S. T. Wood to T. C. Davis, 17 June 1935; exhibit 73, T. C. Davis to C. Rink, 17 June 1935; *Regina Leader-Post*, 17 June 1935.
25. RCP, M. J. Bruton to S. T. Wood, 17 June 1935; SAB, RRIC, exhibit 186, S. T. Wood to J. H. MacBrien, 17 June 1935.
26. SAB, RRIC, exhibit 62, CEC Minutes, 16 June 1935.
27. SAB, RRIC, exhibit 63, CEC Minutes, 17 June 1935.
28. *Regina Leader-Post*, 17 June 1935.
29. *Regina Leader-Post*, 17 June 1935; SAB, RRIC, v. 14, 163–64; exhibit 204, S. T. Wood to J. H. MacBrien, 24 June 1935; NAC, Manuscript Division, R. J. Manion papers, f. 69, "Strike Relief Camp Workers," E. H. Detwiler to R. J. Manion, 16 June 1935.
30. NAC, Manion Papers, f. 69, memorandum, 17 June 1935; R. J. Manion to R. B. Bennett, 17 June 1935; SAB, RRIC, v. 4, 101–2, 206.
31. SAB, RRIC, v. 8, 151; *Regina Leader-Post*, 18 June 1935.
32. NAC, Manion papers, f. 69, minutes of conference, 17 June 1935.
33. NAC, Manion papers, f. 69, minutes of conference, 17 June 1935. CCF member A. A. Heaps had suggested in the House of Commons on 13 June that a handful of trekker representatives be brought to Ottawa to discuss their grievances: *House of Commons Debates*, 13 June 1935, 3592. The CPR recommended the same thing the next day: CPR, f. 15989, W. M. Neal to D. C. Coleman, 14 June 1935.
34. NAC, Manion papers, f. 69, minutes of conference, 17 June 1935.
35. NAC, Manion papers, Manion to Bennett, 17 June 1935; G. Montero, ed., *We Stood Together* (Toronto: 1979), 40–41; R. Liversedge, *Recollections of the On-to-Ottawa Trek* (Toronto: 1973), 108; SAB, RRIC, *R. v. Bell et al*, 112–13. One of the trekkers called Regina police chief Bruton late Monday afternoon with details of the route that the trekkers were supposed to follow en route to the rail yard: RCP, M. J. Bruton to S. T. Wood, 17 June 1935.
36. SAB, RRIC, v. 8, 165; v. 13, 138; v. 15, 62, 112; *R. v. Bell et al.*, 197–202.
37. SAB, RRIC, exhibit 84, Report of Interview between Mr. Manion and Mr. Weir and Relief Strikers Delegation; exhibit 187, Memorandum of Agreement, 17 June 1935; *Winnipeg Free Press*, 18 June 1935; *Regina Daily Star*, 18 June 1935.
38. SAB, RRIC, v. 8, 166–67; *R. v. Bell et al.*, 203; *Toronto Daily Star*, 18 June 1935; *Regina Leader-Post*, 18 June 1935; NAC, Bennett papers, 496606, A. Evans to R. B. Bennett, 17 June 1935.

CHAPTER SEVEN (pages 123–147)

1. *Ottawa Journal*, 19 June 1935.
2. *Montreal Star*, 18 June 1935; *Ottawa Journal*, 19 June 1935; *Regina Leader-Post*, 19 June 1935; *The Worker*, 20 June 1935.
3. Saskatchewan Archives Board [SAB], Regina Riot Inquiry Commission [RRIC], exhibit 64, Citizens' Emergency Committee Minutes, 18 June 1935; *Regina Leader-Post*, 18 June 1935.
4. *Regina Leader-Post*, 19 June 1935.
5. *Regina Leader-Post*, 19 June 1935; SAB, RRIC, v. 23, 140; v. 15, 170; v. 16, 131; E. Drake, *Regina: The Queen City* (Toronto: 1955), 204.
6. *Regina Leader-Post*, 18 June 1935; Canadian Pacific Railway Archives [CPR], Vice President papers, f. 15989, W. Ashman to E. de B. Panet, 19 June 1935.
7. National Archives of Canada [NAC], Manuscript Division, R. B. Bennett papers, C. P. Burgess to H. Hereford, 14 June 1935; NAC, Government Archives Division, Canadian Security and Intelligence Service, RG 146, f. 93-A-00086, pt. 3, M. Black, "Unemployed Single Men's Convergence on Ottawa," 24 June 1935.
8. SAB, RRIC, v. 3, 70; *R. v. Bell et al.*, 70; SAB, J. G. King papers, f. 2, S. T. Wood to J. H. MacBrien, 19 June 1935; S. T. Wood to J. H. MacBrien, 20 June 1935.
9. SAB, RRIC, exhibit 109, M. Shaw to J. Matts, undated.; *R. v. Bell et al.*, 16.
10. *Regina Leader-Post*, 18–21 June 1935
11. *Regina Leader-Post*, 21 June 1935; Regina City Police papers [RCP], M. J. Bruton to R. R. Tait, 14 June 1935; M. J. Bruton to S. T. Wood, 21 June 1935; RCMP Docket, "Re: BC Strikers," undated.
12. SAB, RRIC, v. 5, 13–14; exhibit 193, S. T. Wood to J. H. MacBrien, 18 June 1935; *Regina Leader-Post*, 4 July 1935; NAC, RG 146, f. 98-A-00230, "Regina Riot 1935," S. T. Wood to J. H. MacBrien, 17 June 1935; J. H. MacBrien to S. T. Wood, 18 June 1935.
13. Although the Vancouver strike did not formally end for another six months, the police action was the climax of the labour struggle: R. C. McCandless, "Vancouver's 'Red Menace' of 1935: The Waterfront Situation," *BC Studies*, no. 2 (Summer 1974), 66–68.
14. NAC, RG 146, f. 98-A-00230, "Regina Riot 1935," J. H. MacBrien to S. T. Wood, 19 June 1935.
15. During the Regina Riot Inquiry Commission, Wood testified that only twenty-six additional men arrived in Regina when the trek delegation was away, while eighty odd men were returned to their detachments in the province: SAC, RRIC, v. 39, 33; NAC, RG 146, f. 93-A-00086, pt. 2, J. H. MacBrien to H. Guthrie, 20 June 1935.
16. *Toronto Daily Star*, 21 June 1935; 22 June 1935.
17. G. Montero, *We Stood Together* (Toronto: 1979), 41.
18. Larry Glassford, *Reaction and Reform: The Politics of the Conservative Party Under R. B. Bennett, 1927–1938* (Toronto: 1992), 170.
19. *House of Commons Debates*, 20 June 1935, 3818.
20. *Toronto Mail and Empire*, 18 June 1935. Turnbull supported the Wood plan to take the trekkers just outside Regina and deal with them there: NAC, Bennett papers, 496632, F. W. Turnbull to R. B. Bennett, 19 June 1935. Ralph Webb, the former mayor of Winnipeg,

even went as far as to suggest: "There is not any question of a doubt, although difficult to prove, that the present movement has been started by our friends the Liberals, with the object of embarrassing the government and creating a false picture of the situation.": Bennett papers, 496941–44, R. Webb to R. B. Bennett, 29 June 1935.

21. R. J. Manion, *Life is an Adventure* (Toronto: 1937), 292–3. Manion believed Bennett would have made a "great bishop." Glassford, *Reaction and Reform*, 170; NAC, Manuscript Division, R. J. Manion papers, v. 33, f. 69, R. J. Manion to R. B. Bennett, 20 June 1935.
22. Montero, *We Stood Together*, 41–42; L. R. Betcherman, *The Little Band: The Clashes between the Communists and the Political and Legal Establishment in Canada, 1928–1932* (Ottawa: 1982), 145; *Regina Leader-Post*, 21 June 1935.
23. SAB, RRIC, Report, v. 2, 94–95, 106–7.
24. *Ibid.*, 107–9, 114–15.
25. *Ibid.*, 117–19.
26. *Ibid.*, 119; 124–26.
27. L. Brown, *When Freedom Was Lost: The Unemployed, the Agitator, and the State* (Montreal: 1987), 167; NAC, Manion papers, v. 33, f. 69, Privy Council notes, undated; J. Torrance, *Public Violence in Canada* (Kingston: 1986), 84, 193, 205, 209.
28. SAB, RRIC, v. 9, 24–5; Montero, *We Stood Together*, 41; NAC, Manuscript Division, A. G. L. McNaughton papers, series II, v. 60, f. 380, handwritten notes, 22 June 1935; CPR, Vice President papers, f. 15989, memorandum, 22 June 1935.
29. See, for example, *Ottawa Morning Journal*, 25 June 1935; *Regina Leader-Post*, 22 June 1935; NAC, Bennett papers, 492821, 492823, 492845, 492847, 496637.
30. *Toronto Daily Star*, 24 June 1935.
31. *Regina Leader-Post*, 27 June 1935; CPR, f. 15989, W. M. Neal memorandum, 25 June 1935; G. M. Stone, "The Regina Riot: 1935," unpublished M.A. thesis, University of Saskatchewan (1967), 64.
32. *The Worker*, 27 June 1935.
33. *Regina Leader-Post*, 22 June 1935; *Toronto Daily Star*, 24 June 1935; SAB, J. G. Gardiner papers, vi, 3, "On-to-Ottawa Marchers," report of conference, 24 June 1935.
34. SAB, RRIC, v. 4, 12; v. 14, 98; exhibit 109, M. Shaw to J. Matts, undated.
35. *House of Commons Debates*, 3899–3901, 24 June 1935.
36. NAC, RG 146, f. 98-A-00230, "Regina Riot 1935," S. T. Wood to J. H. MacBrien, 22 June 1935; McNaughton papers, f. 380, handwritten notes, 22 June 1935; memorandum to file, 18 June 1935; SAB, Gardiner papers, f. 46, "Unemployed On-to-Ottawa Trek," A. G. L. McNaughton to H. E. Boak, 22 June 1935. On June 26, despite McNaughton's earlier resistance, tentative plans were made to move the Shilo troops to Regina in the event they were needed: NAC, RG 146, f. 93-A-00086, pt. 3, C. F. Constantine to Officer Commanding Military District No. 10, 26 June 1935.
37. NAC, McNaughton papers, f. 380, A. G. L. McNaughton to H. E. Boak, 24 June 1935; SAB, RRIC, v. 37, 37, 51; exhibit 13, W. Dickson to C. P. Burgess, 24 June 1935; exhibit 193, S. T. Wood to J. H. MacBrien, 18 June 1935; exhibit 204, S. T. Wood to J. H. MacBrien, 24 June 1935; *Regina Leader-Post*, 26 June 1935.

38. SAB, Gardiner papers, vi, 3, "On-to-Ottawa Marchers," report of conference, 24 June 1935; NAC, RG 146, f. 98-A-00230, S. T. Wood to J. H. MacBrien, 25 June 1935 [includes copy of Burgess notice]; SAB, RRIC, v. 3, 71–72, 97–98; v. 37, 51–53.
39. *Regina Leader-Post*, 24 June 1935; *Toronto Daily Star*, 24 June 1935. Commissioner MacBrien feared that the men waiting in Winnipeg, Thunder Bay, and Sudbury might set off for Ottawa without the Regina trekkers: CPR, f. 15989, S. H. Spry, "memo re Camp Strikers and others," 27 June 1935.
40. NAC, RG 146, f. 98-A-00230, J. H. MacBrien to S. T. Wood, 24 June 1935; S. T. Wood to J. H. MacBrien, 24 June 1935; S. T. Wood to J. H. MacBrien (telegram), 24 June 1935; SAB, RRIC, v. 37, 39, 60.
41. NAC, RG 146, f. 98-A-00230, J. H. MacBrien to S. T. Wood, 25 June 1935; S. T. Wood to J. H. MacBrien 25 June 1935; SAB, RRIC, v. 43, 27–28; v. 45, 148–49; exhibit 254, "You Build Your Own Prisons," undated.
42. SAB, RRIC, v. 9, 33; *Regina Leader-Post*, 26 June 1935.
43. SAB, RRIC, exhibit 67, CEC Minutes, 24 June 1935; *Regina Leader-Post*, 24 June 1935; 26 June 1935.
44. *Regina Leader-Post*, 25 June 1935.
45. SAB, Gardiner papers, f. 46, "Unemployed On-to-Ottawa Trek," J. G. Gardiner to R. B. Bennett, 26 June 1935 (two telegrams).
46. SAB, RRIC, v. 4, 112–15; *Regina Leader-Post*, 26 June 1935.
47. *Regina Leader-Post*, 17 June 1935.
48. RCP, A. Rodgers to M. J. Bruton, 26 June 1935.

CHAPTER EIGHT (pages 149-170)

1. National Archives of Canada [NAC], Government Archives Division, Canadian Security Intelligence Service, RG 146, f. 93-A-00086, pt. 3, C. H. Hill to J. H. MacBrien, 21 June 1935; S. R. Hewitt, "Old Myths Die Hard: The Transformation of the Mounted Police in Alberta and Saskatchewan," unpublished Ph.D. thesis, University of Saskatchewan (1997), 180; Saskatchewan Archives Board [SAB], Regina Riot Inquiry Commission, [RRIC], v. 38, 76–79, 112–14.
2. SAB, RRIC, exhibit 212, S. T. Wood to J. H. MacBrien, 26 June 1935; NAC, RG 146, f. 93-A-00086, pt. 3, S. T. Wood to J. H. MacBrien, 25 June 1935; f. 98-A-00230, J. H. MacBrien to S. T. Wood, 26 June 1935; S. T. Wood to J. H. MacBrien, 26 June 1935.
3. NAC, RG 146, f. 93-A-00083, pt. 3, A. G. Manson to C. H. Hill, 27 June 1935; D. F. Taylor report, 17 July 1935; J. T. Jones report, 28 June 1935; SAB, SAB, RRIC, v. 43, 27–28.
4. *Regina Leader-Post*, 26 June 1935; 27 June 1935.
5. SAB, J. G. Gardiner papers, f. 46, "Unemployed On-to-Ottawa Trekkers," R. B. Bennett to J. G. Gardiner, 27 June 1935; J. G. Gardiner to R. B. Bennett, 27 June 1935; R. B. Bennett to J. G. Gardiner, 27 June 1935; J. G. Gardiner to R. B. Bennett, 27 June 1935. Gardiner sent copies of all his correspondence with Bennett to William Lyon Mackenzie King, the Liberal Opposition leader in Ottawa. King was not prepared to take a position on the trek or its stoppage.

6. SAB, RRIC, exhibit 69, Citizens' Emergency Committee Minutes, 27 June 1935; v. 9, 41–43; *Regina Leader-Post*, 27 June 1935.
7. NAC, RG 146, f. 98-A-00230, S. T. Wood to J. H. MacBrien, 27 June 1935; J. H. MacBrien to S. T. Wood, 27 June 1935.
8. *Regina Leader-Post*, 27 June 1935; SAB, RRIC, v. 6, 32; v. 9, 44; v. 39, 139; v. 40, 11; NAC, RG 146, f. 97-A-00086, pt. 3, S. T. Wood to J. H. MacBrien, 27 June 1935.
9. *Regina Leader-Post*, 27 June 1935; NAC, RG 146, f. 93-A-00086, pt. 3, S. T. Wood to J. H. MacBrien, 27 June 1935; SAB, RRIC, v. 15, 78–79. Federal authorities would later point to these permits as evidence of provincial complicity with the trekkers, especially when they were issued after hours at the provincial motor vehicle office. NAC, Manuscript Division, R. B. Bennett papers, 496687, C. P. Burgess to H. Hereford, 27 June 1935.
10. *Regina Leader-Post*, 28 June 1935; SAB, RRIC, v. 15, 122–25.
11. NAB, RG 146, f. 93-A-00086, pt. 3, W. H. Foskett report, 28 June 1935; J. Painter report, 28 June 1935; *Regina Leader-Post*, 28 June 1935.
12. *Regina Leader-Post*, 28 June 1935; SAB, RRIC, v. 15, 53; v. 16, 41, 48–52, 62; v. 43, 29–32; NAC, RG 146, f. 98-A-00086, pt. 3, S. T. Wood to J. H. MacBrien, 28 June 1935. Regina lawyer F. B. Bagshaw later claimed that there was no legal justification for the arrest of the citizens: *Regina Leader-Post*, 24 January 1936.
13. SAB, RRIC, exhibit 124, A. Evans to J. Litterick, 28 June 1935. See S. R. Hewitt, "'We are sitting on the edge of a volcano': Winnipeg during the On-to-Ottawa Trek," *Prairie Forum* 19, no. 1 (Spring 1994), 51–64.
14. SAB, RRIC, v. 4, 124–27; v. 9, 61–62; v. 10, 105–6; G. M. Stone, "The Regina Riot: 1935" unpublished M.A. thesis, University of Saskatchewan (1967), 75–6; SAB, Gardiner papers, f. 46, "Unemployed On-to-Ottawa Trek," 1 July 1935 press statement.
15. SAB, RRIC, v. 10, 107.
16. SAB, RRIC, v. 9, 60; v. 10, 108–10; v. 14, 165; v. 21, 129; exhibit 70, Citizens' Emergency Committee Minutes, 28 June 1935; NAC, RG 146, f. 93-A-00086, pt. 3, S. T. Wood to J. H. MacBrien, 28 June 1935; A. G. Marson to S. T. Wood, 28 June 1935; *Regina Daily Star*, 29 June 1935.
17. NAC, RG 146, f. 93-A-00086, pt. 3, W. S. Edwards to J. H. MacBrien, 28 June 1945; J. H. MacBrien to S. T. Wood, 28 June 1935; SAB, RRIC, 37, 74–75; 41, 1–22.
18. SAB, RRIC, v. 37, 79; v. 38, 63; *Regina Leader-Post*, 28 June 1935.
19. SAB, John King papers, f. 1, J. King to D. Campbell, 28 June 1935; G. Williams press release, undated.
20. *Regina Daily Star*, 29 June 1935; *Regina Leader-Post*, 25 June 1935.
21. Stone, "The Regina Riot," 73–74.
22. *Regina Leader-Post*, 28 June 1935; SAB, RRIC, exhibit 74, T. C. Davis to H. Guthrie, 28 June 1935; Relief Act, Statutes of Canada, 25–26 George V, c. 13.
23. *Regina Leader-Post*, 29 June 1935; SAB, RRIC, v. 15, 126–27; NAC, RG 146, f. 93-A-00086, pt. 3, O. M. Alexander, "Unemployed Single Men's Convergence upon Ottawa," 28 June 1935; S. T. Wood to J. H. MacBrien, 29 June 1935.
24. SAB, RRIC, v. 6, 37; exhibit 75, H. Guthrie to T. C. Davis, 29 June 1935; exhibit 76, T. C. Davis to H. Guthrie, 29 June 1935; exhibit 77, H. Guthrie to T. C. Davis, 29 June 1935;

NAC, RG 146, f. 93-A-00086, pt. 3, S. T. Wood to J. H. MacBrien, 29 June 1935.

25. SAB, RRIC, 41, 41; RG 146, f. 93-A-00086, pt. 3, S. T. Wood to J. H. MacBrien, 29 June 1935.
26. NAC, RG 146, f. 98-A-00230, S. T. Wood to J. H MacBrien, 29 June 1935; f. 93-A-00086, pt. 3, S. T. Wood to J. H. MacBrien, 29 June 1935; SAB, RRIC, v. 4, 127–28; v. 12, 134; SAB, Gardiner papers, f. 46, "Unemployed On-to-Ottawa Trek," press statement, 1 July 1935; *Regina Leader-Post*, 2 July 1935.
27. NAC, Bennett papers, 496694, C. P. Burgess to H. Hereford, 29 June 1935; RG 146, f. 93-A-00086, pt. 3, S. T. Wood to J. H. MacBrien, 29 June 1935; *Regina Leader-Post*, 29 June 1935.
28. *The Worker*, 27 June 1935; 29 June 1935; NAC, RG 146, f. 93-A-00086, pt. 3, S. T. Wood to J. H. MacBrien, 29 June 1935.
29. NAC, RG 146, f. 94-A-00006, pt. 3, M. Black, "C.L.D.L. Meeting," 30 June 1935; S. T. Wood to J. H. MacBrien, 2 July 1935; SAB, RRIC, *R. v. Bell et al.*, 212–13.
30. S. R. Hewitt, "Beyond Regina: The On-to-Ottawa Trek in Manitoba and Alberta," unpublished M.A. thesis, University of Saskatchewan (1992), 57–58.
31. SAB, RRIC, v. 9, 70–71; v. 10, 91; v. 37, 89; NAC, RG 146, f. 93-A-00086, pt. 3, A. G. Marsom to S. T. Wood, 1 July 1935; M. Black, "Picnic held at Wascana Park," 1 July 1935.
32. SAB, RRIC, v. 40, 82; NAC, RG 146, f. 93-A-00086, pt. 2, S. T. Wood to J. H. MacBrien, 23 July 1935.
33. S. R. Hewitt, "Royal Canadian Mounted Police Spy: The Secret Life of John Leopold/Jack Esselwein," *Intelligence and National Security* 15, no. 1 (Spring 2000), 144–68; SAB, RRIC, v. 41, 22; *R. v. Bell et al.*, 664–708; NAC, RG 146, f. 98-A-00230, G. L. Jennings to S. T. Wood, 28 June 1935.
34. SAB, RRIC, v. 3, 77; v. 4, 130; v. 9, 70–72; v. 13, 146–47.
35. SAB, RRIC, v. 3, 77; v. 9, 75–76; exhibit 15, transcript of 11 A.M. meeting, 1 July 1935.
36. SAB, RRIC, v. 3, 80. Wood would claim several months later that the RCMP were actually prepared to see the men demobilize from the exhibition stadium, but were overruled by the government. But in a letter on 2 July, Colonel Wood dutifully noted: "Under your instructions all we could offer them was that they must go to either Dundurn or Craven [Lumsden] camps." SAB, RRIC, v. 40, 46; NAC, RG 146, f. 93-A-00086, pt. 3, S. T. Wood to J. H. MacBrien, 2 July 1935.
37. SAB, RRIC, v. 3, 88; v. 9, 79–82; v. 43, 33; exhibit 244, transcript of 2:30 P.M. meeting, 1 July 1935; NAC, RG 146, f. 93-A-00086, pt. 3, S. T. Wood to J. H. MacBrien, 2 July 1935.
38. SAB, RRIC, v. 41, 23–27; NAC, RG 146, f. 93-A-00086, pt. 3, S. T. Wood to J. H. MacBrien, 1 July 1935; pt. 2, W. Mortimer memo, 12 July 1935.
39. SAB, RRIC, v. 4, 130; v. 9, 85–86; v. 38, 18; SAB, Gardiner papers, vii, 9a, R. C. Marshall file, J. G. Gardiner to R. C. Marshall, 8 February 1938; RG 146, f. 93-A-00086, pt. 3, S. T. Wood to J. H. MacBrien, 2 July 1935. An RCMP Security Bulletin report, dated 19 June 1935, stated: "The Saskatchewan government . . . has been very sympathetic towards the strikers." Quoted in G. Kealey and R. Whitaker, eds., *RCMP Security Bulletins, Depression Years, Part II, 1935* (St. John's: 1995), 352.
40. SAB, RRIC, v. 4, 131–33; v. 9, 86–88.

CHAPTER NINE (pages 171–191)

1. Saskatchewan Archives Board [SAB], Regina Riot Inquiry Commission [RRIC], v. 35, 76; v. 37, 59–60, 106, 112–14; v. 40, 82–83; exhibit 193, S. T. Wood to J. H. MacBrien, 18 June 1935 [name of agent deleted, with word, "confidential," in margin]. Colonel Wood later claimed that he acted when he did largely because of the information he was receiving from the confidential CPR source. The National Archives of Canada Access Section has deleted the name of the CPR secret agent on all RCMP trek-related documents. The author filed a unsuccessful complaint with the Information Commissioner of Canada; it was concluded that disclosure of the agent's identity "could reasonably be expected to be injurious to the prevention or suppression of subversive or hostile activities.": Hon. John Reid to Bill Waiser, 15 May 2002. An attempt to secure the name of the secret agent at the CPR Archives in Montreal was also unsuccessful; an archivist reported that the records do not exist. The CPR also had an agent among prospective trekkers waiting in Winnipeg.
2. SAB, RRIC, v. 37, 109–10; v. 41, 27, 51–52.
3. SAB, RRIC, v. 37, 108, 112–15, 117; v. 40, 82; L. Brown, *When Freedom was Lost: The Unemployed, the Agitator, and the State* (Montreal: 1987), 192–93.
4. SAB, RRIC, v. 37, 107; v. 41, 27, v. 46, 124; v. 47, 3–4.
5. SAB, RRIC, v. 6, 37–38; v. 37, 106, quoted in S. R. Hewitt, "Beyond Regina: The On-to-Ottawa Trek in Manitoba and Ontario," unpublished M.A. thesis, University of Saskatchewan (1992), 91.
6. SAB, RRIC, v. 9, 88–89; v. 12, 140; v. 13, 51–52, 145; v. 27, 86–88; v. 41, 53; *R. v. Bell et al.*, 495; *R. v. Gallinger*, 11–26.
7. SAB, RRIC, v. 37, 111; v. 46, 121–23, 125–28, 143, 149; v. 47, 4, 7; v. 48, 151–52; *R. v. Gallinger*, 93–94; Regina City Police papers [RCP], M. J. Bruton to Chairman, Board of Police Commissioners, 6 August 1935.
8. SAB, RRIC, v. 16, 73; v. 40, 122; v. 41, 54, 58; National Archives of Canada [NAC], Government Archives Division, Canadian Security Intelligence Service, RG 146, f. 93-A-00086, pt. 2, W. Mortimer to S. T. Wood, 12 July 1935.
9. SAB, RRIC, v. 16, 73–75; v. 25, 65; v. 40, 103; v. 45, 102, 13. Colonel Wood subsequently claimed that only "regulation" clubs had been used by his men [v. 37, 120].
10. NAC, RG 146, f. 93-A-00086, pt. 3, M. Black, "Unemployed Single Men's Convergence on Ottawa," 8 July 1935; SAB, RRIC, v. 41, 59; v. 43, 36; *R. v. Forsyth*, 3.
11. SAB, RRIC, v. 41, 59; v.46, 129–30; v. 47, 6, 39–41; pt. 9, *R. v. Gallinger*, 92; RCP, "memo regarding B.C. relief camp strikers and riot in the city on July 1st, 1935," n.d.; H. A. Johnson, "A Night to Remember," *RCMP Quarterly*, July 1969, 40.
12. SAB, RRIC, v. 37, 123–24; v. 41, 54, 59; v. 47, 7; v. 48, 38; v. 49, 118–19.
13. SAB, RRIC, exhibit 112, poster, 1 July 1935; official statement, 1 July 1935.
14. SAB, RRIC, v. 16, 119; v. 46, 144; v. 47, 124; v. 48, 43; v. 50, 108–9; F. Dabbs, *Ralph Klein: A Maverick Life* (Vancouver: 1995), 4–5.
15. SAB, RRIC, v. 18, 9; v. 26, 75; RG 146, f. 93-A-00086, pt. 3, confidential report, "Relief Camp Strikers," 1 July 1935.
16. SAB, RRIC, v. 18, 9, 88–89. The chair of the RRIC would not allow McCarthy to read his poem as part of his testimony.

17. SAB, RRIC, v. 42, 59; v. 43, 38–39; v. 45, 4–5, 103–4.
18. SAB, RRIC, v. 16, 79; v. 17, 97; v. 26, 75; v. 37, 125; v. 41, 60–61; v. 43, 43; NAC, RG 146, f. 93-A-00086, pt. 3, J. Brunet, "B.C. Relief Camp Workers, Regina, Sask Riot, 1–7–35," 2 July 1935.
19. SAB, RRIC, v. 18, 87; v. 20, 62; v. 25, 25; v. 47, 7, 73; *R. v. Forsyth*, 19. Every member of the Regina city police who was involved in the action that evening submitted a report less than two weeks later. Each man denied hitting anyone on the way to the platform or any brutality: RCP "Constable testimonies."
20. SAB, RRIC, v. 21, 163–68; v. 25, 33; v. 44, 26; v. 48, 152–53; v. 50, 106–7.
21. SAB, RRIC, v. 23, 33; v. 25, 145; v. 26, 81; v. 27, 40; v. 38, 15; v. 40, 83; v. 41, 62; v. 46, 60; v. 48, 39–40.
22. SAB, RRIC, v. 16, 82; v. 19, 58; v. 20, 47; v. 34, 156; v. 35, 3; v. 44, 92, 125; *R. v. Mottl and Stevens*, 50–52; RG 146, f. 93-A-00086, pt. 3, J. Brunet, "B.C. Relief Camp Workers, Regina, Sask Riot, 1–7–35," 2 July 1935; pt. 2, S. T. Wood to J. H. MacBrien, 19 July 1935.
23. RCP, M. J. Bruton to Board of Police Commissioners, 6 August, 1935; SAB, RRIC, v. 46, 110–12, 142–43.
24. SAB, RRIC, v. 20, 63, 86–87; v. 36, 21; v. 37, 125–27; v. 43, 43–44; v. 44, 10; v. 47, 8–10; *R. v. Mottl and Stevens*, 54; RCP, "Constable testimonies," D. McDougall, 16 July 1935.
25. SAB, RRIC, v. 43, 106, 127; *R. v. Mottl and Stevens*, 53–54, 510.
26. For a discussion of crowd behaviour, see G. Rude, *The Crowd in History, 1730–1848* (New York: 1964). Rude claims that crowds, when aroused, tend to be violent, impulsive and quick to panic.
27. SAB, RRIC, v. 20, 33; v. 23, 87–88, 96; v. 25, 33; v. 34, 40–41; v. 47, 73, 83–84; *R. v. R. A. Ellis*.
28. SAB, RRIC, v. 22, 111; v. 25, 172; v. 34, 47; v. 46, 100,135; v. 47, 165; v. 48, 153–54; v. 49, 66–72; RCP, R. Anderson to M. J. Bruton, 23 July 1935; NAC, RG 146, f. 93-A-00229, pt. 1, E. A. Wakefield, "Illegal Travelling on Trains," 18 November 1935.
29. Although there are many versions of Millar's death, the majority of the eye witnesses state that Millar was struck first by a shovel and then on the head with a large piece of wood; the autopsy found that Millar had been killed by a single blow from a wide, blunt instrument.
30. SAB, RRIC, v. 22, 7; v. 45, 5–8; SAB, J. King Collection, f. 9, "Biographies."
31. SAB, RRIC, v. 18, 47; v. 20, 91; v. 43, 140; v. 45, 104–7; v. 46, 135–36.
32. SAB, RRIC, v. 18, 55.

CHAPTER TEN (pages 193–212)

1. Saskatchewan Archives Board [SAB], Regina Riot Inquiry Commission [RRIC], *R. v. Kyle, Mynnie, and Coury*, 157–62. Harold Dunn, organizer for the dance in aid of the trekkers, reported that no one showed up: SAB, RRIC, v. 20, 156.
2. The RCMP conducted searches in Vancouver offices that same day. SAB, RRIC, v. 3, 11.
3. *Ibid.*, v. 19, 19; v. 21, 71–72; v. 43, 50; National Archives of Canada [NAC], Government Archives Division, Canadian Security Intelligence Service, RG 146, f. 93-A-00086, pt. 3, M. Black, "Unemployed Single Men's Convergence on Ottawa," 8 July 1935.
4. NAC, RG 146, f. 98-A-00229, pt. 3, H. Cooper, "Illegal Travelling on Trains—1935," 3

January 1936; Regina City Police papers [RCP], f. "Constables Testimonies," A. Apps to M. J. Bruton, 16 July 1935; SAB, RRIC, v. 45, 98.

5. NAC, RG 146, f. 93-A-00086, pt. 3, confidential secret agent report, "Relief Camp Strikers," 1 July 1935; SAB, RRIC, v. 26, 141; v. 45, 91. The CPR police arrested eight trekkers in the yards during the course of the evening: CPR Archives [CPR], Vice President papers, f. 15989, W. M. Neal to D. C. Coleman, 2 July 1935.
6. SAB, RRIC, v. 23, 130; v. 24, 116–17.
7. SAB, RRIC, v. 30, 4; v. 32, 130–34; NAC, RG 146, f. 93-A-00086, pt. 2, S. T. Wood to J. H. MacBrien, 19 July 1935; NAC, Government Archives Division, National Defence, NAC, 24, v. 3047, f. C18-34-1-1B, v. 1, "Mike McAuley," 11 July 1935.
8. SAB, RRIC, v. 24, 158; v. 25, 86; v. 26, 133; v. 32, 69.
9. SAB, RRIC, v. 19, 175; v. 23, 132; v. 30, 55–57, 126; v. 32, 73; v. 35, 39–42; NAC, RG 146, f. 93-A-00086, pt. 2, S. T. Wood to J. H. MacBrien, 19 July 1935; pt. 3, S. T. Wood to J. H. MacBrien, 2 July 1935; J. Brunet, "B.C. Relief Camp Strikers, Regina, Sask," 2 July 1935.
10. SAB, RRIC, v. 21, 151; v. 25, 86–88; v. 34, 139; v. 45, 144.
11. W. Kelly, *Policing the Fringe: A Young Mounties Story* (Regina: 1999), 45, 50–51; NAC, RG 146, f. 93-A-00086, pt. 2, S. T. Wood to J. H. MacBrien, 19 July 1935.
12. SAB, RRIC, v. 30, 25, 84–85.
13. SAB, RRIC, v. 18, 115; v. 29, 141; v. 30, 26, 86–87.
14. SAB, RRIC, v. 36, 28–29; v. 45, 70; v. 50, 93.
15. SAB, RRIC, v. 38, 3; v. 43, 53–54, 146; NAC, RG 146, f. 93-A-00086, pt. 2, S. T. Wood to J. H. MacBrien, 23 July 1935; RCP, f. M. J. Bruton, M. J. Bruton to Board of Police Commissioners, 6 August 1935.
16. SAB, RRIC, v. 25, 25, 29–30; v. 26, 47; v. 30, 27, 87; v. 33, 112–14; v. 44, 60; *R. v. Forsyth*, 75–8. Griffin would later report not hearing any gunshots coming from the vicinity of Eleventh and Cornwall, but a streetcar conductor and several other people in the same area did. The sound of shooting also explains why Griffin stopped his troop; otherwise, they would have continued their sweep westward.
17. SAB, RRIC, v. 18, 116; v. 22, 164–65; v. 25, 26.
18. SAB, RRIC, v. 26, 59; NAC, RG 146, f. 93-A-00086, pt. 3, M. Black, "Unemployed Single Men's Convergence on Ottawa," 8 July 1935.
19. SAB, RRIC, v. 18, 112; v. 19, 163; v. 23, 51; v. 26, 11–12; NAC, RG 146, f. 93-A-00086, pt. 2, G. W. Griffin to C. H. Hill, 15 July 1935.
20. SAB, RRIC, v. 17, 139–40, 189–92; v. 18, 73; v. 19, 113; v. 23, 69, 103; v. 24, 129, 136; v. 26, 37; v. 32, 73; v. 45, 146; v. 50, 23–24. Several citizens witnessed the shooting of Phillips.
21. SAB, RRIC, v. 18, 35; v. 23, 131–33; v. 24, 45; v. 25, 162–63; v. 45, 78; *R. v. Kyle et al.*, 161–62; *Regina Leader-Post*, 25 October 1935.
22. SAB, RRIC, v. 45, 109–13; NAC, 146, f. 93-A-00086, pt. 3, confidential secret agent report, "Relief Camp Strikers," 1 July 1935.
23. SAB, RRIC, v. 21, 72; 47, 51; *Regina Leader-Post*, 2 July 1935.
24. RCP, f. "Constable Testimonies," D. McDougall to M. J. Bruton, 16 July 1935; A. Apps to M. J. Bruton, 16 July 1935; D. J. Matheson to M. J. Bruton, 10 July 1935; R. Anderson to M. J. Bruton, 9 July 1935; J. Dickenson to M. J. Bruton, 9 July 1935; SAB, RRIC, v. 32, 3; v. 48,

70–1, 95; NAC, RG 146, f. 93-A-00086, pt. 3, confidential secret agent report, "Relief Camp Strikers," 1 July 1935.

25. SAB, RRIC, v. 28, 111; v. 35, 155; v. 29, 4–5; v. 45, 113–14.
26. RCP, f. "Constable Testimonies," J. McPhee to M. J. Bruton, 8 July 1935; D. McDougall to M. J. Bruton, 16 July 1935; SAB, RRIC, v. 17, 42–46; v. 23, 104; v. 24, 46; v. 28, 51; v. 45, 114; v. 47, 25–27; v. 48, 71, 96; *R. v. Gallinger*, 120–22.
27. *Regina Leader-Post*, 2 July 1935; NAC, Government Archives Division, Department of Labour, NAC, RG 27, f. 2255, "Medical Aid Ledger," June–July 1935; SAB, RRIC, v. 21, 146; v. 25, 163; v. 46, 90; v. 47, 27–8.
28. SAB, RRIC, v. 19, 164, 174; v. 21, 7, 144; v. 23, 27, 76; v. 24, 151; v. 25, 73, 123; v. 33, 49; v. 35, 155; RCP, f. "Constable Testimonies," W. G. Wilson to M. J. Bruton, 10 July 1935.
29. SAB, RRIC, v. 25, 27; v. 47, 29; NAC, RG 146, f. 93-A-00086, pt. 3, J. Brunet, "B.C. Relief Camp Strikers, Regina, Sask, Riot 1–7–35," 2 July 1935.
30. SAB, RRIC, v. 24, 11; v. 27, 124; v. 43, 55–56, 127; v. 48, 96; *R. v. Dean.*
31. SAB, RRIC, v. 24, 4; v. 36, 99; v. 47, 32; *R. v. Kyle et al.*, 31; RCP, f. "Constable Testimonies," E. McDonald to M. J. Bruton, 11 July 1935.
32. SAB, RRIC, v. 34, 87; v. 36, 99; NAC, RG 146, f. 93-A-00086, pt. 3, H. S. Cooper, "Illegal Travelling on Trains, 1935," 9 January 1936.
33. SAB, RRIC, v. 27, 42–43; v. 34, 84–88, 93–95; v. 36, 86, 100; NAC, RG 146, f. 93-A-00086, pt. 3, H. S. Cooper, "Illegal Travelling on Trains, 1935," 9 January 1936. The mounted police would later insist it was John Wedin, and not Nick Schaack, who was in the barracks cell with Evans. But Wedin had already been sent to the hospital, as confirmed by the admittance records.
34. SAB, RRIC, v. 25, 108–11.
35. SAB, RRIC, v. 18, 146; v. 34, 40–41; v. 43, 11, 55–56; v. 45, 11; v. 50, 109; NAC, RG 146, f. 93-A-00086, pt. 3, CPR secret agent, "Relief Camp Strikers," 2 July 1935.
36. SAB, RRIC, v. 38, 11; *Regina Leader-Post*, bulletin, second bulletin, third bulletin, 1 July 1935; 2 July 1935; SAB, J. G. King papers, f. 1, telegrams, D. Campbell to J. G. King, 1 July 1935.

CHAPTER ELEVEN (pages 213–233)

1. Saskatchewan Archives Board [SAB], Regina Riot Inquiry Commission [RRIC], v. 19, 169; v. 48, 156; *Regina Leader-Post*, 2 July 1935; 3 July 1935; 20 July 1935. By Wednesday noon, three local glass companies had replaced 180 damaged windows and orders were still coming in. Many businesses, however, recovered these costs because they bought riot insurance once it was learned that the trek was to be stopped in Regina: *Regina Leader-Post*, 13 June 1935.
2. National Archives of Canada [NAC], Government Archives Division, Canadian Security Intelligence Service, RG 146, f. 98-A-00230, S. T. Wood to J. H. MacBrien, 4 July 1935; f. 93-A-00086, pt. 3, S. T. Wood to J. H. MacBrien, 2 July 1935; SAB, RRIC, v. 6, 38; v. 38, 18; SAB, J. G. Gardiner papers, f. 46, "Unemployed On-to-Ottawa Trek," J. G. Gardiner to R. B. Bennett, 1 July 1935; R. B. Bennett to J. G. Gardiner, 2 July 1935.

3. SAB, RRIC, v. 4, 138–39; v. 38, 18; NAC, RG 146, f. 93-A-00086, pt. 3, S. T. Wood to J. H. MacBrien, 2 July 1935.
4. SAB, RRIC, exhibit 78, T. C. Davis to H. Guthrie, 2 July 1935; SAB, Gardiner papers, f. 46, "Unemployed On-to-Ottawa Trek," J. G. Gardiner to R. B. Bennett, 2 July 1935.
5. SAB, RRIC, v. 34, 40–1; *Regina Leader-Post*, 2 July 1935; R. Liversedge, *Recollections of the On-to-Ottawa Trek* (Toronto: 1973), 118.
6. NAC, RG 146, f. 93-A-00086, pt. 3, S. T. Wood to J. H. MacBrien, 2 July 1935; SAB, RRIC, v. 4, 139–40.
7. SAB, RRIC, v. 4, 140–41, 208; C. M. Fenwick, "Building the Future in a Steady but Measured Pace: The Respectable Feminism of Marjorie Cooper," *Saskatchewan History* 54, no. 1 (Spring 2002), 20.
8. SAB, RRIC, v. 4, 142; SAB, Gardiner papers, f. 46, "Unemployed On-to-Ottawa Trek," R. B. Bennett to J. G. Gardiner, 2 July 1935; G. Sterling to J. G. Gardiner, 2 July 1935; NAC, Manuscript Division, R. B. Bennett papers, 492887, C. P. Burgess to H. Hereford, 2 July 1935. The Department of Labour eventually paid the trekker hospital charges.
9. *House of Commons Debates*, 2 July 1935, 4124–29.
10. NAC, Manuscript Division, W. L. M. King papers, diaries, 26 June 1926; *House of Commons Debates*, 2 July 1935, 4130–34.
11. *House of Commons Debates*, 4134–43.
12. *House of Commons Debates*, 4156, 4158; NAC, Bennett papers, J. Hone to R. B. Bennett, 12 July 1935, W. L. Woodger to R. B. Bennett, 5 July 1935, S. H. Soper to R. B. Bennett, 5 July 1935, N. Priestley to R. B. Bennett, 25 July 1935; S. R. Hewitt, "Beyond Regina: The On-to-Ottawa Trek in Manitoba and Ontario," unpublished M.A. thesis, University of Saskatchewan (1992), 119–21.
13. Quoted in *Regina Leader-Post*, 3 July 1935; quoted in Hewitt, "Beyond Regina," 118; *The Worker*, 6 July 1935; 9 July 1935.
14. *Regina Leader-Post*, 2 July 1935; NAC, Bennett papers, 492922-3, J. Paul to M. A. MacPherson, 2 July 1935.
15. NAC, Federal Archives Division, Department of National Defence, RG 24, v. 3048, f. Unemployment Relief Regina, Chief of General Staff memorandum, 2 July 1935; Bennett papers, 492949–51, E. C. Leslie to M. A. MacPherson, 6 July 1935; SAB, RRIC, *R. v. Gallinger*, 137–47.
16. *Regina Leader-Post*, 3 July 1935; f. 93-A-00086, pt 3, M. Black, "Unemployed Single Men's Convergence on Ottawa," 3 July 1935.
17. NAC, RG 146, f. 93-A-00086, pt. 3, CPR secret agent, "Relief Camp Strikers," 2 July 1935; CPR secret agent, "Relief Camp Strikers," 3 July 1935; *Regina Leader-Post*, 3 July 1935.
18. *Regina Leader-Post*, 3 July 1935; NAC, RG 146, f. 93-A-00086, pt. 3, S. T. Wood to T. C. Davis, 3 July 1935; SAB, RRIC, exhibit 239, S. T. Wood to T. C. Davis, 3 July 1935.
19. Canadian Pacific Railway Archives [CPR], Vice President papers, f. 15989, W. S. Hall to W. A. Mather, 3 July 1935, W. A. Mather to W. S. Hall, 3 July 1935; SAB, RRIC, v. 4, 156; v. 6, 53; NAC, RG 24, v. 3048, f. Unemployment Relief Regina, Chief of General Staff memorandum, 3 July 1935. The Saskatchewan government was reimbursed by the federal government following the defeat of Bennett in the October 1935 general election.
20. SAB, RRIC, exhibit 80, T. C. Davis to S. T. Wood, 4 July 1935; *Regina Leader-Post*, 4 July

1935; NAC, RG 146, f. 93-A-00086, pt. 2, S. T. Wood to J. H. MacBrien, 4 July 1935; f. 98-A-00230, S. T. Wood to J. H. MacBrien, 4 July 1935; NAC, RG 24, v. 3048, f. Unemployment Relief, n. 12, Chief of General Staff memorandum, 4 July 1935.

21. NAC, RG 146, f. 93-A-00086, pt. 2, S. T. Wood to J. H. MacBrien, 4 July 1935; pt. 1, M. Black, summary of CPR secret agent reports, 8 August 1935; NAC, RG 24, v. 3048, f. Unemployment Relief, n. 12, Chief of General Staff memorandum, 4 July 1935; CPR, Vice President papers, f. 15989, J. M. Chesser to E. de B. Panet, 4 July 1935; SAB, RRIC, exhibit 82, T. C. Davis to trekker delegation, 4 July 1935.
22. CPR, Vice President papers, f. 15989, no author, memo re conversation with Sir James MacBrien re transportation, 4 July 1935; Regina City Police papers [RCP], M. J. Bruton, memo regarding B.C. relief camp strikers and riot in city on July 1st, 1935, undated; *Regina Leader-Post*, 4 July 1935.
23. NAC, RG 146, f. 93-A-00086, pt. 2, S. T. Wood to J. H. MacBrien, 4 July 1935; *Regina Leader-Post*, 4 July 1935.
24. SAB, RRIC, v. 15, 56, 62; NAC, RG 146, f. 93-A-00086, pt. 2, S. T. Wood to J. H. MacBrien; CPR, Vice President papers, f. 15989, J. M. Chesser to E. de B. Panet, 5 July 1935. The registration breakdown was as follows: British Columbia 857; Alberta 172; Saskatchewan 151; Manitoba 54; Ontario 71; Quebec 38; New Brunswick 8; Nova Scotia 6; Prince Edward Island 1.
25. *Regina Leader-Post*, 5 July 1935; 6 July 1935.
26. *Ibid.*
27. *Regina Leader-Post*, 6 July 1935; SAB, Gardiner papers, f. 46, "Unemployed On-to-Ottawa Trek,", J. Hart to J. G. Gardiner, 4 July 1935; Bennett papers, 492903–4, J. Hart to R. B. Bennett, 492905, R. B. Bennett to J. Hart, 4 July 1935; 492918–20, G. G. McGeer to R. B. Bennett, 6 July 1935; NAC, RG 24, v. 3032, f. Unemployment Relief Strikes and Disturbances, W. W. Foster to G. G. McGeer, 3 July 1935.
28. SAB, RRIC, Millar Coroner's Inquest, 1–8; *Regina Leader-Post*, 6 July 1935.
29. *Regina Leader-Post*, 4 July 1935, 6 July 1935.
30. NAC, Bennett papers, 492946–47, J. J. Stapleton to R. B. Bennett, 5 July 1935.
31. NAC, RG 146, f. 93-A-00086, pt. 2, S. T. Wood to J. H. MacBrien, 23 July 1935, 19 July 1935.
32. *Moose Jaw Times-Herald*, 5 July 1935.

CHAPTER TWELVE (pages 235–259)

1. *Saskatchewan Gazette*, 31 July 1935, 2–3; W. H. McConnell, *Prairie Justice* (Calgary: 1980), 207–208.
2. Saskatchewan Archives Board [SAB], Regina Riot Inquiry Commission [RRIC], v. 16, 165, 46, 112; National Archives of Canada [NAC], Government Archives Division, Canadian Security Intelligence Service, RG 146, f. 93-A-00086, pt. 2, S. T. Wood to J. H. MacBrien, 10 July 1935; f. 98-A-00229, pt. 3, S. T. Wood to T. C. Davis, 16 November 1935; *Regina Leader-Post*, 6 July 1935; NAC, Manuscript Division, R. B. Bennett papers, 492949–52, E. C. Leslie to M. A. MacPherson, 6 July 1935.
3. The suggestion that the subject matter of the provincial inquiry was an encroachment on federal jurisdiction was unwarranted. In fact, there is considerable overlap in the division

of powers. Under section 91 (27), the federal Parliament has jurisdiction over criminal law, but under section 92 (14), the provinces have jurisdiction over the administration of justice in the province, which presumably would sanction the provincial riot commission. See NAC, Bennett papers, 492912, J. F. Bryant to R. B. Bennett, 5 July 1935; *Regina Leader-Post*, 16 July 1935. The newspaper carried copies of the correspondence between Davis and Guthrie over the establishment of the commission.

4. Regina City Police papers [RCP], M. J. Bruton to Board of Police Commissioners, 6 August 1935; NAC, Bennett papers, 492249–51, E. C. Leslie to M. A. MacPherson, 6 July 1935; 492991–92, J. H. MacBrien to H. Guthrie, 2 August 1935; NAC, RG 146, f. 98-A-00230, S. T. Wood to J. H. MacBrien, 5 July 1935.
5. NAC, Government Archives Division, Department of National Defence, RG 24, f. 3029, f. Unemployed Relief Strike Movement, "Notes on movement throughout Canada," 12 July 1935; S. R. Hewitt, "Beyond Regina: The On-to-Ottawa Trek in Manitoba and Ontario," unpublished M.A. thesis, University of Saskatchewan (1992), 32–159; NAC, Manuscript Division, R. L. Borden papers, v. 278, 155102–3, "Memo of conversation," 31 July 1935. In the meeting with Borden, it was noted that "The leaders in Communism are clever Jews whose activities should be investigated and dealt with."
6. NAC, RG 146, f. 98-A-00230, S. T. Wood to J. H. MacBrien, 5 July 1935; SAB, RRIC, v. 22, 64–65; v. 45, 91–92; *R. v. Mottl and Stevens*, 123–24.
7. *Regina Leader-Post*, 3 July 1935; 4 July 1935; SAB, RRIC, v. 21, 72; Bennett papers, 492249–51, E. C. Leslie to M. A. MacPherson, 6 July 1935.
8. *Regina Leader-Post*, 9 July 1935; 10 July 1935; 13 July 1935; 16 July 1935; 18 July 1935.
9. *Regina Leader-Post*, 2 July 1935; 9 July 1935; 12 July 1935; NAC, RG 146, f. 98-A-00230, H. E. Sampson to T. C. Davis, 13 July 1935.
10. *Regina Leader-Post*, 13 July 1935.
11. *Regina Leader-Post*, 20 July 1935; 22 July 1935.
12. *Regina Leader-Post*, 31 July 1935; SAB, RRIC, *R. v. Bell et al.*, 6–9, 719, 710–11, 726.
13. *Regina Leader-Post*, 23 July 1935.
14. *Regina Leader-Post*, 8 August 1935.
15. SAB, J. G. King papers, f. 13; *Regina Leader-Post*, 9 July 1935; 6 August 1935.
16. SAB, King papers, f. 13; NAC, Bennett papers, 496826, A. E. Millar to J. S. Stewart, 15 August 1935; *Regina Leader-Post*, 3 September 1935; 21 September 1935.
17. *Regina Daily Star*, 12 September 1935; 13 September 1935.
18. *Regina Leader-Post*, 13 September 1935; D. Lonardo, "Under a Watchful Eye: A Case Study of Police Surveillance During the 1930s," *Labour/Le Travail* 35 (Spring 1995), 21; NAC, Bennett papers, 493004, R. B. Bennett to T. H. Newlove, 4 September 1935; 493005–6, T. H. Newlove to R. B. Bennett, 7 September 1935; 493008–10, R. B. Bennett to T. H. Newlove, 10 September 1935; SAB, King papers, f. 12, Citizens' Defence Committee Minutes, 10 September 1935.
19. SAB, King papers, f. 13, "Report of the Mothers' Committee," undated; "Citizens' Defence Committee Minutes," 20 August 1935; CDC minutes, 27 August 1935; *Regina Leader-Post*, 12 July 1935; 18 July 1935; 4 September 1935; H. H. Mitchell to W. Schroeder, letter provided by Lori Krei, grandniece of Nick Schaack.
20. *Regina Leader-Post*, 19 October 1935; 22 October 1935; SAB, King papers, f. 13, "Citizens'

Defence Committee Minutes," 10 September 1935; SAB, RRIC, v. 25, 110–11; NAC, Government Archives Division, Department of Labour, NAC, RG 27, v. 2255, "Medical Aid Ledger," June to July 1935; Lori Krei to Bill Waiser, e-mail communication, 15 September 1999.

21. N. Ward and D. E. Smith, *Jimmy Gardiner: Relentless Liberal* (Toronto: 1990), 200–202.
22. *Regina Leader-Post*, 6 September 1935; 25 October 1935, 4 December 1935.
23. NAC, Bennett papers, 539212, F. W. Turnbull to R. B. Bennett, 9 November 1935; 539214–15, R. B Bennett to E. Lapointe, 20 November 1935; 539227, E. Lapointe to R. B. Bennett, 22 November 1935. Months later, Leslie provided a strong endorsement of Hogarth's performance. "I do not think," he privately wrote the former prime minister, "that anyone could have evinced greater zeal in digging up and presenting every bit of evidence to justify the actions of the Police or of the Government of that day."
24. SAB, RRIC, v. 1, 7–8; v. 2, 22–23; v. 28, 110.
25. SAB, RRIC, v. 2, 60, 100–101; v. 3, 80–88; v. 4, 194–96; v. 6, 75–78.
26. SAB, RRIC, v. 7, 93–95; v. 10, 17, 28–29, 145; v. 11, 109; v. 13, 60.
27. NAC, Bennett papers, 539223, E. C. Leslie to R. K. Finlayson, 17 December 1935; 539225, R. K. Finlayson to E. C. Leslie, 23 December 1935.
28. NAC, RG 146, f. 98-A-00230, J. H. MacBrien to deputy minister of Justice, 20 December 1935.
29. SAB, RRIC, v. 16, 76; v. 23, 52; v. 24, 107–108.
30. RCP, RCMP docket file, M. J. Bruton notes, undated.; NAC, RG 146, f. 93-A-00086, pt 1, H. Cooper, "Illegal Travelling on Trains, 1935," 11 December 1935; S. T. Wood to J. H. MacBrien, 19 January 1936.
31. SAB, RRIC, v. 38, 43, 60, 91; v. 40, 112–13.
32. SAB, RRIC, v. 46, 126; v. 47, 6, 70; v. 50, 72, 74.
33. *Regina Leader-Post*, 9 March 1936.
34. *Regina Leader-Post*, 10 March 1936.
35. *Regina Leader-Post*, 11 March 1936.
36. NAC, RG 146, f. 93-A-00086, pt. 1, S. T. Wood to J. H. MacBrien, 25 January 1936; NAC, Bennett papers, 539244–45, E. C. Leslie to R. B. Bennett, 16 March 1936; *House of Commons Debates*, 10 February 1936, 65, 124–25; 11 February 1936, 269; 18 February 1936; SAB, RRIC, v. 34, 81–83.
37. *Regina Leader-Post*, 28 February 1936.
38. SAB, King papers, f. 5, f. 6, f. 13, "CDC minutes," 10 July 1935.
39. *Regina Leader-Post*, 14 April 1936; W. H. McConnell, *Prairie Justice*, 75–76; D. Gruending, *Emmett Hall: Establishment Radical* (Toronto: 1985), 28–32.
40. SAB, RRIC, *R. v. Mottl and Stevens*, 1; 506–7.
41. *Regina Leader-Post*, 24 April 1936; 29 April 1936.
42. *Regina Leader-Post*, 23 April 1936; 24 April 1936; 28 April 1936; 29 April 1936.
43. NAC, Bennett papers, 539247–49, E. C. Leslie to R. B. Bennett, 27 April 1936; SAB, RRIC, pt.2, Report, 93, 111, 115–16, 119, 125, 128, 140, 149, 153, 157, 233, 251, 276, 288, 292, 304, 311. The Riot Commission report was transmitted to the provincial government on 23 April 1936.
44. NAC, Bennett papers, 539254, R. B. Bennett to F. W. Turnbull, 5 June 1936; *Regina Leader-Post*, 20 May 1936; *Regina Daily Star*, 16 May 1936; *Saskatchewan Journals*, 2 March 1937, 206.

EPILOGUE (pages 261–275)

1. Saskatchewan Archives Board [SAB], J. G. King papers, f. 6, Citizens' Defence Movement, "A Call to Action," 25 February 1936, f. 12, J. G. King appeal letter, 8 May 1936. The new defence movement also sought advice from the American Civil Liberties Union.
2. SAB, J.G. King papers, "Liberty Draw," 25 April 1936, f. 16, "Has Justice Been Served" pamphlet, undated. The pamphlet stated that the riot resulted in three deaths.
3. *Regina Leader-Post*, 15 June 1936; 16 June 1936; 17 June 1936. For an example of the appeal statements for the convicted trekkers, see SAB, Court of Appeal Dockets, Sidney Stevens notice of appeal, 12 May 1936. All seven appeal statements were virtually the same. On July 24, 1936, the Department of Immigration and Colonization refused a request from Makaroff to suspend Forsyth's deportation order: SAB, J.G. King papers, W. J. Bratt to P. Makaroff, 24 July 1936.
4. SAB, J. G. King papers, J. G. King to M. J. Coldwell, 17 June 1936; f. 20, M. J. Coldwell to A. Evans, 20 February 1936; J. S. Woodsworth to A. Brounstein, 4 June 1936; J. G. King to T. C. Douglas, 8 May 1936, T. C. Douglas to J. G. King 18 May 1936; Canada. *House of Commons Debates*, 6 May 1936, 2554–5; *Regina Leader-Post*, 17 June 1936.
5. *House of Commons Debates*, 20 June 1936, 4004–6.
6. *House of Commons Debates*, 15 February 1935, 858; AB, J. G. King papers, f. 20, J. G. King and P. G. Makaroff to W. L. Mackenzie King and Ernest Lapointe, 20 June 1936; National Archives of Canada [NAC], Government Archives Division, Canadian Security Intelligence Service, RG 146, f. 98-A-00230, J. H. MacBrien to L. P. Picard, 17 June 1936.
7. NAC, W. L. M. King papers, King diaries, 2 July 1935; 3 July 1935; 5 July 1935; v. 205, W. L. M. King to T. C. Davis, 26 July 1935.
8. *House of Commons Debates*, 22 June 1936, 4059–64, 4078–79.
9. *House of Commons Debates*, 4082; G. M. Stone, "The Regina Riot: 1935" unpublished M.A. thesis, University of Saskatchewan (1967), 115–16.
10. J. Struthers, *No Fault of Their Own: Unemployment and the Canadian Welfare State, 1914–1941* (Toronto:1983), 153–61.
11. NAC, Manuscript Division, A. Meighen papers, v. 214, 135348, R. B. Bennett to A. Meighen, 31 October 1935; L. A. Glassford, *Reaction and Reform: The Politics of the Conservative Party Under R. B. Bennett, 1927–1938* (Toronto:1992), 243–44.
12. *House of Commons Debates*, 3 February 1938, 150.
13. SAB, J. G. Gardiner papers, vii, 3b, J. G, Gardiner to T. C. Davis, 28 December 1955.
14. *Regina Leader-Post*, 6 July 1995. The HSMBC plaque text reads: "A defining event of the Great Depression, the On-to-Ottawa Trek has become a poignant symbol of working class protest. In 1935, over a thousand angry unemployed men left federal relief camps in British Columbia and boarded boxcars to take their demand for work and wages directly to Ottawa. As the number of protesters increased, the federal government resolved to stop the movement. The police arrested its leaders at a public meeting on July 1st, sparking the Regina Riot. Although it never reached Ottawa, the Trek marked the failure of the Depression-era work camps as a solution to widespread unemployment."
15. *Regina Leader-Post*, 20 June 1935; 24 June 1935; 27 June 1935.

16. J. W. Brennan, "The On-to-Ottawa Trek and the Regina Riot: A Local Perspective," unpublished paper presented before Northern Great Plains History Conference, September 1997; *Regina Leader-Post*, 30 May 1936; Regina City Police papers [RCP], "Charles Millar Memorial Fund," 26 June 1946; NAC, RG 146, f. 98-A-00229, Charles Millar murder file.
17. A mountain overlooking the South Nahanni River was named in honour of MacBrien in 1952. NAC, R. B. Bennett papers, 286981, R. B. Bennett to G. R. Geary, 2 October 1935; G. T. Hann, "Stuart Taylor Wood, *RCMP Quarterly*, 1, 7; W. K. Wark, "Security Intelligence in Canada, 1864–1945: The History of a 'National Insecurity State'," in K. Neilson and B. J. C. McKercher, eds., *Go Spy the Land: Military Intelligence in History* (Westport 1992), 167; R. Whitaker, "Official Repression of Communism During World War II," *Labour/Le Travail*, n. 17, spring 1986, 135–66; A. Phillips, "The Thirty Years' War with the Commies," *Maclean's*, 1 September 1954. The article claimed that during the riot women slashed Mountie horses with razor blades affixed to long sticks.
18. *Saskatoon Star Phoenix*, 3 April 2001; T. Buck, *Yours in the Struggle: Reminiscences of Tim Buck* (Toronto 1977).
19. B. Swanky and J. E. Shields, *"Work and Wages!": A Semi-documentary Account of the Life and Times of Arthur H. (Slim) Evans* (Vancouver 1977), 255–83.
20. Victor Howard suggests that as many as four hundred men in the Mac Paps (or 25 per-cent of the Canadian volunteers) were former trekkers. V. Howard, *"We were the Salt of the Earth!": The On-to-Ottawa Trek and the Regina Riot* (Regina 1985), 179; V. Hoar, *The Mackenzie-Papineau Battalion: Canadian Participation in the Spanish Civil War* (Toronto 1969), 30, 36, 99.
21. *Saskatoon Star Phoenix*, 14 May 2002; 1 June 2002.
22. NAC, Manuscript Division, R. B. Bennett papers, 492881–83, J. McWilliam to A. Millar, 3 July 1935.

INDEX

About Fifth House Books

Fifth House Publishers, a Fitzhenry & Whiteside company, is a proudly western Canadian press. Our publishing specialty is non-fiction as we believe that every community must possess a positive understanding of its worth and place if it is to remain vital and progressive. Fifth House is committed to "bringing the West to the rest" by publishing approximately twenty books a year about the land and people who make this region unique. Our books are selected for their quality, saleability, and contribution to the understanding of western Canadian (and Canadian) history, culture, and environment.

Look for these other books about western Canadian history from Fifth House at your favourite bookstore.

Alberta Originals: Stories of Albertans Who Made a Difference,
Brian Brennan, $16.95
Booze: When Whisky Ruled the West, James H. Gray, $14.95
Firewater: The Impact of the Whisky Trade on the Blackfoot Nation,
Hugh A. Dempsey, $24.95
Firing the Heather: The Life and Times of Nellie McClung,
Mary Hallett and Marilyn Davis, $19.95
The Golden Age of the Canadian Cowboy, Hugh A. Dempsey, $19.95
Just Another Indian: A Serial Killer and Canada's Indifference,
Warren Goulding, $22.95
The Last Best West: Women on the Alberta Frontier, 1880–1930,
Eliane Leslau Silverman, $14.95
The Last Roundup: Memories of a Canadian Cowboy, Stan Graber, $12.95
Men Against the Desert: A Great Canadian Success Story, James H. Gray, $14.95
The Middle of Nowhere: Rediscovering Saskatchewan, Dennis Gruending, $16.95
On the Road with David Thompson, Joyce & Peter McCart, $18.95
The Palliser Expedition: The Dramatic Story of Western Canadian Exploration, 1857–1860, Irene M. Spry, $14.95
Red Lights on the Prairies: An Unconventional Social History, James H. Gray, $14.95
SaskScandal: The Death of Political Idealism in Saskatchewan, Gerry Jones, $14.95
Scoundrels and Scallywags: Characters from Alberta's Past, Brian Brennan, $16.95
The Silent Song: A Tribute to a Reluctant Pioneer Mother,
Marjorie Wilkins Campbell, $14.95
The Winter Years, James H. Gray, $16.95